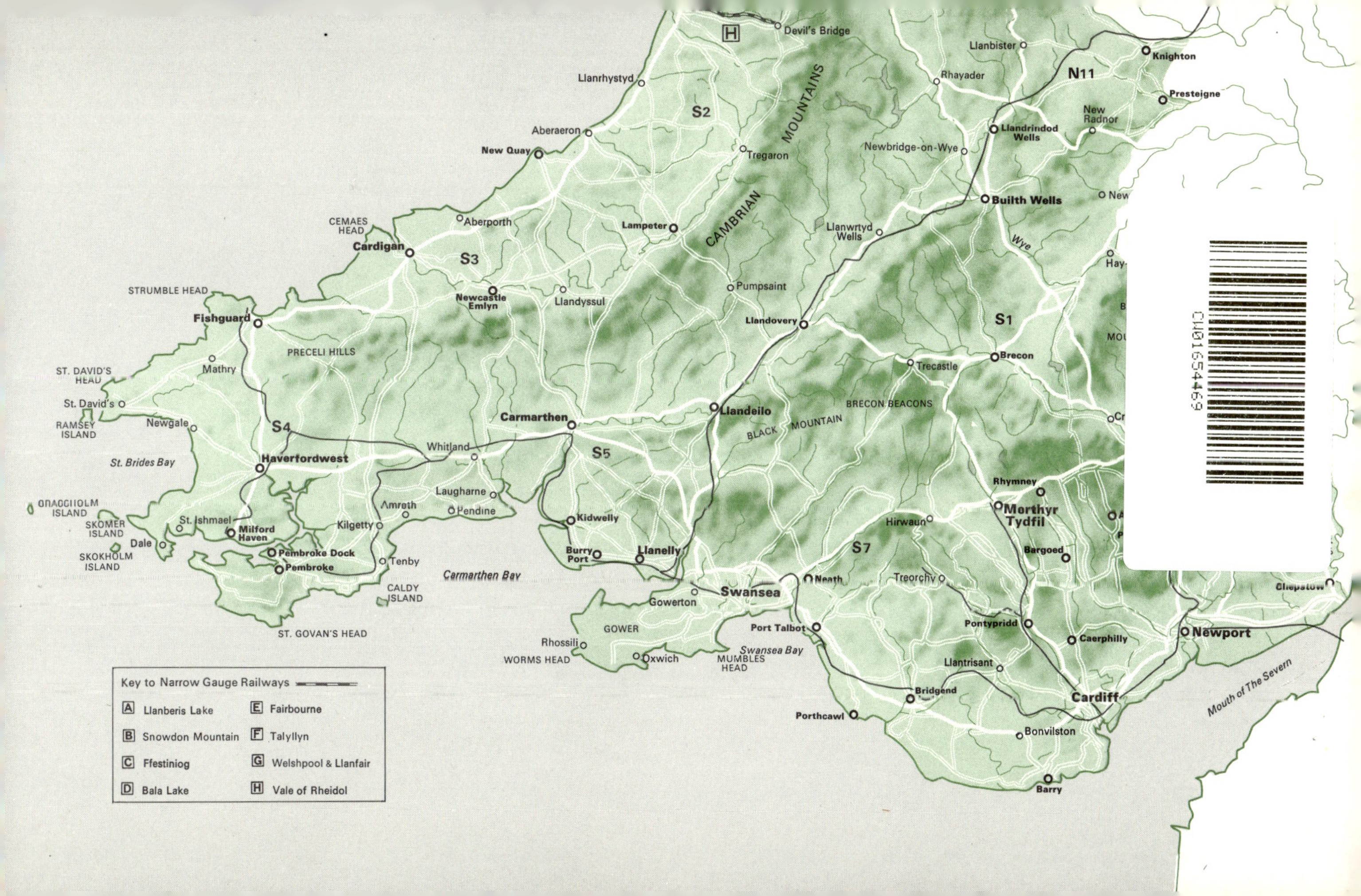

Devil's Bridge
Llanbister
Knighton
N11
Rhayader
Presteigne
Llanrhystyd
S2
MOUNTAINS
New Radnor
Llandrindod Wells
Aberaeron
New Quay
Tregaron
Newbridge-on-Wye
Builth Wells
CAMBRIAN
Llanwrtyd Wells
Wye
Hay
CEMAES HEAD
Aberporth
Lampeter
Cardigan
S3
STRUMBLE HEAD
Newcastle Emlyn
Llandyssul
Pumpsaint
Fishguard
Llandovery
S1
PRECELI HILLS
Brecon
ST. DAVID'S HEAD
Mathry
Trecastle
St. David's
BRECON BEACONS
RAMSEY ISLAND
Newgale
Carmarthen
Llandeilo
S4
BLACK MOUNTAIN
St. Brides Bay
Haverfordwest
Whitland
S5
Laugharne
Rhymney
GRASSHOLM ISLAND
Amroth
Pendine
Merthyr Tydfil
SKOMER ISLAND
St. Ishmael
Milford Haven
Kilgetty
Kidwelly
Hirwaun
Dale
Pembroke Dock
S7
SKOKHOLM ISLAND
Tenby
Burry Port
Llanelly
Bargoed
Pembroke
Carmarthen Bay
Neath
Treorchy
Swansea
CALDY ISLAND
Gowerton
Chepstow
Pontypridd
ST. GOVAN'S HEAD
GOWER
Port Talbot
Caerphilly
Newport
Rhossili
Swansea Bay
WORMS HEAD
Oxwich
MUMBLES HEAD
Llantrisant
Mouth of The Severn
Bridgend
Cardiff
Porthcawl
Bonvilston
Barry
Key to Narrow Gauge Railways
A Llanberis Lake
B Snowdon Mountain
C Ffestiniog
D Bala Lake
E Fairbourne
F Talyllyn
G Welshpool & Llanfair
H Vale of Rheidol

John Nelson Tarn
Harrogate 7.2.74

THE COMPANION GUIDE TO

North Wales

THE COMPANION GUIDES

GENERAL EDITOR: VINCENT CRONIN

It is the aim of these Guides to provide a Companion, in the person of the author, who knows intimately the places and people of whom he writes, and is able to communicate this knowledge and affection to his readers. It is hoped that the text and pictures will aid them in their preparations and in their travels, and will help them to remember on their return.

THE GREEK ISLANDS · SOUTHERN GREECE
PARIS · THE SOUTH OF FRANCE
ROME · VENICE · LONDON
FLORENCE · JUGOSLAVIA
THE WEST HIGHLANDS OF SCOTLAND · UMBRIA
SOUTHERN ITALY · TUSCANY · EAST ANGLIA
SOUTHERN SPAIN · MADRID AND CENTRAL SPAIN
IRELAND · KENT AND SUSSEX

In Preparation

MAINLAND GREECE · BURGUNDY
SOUTH-WEST FRANCE · THE ILE DE FRANCE
EDINBURGH AND THE BORDER COUNTRY
NORTHUMBRIA · DEVON AND CORNWALL
SOUTH WALES · TURKEY

The Guides to ROME, VENICE, FLORENCE, LONDON and THE SOUTH OF FRANCE are available in paperback in the *Fontana* edition

THE COMPANION GUIDE TO

North Wales

ELISABETH BEAZLEY
AND PETER HOWELL

COLLINS
ST JAMES'S PLACE, LONDON
1975

William Collins Sons & Co Ltd
London · Glasgow · Sydney · Auckland
Toronto · Johannesburg

First published 1975

ISBN 0 00 211199 3

Set in Monotype Times
Maps by John Flower
Made and printed in Great Britain by
William Collins Sons & Co Ltd Glasgow

Contents

	LIST OF ILLUSTRATIONS	7
	MAPS AND PLANS	9
	ACKNOWLEDGEMENTS	11
	INTRODUCTION	13
1.	Chester to the Vale of Clwyd	21
2.	Wrexham, the Dee and Glynceiriog, and the Maelor Saesneg	60
3.	Between the Vale of Clwyd and the Conwy	96
4.	Corwen to Conwy	117
5.	The North Coast – Conwy to Caernarfon	128
6.	Snowdonia	146
7.	The Lleyn Peninsula	171
8.	Anglesey	195
9.	Merioneth	220
10.	Montgomeryshire	265
11.	Radnorshire	307
	Glossary of Welsh place names, useful words and pronunciation	341
	Who's Who and What's What	349
	Bibliography	370
	INDEX	373

Illustrations

St Thomas's, Rhyl	*facing page* 32
Plas Têg	33
The High Street, Mold	33
Llanbedr Dyffryn Clwyd (*Martin Harrison*)	48
Ruthin (*Martin Harrison*)	48
Gresford Church	49
The Horseshoe Falls	80
A lane near Cilcain	80
Jesse Window, Llanrhaeadr (*Lord Esher*)	81
The Gates of Chirk Castle	96
Chirk Tunnel	96
Painted House in the Maelor	97
Conwy Castle (*National Monuments Record*)	97
The Pier, Llandudno (*Lord Esher*)	128
Caernarfon Castle by Peter de Wint (*Victoria and Albert*)	129
Penrhyn Castle (*Lord Esher*)	129
Tryfan (*Lord Esher*)	144
Tremadoc Chapel by Kenneth Rowntree (*National Museum of Wales*)	144
Dinorwic Quarry (*Lord Esher*)	145
St Cybi's Well	192
Slate headstone at Llangristiolus	192
Menai Bridge	193
Cottages at Llanddona	208
Newborough Warren	208
Blaenau Ffestiniog (*Martin Harrison*)	209
The Rhinogs (*Lord Esher*)	256
Snowdon from Llandanwg (*Martin Harrison*)	256
Rhaeadr Ddu (*Martin Harrison*)	257
Barmouth (*Martin Harrison*)	272
Maentwrog Church (*Martin Harrison*)	273

Brithdir Church (*Martin Harrison*) 273
Cadair Idris (*Martin Harrison*) 304
Llyn Cau, Cadair Idris, by Richard Wilson (*Tate Gallery*) 304
Powis Castle (*Jeremy Whitaker*) 305
Llandinam Hall 320
Oak Woodland, Radnorshire 320
Pencerrig, by Thomas Jones (*Birmingham City Art Gallery*) 321
Rhulen Church 321

All photographs not otherwise attributed are by Elisabeth Beazley

Maps

New Boundaries	14
Medieval Boundaries	16
Chester to the Vale of Clwyd	22
Rudland Castle	34
Wrexham (area)	62
Wrexham (street plan)	64
Llangollen valley	82-3
Conwy (area)	98
The North Coast	130-31
Conwy (street plan and castle)	132
Caernarfon (street plan)	142
Snowdonia (area)	148
Snowdon (detail)	158
The Lleyn Peninsula	172
Anglesey	196
Beaumaris Castle	200
Merioneth	222
Montgomeryshire	266
Radnorshire	308

Acknowledgements

This book could not have been written without the help and encouragement of innumerable friends and well-wishers. Unfortunately we cannot thank them all by name, and we hope that those who are not named will not think that we have forgotten them.

To start with those who helped most at the latest stage, by reading the galley-proofs, three even read the whole book – Professor Ieuan Gwynedd Jones, Mr D. Morgan Rees, and Dr A. J. Taylor. Parts were read by the Marquess of Anglesey, Lord Esher, the Revd Wyn Evans, Dr Colin Gresham, Mr Richard Haslam, Mr Vernon Hughes, Dr J. D. K. Lloyd, Mr Peter Smith, and Mr Merlin Waterson. All corrected many errors, contributed new material (which we were not always able to use), and cheered us up by their warm response. Needless to say, it would be unjust to attach any responsibility to them for the shortcomings of the finished product. Many of them had already provided invaluable assistance while the book was being written.

We must also thank Professor E. G. Bowen, Mr H. M. Colvin, Mr Alan Crawford, Mrs Mair Jones, Mr Paul Joyce, Dr M. J. T. Lewis, Mr Henry Morris, Mr Trefor Owen, Mr Andrew Saint, and Sir Clough Williams-Ellis, and also the Keeper of Prints, Drawings, and Maps at the National Library of Wales, and Mrs I. M. Rees of the St Davids Branch of the Pembrokeshire County Library.

Lord Esher lent us a large number of his fine photographs: we wish we had had room to use more of them. Mr Martin Harrison made a special tour for us, and contributed the pleasure of his company as well as his excellent photographs. Others who joined in our explorations and made them all the more agreeable include Mrs Paul Carlisle and Mr Paddy Dickinson. Mrs Carlisle also belongs to the noble band who provided welcome hospitality, as do the Marchioness of Anglesey, Mrs J. O. C. Beazley, Mrs M. Bungay, Mr Richard Haslam, and Mrs H. A. A. Howell.

Stalwart work was done by our splendid typists, who had to cope not only with our handwriting but with Welsh spelling: they include Mrs Katie Fforde, Miss Jane Gordon-Cumming (who also made the index), and Miss Betty Stephenson.

Finally, a word of general, but heartfelt thanks to all those, whether Welshmen or non-Welshmen, of all sorts and conditions, who have helped us with information, kindness, and insight.

Introduction

This book was written before the new counties were formed and it will be some time before new maps are in general use, so both new and old county names have been included. The old came about as a result of either Edward I's Statute of Rhuddlan (1284) or of Henry VIII's Act of Union of 1536. The names of the new counties are mostly taken from ancient Welsh kingdoms – Gwynedd, Powys, Gwent, and Dyfed. The name Clwyd is taken from the river of that name. Glamorgan has now been split into three parts. Spelling of place names follows that given in the *Gazetteer of Welsh Place Names* (University of Wales Press) with a few exceptions where another name seems to be in much more common use. Spelling of names is in English, following the custom of this series (e.g. as Joan of Arc is not Jeanne d'Arc nor is Owen Glendower Owain Glyn Dŵr). We have generally worked N–S and E–W but have followed no fixed rules except to make it as easy as possible to follow the Guide.

Unless a house is specifically stated to be open to the public, it is to be assumed that it is not. Since opening times tend to change from year to year, it seemed best only to give rough indications. For precise details, see the annual *Historic Houses, Castles and Gardens*. Houses open on application have generally received grants from the Historic Buildings Council on condition that they are opened. Application usually has to be in writing. For details see *Historic Houses*. Monuments in the care of the Department of the Environment (D. o. E.) are mostly open standard hours (roughly 9.30, Sundays 2.00, – dusk). Some are always open.

Some places described are on private property, so permission should be asked in order to visit them. Some (including parish churches) are not named even on the Ordnance Survey maps.

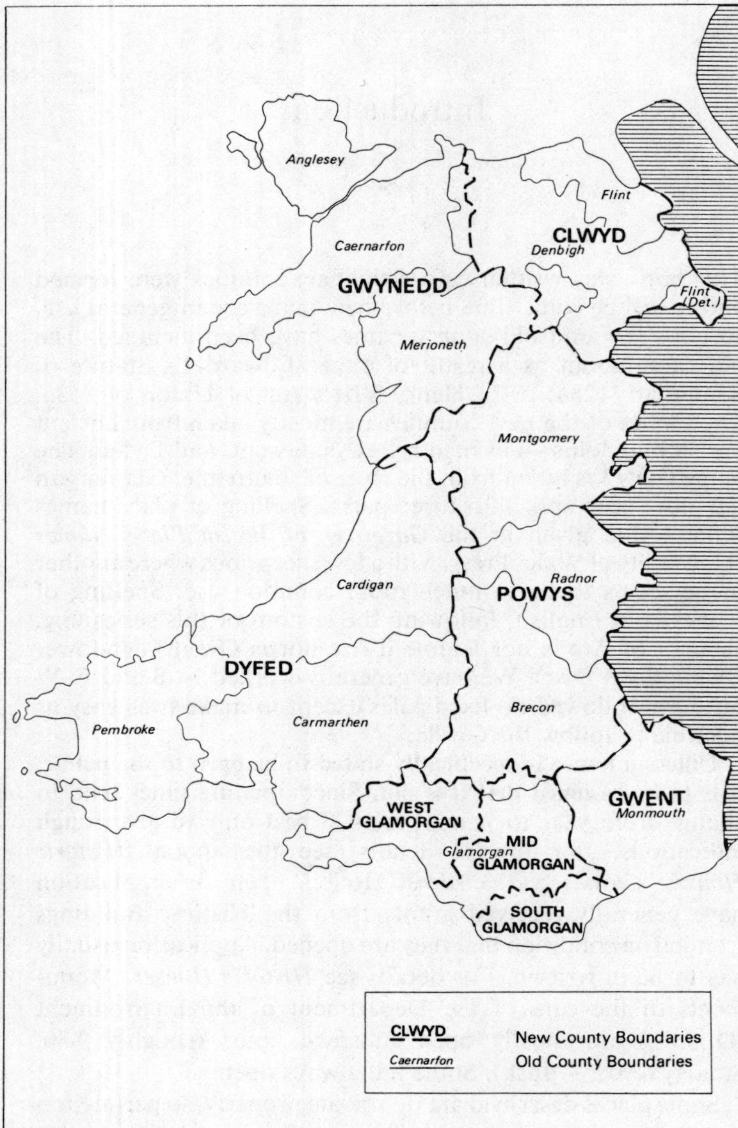
Anglesey
Flint
CLWYD
Caernarfon
Denbigh
GWYNEDD
Flint (Det.)
Merioneth
Montgomery
Cardigan
Radnor
POWYS
DYFED
Brecon
Pembroke
Carmarthen
GWENT
Monmouth
WEST GLAMORGAN
MID GLAMORGAN
Glamorgan
SOUTH GLAMORGAN
CLWYD New County Boundaries
Caernarfon Old County Boundaries

Where we foresee difficulties the O.S. grid reference is given (e.g. 275/321): this system of reference is described on the O.S. maps.

Wales has been divided into two volumes, North and South, and to make the two approximately equal we have had to split Powys, putting Breconshire into the South. This is about as good a division as we could make from the point of view of the reader. North and South Wales are separated by the mid-Wales mountains, cut diagonally by river valleys. Roads are therefore indirect and there is little communication between the two. There is thus a marked difference in the Welsh spoken, but there is an even stronger topographical difference between east and west Wales. Perhaps the only parts of Wales which have a marked physical likeness are the extreme west: Anglesey, Lleyn and Pembrokeshire (akin to Cornwall and Brittany); and the eastern marches which in some ways resemble their English neighbours.

Probably the truest difference in character is between inner Wales, the North and West, and outer Wales, the East and South – that part which has constantly tempted invaders to settle.

Snowdonia, the historic heart of Wales, is unique. The mountains have a scale and grandeur that makes them seem far bigger than an altimeter would suggest. They were for long the eyrie of the Princes and are now the nursery of Himalayan expeditions. In the 19th century their slate roofed cities all over the world and today *Mouton de Pays de Galles* tops the menus in the most expensive restaurants in Paris or Brussels. Snowdonia is the paradise of the industrial north-west, and it still comes as a surprise to hear a Welshman speaking Welsh with a strong North Wales accent switching to English with a marked Merseyside accent. Indeed, Liverpool has long been known as the capital of North Wales; it certainly has plenty of Welsh citizens and there are no big towns in the North.

Much of mid-Wales consists of high sheep walks – lovely rolling grassy hills with big blocks of forestry. If you look closely more small conifers are to be seen poking up through hundreds of acres of 'empty' hill. Clearly the character of the country will soon change dramatically. In 1831 the Reverend John Parker wrote:

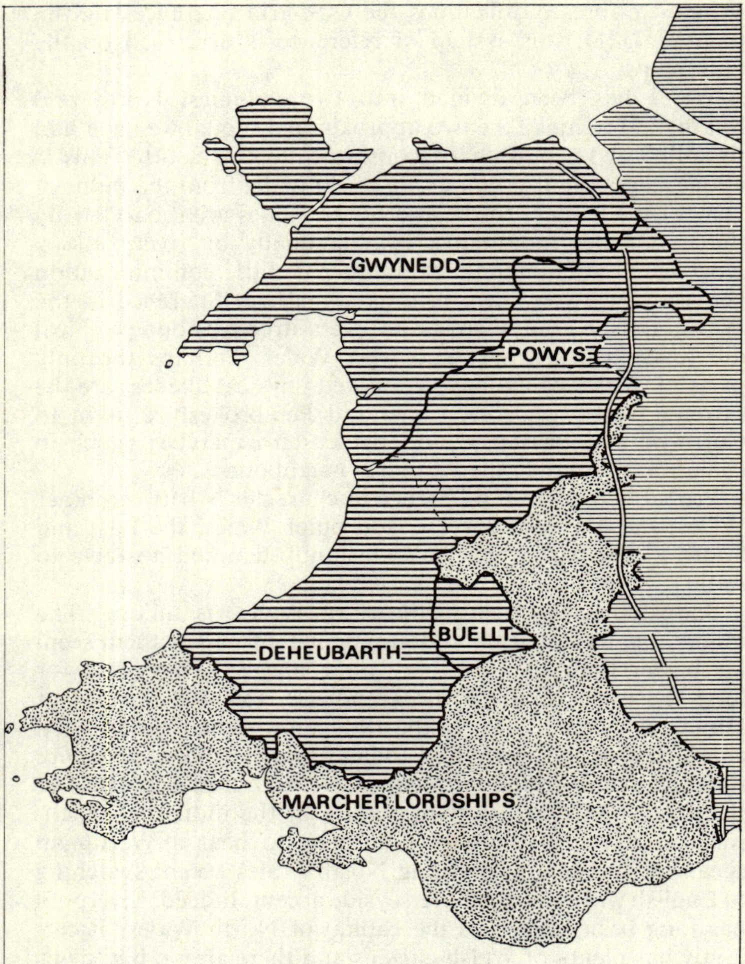

Medieval Wales united by Llywelyn the Great

- Territory giving allegiance to Llywelyn c.1237
- Marcher Lordships
- Border made by the Act of Union 1536
- Line of Offa's Dyke

> 'If they [conifers] were common in Wales, the country would not be worth looking at. These lower mountains cannot overcome such blemishes. We deal here in fantastic beauty, more than desolation and grandeur.'

What would he say now? The Forestry Commission is doing a great deal to absorb tourism but it must be remembered that one of the things that lifts the heart of those who live in Wales and tourists alike is the great spaces of the open hills.

There is much concern about the depopulation of mid-Wales. This seems in many ways an unrealistic worry. Empty farms are a sad sight but it is easy to forget that before the land hunger of the early 19th century few people were attempting to scrape a living on these inhospitable heights, except by sheep rearing based on a lower farm. The *hafod* was a summer dwelling and the *tyddyn* (small holding) up here sprang up literally overnight and provided a very hard life. It is inconsistent to promote farm amalgamation and regret depopulation simultaneously. Although a landscape farmed by thrifty peasants is the ideal to look at, it is not necessarily the best to live in if you are one of the peasants. The thought of a bustling, thriving country community with corn being milled, saddlers making saddles, sycamore and alder being harvested for clog making, oak bark being garnered for tanners, each farm reliant on its neighbours for harvest and sheep shearing, chapels and churches brimming with singing festivals, is a wonderful nostalgic dream. The internal combustion engine coupled with the 'rising standard of living' has hit Wales, as everywhere else, and transformed it more dramatically than anything since the neolithic and early Bronze-Age settlers brought with them knowledge of farming and so of settled life.

Wales has most of the rural problems of the rest of Western Europe with the added complication that these seem inevitably to become inextricably mixed with that of the survival of language. The problem of second homes (illegal in Switzerland except to foreigners) is but one, and it is a serious problem: no one wants to live in a ghost village. Yet it is also true that many outlying cottages would now be derelict if they were not used for holidays. It is a second best solution but often the only one. This is as true of Provence as it is of Wales.

There is a real fear that the language will die. Indeed it

could. In 1974, only 25 per cent of the people of Wales spoke it. Welsh, having been influenced by Latin which was used by the Celtic church and to some extent for administration, settled in its present form in the sixteenth century. Welsh poetry, with its intricate structure and fine use of language, has long been treasured by Welshmen.

Sadly, language has been a bone of contention from the time of Henry VII although at the Reformation Welsh became the official language of the church (Bishop Morgan's Welsh translation of the Bible appeared twenty years before the Authorized version). Even so, once Latin had ceased to have international use, it was essential to have English to get on. Universities were in England and the law was administered in English. Parents as well as schools encouraged its use. There is now a movement to keep jobs for Welsh speakers and interesting experiments in bi-lingual education are under way. The tragedy is that while foreign settlers, whether English, Polish or Italian, are usually happy enough for their children to be taught Welsh, the English-speaking Welsh are becoming increasingly antagonistic to the pressures of the more extreme language protagonists. If there is one thing in which no one, even a Welshman, will succeed, it is in bossing the Welsh about. If they do not physically retreat into the hills, as they did in the Middle Ages, they will quietly go their own way, not telling anyone which way this is.

One minor but important cause of the diminishing use of Welsh is the Welsh love of conversation and speculation: it would be unendurably frustrating to converse with a learner in Welsh in preference to a common language. Death and the Hereafter, as much as rugby football and the price of potatoes, are subjects to discuss over a cup of tea or a pint of beer. Philosophy, genealogy and litigation are traditional hobbies all involving imagination and the use of words. 'Never believe anything you hear and only half of what you say' was the unexpected advice given recently by a postman who was delivering letters to a remote farm in the Cambrian hills; salutary to guide-book writers.

Those who do not know Wales yet should be prepared for a genuine welcome. One of us recently won a week in a holiday camp by completing the sentence 'We like going to Wales because . . .' with 'the people are so friendly.' Hardly original but astonishingly true. They also have a great capacity for enjoying life (although remnants of the austerity of the religious revivals linger in some places). And they have excellent manners, with none of that crushing disregard for the feelings of others in the interests of accuracy prevalent in some races. It is traditionally rude to disappoint people, so do not frame your questions in a way that makes them difficult to answer. Exhausted walkers, for instance, wanting to know the distance to the next village, have been known to receive an encouraging reply despite the actual mileage in question. John Cowper Powys wrote of his fellow countrymen 'The Welsh are such born "introverts" that it is second nature with them to treat people exactly as people like best to be treated.'

Any guide-book writer is confronted by two main tasks – exploring the country, and reading up its topography and history. In Wales both present special problems. Communications are often difficult, and the weather can be bad; cars may overheat on rough mountain roads and steep hills, and thick mist and rain may obscure the view. The problem of research is chiefly that so much has been written, and still is written. Interest in local history in Wales is enormous and scholarly. Booksellers find that second-hand Welsh topography sells like hot cakes, despite the fact that copies of old books have usually been used to destruction (unlike, we are told, those on Scottish topography). The industry which goes into contributions to the excellent national and county journals and the innumerable histories of counties, towns, villages, industries, churches and chapels is vast. Inevitably time, and our woeful ignorance of the Welsh language, have prevented us from making as much use of these riches as we should have liked. Another source inadequately tapped has been the local expert. Time and time again, one is told 'You should see Mr Dai Jones, the council houses'. And, sure enough, Mr Jones turns out to be another invaluable source. Inevitably a vast amount of fascinating material has had to be omitted for lack of space.

Lastly, perhaps, we should explain ourselves and how we have written the book. We divided the country geographically and contributed enthusiastically to each other's sections. The reader may however become aware that, although many of these enthusiasms are shared, equally others belong more to one writer than the other.

CHAPTER ONE

Chester to the Vale of Clwyd

Since this is the nearest part of Wales to the great conurbations of Merseyside, Wirral, and Chester, it is subject to tremendous pressures from industry, commuting, and tourism. It is interesting to compare the old Flintshire, with an area of 164,000 acres and a population of 177,000, with Radnorshire, which had 301,000 acres, but only 18,000 inhabitants. Much of Clwyd, especially the Dee estuary, is spoilt, but it is still easy to get up into the hills – which begin, as usual, on the Welsh border – and find peace, if not solitude. There is plenty of quiet, undramatic country, in moorland and in valleys, particularly the idyllic Vale of Clwyd, wide and richly agricultural. It is not only recently that this part of Wales has been more prosperous than the wilder areas, and its wealth is shown in finer churches and grander country houses, as well as in delightful market towns like Mold and Ruthin.

This chapter covers all of Flintshire except Maelor Saesneg (see Chapter Two), and some parts of Denbighshire, including all of the E side of the Vale of Clwyd. The W side is described in Chapter Three.

From Chester three roads run in a roughly north-west direction, more or less parallel, and only a few miles apart. These are the coast road to Rhyl, the hill road via Holywell to St Asaph, and the more winding road via Mold to Denbigh. In summer all three are almost equally choked with holiday traffic, although the third is usually the emptiest.

CHESTER TO RHYL

The entry into Wales from Chester is dismal, by way of the seedy suburb of Saltney, and over flat ground reclaimed from marsh – the old road curved round farther south, below the

Continued on Chapter 3 map
Continued on Chapter 2 map

higher ground. The coast road is reached by the B5129, along the sharply canalized tidal Dee. Alternatively it can be reached by way of Sealand and the Queensferry bridge. The Connah's Quay conurbation has little to recommend it, and feels all the gloomier since the threat of closure has been hanging over the big Shotton steelworks, but it is worth a visit for two outstanding buildings. The first is at **Queensferry**, ¼ mile SE of the bridge, and reached by a lane passing under the railway (326/680). It is an imposing red-brick factory, with a stout battered tower, designed by H. B. Cresswell (author of the amusing *Honeywood File*). Built c. 1901, it attracted attention for its bold simplicity and lack of period detail. The second is St Ethelwold's Church at **Shotton**, beside the main road. One of John Douglas's finest works (1898–1902), it is in the Early English style, with a most impressive interior – the spire, alas, never built.

The open country beyond Connah's Quay soon disappears as **Flint** is reached, a sore disappointment for anyone with romantic thoughts of Shakespeare's 'Richard II', or Mary calling the cattle home across the sands of Dee. The town is dominated by huge chimneys and tower blocks, yet it retains the rectilinear plan on which it was laid out by Edward I, and there are, of course, 'the rude ribs of that ancient castle' where Richard was taken prisoner. Begun in 1277, it stands looking out over the estuary, in a not unpleasant situation, where it is almost possible to forget the industry, even though the castle is overshadowed by Courtauld's factory. The chief feature of the castle is the great round Donjon, almost certainly based on the Tour de Constance at Aigues Mortes, seen by Edward in 1270. Flint was the first castle built by Edward in Wales. The chief master mason, as at Rhuddlan, Conwy, Caernarfon, Harlech, and Beaumaris, was James of St George (see p. 357). Beside the castle, Edward founded a new borough, to which English settlers were attracted by low rents. Like the Bastides of southern France, these boroughs (founded also at Aberystwyth, Conwy, Caernarfon, Cricieth, Harlech, Beaumaris etc.) were intended to serve as trade centres. Flint was defended, not by walls of stone, but by an earth and timber stockade. The dull parish church was built in 1848 by Ambrose Poynter, who did a lot of work in the district, through the patronage of the Mostyn family. More fun is the crazy English Wesleyan

Chapel (1881), by the turning to the castle, with red, yellow and blue bricks, and lattice windows – designed by Joseph Hall, a member of the congregation.

In the main square stands the quirky Tudor Town Hall of 1840, by John Welch.

Beyond Flint is the awful sprawl of **Bagillt**, which has a dottily-pinnacled church of 1837–9, also by John Welch. Here there used to be a great smelting-works, to which lead ore was brought from Wales, the Isle of Man, and Ireland. Further on is yet more industrialization (revolting smells) below Holywell (see p. 27).

The second road from Chester, the A55, after Broughton junction, climbs round the wooded park of **Hawarden Castle**. Through the trees can be glimpsed the medieval castle, commanding the entrance to Wales. The site was first fortified against the Romans, but the present castle was built by the English in the 13th century. Its interesting ruins, restored in the early 19th century, including a fine stout keep, are pleasantly overgrown, a striking contrast to many in the care of the D. o. E., whose conservation policy does not risk roots in masonry. The main road used to run between the old and new castles, but it was diverted.

The new castle, home of the Gladstone family, was originally a handsome classical structure of 1752, called Broadlane Hall, and designed by Joseph Turner, a Hawarden architect of considerable skill (his work, both as architect and sculptor, is to be seen all over the district). However, in 1809–10 Sir Stephen Glynne, the well-known antiquary, had the house remodelled in a thoroughgoing castellated style by Thomas Cundy (designs by Nash were rejected). The S front is quite convincing, but on the N (and also inside) much of Turner's work survives. In the 1860s W. E. Gladstone took over the house from Sir Stephen, his brother-in-law, who was in financial difficulties. He had a tower added at the NE corner, by Shaw of Saddleworth: in it is his study, the 'Temple of Peace', left as it was at his death in 1898 (and occasionally shown to the public). It contains intriguing relics such as his axes (for tree-felling), and a little box with a joke insect to amuse children. The porch and strong-room were added by Douglas. The old castle is occasionally open, and there is a Garden Centre. The beautiful park is always open to pedestrians, and is entered from the Leopold Gate (1819) in Hawarden village. In the grounds, beside the bend in the main road, is a pretty cottage by H. S. Goodhart-Rendel.

The village contains several buildings of interest. The church is chiefly remarkable for its 19th century history. Restored in 1855–6 by James Harrison, it was burnt out in 1857, and rebuilt by Sir Gilbert Scott. He added the low spire, and the reredos is his. John Douglas added the Gladstone Memorial Chapel, and did other work. In the chapel there is a vast monument, representing the Grand Old Man and his wife at sea on a symbolic boat. It was designed by Sir William Richmond, who also designed the glass and candlesticks. The inscription on the memorial tablet was written by Balfour. (The Gladstones are buried in Westminster Abbey.) Other good glass includes that in the Morning Chapel, by Wailes, and the east and west windows by Burne-Jones. The latter, a touching nativity scene, was a memorial to Gladstone: it was Burne-Jones's last window. There are also two richly carved medieval stalls, and a rood by Sir Giles Scott. The plain brick Rectory houses the County Record Office. West of the church is **St Deiniol's Library**, built in 1899–1906 as yet another memorial to Gladstone. The idea was his, and he transferred 32,000 books to the trustees before he died. The attractive sandstone buildings, by John Douglas, have splendid woodwork inside. The Library is residential, and is the perfect place for anyone wishing to study or write in peace. The little stone Lockup further east on the main road is by Joseph Turner, whose own house, The Elms, stands near by.

Two miles beyond Hawarden is **Ewloe**, with a castle invisible from the road, but well worth crossing a field to visit (D. o. E.). In spite of the English name, the castle is a Welsh one, possibly first built by Owain Gwynedd. The D-shaped Welsh Tower was built c. 1210, by Llywelyn the Last. After Flint Castle was built, Ewloe lost importance. The D. o. E. have rescued the ruins from debris and jungle. They are most romantically sited among steep woods over the confluence of two streams. The next village is **Northop** (Llaneurgain), once attractive, now chopped up by road junctions. The church has a magnificent fifteenth-century tower. The rest was much rebuilt in 1839, and restored in 1877 by Douglas, who put in the excellent woodwork. There is interesting nineteenth-century glass. The old stone school of 1609, in the churchyard, retains all its old fittings, in a state of utter decay. S of Northop is the park – with immense and superb trees – of **Soughton** (or Sychtyn) **Hall** (not open). Built c. 1720 by Bishop Wynne of St Asaph, it was rebuilt in 1868 by the Bankes family to an amazing design, in unspecifiable style, of great elaboration, with arcaded corner towers. Bishop Wynne's stables, and, at right angles to them, coach house, survive: behind the latter were recently discovered the fifteenth-century statues from the porch of the London Guildhall – soon to return there.

Between Northop and Holywell the road passes beneath **Halkyn Mountain**, a bare hilly area which nowhere reaches 1000 feet. The rich lead deposits have been mined since Roman times, producing a strange, pockmarked landscape. There are reservoir pools, little houses of every shape and size scattered all over the place, pubs and chapels here and there. Many of the houses probably began as a *Tŷ-unnos* (house built in a night). According to tradition, if a man was able to get a chimney smoking within one night on common land, he was allowed to build the rest of the house. Great efforts are being made to clear up the dereliction round here. It is thought that, whereas the small round pits are of medieval or later origin, the bigger long adits are Roman. The Roman settlement was probably near Flint. The chief leadworks in post-medieval times was at Gadlys, above Bagillt (p. 24), built in 1703–4 by the famous London Lead Company (or Quaker Company). When the lease expired in 1786 they pulled down the works and transferred business to Alston in Cumberland. From the hilltops there are splendid views across the estuary and towards the Clwydian Hills. At the highest point is Moel-y-Gaer, an Iron Age Fort 600 feet across, now (1973) being excavated before the construction of a reservoir. **Halkyn Castle** was begun in 1824, designed by J. C. Buckler for Lord Grosvenor, so that he could live in it while attending Holywell races. It was later enlarged by John Douglas for the 1st Duke of Westminster, his chief patron, who also commissioned him to build the church, in 1878. The latter is big and solid, with a fine tower and wide nave: the unusual glass, delicately painted in monochrome, is by Heaton, Butler and Bayne.

Holywell is now an ungainly, spreading place. Celia Fiennes, in 1698, was not impressed: 'at Holly Well they speake Welsh, the inhabitants go barefoote and bare leg'd a nasty sort of people.' But it is much more worthwhile than appears at first sight. Beside the main road, on the way in, is the former Workhouse, now a Hospital, with a pretty chapel of 1883 by Douglas. Its most colourful inmate was Baron Corvo (see p. 28). To reach the town, you have to turn off, into its cheerful main street. Off it, to the S, is Panton Place, with nice brick terraces dated 1816, intelligently converted into old people's flats.

Down the hill, past some new flats, is the **Well** from which the town gets its name. It is dedicated to St Winefride (in Welsh Gwenfrewi). She was the daughter of a local prince, living in the early seventh century. A local chieftain, Caradoc, tried to seduce her, but she ran away towards the church of her uncle, the great St Beuno. Caradoc cut off her head. The earth opened and swallowed him up, and Beuno put her head back on again, only a white line remaining to show what had happened. Where the head fell, a spring gushed forth, with healing powers. It became a great place of pilgrimage, and it alone of all the shrines of Wales has remained one ever since. The Well guidebook sternly rejects the legend as 'a commonplace in Celtic hagiography and inherently unlikely'. More sympathetic was Gerard Manley Hopkins, who wrote in his Journal in 1875: 'The strong unfailing flow of the water and the chain of cures from year to year all these centuries took hold of my mind with wonder at the bounty of God in one of His saints, the sensible thing so naturally and gracefully uttering the spiritual reason of its being (which is all in true keeping with the story of St Winefride's death and recovery) and the spring in place leading back the thoughts by its spring in time to its spring in eternity; even now the stress and buoyancy and abundancy of the water is before my eyes.' (He also wrote a poem about the Well, and an unfinished verse drama about St Winefride.) The water is still a magical sight, even though its flow is now much reduced, for in 1917 mining operations at Halkyn diverted the stream, and the well ran dry. Eventually another, less powerful, spring was connected up to it.

The elaborate chapel over the Well was built c. 1490–1500.

Largely financed by Lady Margaret Beaufort, mother of Henry VII, it was not destroyed by Henry VIII because the offerings were a valuable source of revenue. The upper chapel, with an apsidal chancel and richly carved timber roof, is being restored by the D. o. E. and is not yet open. The Well chapel beneath has been leased by the Jesuits since 1873. It is a remarkable structure, of great elegance, even though it has lost ribs and tracery. The water rises within a basin shaped like a five-pointed star (compare Ffynnon Fair, p. 116): from the points rise piers supporting the vault, which is decorated with elaborate bosses, the central one showing scenes from Winefride's life. The rows of crutches, left behind by the cured, which used to line the chapel, have been removed. The numerous carved graffiti bear fascinating witness to the flourishing post-Reformation history of the pilgrimage. They run from the sixteenth to the nineteenth centuries. The earliest dates from 1580, the year after Queen Elizabeth ordered the Council of the Marches to 'pay particular attention to pilgrimages to St Winefride's Well'. The last royal pilgrims were James II and Mary of Modena, in 1686, coming to pray for a son – a prayer that was granted in 1688, with fateful results. Bathing hours are 8–9 for men, 9–10 for ladies. In the large pool outside the chapel there is a rough block called St Beuno's Stone, on which bathers kneel to pray.

The dull **Parish Church**, near the Well, was rebuilt (except the tower) in 1770, and remodelled in 1885 by Mathew Wyatt. Because of its position under the hill, the bells could not be heard throughout the town, so a man went round with a bell fixed to his leg. Bell and knee-pad are kept in the church. Further up the hill is the **Roman Catholic Church**, handsome Italianate, built in 1833 by J. J. Scoles, and much extended from 1895 by Father Beauclerk, S.J.: it was he who got Frederick Rolfe (Baron Corvo), in 1896–8, to paint ten banners for the church (not on show). The story of this extraordinary episode is told in A. J. A. Symons's famous *The Quest for Corvo*: it threw the town into chaos, and resulted in Fr Beauclerk's being moved elsewhere and in Rolfe's moving himself to the workhouse.

Down by the Well, the country seems surprisingly close, with fields on the slopes above, yet along the valley below are a succession of reservoirs which once provided the motive power for the wool and flannel mills and the copper, brass, and lead works. A number of interesting buildings survive. Near the bottom of the valley, close to the main road is **Basingwerk Abbey** (D. o. E.), reached past a pool that once fed a copper works. It was founded in 1132 for the French order of Savigny (who also had Furness, Neath, etc.) but in 1147 became Cistercian. In the next century the monks profited by rapidly declaring their allegiance to Edward I, and even more out of pilgrimages to the Well, which they owned. In the fifteenth century the many guests could choose between the wines of Aragon, Spain and Brittany. The last Abbot was the son of his predecessor. The surroundings of the ruins are surprisingly rural; not much is left, but one can visualize the whole establishment, and the thirteenth-century reader's pulpit in the Frater has real beauty. Nearby is the huge Abbey Paper Mill. On the other side of the main road is **Holywell Junction Station,** a very dignified little Italianate building of brick and stucco. It is one of the few surviving stations designed by Francis Thompson in the 1840s for the Chester and Holyhead Railway (his masterpiece is at Chester).

Up in the hills one and a half miles west of Holywell, is **Pantasaph**, a flourishing modern religious centre. Its origins are interesting. Viscount Feilding (later 8th Earl of Denbigh) married, in 1846, Louise Pennant, who inherited Downing and its estates (see p. 31). He decided to build a church and rectory at Pantasaph, and commissioned designs from T. H. Wyatt (also his architect at Downing and at Newnham Paddox). They were begun in 1849: Manning, also still Anglican, preached at the laying of the foundation stone. The church is much better than most of Wyatt's work: the pyramidal stone steeple is quite effective. But in 1850, before the church was finished, Lord Denbigh was converted to Rome, and wanted it to be Catholic. This gave rise to a lawsuit, which the Church of England lost, and to such bitterness that the subscriptions got up to build an Anglican church produced enough to build two – Brynford (1851–3) and Gorsedd (1852–3), both designed by Wyatt, at his more usual low level of inspiration. To give his new church an authentic Catholic air, Lord Denbigh called in A. W. N. Pugin, who designed the High Altar, font, pulpit, and statues of Our Lady, St David, and St Asaph – all of which were shown at the Great Exhibition of 1851. The pulpit has gone, and the High Altar has been replaced by a lavish new one of 1893, designed by Purdie, and put up, together with an elaborate monument, as a memorial to the 8th Earl. There is glass by Hardman, and also by the great twentieth-century Irish artist, Harry Clarke. The church was entrusted to Capuchin Franciscans, whose Friary was begun in 1858, and other religious institutions have followed. Francis Thompson, drop-out author of *The Hound of Heaven*, spent much time here.

Beyond Holywell, between the A55 and the sea, and extending up to Diserth, is an area of grassy limestone uplands, of great beauty, and full of interest. It feels strangely remote when one considers the proximity of two main roads, and of holiday resorts like Prestatyn. Part of its attraction is due to the presence of numerous sizable houses, most still occupied, and their estates. The most celebrated is near the coast, three miles from Holywell – **Mostyn Hall**. From Carmel, a mile out of Holywell on the A55, a lane drops down to the coast road (A548). This passes the spired EE church of Glanydon, built by Ambrose Poynter in 1844–5 for the Mostyn family. This family, who, with their innumerable branches, have dominated Flintshire history for centuries, still live at the Hall. The house (a mile beyond the church, in a big park – not open) is partly medieval – or rather, one should say houses, for there are two side by side (possibly an example of the 'unit system' – see p. 367). The main house was enlarged by Ambrose Poynter in the 1840s, in the Elizabethan style. There is a window through which the future Henry VII is said to have escaped. The story goes that Richard III's men asked why an extra place was laid at table, but were told that it was a hospitable custom to lay a place for chance guests, and were then entertained while Henry made his getaway.

Mostyn Dock, still in use, was once a prosperous colliery port, also used by the ironworks. The Station, again by Francis Thompson, still stands nearby, though derelict – bigger and grander than Holywell Junction, and with fine decorative panels. The drive from Mostyn Hall up to Whitford crosses the public road by means of the enchanting Gothick Drybridge Lodge: a short tunnel takes the road beneath the castellated lodge through which the drive passes at right angles to the road.

The Mostyn estate adjoins the Downing estate, to which Whitford is the estate village. Downing was the seat of the Pennant family, whose most famous member was the indefatigable Thomas (1726–98), the most famous British travel writer of the century – called by Johnson himself 'the best traveller I ever read'. He was brought up, according to old Welsh tradition, by foster-parents, tenants on his father's estate, but later went to Oxford, and spent the rest of his life pursuing his interests in natural history (he corresponded with Linnaeus and Gilbert White) and topography. He wrote a *Tour of Scotland*, and a *Tour to London*, but best of all are his *Tours in Wales*, still good reading (they should be reissued). He took as his illustrator a self-taught artist from Lleyn, Moses Griffith, whose watercolours – of variable quality, but at their best of great charm and freshness – are now much sought after. Downing was remodelled c. 1858 by T. H. Wyatt, burnt out in 1922, and subsequently demolished. Nothing worth seeing survives: even the ruined Mill which Pennant dressed up in Gothic detail and named the Abbey of Molinduna (a joke which deceived many people) has reverted to bare ruin.

Whitford is a delightful little village, dominated by its grand Perpendicular church, almost entirely nineteenth century – the fine tower is of 1843, by Ambrose Poynter, the rest rebuilt in 1846 and restored in 1876 and 1888. It slopes oddly from W to E. The elegant monument to Pennant, by R. Westmacott Jun., is sadly obscured by the organ. There is also a Gothic one to Lady Caroline Pennant (d. 1824), by Rickman and Hutchinson. Magnificent chandelier of 1755. The churchyard has two lychgates – 'Porch Sir Roger', of 1667, and another of 1624, at the head of three flights of steps. Moses Griffith is buried N of the church.

On top of the wooded hill to the W, **Garreg**, is a ruined tower, identified by Pennant as a Roman pharos, now dated to the sixteenth or seventeenth century. Restored in 1897, it is hard to get at, and there is not much of a view because of the forestry. By the crossroads NW of the hill is Maen Achwyfan, a fine Celtic cross of c. 1000, with elaborate ornamentation, copying Viking patterns.

Further along the coast from Mostyn is **Ffynnongroyw**, where, beside the road, stands one of the last churches built by the great G. E. Street, in 1881–2. It is a simple little building, with some oddities, including a weird font, and arcades reproducing those of one of Street's best early churches, at Wheatley near Oxford (1855). Some will hate it, but Goodhart-Rendel, who called it 'a test for taste', found it 'a tour de force of Street's skill'.

At the corner of the Dee estuary is **Point of Air**, a sandy promontory, with a disused red and white lighthouse of 1777, and coalmines running out under the sea. Talacre is an ephemeral place, all caravans and shanties. Set back on the other side of the main road, up among woods, is **Talacre Abbey**, now a house of Benedictine nuns. The house, a large and richly Tudor stone mansion, was built in 1824–7 for Sir Pyers Mostyn by Thomas Jones. The community began in 1868, as an Anglican sisterhood, under the direction of Father Ignatius (for whom see *South Wales*). In 1912 the nuns went over to Rome (in close association with the monks of Caldey (see *South Wales* again)), and in 1920 moved to Talacre, the birthplace of their patron, Bishop Mostyn of Menevia. The nuns built a plain church in 1932.

From the coast small roads climb steeply to **Llanasa**, comfortably tucked into a valley. The double-naved church, much rebuilt in 1739, was well restored in 1877 by Street, and has some excellent early sixteenth-century glass. On the road to Gwespyr is Henblas, a very pretty stone house of the seventeenth century, and beyond it a handsome chapel (Ebenezer, 1816). Gyrn Castle, east of the village, is a dullish eighteenth–nineteenth-century house. To the west is Golden Grove, a delightful seventeenth-century house, built by a coal-owner: it occupies a splendid position, on the S side of a hill, sheltered by woods. (None of these houses is open.) Further west is the exposed hill-top village of **Gwaenysgor**. The tiny church has a big timber-arched door, the timbers carved with odd patterns, and a good early font. An old man spoke regretfully of the time when the two pubs (now only one) stayed open till 2.0 or 3.0 a.m., and the policeman joined the drinkers – 'Those days are gone.'

Between Gwaenysgor and Trelawnyd is **Gop Hill**, a fine viewpoint, with a colossal mound on top, of uncertain origin, and a cave in the side, used c. 4000–2000 BC: the bones in it included those of both humans and woolly rhinos. **Trelawnyd**

The most original spire of St. Thomas' Church, Rhyl (Sir Gilbert Scott, 1861-9) 'forms a notable landmark on the flat Clwyd estuary'.

Plas Têg. near Mold, 'a real prodigy', built by Sir John Trevor c. 1610.

Mold, a bustling little town. 'The main street leading up from the crossroads to the church is still used for a lively market'.

(or Newmarket) is on the A5151, a road which from Gorsedd follows the line of Offa's Dyke. There is a small church, rebuilt in 1724 ('probably the very worst period of church architecture' – *Handbook for The Vale of Clwyd*, 1856), and remodelled in 1895–7 by Douglas. In the churchyard there is a good medieval cross. On the main road stands a funny pebbledashed chapel of c. 1930 – a stray from Prestatyn.

Tucked into a steep fold of the hills, 2 miles SW of Trelawnyd, is **Cwm**, aptly named: its little church has suffered from too many rich benefactors, just as its setting from too many conifers. The best feature is an elaborate stone tomb, outside the S wall of the church, with strapwork, pilasters, shields, angels, and an arched superstructure, to Grace Griffiths, d. 1642. The inscription seems to read:

LOE . MY . SAD . PLEDGE . ONE . LAST . ADIEU .
IS . HERE . PRESENTED . TO . THY . VIEW .
READER . BEHOLD . MY . LOSSE . SO . DEARE .
SPARE . THY . CENSURE . SPEND . A . TEARE .

The minor road via Cwm is a less disheartening route down into the Vale of Clwyd than by way of Diserth or Prestatyn. **Diserth**, long a popular beauty spot, is a disappointing place. To see its famous waterfall properly, you have to pay 3p, and contend with crowds of trippers. Its double-naved church, restored in 1875 by Scott (certainly not one of his best restorations), is locked, but you can see its best feature, the jumbled fifteenth- and sixteenth-century glass in the E window (including parts of a Jesse), by looking through the S chancel window. Around Diserth there are enormously powerful springs, and above it are great limestone cliffs – as if the hills above were set on defending their peace against the holiday-making hordes below. A mile N of Diserth, on the A547, is **Meliden**, whose little old church is swamped in middle-class suburbia, preparing the way for **Prestatyn** – a younger resort than Rhyl, to which it considers itself far superior. There is certainly no architectural justification for this. The town contains nothing worth seeing. The 1863 church by T. H. Wyatt inspired Goodhart-Rendel to paroxysms of loathing. Holiday camps and a golf course. Prestatyn, rather unromantically, marks the northern terminus of Offa's Dyke.

Half a mile W of Diserth (on the A5151) is **Bodrhyddan Hall** (open June–September), standing in a beautifully wooded

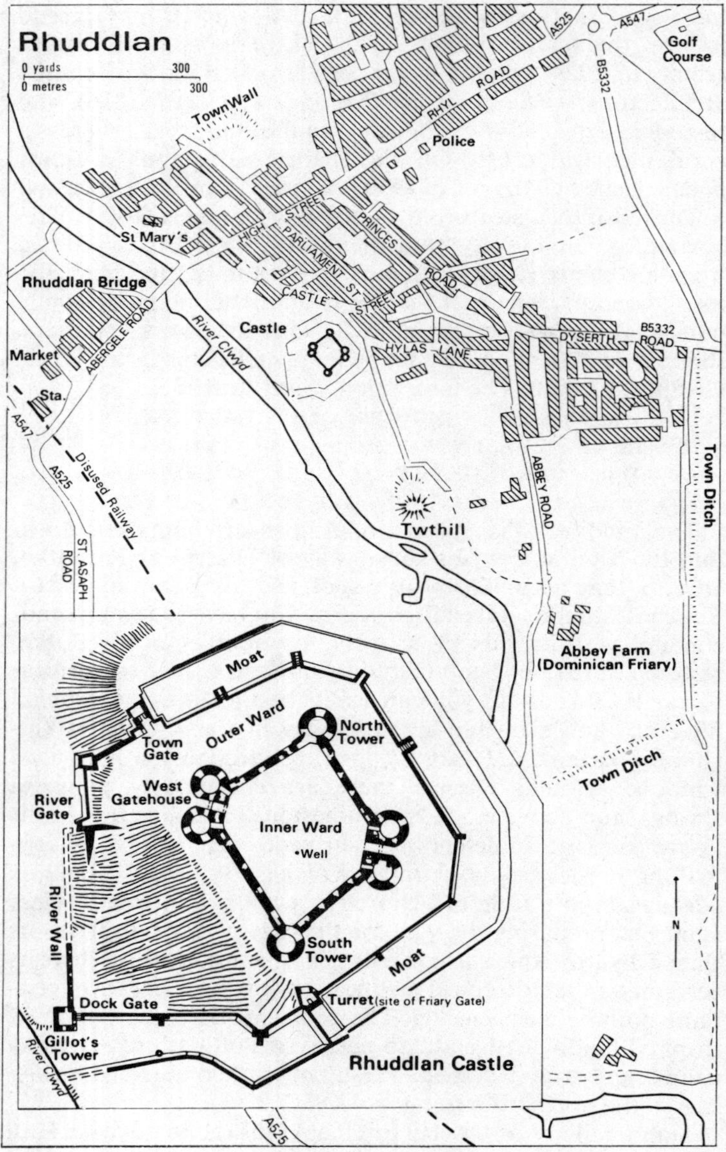
Rhuddlan
0 yards 300
0 metres 300
Town Wall
A525
A547
Golf Course
B5332
RHYL ROAD
Police
St Mary's
HIGH STREET
PRINCES ROAD
PARLIAMENT ST
CASTLE STREET
Rhuddlan Bridge
Castle
River Clwyd
ABERGELE ROAD
HYLAS LANE
DYSERTH ROAD
B5332
Market
Sta.
A547
A525
Disused Railway
ST. ASAPH ROAD
ABBEY ROAD
Twthill
Town Ditch
Abbey Farm
(Dominican Friary)
Moat
Outer Ward
North Tower
Town Gate
West Gatehouse
River Gate
Inner Ward
•Well
Town Ditch
River Wall
South Tower
Moat
N
Dock Gate
Turret (site of Friary Gate)
Gillot's Tower
River Clwyd
Rhuddlan Castle
A525

park. The house was built in 1696–1700 by Sir John Conwy, in plain brick, with quoins, and a recessed centre. In 1872–3 it was brilliantly transformed for Conwy Grenville Hercules Rowley-Conwy by William Eden Nesfield, who added large and picturesque wings at either end, the main entrance being moved to the western one. Nesfield's work is in a bright and cheery 'Queen Anne' style, red brick and white painted woodwork. Inside, there is lots of armour, and some fine portraits. The panelled hall has an inglenook (a feature revived by Nesfield and his colleague Norman Shaw only a few years earlier). On the first floor, the former Library is a stunning disappointment – the books sold, and the shelves painted white and gold and filled with china. In the grounds is Ffynnon Fair (Mary's Well), with a charming octagonal well-house inscribed '1612: Inigo Jones'.

A mile W of Bodrhyddan is **Rhuddlan**, little more than a large village now, but with a resounding history. As the lowest place where the Clwyd could be forded, and later the lowest bridge, its strategic importance is attested from the Dark Ages in the dubious legend of the Battle of Morfa Rhuddlan, at which the Welsh are said to have been defeated by the Saxons, in 796 – mourned in a famous ballad. In 1073 the Normans built a motte and bailey castle: the motte still stands, to an impressive height, beside the river SE of the later castle. It is called the Twthill – a name explained, with glorious implausibility, as derived from *tout*, on the grounds that 'everything' can be seen from it. It really derives from the Old English *tot*=look-out. The Norman Borough was E of the Twthill: its ramparts can be seen along the S and E. In 1277 Edward I began his new castle – so impressive from a distance, so disappointing in detail. The architect, as at Flint (p. 23), was James of St George. Rhuddlan, being more open than Flint to attack by land, has concentrically planned defences. The Inner Ward, roughly square, has gatehouses on E and W, with pairs of stout round towers. A low curtain surrounds the Outer Ward, and beyond that was a dry moat. The outer walls go down to the river where Gillot's Tower (perhaps called after a mason, Gillot de Chalons) protects the Dock Gate. Originally the river flowed beside the wall, and the intriguing suggestion has been made that this tower was intended to recall the similar tower at Constantinople, where the famous Theodosian walls run down to the Bosporus. One of Edward's greatest feats was the canalization of the Clwyd, so that it would be navigable up to Rhuddlan.

Beside the Castle, in 1284, he founded a new borough, NW of the Norman one (again, as at Flint). The main streets of the village follow the lines of the Edwardian ones. Like Flint, the town never had stone walls. The bridge was rebuilt in stone in 1358, and remodelled in 1595. The quay was below it. Edward regarded Rhuddlan so highly that he applied to Rome for permission to transfer the see of St Asaph to it, offering a site and money for a new cathedral, but nothing came of it.

The **Parish Church of St Mary** is a double-naved building with a plain tower, begun c. 1300, but mostly Perp, and restored by Scott in 1868. The battlemented Bodrhyddan mausoleum on the N was built in 1820. The most interesting thing inside is the stone tomb-slab left of the altar, to William de Freney, nephew of Gilbert de Freney, who was sent to England by St Dominic in 1221 to found the Dominican Order there. William became Archbishop of Rages (Edessa) in Syria, but had to return to England when the Muslims overran the country. He spent the rest of his life assisting British Bishops. He died about 1290, probably while assisting Bishop Anian of St Asaph (himself a Dominican), and was no doubt buried at the Dominican Priory (founded in 1258), of which slight remains are incorporated in the farm Plas Newydd, SE of the Twthill.

It was at Rhuddlan that Edward issued the Statute of Wales, in 1284, creating the counties of Flint, Caernarfon, Anglesey, Merioneth, Cardigan and Carmarthen, and establishing the system of government which lasted until 1536. Everyone knows the famous story of how the Welsh nobles said that they would only obey 'a prince of their own nation, of their own language, and whose life and conversation was spotless and unblameable,' and how Edward replied that he would give them a prince born in Wales, who could speak no English, and of unstained life, and at once named his son Edward, recently born at Caernarfon. The story is always associated with Caernarfon, but A. J. Taylor argues that it should more properly be associated with Rhuddlan.

A short mile from Rhuddlan brings you into the suburbs of

Rhyl, but what a difference. Rhyl, to most people, means rock, sandcastles, and skinheads and greasers on motorbikes. Its development as a resort was meteoric. In 1820 there was nothing on the sandy estuary except a few fishermen's huts; by the 1850s the place was a thriving resort with smart Italianate terraces, and churches, chapels, and public buildings going up like mushrooms. In 1854 David Cox painted his *Rhyl Sands* (Birmingham Art Gallery). Rhyl's general architectural character cannot rival Llandudno's, but its ecclesiastical architecture is far more interesting. The earliest church was **Holy Trinity**, humble Perp, built 1835–7 by Thomas Jones, but enlarged in 1849–52 so that it is now cruciform. Some windows have cast-iron tracery, as in Rickman's famous Liverpool churches (it is possible that Jones was associated with Rickman). In spite of enlargement, the church was soon too small, and was handed over for Welsh services when the splendid great **Church of St Thomas**, which overshadows it, was complete. This fine work of Sir Gilbert Scott, in Early English style (1861–9), has a most original spire, 203 feet high, which forms a notable landmark on the flat estuary, and a lofty, dignified interior. Yet another church, **St John's**, was built, further W, in 1885–7 – a surprising building as, although Gothic, it has an octagonal nave. The architect was David Walker of Liverpool (who had been Poundley's partner – see p. 49).

The Catholics also built an exceptional church – the **Assumption** (Wellington Road). The priest in charge, a Jesuit from St Beuno's, was Father Wynne (of the Voelas family – p. 118), and he got his old friend Hungerford Pollen to design it, in 1863. Pollen was a remarkable man – painter and architect, associate of the Pre-Raphaelites, designer of Newman's University Church in Dublin. The Rhyl church has been badly treated, and is threatened with destruction, but is still interesting. It is a small, apsidal Romanesque building. The polychrome brickwork has been cement-rendered, but the statues by O'Shea survive (he was the crazy Irish genius famous for his work at the Oxford Museum – where Pollen also worked). Inside, the all-over decorative painting by Pollen has gone, but his magnificent marble and alabaster altar and reredos, carved in flat relief, are still there. Rhyl also possesses innumerable chapels, in every conceivable style.

The showy Town Hall is a poor effort by Wood and Turner of Barrow-in-Furness (1874).

CHESTER TO MOLD

The third road from Chester leaves the A55 at Broughton junction and goes off towards Mold (A549). The direct route goes through the hilltop town of **Buckley**, a sprawling industrial place, chiefly celebrated for its clay, once used to make bricks and also coarse pottery. Along the main road, the place has little to offer – chapels, and Emmanuel Church, 1842, by John Lloyd, copied from Casterton church in Westmorland – though why anyone should want to copy that feeble effort of 1831 by George Webster is hard to comprehend. However, off to the N stands the much grander **Church of St Matthew**. It has had a curious history. Built in 1821–2 by John Oates of Halifax, it was altered in 1845 by James Harrison, then again in 1864–5. It was completely remodelled in 1897–1904 by John Douglas. He added the chancel (in memory of Gladstone) in 1902, heightened the tower, and rebuilt the nave. The exterior is in his late style, with a half-timbered clerestory. The porch (1902) was paid for by the Vicar's wife, Mary Drew, who was Gladstone's daughter, out of the profits of the publication of her correspondence with Ruskin. The spacious interior is astonishing, but not really successful: the arcade piers are of steel encased in oak, and the clerestory and baptistery have elaborate painted decoration. The glass in the chancel and baptistery is by Henry Holiday. The tower clock was designed by Lord Grimthorpe (designer of the Big Ben clock). By the church is the bare Common, where many of the scattered cottages probably began as *Tŷ-unnos* (see p. 26). Little is left of the brickworks, but parts of the tramways survive by which coal, lead and bricks were taken down to the Dee.

Through traffic to Mold cuts out Buckley by going to the south. By the roundabout, at a place called **Penymynydd** on the map, but **Pentrobin** on the signs (a confusion not uncommon in Wales), stands a spindly Early English church, with a spire, designed by John Buckler in 1843. It is well worth a visit, not so much for its architecture (though the octagonal vaulted vestry is fun), but for its rich decoration, all carried out by the Curate-in-Charge, Rev. J. E. Troughton, who was here from 1843 until 1864. According to a tablet set up by Gladstone, 'he used his rare gifts of genius and taste in himself adorning all the interior . . . by colouring and frescoes and sculptures and window staining, with much labour but with no detriment to the faithful discharge of his manifold Parish duties.' The glass is rather good, but the paintings (including a Doom over the chancel arch, and Adam and Eve on the W wall) have been badly restored. Tall rich sedilia in the chancel, and funny angels on the roof. The decorative scheme was designed by R. P. Pullan, brother-in-law of William Burges. The atmosphere is rich and holy. Beyond Pentrobin the huge Padeswood cement works disturb the rural peace.

Mold is a busy little town, which has precariously retained a good deal of character. By-passes have eased the traffic, and the main street leading up from the crossroads to the church is still used for a lively market, which, like so many Welsh markets, boasts a bookstall. The Welsh name of Mold – Yr Wyddgrug – means 'mound', and refers to the motte-and-bailey castle of which the motte still stands in the public park called Bailey Hill, just N of the **Parish Church**. The church is a splendid building, dominating the main street, and indeed much of the Alun valley. It is less uniform than appears at first sight, for it has been fortunate in its history. To the great aisled nave, built c. 1500–1570, was added, in 1768–73, a grand tower, probably by Joseph Turner, who entered into the medieval spirit in a way unusual for his time – even the frieze of animals and grotesques is carried on convincingly from the nave. Finally, in 1856, the chancel, with a canted apse, was added by Sir Gilbert Scott, equally successfully (and Perp was not in favour in the 1850s). He also completed the clerestory. There are good timber roofs (that over the N aisle medieval), and plenty of rich stone carving, especially on the E window of the S aisle. The chancel windows are by Wailes, while the reredos, of 1878, is a tactful addition by Douglas. There is some fifteenth–sixteenth-century glass, and other good nineteenth-century glass, the best window being that in the S aisle, to Henry Raikes, d. 1863 (maker unknown). The War Memorial Chapel in the N aisle, by Sir T. G. Jackson (1921), has a curious Art Deco floor. The monuments include a statue by Sir Henry Cheere of Robert Davies, d. 1728, and a small one on the W wall to Rev. William Wynn, d. 1776, by Rysbrack. The new organ by the chancel looks best from a distance. Outside the church, near the N wall, is the restored table tomb of Richard Wilson.

Facing the road junction nearby stands an enchanting **Wesleyan Chapel** of 1828, delicately Gothick and showing off the pinky-yellow strong-grained stone even better than the church. SE of the church is the old County Hall, of 1833–4, by Thomas Jones, in Tudor style. It has lost its tall lantern. It seems a far cry from this humble building to the enormous new white County Hall (1967), built right outside the town to the N, and said to represent Flintshire's bid to get the upper hand in local government reorganization. Beside the main crossroads is the old Town Hall, once a handsome eighteenth-century structure, crudely enlarged in the nineteenth. Along the Ruthin road is the grand Welsh Presbyterian Church, with a Corinthian portico (1863, by W. W. Gwyther of London).

Around Mold there is a group of country houses of exceptional interest, mostly seventeenth century, and most – unlike their counterparts around Wrexham – still surviving as private houses. Two miles N, high up on the hillside above the A541, is **Gwysaney**, a tall plain house of the early seventeenth century (not open). A mile W on the minor road to Gwernafield is **Rhual** (open on written application), a charming house of 1634, with a particularly attractive forecourt, enclosed by symmetrical curved walls topped by iron tulips. Unfortunately the brickwork on the main front has been rendered. In the field across the road stands the 'Alleluia Monument', an obelisk set up in 1736 by Nehemiah Griffith of Rhual, to commemorate the famous victory (*Victoria Alleluiatica*) supposed to have been won here by the Britons over the Saxons and Picts in the early fifth century. The Britons asked the help of St Garmon (Germanus, Bishop of Auxerre, who had come to Britain to fight the Pelagian heresy). He baptized them in the Alun, and then led them to battle, teaching them the warcry 'Alleluia'. This was too much for the enemy, who fled and were cut to bits. A curious local echo no doubt helped.

A mile W of Rhual is **Gwernafield** (called **Waen** on the map), a dull place, whose little church of 1870–2 by David Walker possesses some character but is chiefly worth a visit for the eighteenth-century churchyard gates, and the superb

Grecian marble monument inside, showing two children on their deathbed, with an angel. They were the children of Thomas Lloyd, of Leghorn, and the monument was made at Rome in 1843 by W. Theed, one of the best Victorian sculptors.

S of Mold there is a whole cluster of good houses. **Pentrehobin** (not open), beside the A541, is sixteenth–seventeenth century, and is best known for its **Lletyau,** a row of eight small cells with brick vaults, said to have been built as lodgings for poor travellers after the Dissolution. This seems very improbable, but local feeling on the subject is so strong that one hardly dares question it. Half a mile W is **Tower**, basically of 1380, but much Victorianized. In 1450 a Mayor of Chester was seized by a Welsh chieftain in Mold market, brought here, and served with a pie. In it he found a rope, with which he was promptly hanged – from a staple in the stone vault which still survives.

A little beyond Pentrehobin, on the main road, are the Black Gates of **Leeswood.** These magnificent early eighteenth-century iron gates are the work of the famous local smith Robert Davies, of Croes Foel (see p. 71). They stand between a charming pair of lodges, their pediments carved with weapons and musical instruments (representing the arts of war and the arts of peace). The even finer and grander White Gates are up the lane running due S from the A541, ¼ mile back towards Mold. They are not really gates, but an ornamental screen closing the view from the house. The profusion of ornament – flowers, dolphins, and so on – is amazing. The house itself (not open) was built in the early eighteenth century as a grand mansion, with a pilastered front between wings, out of lead mining revenues, but when these dried up early next century the top storey and wings were prudently removed and the front rendered. The garden laid out by Switzer survives, with its yew walks and artificial mound – almost the only garden of its type remaining.

Further on, near the road junction, is **Fferm**, an attractive passage house (open on written application), probably built in 1607. Half a mile beyond, one is suddenly confronted with the most amazing of all these houses, **Plas Têg**, a real prodigy. It is built on a square plan with a large square tower at each corner, surmounted by a shaped roof and cupola, and with gables between. The house is something of a mystery. Built for Sir John Trevor, c. 1610, it is sophisticated in plan, but provincial in detail. The traditional attribution to Inigo Jones is regarded as no more reliable than any of the numerous other Welsh attributions to him, but it is curious that the arms on a portrait of Jones are almost identical with those of the Trevors of Plas Têg. Inside there is little to see except the staircase. Recently bought back into the family by Mr Patrick Trevor-Roper, the house is open on written application.

Trevor was Secretary to Lord Howard of Effingham, and a naval administrator. His monument is in the church at **Hope**, on the other side of the Alun. It is a good double-naved church, with a big tower, mostly Perp. Some fifteenth-century glass. Hope is also the church of **Caergwrle**, immediately S. Not much is left of its thirteenth-century castle, though the steep site gives good views. Below it, to the W, just across the river, are sad remains of the late nineteenth-century spa – a ruinous Ruabon brick building in the middle of a field and a few pipes. Hope Mountain, to the E, only reaches 1085 feet, but is quite a landmark. On the other side of it, feeling very remote and pastoral, even though it is only a couple of miles from Brymbo Steelworks, is the village of **Llanfynydd**, with a crude church of 1842–3 by John Lloyd. Along the E side of the Cegidog valley ran Offa's Dyke, and along the W ran a railway, now disused, though a good viaduct survives at Ffrith.

Two miles NE of Llanfynydd, across the A5104, is the workaday village of **Treuddyn**, with a horrid little church of 1875 by T. H. Wyatt. Still, it is worth getting the key from the vicarage to see the remarkable fourteenth-century glass, including one panel in the apse – the left lower panel on the N – which is early fourteenth-century, richly coloured, and said to be the earliest glass in North Wales.

Further N is **Nercwys** (or **Nerquis**), spread out along the hillside with views over the Alun valley. The attractively-set church has a nice shingled spire, added by John Oldrid Scott at his restoration of 1883. It has some odd features, and a lot of interesting fittings. The most exceptional is the so-called Cadair Fair, a very elaborate wooded structure, late medieval, whose name – 'Mary's Seat' – suggests that it was a shrine to contain a statue of the Virgin, but which looks more like part of a rood-screen. Scott made it into sedilia. It is prettily painted in red, blue and gold. Several excellent windows by Burlison and Grylls: their E window ingeniously incorporates medieval glass, including a lion and a boar, the badges of Richard III. There are two surprisingly old-fashioned monuments – a marble one in the chancel, with kneeling figures, to Robert Roberts, d. 1725, which looks seventeenth-century, and a small engraved plaque under the tower, to Walter How, d. 1907, looking early nineteenth century. Also a well-preserved medieval pulpit of carved wood.

Outside the church, to the W, is a splendid eighteenth-century marble monument, bearing a sarcophagus with cartouches, to Elizabeth Hyde. She lived at **Nercwys Hall** nearby. This house, after falling almost derelict, has been completely restored over the last few years by Mr and Mrs A. W. Furse (open on written application). The contract for its building, made by John Wynn with Raphe Booth of Chester, freemason, in 1637, survives: the house was to be 'like Rhual'. It was built in 1638–40. In 1797 wings were added at either end, of a strange nature, for towards the front they were Gothick, with semicircular castellated projections, towards the garden they were Jacobean, with gables, while the side towards the stables had plain sash windows. These wings have been removed, as has the Gothick porte cochère (re-erected at Portmeirion). Of these romantic additions, there survive the screen walls to the stables, and a chimneypiece in the Hall, together with the derelict Orangery to the S, with cast-iron tracery (designed by Benjamin Gummow c. 1815), and the little castle folly to the N. Part of the latter has collapsed, improving the effect (the same happened to one of Brunel's castellated bridges near Bristol, and he ordered it to be left ruinous). Inside the house there is a fine panelled room of the mid-eighteenth century, and another with a moulded plaster ceiling. Along the top floor runs a long gallery.

CHESTER TO BODFARI

The main road from Mold to Denbigh follows winding, wooded valleys, past limestone quarries, in close company with the old Chester–Ruthin railway (now closed). The first stop, three miles out, was **Rhydymwyn**, worth a visit for its church, a first-rate early work of J. L. Pearson (1861–4). Tall and lavishly detailed, it has great dignity, and the grey and yellow stones are well contrasted. Characteristic fittings include the red and white inlaid reredos (note Judas's money-bag). The village is industrialized, but its industry has a respectable history, for at Llyn y Pandy, further up the Alun, John Wilkinson (see p. 70) worked a big lead-mine, drained by four Boulton and Watt engines. There is little trace of it now, nor of the nearby Penyfron mine, in the quiet wooded valley, though the Leete can be followed to Loggerheads (see p. 148).

Further W, reached by steep, twisting roads, is the delightful village of **Cilcain**. The double-naved church has been much rebuilt. The N aisle was rebuilt in 1746, and screened off at the big restoration in 1887–8 by John Douglas. He added huge buttresses and a new top to the old tower, giving it great character. He also made new S windows and porch, and put in plenty of carved woodwork. The magnificent medieval roof, with splendid angels and rich carving, was well restored in 1845 by Ambrose Poynter, and again by Douglas. There is good glass of 1546 in the E window, and beside it a fine marble tablet of 1731 to three Roger Mostyns, signed T. Wynne. The cottage opposite the lychgate was a school, and has a nice inscription of 1799. From the lane running up past the Vicarage starts one of the best paths up Moel Fama (at 172/648).

Beyond Rhydymwyn, the villages lie off the main road. First comes **Nannerch**. The church of 1852–3, by T. H. Wyatt, has a broach spire, and an E window of 1853 by Gibbs. It contains a superb brass chandelier bequeathed in 1826, but, even more remarkably, a grand marble monument, with sarcophagus and putti, to Charlotte Theophila Mostyn, d. 1694 – the work of Grinling Gibbons. She was the granddaughter of Sir Kenelm Digby. Further on, up on a bare hilltop N of the road, is **Ysgeifiog**, with a big plain lancet church of 1836–7 by John Welch.

Also up on the hills, a mile N of the road, is **Caerwys**, a small, quiet village now, but preserving in its strict grid lay-out unmistakable evidence of its past. The borough was founded in 1290, and became an important market town, but later it declined owing to poor communications. The NE part of the grid is only now being built up, with council houses. Many

Eisteddfodau have been held here, the first reputedly in 1100, but the town's finest hour was in 1568, when an Eisteddfod was set up by Queen Elizabeth, to test the claims of vagrants calling themselves bards and harpists. The village enjoys great views W and S. The double-naved church, whose tower was heightened in 1769, contains old woodwork (some jolly medieval dragons), but is not exciting. In the churchyard, on the N, stands a monument to Llewelyn Edwards, 'who with two cousins of his was drowned in Crossing the Sands from Parkgate to Flint on the 20th April 1832 aged twenty years', also to Jane Roberts, one of the cousins, aged eight. Such tragedies were not uncommon in North Wales, when the crossing of tidal estuaries like that of the Dee was a normal means of travel. The Piccadilly Inn, N of the village, owes its name to a successful bet on a horse so called at Holywell Races.

The lanes between Caerwys and Tremeirchion give glorious views across the Vale of Clwyd to Snowdonia and the sea. **Tremeirchion** is a neat hillside village. Its church – the only medieval one in Britain dedicated to Corpus Christi – is well placed among yews between vicarage and pub. A small, plain building, it houses an elegant and well-preserved fourteenth-century canopy tomb (to see the front, lower the hinged pew-back). It is thought to commemorate Dafydd Ddu Hiraddug, Canon of St Asaph, a poet and scientist. There is some fifteenth-century glass in the vestry, but more interesting still are the seventeenth-century panels in a S window, brought from the Vicarage, with portraits of James I, Charles I, and Archbishop John Williams (buried at Llandygai – see p. 136). E window by Olliphant. Dr Johnson visited the church in 1774, and tells how a curious mistake had been made in a painted text. Instead of St Paul's words, '*Y Gwŷr, cerwch eich gwragedd*' (Husbands, love your wives), was written '*Y Gwŷr, curwch eich gwragedd*' (Husbands, beat your wives). The reason for his visit is given by the tablet set up in 1909 to Mrs Piozzi, formerly Mrs Thrale, his close friend. She was a member of the ancient local family of Salusbury, whose seats were Bachegraig and Lleweni. Johnson came up here to stay with her on several occasions.

After her marriage to her Italian music master, Gabriele Piozzi, she settled here with him. They did not live at Bachegraig, which she had inherited, but built a new house, Brynbella – a tragic decision, for, however charming Brynbella may be, **Bachegraig** was unique. What is left of it stands a mile SE of Tremeirchion, on the hillside, now used as a farmhouse. It was built in 1567–9 by Sir Richard Clough, a merchant, and an associate of Sir Thomas Gresham, builder of the Royal Exchange. He traded with the Low Countries, and this explains (as in the case of the Exchange) the Netherlandish look of the house, and also the use of brick – possibly the earliest use of it in Wales. (The story that the bricks were brought from Holland is untrue: they were made locally.) It was built round three sides of a courtyard. The main entrance was through an archway, below a square tower with pyramidal roof, in the W wing. From the arch a loggia ran S, and then along the S wing. Both these wings survive, although the tower has gone, the arch and loggia have been walled up, and the windows altered. The E wing was the principal one, and rose to a height of six storeys. The chief floor contained a huge parlour, and above was a steep pitched roof with rows of dormers and tall chimneys, then a rectangular gazebo, and on top of all a cupola. The house seemed so freakish to the locals that they assumed it was built by the Devil. Tradition maintained that Clough intended the buildings to serve as a trade-centre, and that he planned to make a canal from Rhuddlan, or else to make the Clwyd navigable. Johnson was taken to see the house, then derelict, and rather liked it – 'I wish it well', he recorded in his Journal. Piozzi repaired it in 1800 and 1803, but in 1794 he had begun his new house, nearer Tremeirchion, called (in an apt mixture of Welsh and Italian) **Brynbella**. This elegant Italianate villa, beautifully situated in a wooded sloping park, was designed by Clement Mead, though Piozzi himself took a hand. By 1817 the main wing of Bachegraig was demolished.

Across the road from the SE corner of the park of Brynbella is **Ffynnon Beuno** (Beuno's well): the water – if there is any – comes through the mouth of a weird stone figure. It is thought that St Beuno must have passed this way, and the Jesuit College just N of the village is dedicated to him. It was built in 1846–9 by Joseph Aloysius Hansom, and extended later. Surrounded by trees, it is sober collegiate Gothic – 'decent outside, skimpin within, Gothic like Lancing College done worse,' wrote its most famous student, Gerard Manley Hopkins. He was here from 1874 until 1877. It was while he was here that he learnt Welsh, and became fascinated by the strict metres and word-music of Welsh poetry, which strongly influenced his own writing. He was also deeply impressed both by the beauty of the surroundings – 'in its way there can hardly be in the world anything to beat the Vale of Clwyd' – and by the widespread evidence of the area's rich religious history. Outside the College stands a good medieval cross from Tremeirchion. A conspicuous landmark is the tiny chapel of Our Lady of Sorrows, with apse and flêche, built on a rocky hill just to the S – giving the Vale a continental touch. Up on the hill E of the Tremeirchion–Bodfari road is the intriguingly named hamlet of **Sodom.**

At **Bodfari**, the village centre forms a picturesque group, with the tall church tower at the head of a steep flight of steps, and jokey lychgate below, a stuccoed Tudorish house on the left, and the pub on the right. Best not to look too far, though – the pub is so popular that it has carparks tiered like a quarry, and the church was rebuilt by T. H. Wyatt in 1865 – for which he was denounced by Goodhart-Rendel as 'an unutterable cad'. Below the village, the A541 (from Mold) comes down into the Vale.

MOLD TO RUTHIN

The road from Mold to Ruthin (A494), climbs steeply up to Gwernymynydd, and then drops down into Denbighshire, towards the upper part of the Alun valley. A mile off to the S is **Maeshafn**: remains of a lead-mine opened in 1755 are scattered along the valley, including waterwheel pits. Unfortunately a fine stone and brick chimneystack was recently demolished as 'unsafe'. Just off the main road, before Loggerheads, is Glan Alyn School, occupying **Colomendy Hall** and its park. Here Richard Wilson died, for the house belonged to a relative, to whom his brother was agent. The house was rebuilt c. 1800. The school is a remarkable institution: it is run by Liverpool Corporation to provide a country environment for children in need of it, and also courses in environmental studies. Well sited modern buildings have been designed by the firm of Colwyn Foulkes. The school is run with immense dedication. Down by the river is the famous **Loggerheads Inn**. Its sign, painted by Wilson, has recently been restored and replaced on the outside. The name is properly 'We Three Loggerheads' (blockheads), but Wilson only painted two, the idea being that the spectator is the third.

From the Crosville Bus Co. Tea Gardens opposite, a path called the Leete follows the river through woods and beneath limestone cliffs to Cilcain and Rhydymwyn: as the name implies, it follows the course of a leet which supplied the Llyn y Pandy works (see p. 44). In dry weather the river disappears into swallet holes – three times, according to legend, because King Benlli was punished for his wickedness by a burning sensation, but each time he tried to cool himself in the river it disappeared underground. Loggerheads is one of the classic starting-places for Moel Fama, but as this route involves passing through the Clwyd Forest, the Cilcain or Bwlch Pen Barras paths have advantages.

A mile WNW of Loggerheads (actually in Flintshire) is **Brithdir Mawr** (not open), beautifully sited, at right angles to the steep hillside. The house is a fascinating survival. It was built in 1589, on what was then the old-fashioned open hall system, and remains almost intact. Typical of Flintshire vernacular, it is built of stone, with wooden partitions. The large hall had a central open fire. The wooden windows with close-set mullions survive. Originally they had no glass, but a fragment of semi-transparent horn was found in one.

Beyond Loggerheads, the road follows the Alun valley through **Llanferres**, whose church, rebuilt in 1843 by Thomas Jones, has a jolly little bell-turret. Then it climbs over the Clwydian range. From the top the view is breathtaking. The vale lies spread out before you, with Ruthin down below: beyond the green vale, and the wooded hills beyond, rise the mountains of Snowdonia. It is also possible to cross the range by the more direct, but much steeper road over **Bwlch Pen Barras**. In summer-time the top of the pass is crawling with trippers. From here a rapid ascent can be made of Foel Fenlli (1676 feet), a heathery Iron Age hill-fort, or a longer, but less strenuous climb to **Moel Fama** (1820 feet), the highest point of the Clwydian hills. The western slopes are purple with heather in summer, brown in winter. The conifer forest on the east has fortunately been kept below the skyline.

Llanbedr Dyffryn Clwyd has 'one of the most characterful little churches imaginable', built in 1863 by Poundley and Walker. Behind are the Clwydian Hills.

Ruthin, 'one of the most attractive small towns in Wales'. Behind the Clwydian Hills rise to their highest point, Moel Fama.

The pinnacled tower of Gresford Church, rebuilt in the late fifteenth century.

The summit is crowned by the huge ruin which makes the mountain so instantly recognizable from far and near. It is the bottom part of a 'Tower', really a vast Egyptian-style obelisk in three set-back stages, erected to commemorate the Golden Jubilee of George III's reign in 1810. It was designed by Thomas Harrison of Chester, whose fertile brain was inspired by the commission to produce one of the most amazing series of designs ever conceived – including triumphal arches carrying quadrigae, Greek temples, telescopic castellated towers, pyramids, and even a gigantic ziggurat. The design chosen was one of the simplest, but even that, despite its immensely solid masonry (the builder, Thomas Penson, fell out with Harrison – which is not, perhaps, surprising), it collapsed in 1862. Various subsequent proposals for its re-erection never came to anything. Finally, in Investiture Year (1969), the contractors for the St Asaph by-pass offered to tidy up the ruin. Crude concrete staircases at each corner now lead to a platform on the top, complete with orientation tables. G. M. Hopkins did not like the Tower – 'an ugly and trumpery construction, make-believe-massive, but so frail that it was blown over . . . and it cumbers the hilltop and interrupts the view.' Below Moel Fama is Moel-y-Gaer, another of the fine series of forts along the range.

Both roads across join at the bottom of the hill, at **Llanbedr Dyffryn Clwyd**, where the traveller warily rounds a bend to be greeted by one of the most characterful little churches imaginable, in chunky grey and yellow stone, with a slate-patterned roof, a tough little bell-turret over the porch, and lots of vigorous carving (especially the gargoyles round the apse). It was built in 1863 by Poundley and Walker. John Wilkes Poundley (1807–72) was a remarkable man – a surveyor from Kerry, in Montgomeryshire, who became Surveyor to that county in 1861, and over the next few years designed a series of fascinating buildings, right up-to-date, the best of which are equal in merit to anything then produced in the provinces. This is one of his best. Inside there is some splendid glass (especially the W window), and a portrait tablet of Edward Lloyd, by John Gibson, made at 'Rhufain' (Rome) in 1863. The church was built by John Jesse FRS, whose son had the Hall enlarged by Poundley in 1866. Jesse had inherited the Hall from Joseph Ablett, a Manchester businessman, patron of Gibson, friend of W. S. Landor and Leigh Hunt, who fined his servants if they spoke Welsh. Ablett insisted on being buried on the N side of the old church (whose ruins are near the Hall), hoping to overcome the traditional superstition against that position, and Landor wrote his epitaph (not inscribed on the tomb). The former Vicarage, NW of the church, is a most attractive brick house of c. 1700, unusual for Wales.

It is a mile from Llanbedr to **Ruthin** (see p. 52), but it is also possible to approach the Vale of Clwyd from Mold by way of the A5104 and A525. The A5104 leaves the A541 at Leeswood. **Pont y Bodkin** is a workaday little place, with some handsome industrial buildings, probably by Charles Mathews, an architect who later turned to acting. A few miles more bring you, rather surprisingly, onto lonely moorland, over 1000 feet up, glorious with heather. Yet only a couple of miles N the country is quite different, in the limestone district round the hilltop hamlet of Eryrys, and the cosier village of **Llanarmon-yn-Iâl**, beautifully sited, with views of Clwydians and Berwyns, the outcropping limestone round about pock-marked with caves. Iâl, or Yale, was the name of the medieval commote (see p. 51). There is a motte castle, Tomen y Faerdre, on a natural outcrop. The church was rebuilt in 1736. The twin naves are separated by a row of wooden classical columns, said to have been transformed from rough trunks at the time of the restoration by John Douglas in 1870. There is a wonderfully elaborate brass chandelier, with a figure of the Virgin among its leafy branches, of the early sixteenth century – a remarkable survival. Handsome eighteenth-century font and Douglas pulpit. Good monuments include an effigy of Evan Lloyd, d. 1639.

At **Llandegla**, ½ mile N of the junction of the A5104 and A525, the small church, rebuilt in 1866 (probably by John Gibson), contains a chandelier similar to the one at Llanarmon, and an amazing E window, made in 1800 for St Asaph Cathedral by the well-known glass-painter Francis Eginton of Birmingham. It shows Christ in an orange robe, with a gang of unecclesiastical putti holding emblems of the Passion. One is forging the nails on an anvil. They are clearly based on Pompeian wall-paintings of cupids.

The A5104 leads down to the A5, along a broad valley.

2½ miles from the junction, up above the R side of the road, stands **Plas-yn-Yale** (Iâl), a substantial eighteenth–nineteenth-century farmhouse. It occupies the site of the ancestral home of the Yale family, of whom the most famous was Elihu, founder of Yale University. He is buried at Wrexham (see p. 66). Two miles further on, the quiet village of **Bryneglwys** is across the other side of the valley from the road. The small church is well placed up on a bump. Attached to the SE is the Yale Chapel, late sixteenth-century, separated internally by great oak piers. It contains some family tablets. The church was excellently restored in 1876 by Arthur Baker. His characteristic woodwork incorporates Jacobean bits. The little Church Hall has Gothick windows, and a door in the apsidal end. It is six miles from Bryneglwys down to the A5 at Rug, just W of Corwen (p. 117).

A mile SW of Llandegla, near where the B5431 joins the A525, is **Tomen y Rhodwydd** (mistakenly called on the One Inch map Castell yr Adwy). It is a textbook example of a motte-and-bailey castle, excellently preserved, and nicely rural with long grass and hawthorn trees. Built as the castle of Iâl by Owain Gwynedd, in 1149, it was well placed to guard the head of the deep and winding **Nant-y-Garth Pass**. This romantically wooded route provides another way into the Vale of Clwyd, less dramatic than those further N, but still effective as you emerge from the pass into the level Vale, with the Clwydian range flanking your right, and wooded hills on the left.

Beside the A525, 3 miles S of Ruthin (at 141/537), is **Jesus Chapel**, 'Founded and Endowed by Rice Williams of Eyarth ucha Gent: 1619. Consecrated: 1623. Rebuilt: 1787.' Williams was a verger at Westminster Abbey. It is a charming little building, with primitive columns on either side of the door, and contemporary altar table and pulpit, but it has been fearfully done up, and the surroundings are gruesomely neat. A mile further on is **Llanfair Dyffryn Clwyd**, not much of a village, but with a good double-naved church, with a stout tower, excellently restored in 1872 by J. D. Sedding. He put in the good simple wood and ironwork, but his reredos has been nastily painted. In the S aisle there is a ravishing window of 1893 by Christopher Whall (Christ blessing the children). There is a wooden lychgate of 1708, and stone almshouses.

One and a half miles NNE of Llanfair, at 140/577, is **Llanrhudd**, mother church of Ruthin. Badly restored in 1852 by Kennedy, it retains a good medieval roof and screen, and a curious communion table supported by comical lions. Monuments to the once-great Thelwalls of Bathafarn include one to John, who gave his fourteen children names like Perse, Bevis, and Lowrie, and another to Ambros, Yeoman of the Robe to James I and to Charles when Prince of Wales, who 'yielding to age and troublesome times retired to the place of his birth', and died in 1653. Opposite the church lived Stanley Weyman, author of *Under the Red Robe*.

Ruthin (Rhuthun) is one of the most attractive small towns in Wales. It is situated on a ridge, with the Clwyd flowing along the eastern side. The Castle is at the southern end of the ridge, and the Parish Church is off the main square at the north. The main streets wind down from the square, and contain an unusual number of interesting and pleasing buildings. The Borough was founded in 1282, and soon became a prosperous market town. In 1400 it was looted by Owen Glendower, and in 1402 he even captured and held to ransom his old enemy, Reginald, 3rd Lord Grey of Ruthin. The best building in St Peter's Square is the Castle Hotel, with a handsome brick front of the eighteenth century, and, beside it, what was once the town house of Sir Richard Clough. Like Bachegraig, it has a steep tiled roof with a proliferation of dormer windows. In the middle of the Square, where the Old Town Hall stood, is a merrily striped Jacobean clock tower, built in 1883 by John Douglas. Beside Barclay's Bank is a rough stone called Maen Huail: on it King Arthur is said to have had a rival for the affections of a Ruthin lady decapitated. The half-timbered National Westminster Bank, over-restored, was the old Courthouse and Prison.

The Square is dominated by the elegant stone spire of **St Peter's Church**, added by R. K. Penson when he carried out his restoration in 1856. Approached through fine gates, of 1727, by the Davies family, the church is a rather odd double-naved building. Each nave has a magnificently carved wooden roof, with superb bosses – the N one is finer. The chancel was pulled down in the seventeenth century. It was a collegiate church, and the college was refounded in 1590 as almshouses, called Christ's Hospital, by Dr Gabriel Goodman, Dean of

Westminster, who was a native of Ruthin. (He assisted Bishop Morgan with his translation of the Bible.) The Rector is still called Warden. There is a monument with a bust of Goodman. Glass by Wailes and Powell. In the N aisle, there is a charmingly naïve picture of the church (including a lion) made of bog-oak inlaid with bone by W. Roberts, a porter at the Castle. E of the church stands Christ's Hospital, rebuilt in 1865, and N of it is The Cloisters, a picturesque house incorporating parts of the old College.

Down Castle Street, E of the Square, is the **Town Hall**, its vigorous tower, with pyramidal roof, forming a striking landmark. Built in 1863 by Poundley and Walker (who else?), its roughly dressed masonry contrasts with elaborate sculpture, including a harvest scene over the centre window (presumably to symbolise the Vale's agricultural richness). It incorporates a Fire Station and Market, cleverly designed to fit the sloping site. In the Council Chamber is another bog-oak and bone picture, this time of the Corporation arms, presented by Mr Roberts 'on the coming of the railway in 1862'. Right out to the E of the town, on the Mold road, is the Grammar School, also founded by Goodman, but rebuilt here in 1889–92, in John Douglas's characteristic Jacobean style. In Well Street are the stone seventeenth-century Plas Coch, the half-timbered Wynnstay Arms, and the neat bow-fronted Congregational Chapel of 1820. Hidden away in Record Street, which links Well Street and Castle Street, is the exceptionally refined County Hall, built as a Court House and Record Office in 1785–7, by Joseph Turner: it has a handsome portico. Castle Street is full of old houses, one with a projecting timber porch, another with a colonnade.

The **Castle** consists of a motley assemblage of buildings, set in Victorian grounds. Little is left of the medieval castle, founded by Edward I, and given in 1282 to Reginald de Grey, except parts of the curtain wall and towers. The rest was destroyed in the Civil War. The jumbled ruins near the gate are just a kind of super-grotto. A new house was built on the site in 1826, and this was much enlarged in 1849–52 by Henry Clutton, for Frederick West. He built the principal block, in red sandstone, with a great octagonal tower. The entrance front, with canted oriels and asymmetrical doorway, is effective, and there are elaborate chimneypieces and ceilings inside.

West's grandson, George Cornwallis-West, married, among others, Lady Randolph Churchill and Mrs Patrick Campbell. In 1921 he sold the Castle, and it became a luxury clinic. Now it is a hotel, celebrated for its nightly medieval banquets – 'quaff wine from pewter goblets – eat nourishing medieval dishes with a dagger – be pampered by ladies of the court', to quote its publicity.

Down Clwyd Street, W of the Square, is the Gaol, whose handsome stone front bears the inscription, 'The Magistrates, sensible of the miserable state of the antient prison, in compassion to the unfortunate, caused this building to be erected in the year 1775: Joseph Turner architect.' Vast Victorian additions form a conspicuous landmark. Nearby is Castle Mill, basically thirteenth century, with original features. From here a delightful footpath winds round the wall of the Castle park up to the Castle gate, providing intriguing views of the town.

RUTHIN TO THE A5

The main road from Ruthin to Corwen (A494) follows the Clwyd valley as far as Derwen. Beyond the narrow wooded defile, two miles out of the town, the valley widens and the road skirts a park. Among a lot of new planting (mostly conifers) a surprisingly new-looking stone arch suddenly appears in a style instantly recognizable to anyone who knows Portmeirion. The house is **Nantclwyd Hall**, and the whole astonishing set-up can be seen from a lane which climbs steeply behind it. The handsome late seventeenth-century house of brick was much enlarged in the nineteenth century, but these additions have been demolished, and a large new façade built, also arches, fibreglass temples, a dovecote, formal gardens, lakes, bridges, and so on – all over the last fifteen years or so, and all designed by Clough Williams-Ellis. Statuary from Scarisbrick, ornamental birds.

Half a mile S of the A494 is **Llanelidan**, feeling pleasantly remote, with a well-restored double-naved church, next to the smart bargeboarded Leyland Arms (1844). The church has fine carved woodwork, and some excellent seventeenth–eighteenth-century monuments. One of the Lloyds of Nantclwyd Isa is said to have gambled away three fortunes playing fives against the churchyard wall. Two miles E, up on the hill above the other side of the main road, is **Derwen**, where the small, unprepossessing church retains two features of exceptional quality – the fifteenth-century roodscreen and loft, almost perfect and unusually fine, and the stone churchyard cross, carved with a Crucifixion and other figures. In 1914 the Royal Commission on Ancient Monuments described it as 'one of the finest in the Principality.' It stands in the open, facing over miles of lovely country.

Beyond Derwen, the country is disfigured by modern quarrying. This is now Merioneth – that curious northern extension of Merioneth which seems more naturally part of Denbighshire (and which, in 1974, was put in with Clwyd). **Gwyddelwern**, a rather dismal village, has a small old church, much restored in 1880, when the startlingly grandiose spire was added. The A494 joins the A5 at Rug (p. 117), just outside Corwen.

From Ruthin the A5 can also be reached further W, at Cerrigydrudion, by way of the B5105. Just outside the town is the church of **Llanfwrog**, with a stout tower. It was sensitively restored in 1870 by J. D. Sedding: he added the nice slate-hung porch, with bottle-glass windows. Two miles further on is **Pool Park**, now a mental hospital. It was built in 1828, for Lord Bagot of Blithfield, designed by John Buckler, and executed by Benjamin Gummow. Elizabethan in style, it was originally black and white outside, but is now rendered. Half a mile E, in an upland valley, is the little village of **Efenechtyd.** The tiny church, beautifully restored in 1873 by Arthur Baker, contains a most unusual medieval font, hewn out of solid oak. A brass tablet commemorates Rev. John Price, d. 1723 – 'one time rector of this parish, who for the love he bore to it chose rather to be interr'd here than in other places that he had an unquestioned right in'. Sensible man. Just S of the church is an unexpectedly grand early eighteenth-century house, of seven bays, with stone quoins. It is reached by a cobbled path from gate-piers surmounted by iron busts of cheerful blackamoors.

Also off the road, two miles S, is **Clocaenog**, whose church retains its rood-screen. The village gives its name to a huge conifer forest. On the hilltop, a mile NW, the Forestry Commission maintains a monument inscribed: 'As a memorial of his having completed the large range of mountain plantations which in part skirt the base of this hill, William, second Lord Bagot, erected this pile of stones in the year 1830.' Beyond the forest, at **Llanfihangel Glyn Myfyr**, the B5105 crosses the Alwen by means of a handsome stone bridge, built by Thomas Penson the elder. Tyddyn Tudur, near by, was the home of the talented Jones family, the most famous of whom were Owen, b. 1741, the antiquary and founder of the Gwyneddigion Society in London, and his son, of the same name, the famous architect, decorator, and illuminator. It is three miles from Llanfihangel to the A5 at **Cerrigydrudion** (p. 117).

Llanfihangel is in Denbighshire, but the area of Merioneth between the A494 and the B5105 contains some marvellous country – quiet, wooded valleys, between open, grassy hills, and two delightful little villages, **Melin-y-Wig** and **Betws Gwerful Goch.** Gwerful Goch was grand-daughter of Owain Gwynedd, who reigned 1137–70. Her husband is said to have rebuilt the church. It was again rebuilt – excellently – by John Douglas in 1879. He retained the porch of 1606, and some odd medieval carvings, in the reredos. It was reported in 1864 that the cottages in the village were in a shocking state, but there were no less than three chapels. It is two miles from Betws to the A5 at **Maerdy** (p. 117).

THE EASTERN SIDE OF THE VALE OF CLWYD

This is prosperous agricultural country, thickly populated, and that this has long been so is testified by the remarkable number of old churches and houses. Going up the B5429, from Llanbedr Dyffryn Clwyd (p. 49), the first village (if it can be called that) is **Llanhychan** (114/622), with a small church, sensitively restored in 1878 by Arthur Baker, a pupil of Sir Gilbert Scott who did a great deal of excellent work in North Wales. He added the timber porch. Inside are all sorts of interesting odds and ends, such as the medieval carvings on the lectern, and the 1920s folk-art carvings on the organ. Plas Llanhychan is an old house rebuilt by Baker in 1881. He fitted in the staircase so ingeniously that the corny old tale about the architect forgetting the stairs soon got around – as he himself wryly recalled. Almost a mile further on is Rhydonnen, a farmhouse with imposing gate-piers, a half-timbered wing, and a yew tree. A mile SW is **Llanynys,** one of the finest churches in the Vale. It has only a handsome vicarage and a tarted-up pub to keep it company. Founded in the sixth century, it is a big double-naved building, the naves separated by fluted wooded columns (c. 1768). Richly carved roof supports, and three chandeliers – two of wood (one 1748, the other very plain), the third a pretty nineteenth-century one of brass (from Rug). Altar table of 1637, as at Llanrhudd supported by lions (very male). A splendid great wallpainting of St Christopher faces the door (so that everyone would see it, for anyone looking on an image of St Christopher would be safe from harm that day). A description of it stands on a really superb Rococo easel. In the church, brought in from outside, stands a remarkable hexagonal sepulchral cross, probably fourteenth century: on one side is a figure of a bishop, and on the other a Crucifixion. The wooden dog-tongs are in working order. They were intended for the removal of fighting dogs: one vicar, however, is said to have stopped in mid-sermon, seeing his dog fighting another one, in order to cheer it on. The church is well cared for, and it is a pity about the horrid partition in the S aisle.

Around Llanynys are lush watermeadows, with numerous stone bridges over the Clwyd and Clywedog. A mile W of Rhydonnen, up on the side of Moel Fama, is **Llangynhafal.** The church is up a lane, with a half-timbered farmhouse beyond, and then the bracken-covered slopes. Again double-naved, and Perp, it has been recently done up, the outside newly plastered, and the inside (according to a parishioner) 'sprayed with dry-rot'. Excellently restored in 1884 by Arthur Baker, it has first-rate old roofs. The most unusual feature is the gilded pelican, about two feet high, with four silver babies drinking its blood, set up over the altar. It is said to date from about 1690. There is a brass to John Jones, d. 1760 – 'His visitation was very sudden, which made his death to his friends excessive grievous.' In the churchyard stands a topiary cock. At the farmhouse, Plas yn Llan, Wordsworth stayed with his Cambridge friend Robert Jones, with whom he made a tour of Europe in 1790 and of North Wales in 1791.

The next village on the B5429 is **Llandyrnog,** a neat little place, with its double-naved church raised up above the street. It was lucky enough to be restored in 1878 by W. E. Nesfield

– H. R. Hughes of Kinmel (see p. 104) was one of the chief contributors. It has a pretty bellcote, superb ironwork on the doors, and a charming timbered porch, its pink plaster panels decorated with moulded sunflowers. The rich woodwork includes 'sedilia' of 1877, a classic piece of Arts and Crafts furniture, with Nesfield's characteristic 'pies' (a device taken from oriental porcelain). One window contains jumbled remains of a medieval Seven Sacraments window, and there is an especially fine Annunciation in the tracery. Others contain good nineteenth-century glass. There are splendid tiles in the sanctuary.

By the crossroads SW of the village is a derelict Baptist Chapel, 1836, and handsome: the ground for it was given by John Madocks, of Glanywern, the dignified house (c. 1810) overlooking the river a mile N. Near the roundabout is Capel Dyffryn, also 1836, a charmingly neat Methodist Chapel, painted white and grey. Up to the NE, on the slope of the hill, is **Llangwyfan**: the little church is reached past the big Sanatorium, built as part of the Welsh memorial to Edward VII, along with the one at Bronllys (see also *South Wales*). The church is attractive, with medieval features, and an E window, said to be eighteenth century, containing rich glass by A. Gibbs. Outside the churchyard are stocks – not common in North Wales.

A mile further NE is **PenyCloddiau**, one of the largest and highest hill-forts in Wales (area over 50 acres, height 1320 feet–1440 feet). The B5429 joins the Mold–Denbigh road at Bodfari (see p. 47). A mile SW of the junction stands what is left of **Lleweni Hall**, reached by long rough tracks across the flat valley. Once it was one of the greatest houses in North Wales, seat of the powerful Salusbury family, and one of the most interesting architecturally. It is known to have had a great hall with carved angels on the roof. It was sold c. 1775 to the Hon. Thomas Fitzmaurice, brother of the Marquess of Lansdowne. He seems to have been an odd fish – 'distinguished by eccentric philanthropy' (*Black's Guide*, 1869). He added to the house, which, to judge from engravings, must have been one of the strangest sights imaginable, for it consisted of a whole series of different parts, of different dates and in different styles, tacked on to one another. He also built a Bleachworks near by. This was no ordinary enterprise, for it was designed by Thomas Sandby, and it was an elegant brick building, on a semicircular plan, 400 feet long. The pools in front were graced by Coade stone statues. Fitzmaurice's scheme was to provide employment both here and on the family estates in Ireland: the Irish tenants grew the flax, the Welsh ones bleached it. As for the selling of it, he caused great astonishment by driving over to Chester in a coach-and-six, and then serving behind the counter himself. We hear of a grand illumination put on at the Bleachworks in 1790, but after Fitzmaurice's death in 1793 the place declined, and was put up for sale in 1809. The house has been demolished, except for a plain brick part which contained offices. The last fragment of the Bleachworks disappeared recently. What survives is a large and handsome brick building, built round three sides of a courtyard, with blank arches along the sides, said to have been stables, and presumably designed by Sandby.

CHAPTER TWO

Wrexham, the Dee and Glynceiriog, and Maelor Saesneg

A483, the main Wrexham road, is the main road south into Wales from Chester. It runs to the west of the water-meadows of the ever-winding Dee, which is here the Welsh border. This is the trunk road south through Wales all the way to Swansea. Improvements continue throughout its length but shepherds, with a nice regard for priorities, still herd their flocks along its middle stretches filling its entire width with unhurried sheep. Since this is a guide to Wales itself rather than a book which tells how to travel quickly through it (an impossible undertaking since the mountains get in the way), such occurrences will be no inconvenience.

Rossett, the first village in Wales, is geographically a Cheshire village, but there is an undefinable border feeling even here: somehow grittier and less lush. It is sited on the ubiquitous little river Alun which here drove two mills, both beside the main road. The black and white mill with the huge water wheel (and much surviving machinery) is now derelict. It dates from 1661 and last worked in 1961. Incidentally some of the black and white is painted decoration of no structural relevance; a nice border tradition (there is a charming corrugated iron cottage nearby in the Maelor entirely done in this manner). The brick mill opposite (1791) is also retired. Weirs constructed for these mills are close to the Hope road. The handsome church (1891) is by John Douglas, as is the Presbyterian chapel (1875).

Trevalyn Hall (1576) just to the east of the main road, a brick house with stone quoins (now rendered), was built by John Trevor, who has a curious monument in Gresford church (p. 61). It has human scale and unexpectedly wide views (Beeston Castle and the Welsh hills) and interesting early classical details – note the porter's lodge (moved to its present position by Thomas Jones in 1836). The topiary garden is nineteenth century.

Marford, astride the main road and so impossible to miss, is a delightful Gothick estate village (1805), built by George Boscawen, whose wife inherited the Trevor property. The tea-cosy type cottages with their curious lattice iron windows were originally thatched. The coach-house doors and some of the windows of the inn have nice ogee arches. The character of the village has been kept remarkably intact since the 1920s by a builder, Mr Randles, who lives in one of the cottages and owns others.

At Marford the road climbs up diagonally from the Cheshire Plain on to the foothills of the Welsh mountains, here well disguised by sadly suburban houses (better to look out at the splendid views): a foretaste of the scruffy sprawl generated by Wrexham and its industrial hinterland.

Gresford is unattractive from the main road, but a short divergence to the north (taking care not to end up in the cul-de-sac housing estate) brings you past a fine duck-pond to the glorious church, one of the best in North Wales. It is well set in an iron-railed churchyard full of big yews and good tombs. The church was almost entirely rebuilt in the late fifteenth century, and is characteristically light and spacious. The pinnacled tower contains eight bells, the two oldest of 1623, which form one of the 'Wonders of Wales' (see p. 365). The most exciting feature inside the church is the glass: the east window (Te Deum) was given in 1500, and there are several others with glass of about the same date. Money was left for its repair in 1634, and it was again restored, by Clayton and Bell, in 1867–8, at the time of the church's sympathetic restoration by G. E. Street. The church also retains its oak screens and choir-stalls, with vigorous misericords. The north-east chapel contains monuments to the Madocks family, including John (d. 1793), the father of William of Tremadoc fame (see p. 192). Its altar and fittings are by W. D. Caröe (1913). There are many other fine monuments, some medieval: NB the Trevor ones in the SE chapel (also a lively Early Victorian effort complete with brasses, by Messrs. Waller); those in the chancel to W. Egerton (1827), with a bust by Chantrey; and John Parry (1797), by R. Westmacott Jr., with an infant mourner; and at the W end the figure of Resignation, to John

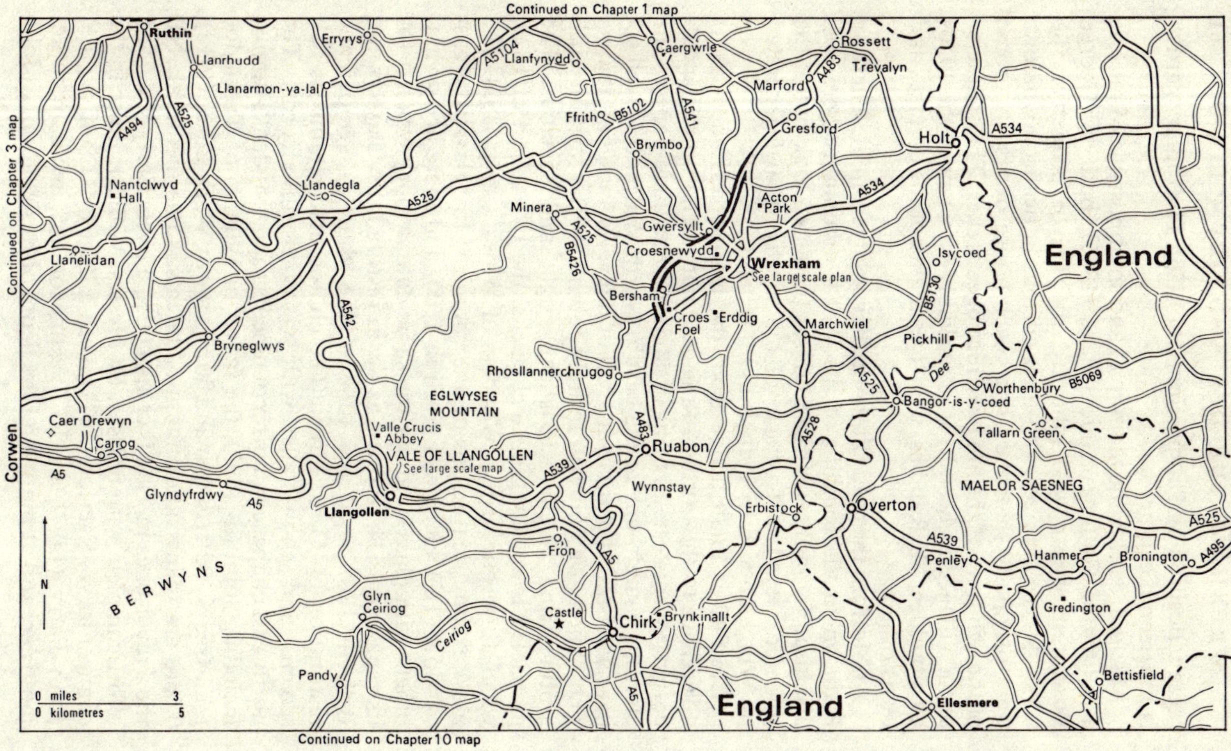

Continued on Chapter 1 map
Continued on Chapter 3 map
Continued on Chapter 10 map
Corwen
England
England
Ruthin
Erryrys
Llanrhudd
Llanarmon-ya-Ial
Llanfynydd
Caergwrle
Rossett
Trevalyn
Marford
Gresford
Holt
Ffrith
Brymbo
Nantclwyd Hall
Llandegla
Llanelidan
Minera
Gwersyllt
Acton Park
Croesnewydd
Wrexham
See large scale plan
Isycoed
Bersham
Croes Foel
Erddig
Marchwiel
Pickhill
Dee
Bryneglwys
Rhosllannerchrugog
Worthenbury
Bangor-is-y-coed
Tallarn Green
EGLWYSEG MOUNTAIN
Caer Drewyn
Carrog
Valle Crucis Abbey
VALE OF LLANGOLLEN
See large scale map
Ruabon
Glyndyfrdwy
Llangollen
Wynnstay
Erbistock
Overton
MAELOR SAESNEG
Fron
Penley
Hanmer
Bronington
Gredington
BERWYNS
Glyn Ceiriog
Castle
Chirk
Brynkinallt
Ceiriog
Pandy
Ellesmere
Bettisfield
A5104
A483
A534
A541
B5102
A494
A525
A542
B5426
B5130
B5069
A528
A539
A5
A495
N
0 miles 3
0 kilometres 5

Williams (1851), by W. Theed. Good fittings include the interesting fifteenth-century font; eighteenth-century chandeliers; and the pulpit by Street. A curiosity is the eighteenth-century glass (heads of putti) in the S porch windows bought in Italy in the early eighteenth century by a Gresford boy who had made good.

Returning to the main road, beyond Gresford Colliery (scene of a terrible disaster in 1934 in which 265 men died), are the suburbs of Wrexham. Here (on the left) stands a grand Greek Doric entrance screen, by Thomas Harrison of Chester (c. 1810), shaming the 1960s estate that cowers behind it. It once led to **Acton Park**, a house partly rebuilt by James Wyatt in 1786–7, but demolished after the park had been bought for housing by the Corporation. The southern part was laid out by Sir Patrick Abercrombie. The attractive houses on the opposite side of the road from the Acton gates are by T. Alwyn Lloyd (1914–16): they form part of a Garden Village which, like so many, was never completed to its original standard owing to the 1st World War.

WREXHAM

Ahead lies **Wrexham**, where the remains of an attractive old market town lie choked in a far-spreading mass of unlovable suburbia. From the Middle Ages until the railway age Wrexham was the clearing house of North Wales. Its medieval importance is attested by the grandeur of its parish church. For hundreds of years the town's markets were among the most important in the Principality, and its narrow lanes and prosperous public houses rang with English and Welsh tongues bargaining over Welsh wool and flannels, cattle and sheep, butter and cheese. But the region was also rich in minerals, lead in Flintshire, and coal and iron around Wrexham (whence the forges and foundries for which it was to become famous). This wealth meant a completely different pattern of life from that of most of Wales for both the poorest labourer and the richest landowner. The poor, having alternative employment, were not so poor; the rich owned both minerals and good agricultural land. Indeed Wrexham was the lively social centre of the region (including parts of the neighbouring counties of Shropshire and Cheshire). Great houses, so rare

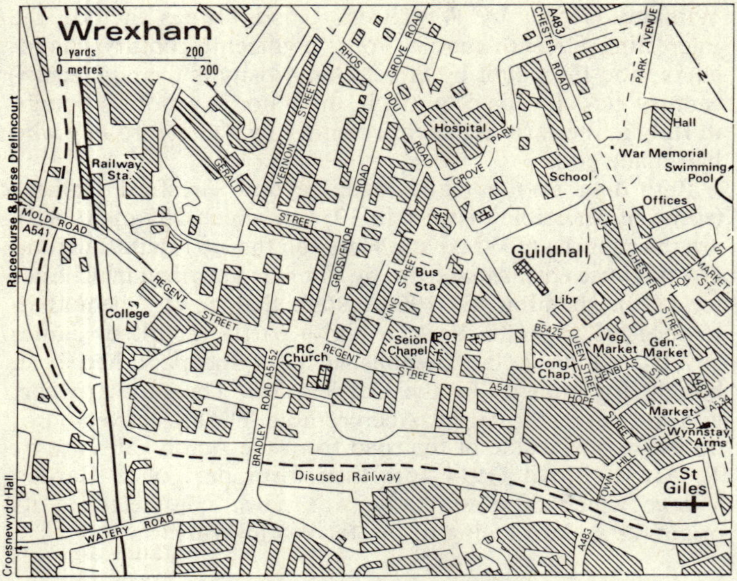

in the rest of Wales, were numerous, private theatres not uncommon, and it was worth leaving London for the balls of the Wrexham season; the good agricultural land was fine fox-hunting country. This humming, thriving town was doomed to be spoilt in the nineteenth and twentieth centuries by its own industrial success. In the eighteenth century industry became more and more dominant. The North Lancashire ironmaster Isaac Wilkinson took over the old ironworks at Bersham in 1753, and he was succeeded by his more famous son, John, in 1762. In 1793 John set up works at Brymbo. The Wilkinsons were by no means the only ironmasters. Copper and lead were also worked, and coal-mining became increasingly important. Other industries included brewing and tanning. With so much industry, it follows that much of the area is correspondingly grim: it is not surprising that many people think of it as a conglomeration of mines, dereliction, and innumerable terraces in dirty Ruabon brick, all remembered through a haze of the grey rain that seems to fall so often. Once industry had begun to overwhelm the district the landowners moved to greener fields. Wrexham was once surrounded by a whole ring of country houses of exceptional historical and architectural interest. Going clockwise from the north these included Acton Park (see above), Cefn Park (early nineteenth century), Erddig, Cadwgan Hall (fifteenth–seventeenth centuries), Plas Power (see below), Brymbo Hall (see below), Stansty Park (eighteenth century), Gwersyllt Park (a handsome Palladian villa), and Gresford Lodge (a delectable domed house of c. 1790 by James Wyatt). Of these, apart from Erddig, only Cefn survives – the least interesting of all. None of the grand town houses of the Wrexham gentry survives. At least the future of Erddig is now at last secure (see p. 71).

All the same, Wrexham deserves to be better known, before it is too late, for the commercial pressures which have already destroyed so much of it threaten continually. The surprising thing, considering the size and importance of the place, is that it still possesses any atmosphere at all. Much of the town has been dismally ill-treated – not least by the construction of the Wrexham–Ellesmere Railway in 1893, brutally cutting through its heart.

Yet it is still worth exploring, and the **Parish Church of St Giles** is the place to start. Like Gresford, it is well sited, but in a way specially suited to a town church, for it is at once withdrawn, behind fine iron gates (c. 1720 by the Davies brothers) in an atmospheric churchyard (the atmosphere often dominated by the nearby brewery), with narrow passages leading off it, and yet its noble tower faces the town's principal crossroads down a short street. This superb early sixteenth-century tower (another of the 'Wonders of Wales') combines strength and dignity of outline with great richness of detail. The rest of the church is its equal in splendour, if not in refinement. Particularly unusual is the canted apsidal chancel: when this was made the original east window was opened out to form a chancel arch, and odd stumps of tracery still hang from it. The chancel was refitted in 1914, by Sir T. G. Jackson. The iron screen is supposed to have been given by Elihu Yale (as also the painting in the ante-nave). The most striking object in the church is the large monument in the N aisle to

Mary Myddelton (d. 1747), by L. F. Roubiliac, England's greatest Baroque sculptor, with its dramatic figure rising from the grave, and collapsing pyramid. Roubiliac also did the delightful tablet to the Rev. Thomas Myddelton and his wife, in the chancel. In the S aisle is a tablet to Ann, wife of 'John Wilkinson, Iron Master', d. 1756: it is signed by T. F. Pritchard, designer of the Coalbrookdale Ironbridge – hence no doubt the connection. There are numerous other nice tablets, including one to Owen Bold, d. 1703, by Stanton (W end of S aisle), and an attractive relief (1867) by Thomas Woolner, the Pre-Raphaelite sculptor, to Mrs Peel (ante-nave). Also worth noting is the brass on a nave pillar to Humphrey Lloyd, d. 1673, by Silvanus Crue, a Wrexham goldsmith, whose beautifully engraved brasses are to be seen in several local churches (e.g. Holt, Llangollen and Llanrwst). The church was restored in 1867 by Benjamin Ferrey, and in 1902–3 by H. A. Prothero of Cheltenham. Outside, near the tower, is the tomb of Elihu Yale, d. 1721, with its famous epitaph:

> Born in America, in Europe bred,
> In Afric travell'd, and in Asia wed,
> Where long he liv'd, and thriv'd; at London dead.
> Much good, some ill, he did; so hope all's even,
> And that his soul, through mercy's gone to heaven.
> You that survive, and read, take care
> For this most certain exit to prepare:
> For only the actions of the just
> Smell sweet and blossom in the dust.

(The last two lines are from James Shirley's *Ajax and Ulysses*). Yale's family came from Bryneglwys (p. 51). On his return from India Yale settled at Plas Grono, near Erddig (see p. 72). He was a considerable benefactor of the church. The tradition has been maintained by the university which was named after him in gratitude for his benefactions – for example, some of the graduates restored the NW porch in 1901. Yale has even gone to the lengths of erecting on its campus, in the 1920s, a reproduction of Wrexham tower.

Our perambulation of the town will start with the short street leading from the church: this brings us to the crossroads formed by High Street, Hope Street and Town Hill. (Here stood until 1939 the Town Hall, built in 1713, with an arcaded ground floor. It was demolished to widen the road – a sad loss.) **High Street** to the E is handsomely closed by the eighteenth-century Crest Hotel, formerly Wynnstay Arms (the name recalling the powerful Williams-Wynn influence on the town's history), and contains some fine commercial buildings, especially the former Provincial Welsh Insurance Co. (1858) by R. K. Penson. Opposite is the Jacobean Market by his father Thomas Penson (1848). From the Market you can go out to Hope Street by way of an arcade (1891) very like those of Cardiff, and, in **Hope Street**, as well as marvelling at the redness of the Arcade's façade, admire the National Provincial Bank, a characteristically dignified palazzo of 1876 by John Gibson, a pupil of Sir Charles Barry (his numerous banks are much more satisfying than his churches – which include the famous so-called 'Marble Church' at Bodelwyddan). There is a back entrance to the Market in Henblas Street, and beyond that is the General Market (1876) with fine iron roof and Ruabon red façade, and, finally, in Guildhall Street, the Vegetable Market, biggest of them all. The markets cover the sites once occupied by squares surrounded by stalls whose names indicated the importance of the town as a centre of trade; these included Birmingham Square (hardware merchants – later taken over by clothiers and renamed New Yorkshire Square), and Manchester Hall (cotton traders).

Coming out of the Vegetable Market into **Queen Street**, one is opposite the Ionic-pilastered Ebenezer Congregational Chapel (1862) – reassuring in its typical Welshness. The half-timbered block on the corner of Queen Street and Hope Street is more like a stray from Victorian Chester. In Hope Street stands another alien intruder, but this time a real stunner – the twin-steepled Germanic façade of Seion Presbyterian Chapel, by the interesting Liverpool architects and polychrome experts W. and G. Audsley; red and black brick, with chunky carved capitals (1867). Beyond this is Our Lady of Dolours RC Church, an uninspired effort of 1857 by E. W. Pugin. In 1907 it became Pro-Cathedral of the Diocese of Menevia. It is just worth going inside to see the pretty effigy of the founder's wife, 'executed by a self-taught artist'. Beyond the crossroads is the Grecian former Infirmary (1838), and opposite that is the Italianate Grosvenor Lodge (1869), by the local architect J. R. Gummow, one of a number of

Wrexham villas which he proudly published in 1874 in his *Hints on House Building*. Return down Regent Street and go up King Street to see the remarkably urbane brick terrace of c. 1800. A call at the Bus Station Café will be rewarded by a collection of views of old houses in the Wrexham area. This brings us to the Civic Centre, dominated by the big new Guildhall (1961), decent but tame. Outside it stands, of all things, a large bell from the Incomparable Temple at Mandalay, sent back in 1885 by the Royal Welch Fusiliers. Their War Memorial, by Sir Goscombe John (1924) is nearby. Finally, you can wonder at the Edwardian fashion for architectural competitions, which resulted in Wrexham's possessing a Baroque Library by one Vernon Hodge of Teddington (1906).

The immediate surroundings of Wrexham contain little worth lingering over, but further out there are several fascinating places. In exploring these it comes as a continual surprise to find pockets of real countryside surviving between the factories, pits and housing estates. It is best to start by going northwest up the A541 – but first, for a rewarding diversion, at the crossroads beyond the Technical College turn left (B5101). A mile along the road, at **Berse Drelincourt**, there stands on the right a chapel. At first sight it looks uninteresting, with its grey pebble-dash. However, as the inscription over the original entrance-door (immediately opposite the gate) tells us: 'This Chapel was built and endowed by Mary Drelincourt, 1742.' This good lady was the widow of a Dean of Armagh (whose father had been a Huguenot minister in Paris). They had a house over in the Vale of Clwyd, but also owned land here, where they had previously set up a charity school for twenty-four girls. The chapel – known since as 'Madam's Chapel' – was connected with this scheme: the curate was to be in charge. It is a plain building and has been considerably altered, but retains its charm. Inside there is a plaster ceiling with curious coving down the centre, and a big plaster shell surmounts the former entrance. Mrs Drelincourt has a large marble monument. There are two brass candelabra, one of them an unusual piece of 1688 (brought from Wrexham). Opposite the chapel there used to be an avenue (now, alas, gone), which linked up with another at right angles leading to the front of Mrs Drelincourt's house – after her death that of the curate. This is a delightful building: a neat little brick and stone house of c. 1740, with a forecourt in front, originally flanked by wings, one of which contained the school, and the other the schoolmistress's residence.

Half a mile SE (on the other side of the bypass) is **Croes-newydd Hall**, built in 1696, and handsome, though very naked-looking without its avenue. This is where Miss Myddelton, the lady commemorated so dramatically by Roubiliac at Wrexham, lived, as tenant of poor Peter Ellice, who had spent so much on rebuilding the house that he could no longer afford to live in it.

Returning to the A541, on the left is the site of Stansty Park (demolished), and beyond, up on the slope, appears the broach spire of **Gwersyllt Church**. This was built in 1850–51 by Thomas Penson: as well as designing it, he contributed to the cost, and he and several of his family are commemorated by stained glass windows (by Wailes). In 1841 Penson rebuilt an old house called **Summer Hill** (½ mile SW of the church) in the Jacobean style, and settled there.

Over the ridge W of Gwersyllt lies **Brymbo**, now dominated by the huge Brymbo Steel Works. Its origins go back to 1792, when the estate of the seventeenth-eighteenth century Brymbo Hall (demolished in 1973) was bought by the famous iron-master John Wilkinson, largely for the sake of its coal resources. He established works here, during his dispute with his brother William, and, unlike the Bersham works (see below), they carried on after his death in 1808, being taken over in 1885 by the Brymbo Steel Company. In the middle of the new works one of the original stone and brick blast furnaces survives. Brymbo is an odd sort of place, scattered up and down the hillside. A mile W of the Steelworks, at Mount Sion, there are remains of a smeltery built by Wilkinson in 1793, to smelt lead from his mines at Minera (p. 70) and Llyn-y-Pandy (p. 44). They include the base of a 'bottle chimney', for the emission of the arsenical fumes, and flues which connected it with the furnaces in the hillside below. Nearby is the reservoir which supplied the works.

Half a mile SW of Mount Sion, on the B5102 (a road built c. 1800 by Wilkinson), there is a crossroads called **Pentre Saeson**. The name means 'village of the Englishmen': here a charter of 1411 permitted the burgesses of Holt (Englishmen – see p. 72) to dig coal. It was exploited later by Wilkinson.

Another mile SW, on the other side of the A525, is **Minera**, an important lead-mining centre from Roman times until this century. The most interesting remains are at New Brighton (274/510), just E of where the road over Esclusham Mountain (p. 88) joins the B5426. They include a beam-engine house and chimney.

From a mile down the B5426, a pretty road leads E to **Bersham**, crossing Offa's Dyke and following the wooded valley. It passes the lodge of Plas Power, remodelled in 1858 by John Gibson for the Fitzhughs, but now demolished. There is opencast mining in the park. The Fitzhughs also built the extraordinary church, again by Gibson, in a somewhat overpowering Romanesque style (1875–6; tower 1892). Not only is the church kept locked, but the churchyard too – and a very Victorian churchyard it is, with its shrubs and trees instead of graves. To see the interior apply at the barge-boarded cottages further on (also by Gibson).

Bersham is now something of a beauty spot, but in fact it is a remarkable (and encouraging) instance of reversion from industry to rural peace. The stream once had to work for its living. There were ironworks here from the late seventeenth century, and (as mentioned above) these were taken over in 1753 by Isaac Wilkinson. Under John Wilkinson they were especially famous for armaments: they supplied both sides in the Russian-Turkish War of 1768, and malicious rumour claimed that Wilkinson supplied arms to the rebellious Americans, by way of France. Certainly he was an intransigent liberal (he was brother-in-law of Joseph Priestley), and his brother William actually set up foundries in France. The works were wrecked as a result of a bitter dispute between John and William: both brothers called in roughs to smash them up. Before long they fell into ruin. Surviving remains include several leets, the weir on the stream, and also the chief building, which was converted into a corn-mill in the 19th century. It now forms part of Mill Farm, by the junction E of the church. The ruinous brick building still contains the mill-wheel. In the hillside beyond the octagonal horse-gin there is a ruined blast-furnace (probably early eighteenth century). A quarter of a mile E (on the other side of the new road) part of a row of single-storey workers' cottages stands up above the B5099. Called Bunker's Hill, they were built in 1775 by Wilkinson.

Two miles S of Wrexham, just beyond the roundabout where the new road joins the A483, is **Croes Foel**: beside the old B5098 (R), a plaque was set up, when their smithy was demolished, to commemorate the fact that this was where the Davies family made their famous wrought-iron gates (to be seen at Wrexham Parish Church, Leeswood, Chirk, Erddig, Eaton Hall, etc.). A mile E of here stands **Erddig**. This remarkable house, together with its beautiful wooded park and 2,000 acres of land, was given to the National Trust in 1973 by Mr Philip Yorke, last Squire Yorke of Erddig. It will not be open for some years: very extensive restoration has to be carried out, partly to remedy the effects of subsidence caused by coal-mining. This was one of the most generous gifts ever made to the Trust, for apart from the house itself, the value of the land is such that the sale of one small part of it, near the town, brought in nearly £1m. to endow the property. Furthermore, many of the contents of the house are of outstanding rarity and quality. It was built in 1684–7 by Thomas Webb for Joshua Edisbury. He ruined himself financially, and in 1713 it was bought by John Meller, a Master in Chancery, and son of a London draper. He added the wings in 1723. From him it was inherited in 1733 by his nephew Simon Yorke. In 1774 the W (entrance) front was recased in stone: it seems that a design produced by James Wyatt was altered (to its detriment) by a Mr Franks. At the same time internal alterations were made by Wyatt and by Joseph Turner. In 1826 a stately new dining-room was designed by Thomas Hopper. Little structural work has been done since then.

Lavish furnishings bought for the house by John Meller in 1720–26 include fabulous mirrors and a magnificent bed with Chinese silk hangings (recently on loan to the Victoria and Albert). There is also a Chinese Coramandel screen sent to Mrs Edisbury from India as a present (with some 'mango atchar' for her husband) by Elihu Yale. However, for many people the most memorable thing about Erddig is the marvellous atmosphere built up over the years and lovingly preserved – exemplified in the portraits of servants, the vast collection of bicycles, the children's toys, and so on. The E side of the house was not recased, and so is of brick, more or less in its original state, and faces down an ornamental canal. The formal planting on each side is to be restored. The fine iron screen across the end, until recently lodge gates, was made by the Davies family (originally for Stansty). Late eighteenth-century travellers were amazed that Mr Yorke should be content with such an old-fashioned garden, utterly unpicturesque. The oddest feature in the grounds is a stone 'cylinder bowl' into which the water of a stream cascades (known as 'The Cup and Saucer'). The park was landscaped in 1772–89 by William Emes. N of the house, on a wooded spur above the river Clywedog, there is a fine motte and bailey.

When he returned from India, Elihu Yale lived at Plas Grono, just outside the park. A later resident (the house was demolished in 1876) was C. J. Apperley – the famous sporting writer 'Nimrod'. His *My Life and Times* gives a fascinating picture of life in the district. In it he tells how on one occasion a nightingale sang in the famous Erddig woods for six weeks. 'Being really a *rara avis* in that part of the world, half Wrexham would be in the wood until a late hour of the night, and some throughout the entire of it. Several unpropitious matches, as well as a considerable augmentation of the population to be provided for from the parish rates, were the result of the amorous power of his soft lay.'

THE COUNTRY E OF WREXHAM

The A534 (to Crewe) leaves Wales at **Holt**, 5 miles ENE of Wrexham. This has long been an important crossing of the Dee, here the Welsh border. There is a fine painting of the **Bridge** by Richard Wilson in the Birmingham Art Gallery, in which a gatehouse, midstream, is shown (now gone). The present eight-arched structure dates from the early fifteenth century, but an earlier bridge served the borough founded in the late thirteenth century by John de Warenne, Earl of Surrey. He also built the Castle, whose remains survive on a small boss by the river (follow the path by the school). The thirteenth-century **Church** derives much of its present character from a 1500 rebuilding when the aisles were added. It has a most satisfying symmetry which is reinforced by the flight of steps down under the W tower, the whole unfolding below as you enter. It was sympathetically restored (1871–3) by John Douglas. Ewan Christian restored the chancel. The octagonal font is elaborately decorated with the arms of successive lords of Holt castle. An acrostic on a seventeenth-century brass commemorates Thomas Crue d. 1666. It was engraved by his kinsman Silvanus Crue, who signed it in Greek. NW of the village, by the river, the Romans had a large works depot, producing tiles and pottery. It was associated with the legionary fortress of Deva (Chester), and flourished at the end of the first century AD and beginning of the second.

South from Holt B5130 makes a useful ring road, by-passing Wrexham to its E on the fringe of the industrial estate. **Isycoed** (404/502), a hamlet just off to the L, seems to have escaped from Cheshire. Its plain brick 1829 church by John Butler has a low square tower topped by a little lead-domed octagon. It has been refitted inside. **Pickhill** (400/473), a 1720s house with a brick and pilastered façade of great distinction, buried in the country a couple of miles on, is perhaps by Richard Trubshaw. He was a member of a celebrated family of Staffordshire masons and architects, and also a champion wrestler.

The B5130 crosses the A525 (Wrexham-Whitchurch) at Cross Lanes. Turn R here for **Marchwiel**, 1½ miles towards Wrexham. The church is the parish church of Erddig (p. 71). It was rebuilt in 1778, and the matching tower of 1789 seems (surprisingly) to have been designed by James Wyatt. A transept was added in 1829. The old tower had been known to be unsafe for many years, and this led to a curious mishap. Squire Philip Yorke was celebrated for his tremendous sneeze. One of these occurred in church: an old man, who had fallen asleep during the sermon, thought the tower must be falling, and died of shock. There is an armorial window of 1788 by Francis Eginton, a delightfully worded memorial to Simon Yorke, d. 1767, and one to Philip Yorke, d. 1804 (the sneezer), by Richard Westmacott Jr. A mile SE from Cross Lanes, the A525 crosses the Dee into Maelor Saesneg.

MAELOR SAESNEG (*Flintshire Detached*)

This odd little bit of Flintshire, on the English side of the Dee, and cut off from the rest of the county by a big wedge of Denbighshire, has long been a delight to lovers of eccentricities and a problem to schoolchildren learning geography. The tidy-minded bureaucrats were bound to bring this happy state of affairs to an end one day, and local government reorganization has done the trick. Not even the reorganizers, however, have dared to do what would seem to most people the obvious solution – hand the Maelor over to England. Its place-names are mostly English, the look and feel of the country is much more like the adjoining parts of Cheshire and Shropshire than Wales. The very word *Saesneg* is the same as *sassenach* (meaning 'English'). Welshmen may feel glad to have kept it, for it is a quietly rural part of the world with plenty of charm and interest, even if it does lack true Welsh drama. In some ways it is more like Cheshire than Cheshire, with lush green fields and fine trees, big neat hedges and marl ponds, lanes rife with cow parsley and bluebells.

The Maelor is entered from Wrexham by way of the medieval stone bridge over the Dee at **Bangor Is-coed**. Near it is the church, with a cheery brick tower built in 1726 by Richard Trubshaw (see p. 73). The rest was restored in 1868 and 1877 by John Douglas – appropriately, since he was married here. The E window is by Gibbs (1868). Somewhere near here, perhaps between Bangor and Overton, was the great Celtic monastery of Bangor, said to have had more than 2000 monks in the sixth century. When the battle of Chester was fought, in 613, they prayed for the Welsh, but the Northumbrians won and punished them by massacring all except a few who fled to Bardsey. The massacre was regarded as the fulfilment of a threatening prophecy made by St Augustine in bringing to a close the meeting where he unsuccessfully attempted to persuade seven British bishops (probably including Asaph and Tysilio), under the leadership of Abbot Dunawd of Bangor, to accept his demands. The most famous monk of Bangor was Pelagius, whose heretical views were considered so dangerous that Pope Celestine I sent St Germanus of Auxerre to Britain to suppress their influence (see p. 40). The kernel of them was his denial of the doctrine of original sin.

Along the B5069, towards Malpas, is **Worthenbury**, with a splendid church of 1736–9, also by Richard Trubshaw. Built of warm red brick, it has a grand west tower and an apsidal chancel. The details are fun, but by no means according to strict classic norms – especially the E end. The setting, among fine mature trees, is suitably dignified. The interior is remarkably perfectly preserved, pews and all: the two chancel pews (for the Puleston family) have fireplaces. Excellent brass chandelier of 1816. The glass in the E window is an odd assortment, installed by Betton and Evans of Shrewsbury soon after 1822: it includes fourteenth-century glass from the E window of Winchester College Chapel (Betton and Evans had been asked to clean that window, but instead they installed a copy), also bits from Emral Hall chapel, and panels made by themselves – a large coat of arms of Sir Richard Puleston Bt., and two copies from engravings (St Leonard, and Sir Roger Puleston). Emral Hall, remodelled by Trubshaw in 1724–7, but incorporating earlier parts, has, alas, been demolished: a barrel-vaulted ceiling showing the labours of Hercules in plasterwork was bought by Clough Williams-Ellis and installed in the Town Hall at Portmeirion, after an adventurous winter journey. One load had to be abandoned on the mountains and left there for a month.

S of the A525, two miles from Bangor, is **Halghton Hall** (open on written application) now a farmhouse: it is a brick seventeenth-century building chiefly remarkable for its weirdly elaborate doorway, in a sort of provincial proto-Baroque. Two miles N of the road is the hamlet of **Tallarn Green**, where two spinster daughters of Lord Kenyon employed John Edge to build the church (1872), but later more wisely got Douglas to build their own house (The Gelli), the Vicarage, and some simple half-timbered cottages – delightful revivals of vernacular tradition. At Sarn Bridge, at the N end of the village, on the Cheshire border, is a good brick mill, its iron wheel split in half. Only a mile from the Shropshire border, half a mile N of the main road and hidden away in a quiet valley, is **Whitewell** (Is-coed) (495/414). Approaching from the west, one sees a nice group – first the small brick stables of 1849, then the thatched carriage shelter, seventeenth-century and a rare survival, then a cottage, and finally the little whitewashed church with its pyramidal spire. Built in 1829 by John Butler, it has an odd plan – the N transept is the same length as the nave, while the S one is the same length as the chancel. The junction of the roof beams at the crossing is concealed by sprouting acanthus leaves. Good marble tablet to Rev. Richard Congreve, d. 1782, by Van der Hagen. In the churchyard stands a square monument made of iron plates. The well from which the place takes its name is across the stream.

Just before the border, the Ellesmere road (A495) goes off S: the first village is **Bronington.** The church is up a lane, by a dark pond overhung with rhododendrons. It is an odd building of brownish-red brick which began life as a barn, but was remodelled in 1836, 1864, and 1901. Three miles further on, down a side turning (L), is **Bettisfield**, with a first-rate church of 1874 by G. E. Street. It has an elegant octagonal spire, and a finely-detailed interior: the dado on the E wall is of superb Minton tiles. The church was built by Lord and Lady Hanmer, whose family seat was Bettisfield Park. The Hanmer family have lived in the Hanmer district since the fourteenth century. The most celebrated of them (apart from Owen Glendower's wife) was Sir Thomas Hanmer (1612–78), Cupbearer to Charles I, a connoisseur and horticulturist: he married Elizabeth Baker, Lady-in-Waiting to Henrietta Maria, whose brother's bust, by Bernini, is in the Victoria and Albert Museum. Van Dyck's portrait of Sir Thomas, described by Evelyn as 'one of his best', was a star of the exhibition 'The Age of Charles I' in 1972.

Hanmer itself is two miles N of Bettisfield, on the A539. It takes its name from the pretty mere. It is a small village of handsome brick houses. The grand church looks down to the mere, along an avenue closed by low eighteenth-century gates (formerly the chancel gates). Richly Perp, with a strong tower, it was gutted by fire in 1889, and skilfully rebuilt by Bodley and Garner – all except the chancel, built in 1720 (but the E window probably of 1881), which was not restored until 1936 (by W. D. Caröe). The elegant S porch, the arcades and roofs, and the fittings are all by Bodley and Garner. In the S chapel hangs a splendid iron and brass chandelier (? c. 1890). Hanmer Hall, a little to the NE, has grand eighteenth-century stables. The mere lies in the park of **Gredington** (not open), the seat of Lord Kenyon, largely rebuilt in 1810–15 by Thomas Harrison. Two miles W of Hanmer is **Penley**, where the neat little sandstone church of 1899, by Hodgson Fowler of Durham, stands opposite the delightful school, big and low, with a huge thatched roof. A plaque says 'Madras School founded by George 2nd Lord Kenyon 1811.' The Madras system involved setting the older pupils to teach the younger ones. Llannerch Panna is a handsome half-timbered house of 1878 by Douglas, built for a Kenyon son as a wedding present. Three miles further is **Overton**, a large and good-looking village, with a dignified townish air. The church is right in the middle, surrounded by yews which form one of the 'Seven Wonders of Wales' (see p. 365). The N aisle was added in 1819, the S one in 1855, and the whole lot was poorly restored in 1870–1 by W. M. Teulon and E. E. Cronk. There are numerous good tablets of the eighteenth and nineteenth centuries: a lavish Gothic one, showing their three mourning daughters, to Thomas and Jane Bennion (d. 1803 and 1840) is signed 'London Marble Works by Patent Machinery'. There is a mosaic of water and fish around the font, and a striking eighteenth-century chair.

Half a mile W on the Wrexham road is a gate, hidden by trees and easily missed, opening on to a path which leads romantically through trees: suddenly one finds oneself standing in a **Cemetery**, precariously terraced along the side of the steep hill, with trees below concealing a great loop of the Dee, and a tremendous view beyond over to the Denbighshire hills. The neat little Gothic chapel, with a spirelet, was built in 1872, by W. M. Teulon: it is now derelict, and its good stained glass nearly all smashed by vandals. All in all a most memorable spot. The road passes the park of Bryn-y-pys (demolished) and goes down to **Overton Bridge**, the other side of which is Denbighshire. The single-arched stone bridge was begun in 1814 by Thomas Penson Sen. (a scheme for an iron bridge by Hazeldine was rejected), but collapsed before it was finished. Penson lost his job as County Surveyor, and his son, another Thomas (then only twenty-two years old), completed it. It spans a particularly beautiful stretch of the Dee.

Just across the bridge, a road leads L to **Erbistock** (one mile), a delightful arcadian survival on the banks of the river. It is one of the few places where it is possible to reach the river, and the Boat Inn is very popular. The little church of 1861 stands above parked cars and evergreens, and the steep bank opposite is richly wooded. From Overton Bridge, it is three and a half miles to Ruabon (p. 77) by the A539, skirting the park of Wynnstay, or six miles to Wrexham by the A528.

SOUTH FROM WREXHAM

Travelling down the A483, anyone wishing to get the feel of the area is well advised to turn off into the splendidly named colliery township of **Rhosllannerchrugog**. Its inhabitants are proud of their Welshness, and tell how an English bank manager eventually almost forgot how to speak English. Dense rows of Ruabon-brick terraces are enlivened by numerous chapels. Tucked away in a big churchyard is St John's Church, by Thomas Penson (1853): Norman, of stone, it has a funny little tower, and lots of gaily grotesque carving. The village is famous for its choirs, and the National Eisteddfod has been held here twice. Beyond Rhos to the west are the surprisingly wild foothills of Ruabon and Esclusham Mountains, where just a couple of miles from the village you can walk up through the heather past Mountain Lodge – intriguingly set on a raised circular plateau of grass surrounded by a ring of trees – over the bare top to World's End.

Returning to the main road, the next village is **Ruabon** (Rhiwabon). The northern part is dreary: the attractive part is around the crossroads by the church, where the road begins to curve downwards. On the left is the handsome eighteenth-century Wynnstay Arms (with a fine iron sign-bracket), and by its side runs a wide street, with neat Gothick cottages on each side, terminated by an eighteenth-century arch. From this used to run the magnificent avenue (now almost entirely gone) which formed the main approach to **Wynnstay**, the principal seat of the Williams-Wynn family, who dominated North Wales for two centuries. The estate was originally called Watstay, but was acquired by marriage by Sir John Wynn, fifth and last Baronet of Gwydir, who changed its name to Wynnstay. On his death in 1719, it went to his cousin Sir Watkin Williams, 3rd Baronet, who took the name Wynn. Since then every Baronet has been christened, or has taken the name Watkin. The first Sir Watkin Williams-Wynn – known as 'the great Sir Watkin' – was an influential Jacobite, and was rumoured to have promised support to Prince Charles in the '45. He persecuted the Methodists, who were delighted when he died in a fall from his horse in 1749. The second Sir Watkin, born in the year of his father's death, never rode a horse in his life, but was one of the greatest patrons of the arts of the century, an outstanding connoisseur of painting, architecture and music. The splendid portrait of him and his companions on the Grand Tour in 1768, by Pompeo Batoni, is now in the National Museum. In his famous theatre (of which nothing seems to be left) he put on every winter a week of plays, on one occasion under the direction of his friend Garrick. His son, the 5th Baronet (1789–1840), who inherited debts of £160,000, continued the theatricals until 1808. In his time R. B. Sheridan and his family used to come and act.

The 5th Baronet was known as 'Prince of Wales', and in his time the poor of North Wales are said to have been accustomed to say 'If God was to die we should still have Sir Watkin.' In 1883 the family possessed 145,770 acres, mostly in Montgomeryshire, Merioneth, and Denbighshire. But the land was so poor that all this brought in – as was noted with astonishment by contemporaries – only £55,000 a year (enough, though, to keep the wolf from the door). Members of the family often sat in Parliament, as staunch Tories. Most of the family have been keen sportsmen, and Sir Watkin Williams-Wynn's Hounds (the famous 'Wynnstay') still hunt this country. Wynnstay itself was the social centre of a great area, renowned for its lavish hospitality to rich and poor, and from it the family wielded enormous influence.

Today the house is a school (Lindisfarne College), and Sir Watkin lives at Llangedwyn (p. 270). The huge park has suffered sadly, but there is still much of interest. The whole estate is private, but parts can be visited with permission from the School Headmaster, the Estate Office (in Ruabon), and tenants. The house is now approached from a lodge a mile along the A539 (L of the arch). It has a magnificent site, high above the winding valley of the Dee, and enjoying tremendous views of the hills. The old house of 1616 was rebuilt by the 3rd Baronet in 1736–9, to designs by Smith of Warwick. Of this house the Stables, with Gibbsian window-surrounds, survive. The 4th Baronet obtained designs for another rebuilding from an astonishing galaxy of architects, including Robert Adam, Capability Brown, T. F. Pritchard, John Wood,

James Byres, and James Gandon. The choice fell upon James Wyatt, but not much had been done when Sir Watkin died at the age of forty in 1789. His mother commissioned Wyatt to design as a memorial the elegant column, surmounted by a bronze urn, which stands NW of the house, and can be seen from the A483. In about 1820 the house was tidied up with a severe classical dress by an unknown architect, but in 1858 it was gutted by fire. Not long before, it had happened that Sir Watkin was travelling by train, and fell into conversation with a fellow-passenger. This turned out to be the architect Benjamin Ferrey (biographer of Pugin). As a result, Ferrey got, not only a great deal of work on the family estates, but the job of rebuilding the house. (Later he used to tell his pupils that this showed how wise it was always to travel first-class.)

The new house is built on the foundations of its predecessor, which explains its peculiar T-shaped plan. The style – French Renaissance, with tall towers with steep-pitched roofs – was requested by Sir Watkin. From a distance it looks fine, but close to it is less satisfying. Inside there are some coffered ceilings and elaborate chimneypieces, but the best thing is the lovely organ in the Great Hall. Its case was designed by Adam for the Music Room of 20 St James's Square, the elegant town house which he built for the 4th Baronet. The organ itself is by Snetzler (1775).

The improvement of the park was begun in 1777 by Capability Brown, and continued after his death in 1783 by a local man, John Evans, who made a celebrated lake and cascade (now gone). The park contains several interesting buildings. Near the house are the Chapel, converted from an Orangery in 1876, and the Dairy, designed in 1782 by Brown. It has a refined portico, and was originally lined with Wedgwood tiles. Half a mile NW of the house is the Bath House (c. 1780), above the now jungly valley where the lower lake was. Its elegant portico stands above steps which descend into the great bath tank. A mile E of the house, on the A539, is a porticoed lodge, near which are the cupola-topped Kennels (1843, George Tattersall). Away to the SW, on the hill above Cefn Bychan, is the castellated Waterloo Tower, built to commemorate the victory. Down below it, at Newbridge (just off the A483), is a grandiose entrance to a long-disused

The Horseshoe Falls, Llangollen. Telford constructed this beautiful curving weir to take off water from the River Dee for the Llangollen Canal.

A typical Flintshire lane near Cilcain.

The chief glory of the church at Llanrhaeadr-Yng—Nghinmeirch is the wonderful Jesse window, dated 1533.

drive. The mannerist lodge has three deeply-recessed arches along the ground floor. It is by C. R. Cockerell, who in the same years (1827–8) worked at the house. Finally, most remote of all (in private woodland), there is the Nant-y-Belan Tower, or what is left of it. This mausoleum was built on a platform over the romantic valley, one and a half miles S of the house, to commemorate the brother officers of the 5th Baronet, who had died in Ireland fighting with his 'Ancient British Fencibles' in 1798–9. Before the trees grew up, it had a tremendous view. The tower itself, based on the Tomb of Caecilia Metella on the Via Appia, was designed by Sir Jeffry Wyatville. Unfortunately, the cliff has given way and taken most of the tower with it. Down below the Dee runs peacefully over great flat rocks between the steep wooded banks.

The **Church** at Ruabon was unkindly restored by Ferrey, in 1870, but is well worth a visit for what it contains. First there is the font, an astonishingly elegant piece to find in such a place: it was designed by Robert Adam and presented by the second Sir Watkin on his son's baptism in 1772. Then there are the monuments. In the NE chapel is an early sixteenth-century alabaster tomb with effigies of Sir John Eyton and his wife. There too is the large marble monument, erected in 1719, with a standing figure of Henry Wynn and kneeling ones of his disconsolate parents. This is by the local sculptor Robert Wynne of Ruthin, who could do delightful tablets, but was not up to work on this scale. Visitors, from Pennant onwards, have criticized it severely. Not so the monument in the SE chapel to the first Sir Watkin, which is by J. M. Rysbrack (erected in 1751), and has a recumbent figure. Next to it is an elegant tablet to a Wynn who died in 1763. Finally, now at the W end of the N aisle, there is the statue by Joseph Nollekens, on a superb pedestal, of Lady Henrietta Williams-Wynn. She married the second Sir Watkin in April 1769, but died in July of the same year, aged twenty-one. Their portrait had been painted by his friend Reynolds a month before their marriage.

Below the church, on the right of the main road, is a circular Lock-Up, handsomely rusticated, said to have been used for housing prisoners en route for Shrewsbury gaol.

Beyond Ruabon the A539 diverges to the right, over the railway, and crosses the shoulder of the hill towards Llangollen.

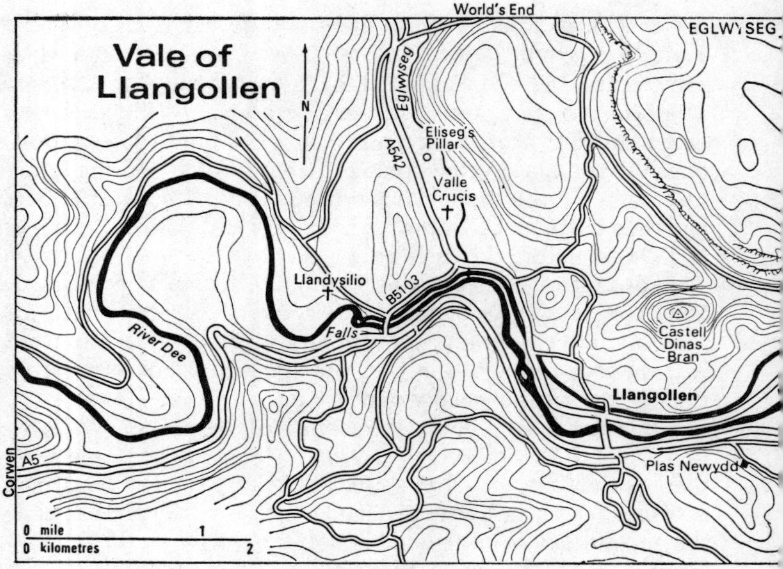

THE VALE OF LLANGOLLEN

The Vale of Llangollen is the pastoral valley of the Welsh Dee, which is about to become a lowland river winding in ever changing ox-bows through its water-meadows to Chester. Above Llangollen, the small town at the head of the Vale, the Dee is joined by the Eglwyseg; both the main valley and that of the little tributary stream and the heights which enclose them are very well worth exploring.

Indeed Llangollen has for so long been a mecca for tourists that it might seem impossible to add to the vast amount of advice which generations of guide-book writers have produced. They have made it difficult to see the Vale with twentieth-century eyes. So strongly is it pervaded by their romantic dream that this cannot completely dissolve even when the smells from the chemical factory at Cefn Mawr linger round the heights of Dinas Bran or the roar of traffic on A5 continues, as it may in the holiday season, far into the

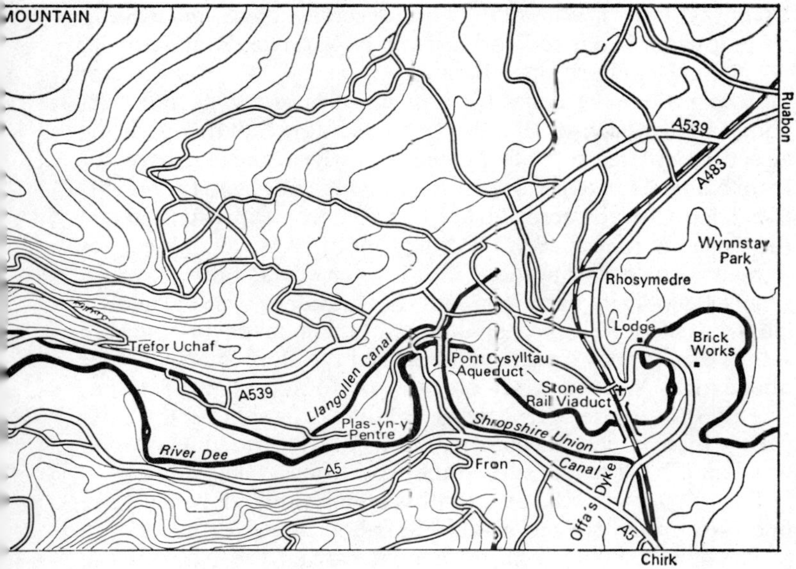

night. It is as latter-day eighteenth-century tourists that we want to see the Vale. One answer is to go in the early spring when the celandines and aconites carpet the sunny patches in the bare woodlands; or perhaps in early November, after the first sharp frosts have turned the oak to burning gold and mists hang over the valley floor until mid-morning so that the great limestone cliffs which wall it in rise sheer from a milky sea. Pack some good books, for the evenings will be long by the big coal fire.

For walkers Llangollen provides enormous variety, including plenty of level strolls on the green lawns of the limestone terraces where once the quarry tramways ran, or along stretches of canal tow-path, some idyllic. The Vale abounds in aspects and prospects and seems to have been created to be admired.

It also provides a mine of interest to the industrial archaeologist, which is visually of the highest order. The east end is spanned not only by Robertson's monumental railway viaduct (p. 91), but also by Thomas Telford's superb aqueduct,

Pontcysylltau (1794–1805). This deserves close inspection: an enjoyable if not too hair-raising experience. Bear R on to A539 S of Ruabon; one and a half miles on, turn L at Trefor and park near the canal (do not drive on down to the river yet). The towpath of the Shropshire Union Canal, which the aqueduct carries over the Dee, is easily accessible here (or from below Fron at the opposite end), but a fair head for heights is needed to walk across what our forebears aptly christened the 'stream in the sky'. Pontcysylltau was an object of immense curiosity and admiration when it was built. It was a pioneer work in cast iron on the grandest scale. Details: length 1000 feet; a massive embankment leads to nineteen sets of airy arches which span between the stone piers 127 feet above the Dee. Each set consists of four cast iron arches, side by side; these carry the trough of the canal and the tow-path which is cantilevered over it. (Chirk Aqueduct, which was being built at the same time, has stone arches).

The great work was eventually ceremoniously opened on a fine November afternoon in 1805 when it was crossed by a procession of boats. The third boat carried the band of the Shropshire Volunteers, playing heartily to the great satisfaction of a vast concourse of people gathered to witness this amazing event.

At **Fron**, to the south of the canal just off A5, there is a massive ruined limekiln and an attractive 'Van Gogh' type of lifting bridge (in use).

William Hazeldine, Telford's colleague who provided the iron for the aqueduct (and was later to work with him on the other famous structures, such as the Menai Bridge), had built a foundry immediately north of the aqueduct (the site of the present chemical works). Remains of a boat-building yard survive; the canal basin is now used by canal enthusiasts. Here the Shropshire Union is joined by the **Llangollen Canal** and there are few better introductions to the Vale than to boat right up it to the head of the canal above Llangollen (about six miles) or to walk along the tow-path. It glides through the meadows under sturdy canal bridges (typical of Telford's work), separate from the road traffic and close under the cliffs of the Trefor Rocks and the steep slopes of the castle at Dinas Bran, giving a sense that it is penetrating foreign territory. In places the canal runs close to, but in its lower stages, high above the Dee. At **Plas-yn-y-pentre**, where the two are very close, there is a big mill with a fine water wheel (no longer used), a horse mill and a dovecot; once probably typical of a prosperous small *plas* in these parts. The house itself is a characteristic border mixture with black and white first floor, stone and brick below.

Back on A539, two miles on, it is well worth stopping at **Trefor Uchaf** to look up the steep inclines which brought the lime down from the great kilns (1881) above. An attractive minor road follows the contours below these cliffs right along the north side of the Vale. The cliffs and kilns are easily accessible from it. The rocks here are so angular and perpendicular that it is difficult to believe that they are not man-made, and the tramways, with their short springy turf, make most comfortable walking.

Llangollen, a friendly Victorian-looking small town, is of course world-known for the International Eisteddfod (annually in July). Appropriately this great gathering takes place in a marquee; a permanent building would look forlorn for the rest of the year, and could kill the sense of occasion that a good tent can create. Then the town is a babel of tongues renewing old friendships and singing new songs and every house and hotel is full to bursting.

The Trefor Bridge, which crosses the Dee in the middle of the town, was built originally by Bishop Trefor in the fourteenth century. The present structure probably dates from Elizabethan times and has been several times widened. The once numerous wool and flannel mills along the Dee have mostly closed but Llangollen has thrived on tourism since the late eighteenth century when it was a popular coach halt on the road to Holyhead (and so to Dublin). It was in 1780 that the indomitable and eccentric Ladies of Llangollen took up residence at Plas Newydd (across the bridge, above A5, on the E side of the town). This they gothicized, making a picturesque black and white 'cottage'. From a gazebo in the garden they could spy coaches coming up the Holyhead Road. For nearly half a century anyone who was or aspired to be anyone called on their way through Llangollen (visitors included such celebrities as Wellington, Burke, Castlereagh, Wordsworth, Shelley, Byron and Scott). Lady Eleanor Butler, the Hon. Sarah Ponsonby and their faithful maid Mary

Carryll had escaped from provincial life in Ireland to set up house here. They soon became generally accepted as part of the North Wales scene but from the start there were busybodies who enjoyed anxious speculation and gossip. Several books have been written about them which tell of a remarkably ordered life, gardening, writing, chatting and playing backgammon together (see *The Ladies of Llangollen*, Elizabeth Mavor, Penguin). Unfortunately, their surviving journals are dull, despite their wide acquaintance. They also interested themselves in local affairs, opposing such things as Telford's new road (but recanting on receiving a carefully reasoned letter from him, to which they sent a disarmingly generous reply). The house, now owned by the local council, is open. It has been altered over the years but a tradition was established that visitors should bring a present of wood-carving, so it is like a sampler of carving from all over Europe.

Their tomb, designed by Thomas Parker, father of John Parker (p. 291), is triangular in plan so that each has her own side. It is outside the west door of the parish church, in the middle of the town. **St Collen's** is a typical double-naved church to which an aisle was added in 1865. The old naves have robustly carved open roofs, the central being particularly fine with angels on the hammer beams (switch on the light). The roof does not match up with the arches. The Ladies' memorial inside the church was commissioned by Dr Mary Gordon, a disciple of Jung, on the proceeds of her fictional biography of them, *The Chase of the Wild Goose* (1936). It is by Violet Labouchere, and makes them look like a pair of suffragettes. The models were in fact the donor and the sculptor.

The Ladies enjoyed from their windows a romantic view of **Castell Dinas Bran** which has a commanding site on a steep green hill to the north of the town. This isolated outcrop is almost as high as the limestone cliffs behind and it is worth climbing, both for the meagre but romantic thirteenth-century ruins which have a not over-tidy 18th-century atmosphere, and the view of the Dee Valley. The castle stands within an Iron Age fort, and is said to have been built by Gruffydd ap Madoc whose father founded Valle Crucis. The beautiful Myfanwy Fechan, inspiration of the fourteenth-century bards, lived here.

Several steep lanes and wooded walks also lead south from Llangollen into the narrow belt of upland which separates the Vale from the valley of the Ceiriog. This farming upland is really an easterly extension of the foothills of the Berwyns and is more often approached from Chirk. There are great views into England from the windy road which runs along the top.

A542 continues W from Llangollen on the N bank of the Dee and soon turns N up the Eglwyseg valley between the high tops of Maesyrychen Mountain and the Eglwyseg cliffs. Both have been quarried for generations and were connected with the canal by dramatic tramways and inclines. One mile up from Llangollen (the site is now a petrol station) is the quay from which stone was loaded for the journey to Paddington. The tramway crossed the road here (you can see its causeway in the nursery garden opposite). It then rejoined the road after the latter rounds the corner and created the raised bank on your left before taking to the fields and making up the mountain in a grand series of inclines to the quarries above. A very steep walk only for the fit.

Just off the main road to your R is **Valle Crucis**, a lovely ruin of a Cistercian abbey which lay in the heart of its vast sheepwalks. (At one time the monks had 25,000 sheep.) It was founded in 1201 and the choir is said to have rivalled that of Salisbury. Standing here on a spring evening watching the changing light on the wooded hills through the empty thirteenth-century windows it is possible to regain something of its medieval seclusion. In summer this is more difficult owing to the immediate proximity of a caravan site. The east end, with its unusual pilaster buttresses dividing to frame the upper lancets, is reflected in a formal fish pool; some discerning eighteenth-century admirer of the abbey here erected a cottage (now a tool shed) from which to enjoy this dream-like view. There are extensive buildings (some still being excavated). The west end was repaired by Gilbert Scott.

The Pillar of Eliseg, a little higher up the valley, of scholarly rather than visual interest, is the remains of an eighth–ninth-century cross, whose Latin inscription (now undecipherable) was read in 1696; it recorded the ancient glories of the royal house of Powys and was erected in honour of King Eliseg, a contemporary of Offa who built the Dyke. The abbey takes its name from this cross.

The main road, A542, continues north up the easily graded Horseshoe Pass and so over to the Vale of Clwyd (p. 50). On each side is heather and grouse moor and, wherever a car has stopped, sheep. From Cyrn y Brain to the E of the road, right along Llandysilio Mountain, there are splendid views of unfolding ranges right into the heart of Snowdonia.

On each side of the pass lanes lead off R to the valley of the Eglwyseg, which are well worth following. They join the lovely road which has followed the contours below the sheer cliffs of Eglwyseg and Trefor Rocks from above Trefor Uchaf, near the mouth of the Vale (p. 85). It is now enticingly sign-posted to **World's End**, but in fact continues over Esclusham Mountain to Minera, W of Wrexham. Indeed those flat, heathery tops feel like the roof of the world. It was at World's End that, between the Wars, the Duke of Westminster used to hold what might be described as a folly in terms of a pheasant shoot. The birds, driven from the steep slopes on one side of the valley, made straight across almost out of range of the guns. As the day proceeded the drives got higher. Winston Churchill was among the distinguished guns who gathered at Plas Uchaf, the simple stone and timber house of Tudor origin (sympathetically restored in recent years), which lies beside the road. A gruesome legend tells that Queen Elizabeth came here to have a baby, which was instantly thrown on the fire. A more authentic claim to fame is that Colonel John Jones, who was among the signatories of Charles I's death warrant (see p. 249), lived here. It is a strangely remote valley so close to the unremote.

Where A542 turned N, away from the Dee, a minor road, B5103, clings to the main river. **Llandysilio Church** has an attractive wooded site above the river. It is much restored and reflects the affection of the Victorians for this valley. Theodore Martin (Prince Albert's biographer) was a parishioner and Robert Browning read the lesson for ten weeks during his stay. There is a tiny single-light window in the north of the nave, with glass of 1460.

The **Horseshoe Falls** are just below the church. Although the Llangollen Canal always carried narrow boats (and now pleasure craft) its primary function was to act as a feeder for the Shropshire Union. It takes its water from the Dee here. To this end Telford constructed the beautiful curving weir which forms a lovely still-seeming pool above its long crescent line. This is quite unlike the raging mountain torrent which visitors to picturesque Wales might expect from the name; the fall of the weir is about 18 inches.

The Dee now makes a great loop. Further up it runs through a lovely wooded valley, in the best tradition of the romantic but more gentle picturesque. The road along the N side is unhurried, at times right down at water level; it is a most beautiful stretch of this famous salmon river.

From Llangollen Telford's Holyhead Road (A5) follows the S side, cutting bends wherever he could plan it so. Three miles beyond Llangollen, the road entered Merioneth (until 1974). The first village is **Glyndyfrdwy**. Right in the middle there is a good seventeenth-century stone farmhouse, its yard opening on to the A5. Nearby, an incline carried a tramway (built c. 1850) from the slate quarries up Nanty Pandy down to the railway. Parts of the old wooden rails survive higher up. The road which climbs to the upper quarries, from half a mile beyond the village (only motorable in dry weather), provides an easy start for the gentle climb up Moel Fferna (2071 ft), part of the humpy, heathery Berwyn Range. The views of Snowdonia can be glorious.

A mile beyond, a motte, between road and river, is marked on the map as 'Owen Glyndwr's Mount'. He certainly had a residence here, but it is not known precisely where it was. It was at Glyndyfrdwy that he was proclaimed Prince of Wales in 1400. The B5436 crosses the river here to **Llansanffraid Glyndyfrdwy** (or Carrog). The old church down by the river was swept away by a flood in the early seventeenth century, and a new one was built higher up in 1611. This was rebuilt in 1852, and a large and distinguished chancel was added in 1867 by G. E. Street. It has deeply-splayed windows, the E one containing good Clayton and Bell glass. The B5436 goes over the hills to Bryneglwys (p. 51), while the B5437 runs along the N bank of the Dee, below **Caer Drewyn**. This Iron Age promontory fort covers eight acres, and much of the stone rampart survives.

The A5 continues into **Corwen**, a pleasant little town, mostly of grey stone. It lies snugly beneath steep wooded slopes, where the narrow Dee valley opens into the wide and fertile Dyffryn Edeirnion. On the main road is the former Workhouse, early nineteenth-century: its grand frontispiece has Doric columns, and a few windows retain their original iron glazing bars. Beyond, the main road widens to form the Market Place, surrounded by eighteenth and early nineteenth-century houses. An assertive half-timbered bank built in 1928 is absurdly out of place. The Church is set back up above, in a good big churchyard. It is not an attractive building. The W tower is crude, and the rest was largely rebuilt in 1871 by T. H. Wyatt. The S aisle arcade is unusually tough for him. Three medieval lancets survive in the E wall. In the chancel is the tomb-slab, with half-effigy in low relief, of Iorwerth Sulien, vicar c. 1400. The old nave roof and Norman font remain. On the S wall a monument in coloured marbles, with a portrait of Maria Lloyd (d. 1780), is signed by Van der Hagen, and inscribed:

> Nor love thy Life; nor hate; but what thou liv'st
> Live well; how long or short, permit to Heav'n.

Outside the church, to the SW, stands Carreg-y-big (the pointed stone): the Celtic cross on top was a later addition. A legend (not peculiar to Corwen) tells that attempts to build the church anywhere other than where stood Carreg-y-big were divinely frustrated. Another stone, now used as the lintel of the chancel S door, bears a rough mark the shape of a dagger. This is said to have been made by the dagger of Owen Glendower: some say he threw it from a nearby height. This sort of feat is usually attributed to King Arthur, and like other Owen legends it shows how deeply he entered into folk-myth. On the S side of the churchyard is the College, built in 1750 as almshouses for six clergy widows, and now a Bed and Breakfast.

For the A5 beyond Corwen, see p. 117. For the B4401, to Bala, see p. 221.

RUABON TO CHIRK (A483)

Beyond the divergence of the Llangollen road (A539), the A483 skirts Wynnstay Park (see p. 80). On the left of the road stands a remarkably fine stone engine-house, with tall round-headed windows. It was part of a colliery. Further on is Rhosymedre – celebrated as the name of a hymn tune. Just on the bend at **Cefn Bychan**, where the road starts to go down, is a nice unpretentious chapel of 1826. Here the Dee Valley is crossed by the magnificent great stone viaduct built in 1848 to carry the Chester and Shrewsbury Railway. Stephenson had advised that this route was impracticable, but the young engineer Henry Robertson carried it through. It was suggested that the viaduct should bear the inscription 'Where old Stephenson's heart quailed, young Robertson has not failed.' Down in the valley is Cockerell's lodge to Wynnstay (see above). Climbing up the hill, on the left is the Castle Brick Works, which formerly belonged to J. C. Edwards & Co., one of the best-known of the many firms producing the shiny red brick and terracotta products for which Ruabon is so famous. Good specimens of their products can be seen in the row of houses near the entrance, built for foremen in 1882. From here there is a glorious view down the Vale of Llangollen: the sight of it on a misty morning, with Castell Dinas Bran rising out of a grey sea, is unforgettable. After crossing railway and canal the road joins the A5: two miles south is Chirk.

Chirk is a gateway to Wales for travellers from the south. The Ceiriog, which joins the Dee three miles downstream, here forms the border with Shropshire and, thanks again to Thomas Telford and Henry Robertson, the view upstream as you enter the Principality on A5 provides a good curtain-raiser to what lies ahead. The valley is spanned by an **Aqueduct** (1796–1801) and **Viaduct** (1848), side by side only a few feet apart. Both are worth closer inspection and this is easy. Take the Glyn Ceiriog road (west from Chirk village). After 500 yards, a short path to the left runs down to the aqueduct which can be seen as a shining ribbon through the trees. Above strides the viaduct with some handsome classical detail. There is a complete illusion of being at ground level, and only on reaching the aqueduct proper is one aware that the Ceiriog is rushing seventy foot below. Telford constructed this aqueduct with an iron base instead of the puddled clay which had until then been customary (the side plates were added in 1880). Through the canal tunnel, which opens into the boat pool beside the aqueduct, the pinpoint of green light which you see is a quarter of a mile away. Eerily clear voices of invisible boatmen may suddenly surprise you. A shimmer of light reflects from the water on to the tunnel's flaring mouth;

lovely ochres and pale lichen and white salts on the weathering red brick are again reflected in the still canal. A notice reads: OPEN TO APPROVED CANOEISTS. It is possible for brave pedestrians to walk through the tunnel, but the tow-path may not be entirely sound.

The small stone road bridge which carries the A5 into Wales is also by Telford. To the visitor Chirk village, with its pollarded chestnuts, nice Gothick cottages, and redbrick Georgian house (on the site of the bailey of the old castle, Castell y Waun, which guarded this important river crossing) may seem surprisingly English. It is situated between two great estates – that of the Castle, up on the hill one and a half miles to the west, and that of Brynkinallt hidden away in its beautiful park, sloping down towards the Ceiriog, to the east. The **Church** was originally twelfth century; a north aisle and sturdy tower were added in the late fifteenth century and the whole brought up-to-date. The carved corbels in this aisle are odd. Good monuments: the grandest (1721) has standing figures of Sir Richard and Lady Myddelton, and a reclining figure of Sir William, together with all manner of other details (note the red hand at the top – the family crest). This one is by Robert Wynne of Ruthin. There are also two monuments, both made in 1676, by the eccentric London sculptor John Bushnell – one to Elizabeth Lady Myddelton, the other (with busts) to Sir Thomas and Lady Myddelton.

At the crossroads in the village stands the War Memorial by Eric Gill, commissioned by Lord Howard de Walden, then tenant of Chirk Castle, and carried out in 1919–20. On the S. face is a bas-relief of a 'soldier on the look-out – the most typical attitude representing the war of entrenchment', as Gill himself put it. Further N on the main road is the school, of which the earliest (S) part is an excellent work of A. W. N. Pugin (1843–4). New industries have come to Chirk (partly to replace closed mines): the village sprawls to the north and smells of chocolate come from the west.

Chirk Castle (open regularly in summer, and well worth a visit) is approached through magnificent iron gates, one of the finest works of the Davies brothers of Bersham (these can be seen at any time). Made in 1719–21, they originally closed a forecourt immediately in front of the main entrance to the Castle. In 1770 they were moved to a site some way north of the present one, where the pair of elegant classical lodges that flanked them still stand. Only in 1888 were they moved to their present position. The fine park (crossed by Offa's Dyke) was landscaped in the late eighteenth century by William Emes, who also worked at Erddig, Baron Hill, etc. On the way to the castle is the pretty half-timbered Home Farm. The Castle itself was built by Roger Mortimer c. 1300, and is closely related to the series of castles built by Edward I to consolidate his Welsh conquests. It is quite exceptional in having been occupied ever since. In 1595 it was bought by Sir Thomas Myddelton, a merchant associate of Sir Walter Raleigh, and descendants of his still live here. The plan is rectangular, with a courtyard in the middle. It is only half the size that was intended, and the entrance front is far the most impressive, with its three great round towers, and the tall recessed arch over the gateway. Inside, as might be expected, the interiors are mostly of the seventeenth, eighteenth and nineteenth centuries. There is a splendid Long Gallery, with panelling richly carved by Thomas Dugdale, completed in 1678. There are also fine eighteenth-century rooms, mostly the work of Joseph Turner of Chester, and carried out in 1766–73. The Great Saloon has a magnificent coffered ceiling with painted panels, and the staircase hall is an ingenious treatment of an odd-shaped space. In the early nineteenth century the east wing of the Castle (now private) was remodelled by Thomas Harrison of Chester, who put Gothic vaults of plaster into the rooms, and built an open Gothic cloister along the exterior on the courtyard side. Then, in the 1840s, A. W. N. Pugin was called in: he converted the cloister into a passage by adding a new front, and remodelled the entrance hall. He was also responsible, together with the famous interior decorator, J. G. Crace, for redecorating the eighteenth-century rooms: their cheerful colour scheme for the Great Saloon survives. Many fine pictures, furniture, historical relics etc.

Paths through the park are open from 1 March to 30 September, from Castle Mill in the Ceiriog valley to Tyn-y-Groes and Llwyn-y-Cil.

Brynkinallt, on the other side of Chirk, the home of the Trevor family, is a restored Jacobean house – '1612', as it proudly says on the (sadly disappointing) iron gates, kept firmly closed. It is worth going round the north side of the park and down into the valley to **Pont-y-Blew**, a wonderfully secret and remote place. The attractive old bridge is amazingly narrow. The atmosphere of rural peace is so great that it is hard to believe that from the seventeenth century until the twentieth there was a forge here. But if you go on up the hill on the Shropshire side towards St Martin's, you will be astonished by the sudden appearance of a vast slag heap, and all the mess of a colliery only recently closed.

THE CEIRIOG VALLEY

Across A5 to the west the B4500 up the **Ceiriog Valley** follows close to the north bank of the river: it is more secretive than that of the Dee, narrow and winding with wooded slopes, long the retreat of Wales-loving romantics and now also of pheasant syndicates. Travelling west, stone soon entirely replaces the occasional brick in the farms and cottages, woodland and pasture give way to sheep and quarries, many no longer worked.

Glyn Ceiriog (Llansanffraid Glynceiriog), a quarry village, has a lovely site on the bend of the river but it is its drear modern housing which unfortunately catches the eye. The Parish Church stands above to the north on the 1 in 4 lane (well worth following) which leads over to Llangollen. Its 1790 tower and some simple woodwork now incorporated in the altar rails and chancel panelling of that date seem to be all that has survived the 1838 rebuilding of what Lewis describes as a 'Grecian style' church. There is early Victorian armorial glass by David Evans.

Pandy (the name means fulling-mill) has sturdy stone cottages and a pleasant stretch of old tramway (National Trust owned, so accessible) running immediately by the river up to Pont-y-Meibion. Here, at the farm of this name above the bridge, lived Huw Morus, Eos Ceiriog (the nightingale of Ceiriog). Born in 1622, Morus lived through six reigns but was famed throughout Wales during the Civil War for his support of the Royalist cause. This he gave as a poet and satirist rather than as a soldier; his poems fired the Principality to the support of the King. The farm, like others in the valley, now thrives on pony trekkers rather than poets or sheep.

Llanarmon Dyffryn Ceiriog, the highest village on the river (now a mountain stream) is an excellent centre for exploring this side of the Berwyns. Two attractive-looking stone inns with iron Gothick windows suggest that this sentiment is not new. The stone cottages and bridge are plainly right and the whole has an upland, as against valley, feel. The 1846 church, by Thomas Jones of Chester, is pleasantly simple (except for the new reredos), and the ancient yews flanking the path give the site its time scale. So, in quite different ways, does the tiny obelisk, less than two foot high, which commemorates one Robert Evans who lived from March until December 1900. The church is dedicated to St Germanus, famous Bishop of Auxerre, who is said to be buried here (unlikely, since he died at Ravenna, in 448).

The lane signposted Swch-cae-Rhiw follows the Ceiriog yet further. There are few buildings, but at Pentre Bach is a chapel, trim, cheerful and small. It was founded in 1815 for the upland farm families but was rebuilt fifty years later; sensibly plastered and painted only where it shows and brightly lit by friendly roundheaded windows. At Swch-cae-Rhiw ask at the corrugated iron farm-house (which you thought to be stone until you were close) if you want to take the path over the heather to trace the rushing stream to its source. A mile north the young Ceiriog cuts a deep gorge in the rock and drops by a series of exceedingly beautiful falls. Small weather-beaten mountain ash confuse all sense of scale: a ten-foot drop might well be fifty. Their berries blaze in the moist air and make their marvellous discord with the purple heather. A little higher up and the flattish tops begin to fall towards the ancient trackway of Saeson and the young Forestry Commission plantations of Ceiriog Forest before climbing further into the long range of empty moorland which forms the NE flank of the Berwyns. Alternatively you can follow another old trackway westwards over the top, where a memorial commemorates a member of the RSF, and down towards Llandrillo and Cynwyd (p. 221). 'RSF' stands for Rough Stuff Fellowship: anywhere in Wales you may meet a member of that glorious band of indefatigable cyclists, bravely carrying his bike over boggy moorland until he reaches a cyclable path.

From back at Llanarmon, several minor roads run S over the hills to the B4580 (Oswestry–Llanrhaeadr) – see p. 265.

CHAPTER THREE

Between the Vale of Clwyd and the Conwy

Whereas the eastern side of the Vale of Clwyd is sharply demarcated by the Clwydian range, the western side rises more gently into rolling hilly country, much of it wooded, much of it limestone, into which run numerous valleys, remote and delectable, and networks of country lanes. Further N is the high open moorland of Mynydd Hiraethog, and beyond that more hospitable hilly country bordering the Conwy valley. The whole area is quiet and extraordinarily little known: it is one of the characteristic contrasts of Wales that just a few miles inland from the busy coast are some of the most secluded valleys imaginable.

Going down the A525 from Ruthin towards the sea, at Rhewl the road crosses the Clywedog by a bridge of 1819. This lovely wooded river leads up to the tiny village of **Gyffylliog,** cosily set in the deep valley. Its little church was restored by Baker in 1876. It was to this remote spot that Charles I summoned his local supporters in 1645. By the church is the stone 'Hearse House 1823'. Back on the A525, a mile beyond Rhewl is **Bachymbyd**, a brick house of 1666, and a little further on stand the Three Sisters, huge chestnuts planted by three daughters of Sir William Salusbury of Bachymbyd, to commemorate their mutual affection, when one of them was due to be married.

The next village is **Llanrhaeadr-yng-Nghinmeirch**, now by-passed. The big double-naved church stands among trees. Excellently restored by Baker in 1879–80, it has a fine timber porch, but its chief glory is the wonderful Jesse window, dated 1533. It is said to have survived the Commonwealth by being hidden in the old chest kept nearby, and buried in a wood. It was re-erected in 1661. The carved roofs are unusually fine. There is a large marble monument, with effigy, to Maurice

Chirk Castle 'is approached through magnificent iron gates, one of the finest works of the Davies brothers of Bersham, made in 1719-21'.

The tunnel on the Llangollen Canal at Chirk: 'a shimmer of light reflects from the water on to the tunnel's flaring mouth'.

A cottage in Maelor Saesneg, where the 'half-timbering' is entirely painted on—a local tradition.

An old photograph of Conwy Castle and Stephenson's tubular Railway Bridge of 1846-8. Beyond are Degannwy and the Great Orme.

Jones of Ddol, d. 1702, ('His conversation was diverting and innocent, pleasant and instructive'), put up by his widow, a daughter of Sir Walter Bagot. She also built the pretty Almshouses by the church in 1729 (restored in 1820 and 1963). In the wood behind the church is St Dyfnog's Well, with a large stone tank: it was held to be good for the scabs and the itch. On the opposite side of the road from the church is the Hall, its avenue now bisected by the bypass. The stone Jacobean front was added in 1842 by Thomas Penson, but is said to be based on the original front. Behind it is an elegant late eighteenth-century wing, built by Richard Parry, who commissioned grand designs for rebuilding from Robert Adam, but settled for something more modest.

Two miles from Llanrhaeadr, down a road leading E, is **Whitchurch** (Eglwys Wen – or, strictly, Llanfarchell), the mother church of Denbigh, yet another big Perp twin-naver. It contains a large painted alabaster table tomb with figures of Sir John Salusbury of Lleweni, d. 1578 (see p. 58) and his wife, erected by her in 1588, and fine hammer-beam roofs. Always locked. In the churchyard is buried Twm o'r Nant (Thomas Edwards) (1739–1810). He had a difficult life, and followed many occupations, but he is chiefly famous for his 'interludes' (folk-dramas, often satirical comments on contemporary life).

Denbigh (Dinbych), although not quite so attractive as Ruthin, has lots of character – 'a taking picturesque town', said Gerard Manley Hopkins. The main street climbs up from the road junction towards the **Castle**, which stands at the highest point. In 1282 Edward I gave the district to Henry de Lacy, Earl of Lincoln: he built the town walls, and began the castle (D. o. E.). Much the most impressive feature is the Gatehouse, built on an ingenious triangular plan, with two hexagonal towers outside and a larger octagonal one inside. Over the outer gate is an elegant niche holding a decrepit statue, probably of Edward I. The Castle gives a splendid view over the neighbourhood. Almost the whole of the **Town Walls** survive including the big Burgess Gate N of the Castle. In 1563 the Castle came into the possession of the Earl of Leicester, and he began to build a church NE of the Castle, called **Leicester's Church**, which – so it was said – he intended to replace St Asaph Cathedral. The nave would have been

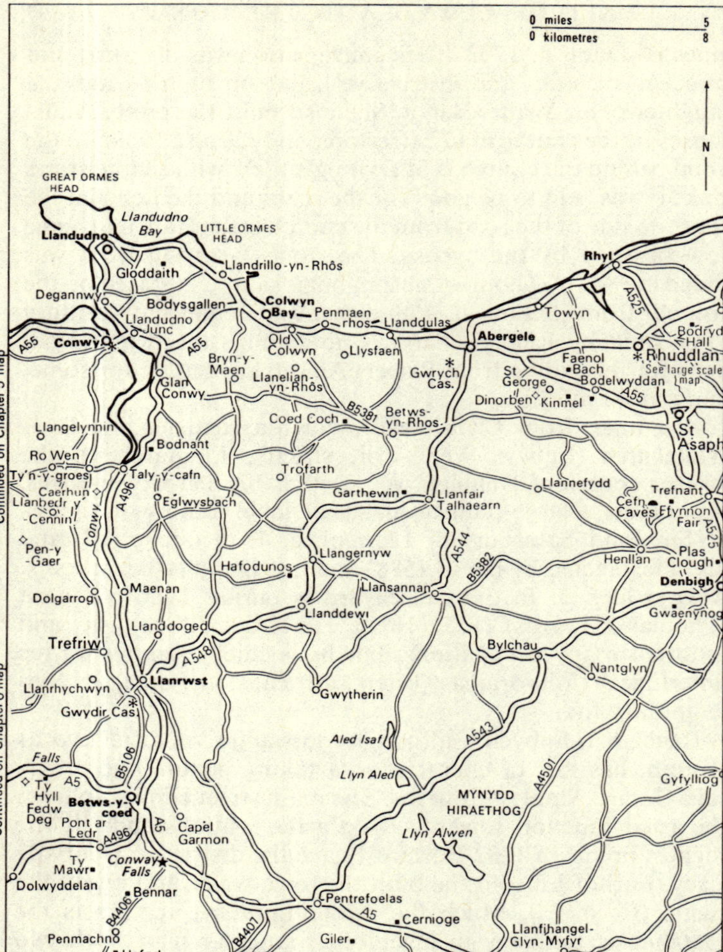

Continued on Chapter 5 map
Continued on Chapter 6 map
Continued on Chapter 1 map
Continued on Chapter 2 map
Continued on Chapter 9 map

170 feet by 70. The wall of the N aisle, with large roundheaded windows, still stands, looking rather like an aqueduct. Nearby is **St Hilary's Chapel**, used both as castle chapel, and, since Whitchurch was so far out, as the parish church. Built c. 1300, it was unroofed in 1904. On the other side of Leicester's Church is an extremely comic Victorian gatehouse, tall and elaborate, built of multicoloured brickwork.

The main street is remarkable for its arcades, a most unusual feature in Wales. Numerous good buildings include a nice iron-and-glass shopfront, on two storeys. Below the rustic eighteenth-century **Town Hall** is the English Presbyterian church, a tough High Victorian nut, in sharp contrast with the elegant Georgian houses further down. The S side of the street is interrupted by a curiosity which could only properly be described by Barbara Jones – that connoisseur of the curious. It is a small garden in which stands a column 50 feet high, bearing a statue of Sicilian marble, by W. and T. Mills of London. Erected in 1874–6, and designed by Martin Underwood, this jokey affair was set up to Dr Evan Pierce, during his lifetime. Nice reliefs on the base, by M. Raggi, show works of mercy. In the bedraggled little garden are two funny iron fountains, decorated with lots of birds and the names of the Queen's children, presented in 1887 by Dr Pierce himself. The flowerbeds have terracotta borders (like pastry). Perhaps we ought not to laugh: the reason for Dr Pierce's celebrity was his heroism in a cholera epidemic. Yet another oddity is the surprising classical building, further down and just off to the N: it has the Royal Arms over the door, but with its pastel shades and flashy tapering columns, looks like a stray from Monte Carlo. Neither of the town's two churches is up to much. **St Mary's**, N of the Castle, is of 1871–4, by the local firm Lloyd-Williams and Underwood. The bishop refused to consecrate the church at first, owing to Protestant objections to the reredos, which shows the Crucifixion (by Earp). **St David's**, to the E, was rebuilt in 1895 by R. Lloyd-Williams, retaining the tower of 1858 by T. Penson. It is next to **Howell's School**, one of the two great girls' schools (the other is at Llandaff) founded in 1860 by the Drapers' Company – rather belatedly applying the income from the wealth of Thomas Howell, d. 1540, a Monmouthshire man, and merchant at Seville, who left his estate to provide dowries for female orphans. The original buildings are by Herbert Williams. They were remodelled and enlarged in the 1920s, in striking fashion, by Leslie Moore and Heaton Comyn. A splendid footpath leads up from the School, under the Walls, to the upper town. On the road out of the town, towards St Asaph, behind a filling station, stands the ruined but elegant chancel of a **Carmelite Friary Church.** Founded in the thirteenth century, it was burnt out in 1898. S of the town is the huge and grand **North Wales Mental Hospital**, opened in 1848. It was financed by Joseph Ablett (see p. 49). The original buildings, by Fulljames of Gloucester, in effective Jacobean style, have been much added to. Further S again, above the river Ystrad, is the motte-and-bailey called Llys Gwenllian.

Just W of the town (S of the A543) is **Gwaenynog**, where Samuel Johnson stayed. In the park, down by the river Ystrad, is 'Dr Johnson's Cottage' (now ruinous), so called because he liked to visit the spot. Nearby his host set up an urn to commemorate his visit – which he thought a dubious compliment: 'Mr Myddleton's erection of an urn looks like an intention to bury me alive.' Two celebrated men born in Denbigh were H. M. Stanley (b. 1841, and brought up, under his real name John Rowlands, at St Asaph Workhouse), and, of greater local significance, Thomas Gee (1815–1898). Gee was a printer by trade, and published many Welsh works, of which the most important were an Encyclopaedia and the weekly *Y Faner*. He was a stout Nonconformist and Radical, and used his paper to further his campaigns for educational reform, for the rights of tenants, and for Disestablishment. He was also a pioneer of Welsh nationalism.

A mile out of the town, just beyond where the Mold road (A543) leaves the St Asaph road (A525), is **Plas Clough**, another house built by Sir Richard Clough (see p. 46). This one, of 1567, has stepped gables. Two miles further on is **Trefnant**, which has a church, parsonage and school by Sir Gilbert Scott. The church, built in 1853–5 in a very refined Dec, is a treat. The rich interior has columns of Anglesey marble. As for the capitals, 'every group of leaves was carved by Mr Blinstone of Chester, from natural specimens gathered from the woods and hedges around' (W. Davis, *Handbook for the Vale of Clwyd*, 1856). This application of Ruskin's teaching is surprising for Scott, and surprisingly early (earlier than the

Oxford Museum). 'Good work', commented Hopkins (who found the church 'pretty'). E windows by Wailes.

Another two miles bring you into Flintshire, and to **St Asaph** (Llanelwy). It ought to be an attractive place, with its bridge over the Elwy, and the village street leading up from the parish church below to the cathedral at the top. It looks attractive in old pictures. Furthermore, it now has a bypass, to the N. But somehow it fails to attract. Take the **Cathedral**, for a start. Founded in 560 by the Scottish St Kentigern, who, on returning to Glasgow (where he is known as Mungo) left his pupil St Asaph in charge, it was rebuilt in the fourteenth and fifteenth centuries. It was proposed in the thirteenth century to move the see to Rhuddlan (see p. 36), and in the sixteenth to move it to Denbigh (see p. 97); in the 1830's it came near to being united with Bangor (see p. 280). Yet it survived. And the Cathedral itself has not had a bad press. Johnson wrote, in 1774, 'The Cathedral, though not large, has something of dignity and grandeur'. Hopkins wrote, a century later, 'Though it is no bigger than a large parish church, it has an imposing rather Cathedral-like look.' It was well restored in 1868–75 by Sir Gilbert Scott, who gave it a dignified if plain exterior, and a richly furnished interior. (Not that Hopkins was pleased – 'its historical interest is gone, and you cannot tell what is old, what new'.)

Scott restored the Early English lancets of the Choir, which had been walled up in the late eighteenth century. The Dean and Chapter would not let him probe the walls sufficiently deeply, so that details showing the original form of the windows were only discovered after four had already been conjecturally rebuilt. Scott wrote ruefully in his *Recollections*: 'I restored the remaining windows on either side correctly and left the others to take their chance; monuments of weak compliance, and beacons to warn others against such foolish conduct. There ought to be a brass plate set up recording our shame and repentance.' Since Scott's time, St Asaph has suffered the fate of so many small cathedrals, in being too small for the amount of money and enthusiasm lavished on it. Hence the dreadful painting and gilding spattered around all over the excellent timber roofs, the Bishop's Throne, and so on, and – worst of all – the repulsive organ case under the crossing. Far the best thing in the Cathedral is the moving reredos, showing the Way of the Cross: designed by Scott, it was superbly carved by Earp. The E window is poor work by Ward and Hughes. Fifteenth-century canopied stalls (foolishly tampered with in 1906). Heraldic glass by Eginton survives in the S transept: it surrounded his E window (for which see Llandegla, p. 50). Some good monuments include one to Sir John Hay Williams, d. 1859, signed by an Athenian sculptor (Λ. ΔΡΟΣΗΣ, ΑΘΗΝΑΙΟΣ, 1873), and, below it, a gorgeous brass and enamel tablet to Lady Sarah Hay Williams. The monument to Sir John Williams, d. 1830, by Westmacott, has his usual pair of simpering angels. The seated figure of Dean Shipley, by Ternouth, reminds us of the fact that the chief fame of the see in the eighteenth and early nineteenth centuries (with some exceptions) was as one of the most notorious cases of absenteeism and corruption in the Church of England. Shipley was Dean from 1774 until his death in 1826: it was no coincidence that his father was Bishop from 1769–87 (his father was simultaneously Dean of Winchester).

But even the Shipleys pale before the Luxmoores. It can hardly be an accident that the large canopied Gothic tomb of Bishop Luxmoore, by Thomas Jones, has disappeared, or that the marble tablet, which is all that was left of it, is now covered with a curtain. No one at St Asaph is likely to wish to remember him. He was Bishop from 1815–30: he too gave one son the Deanery, to add to his other preferments, in 1826, and another son a Canonry and various benefices. It is said that he and his family managed to rake in no less than £27,000 a year out of the dioceses of St Asaph and Hereford (his previous see), and even after his death his relatives got £7,000 a year out of the diocese of St Asaph alone. It must be added that, as far as absenteeism was concerned, there was medieval precedent. Geoffrey of Monmouth (see *South Wales*) had been appointed bishop in 1151 (before he was ordained priest), but there is no evidence that he ever visited his see between then and his death four years later.

Outside the Cathedral (NO SMOKING in the tidy precincts) stands an elaborate but uninspired memorial cross set up in 1902 (architects Prothero, Middleton and Phillott of Cheltenham) to commemorate William Morgan, Bishop 1601–4, and his collaborators in translating the Bible. On the W of the

Cathedral green are the grounds of the former **Bishop's Palace**, sloping down to the very refined front built in 1791 by Bishop Bagot – the first bishop to reside in the diocese for more than a month or so each year since about 1750. It has a central bow surmounted by a shallow dome. The western part of the Palace was added by Edward Blore in 1836, in rather unsympathetic Tudor. Just above the Palace gate are brick almshouses built by Bishop Barrow in 1680, rebuilt in 1795 – very plain and tiny. The double-naved parish church was also rebuilt by Scott, in 1872. There are some good eighteenth-century monuments, and on the roof wooden hearts where you would expect shields. The fine bridge was built in 1770 by Joseph Turner, and on the other side is the big Tudor-style Deanery, built for Luxmoore Jun. by Thomas Jones.

Two miles W of St Asaph, the main road (A55) passes by the famous 'Marble Church' of **Bodelwyddan**. This fantastically lavish and ornate building is, with its 202 foot W spire (based on King's Sutton in Northants), a landmark for miles. Shining white, it is not built of marble (though there is plenty of marble inside), but of local white limestone. It was built in 1856–60, and the architect was John Gibson – it makes a striking contrast with his church at Bersham (see p. 70). It was paid for by the Dowager Lady Willoughby de Broke, in memory of her husband (she was a Williams of Bodelwyddan Castle). Inside, everything is expensive and richly carved. The pulpit, chancel, bosses, and stall ends are by Earp, the lectern (1882) by Kendall of Warwick, the Carrara marble font, showing the donor's daughters holding a shell, by Peter Hollins, the E window by O'Connor, and so on. But it does not really come off. Goodhart-Rendel found it all 'a sad waste of money'. Beside the church are rows of neat graves, of soldiers who died at the nearby army camp – many, it is said, in a riot. The village has estate cottages, the estate being that of the **Castle**, which stands, high up in the big park, surrounded by an impressive cyclopean wall, across the road from the church. It is now Lowther College, a girls' school. Said to be basically Elizabethan, and retaining seventeenth- and eighteenth-century features, it was grecianized c. 1800, but then after 1830 – to keep up with changing fashion – completely castellated for Sir John Hay Williams by Joseph Aloysius Hansom. The most entertaining feature is a huge stone man in armour carved out of limestone (just right for the Commendatore in *Don Giovanni*). A mile beyond the church, N of the road, is **Faenol Bach**, a delightful house of 1571, enlarged 1626, with stepped gables and numerous tall chimneys. At that time, when open hearths were still the rule, 'a tall chimney was as much a prestige symbol as TV aerials at a later date' (*Farmhouses and Cottages*, Flintshire Record Office, 1964).

Immediately adjoining the Bodelwyddan estate is the park of **Kinmel**, but the house is actually in Denbighshire. It is now Clarendon School (also for girls). The original house was built by Samuel Wyatt for Rev. Edward Hughes, who had bought the estate in 1786 with profits from the Parys Mountain mines (see p. 206). It was burnt in 1841, and rebuilt in Greek revival style by Hopper, but in 1868–74 it was completely transformed by W. E. Nesfield. It is a wonderfully rich and satisfying example of his work, a pioneer of the so-called 'Queen Anne' style, in warm red brick and stone. To some extent it is based on Hampton Court, which architect and clients visited together in 1868, but the plan is unclassical, the steep roofs are French, and the detail – including features of Japanese origin such as 'pies' (see p. 58) – Nesfield's own. The work was done for H. R. Hughes, whose initials seem to have corresponded to his own ideas of his status. There was even a special room for ironing the newspapers. The remarkable stable block of 1855 is probably by William Burn. Beside the road is an elaborate stone lodge (1868), in the style of the house, with big dormers in the steep roof, decorated with lots of sunflowers and pies. Down the lane opposite is the Home Farm, also by Nesfield (1866). In the village of **St George**, half a mile S of the main road, there is a peculiar lodge of 1808, and a dull church (1887–94, C. H. R. Mileham), in whose churchyard stands the crisp Gothic mausoleum of Lady Dinorben, d. 1835, by Thomas Jones, looking out to sea. The Iron Age fort of **Dinorben**, to the W, has been excavated.

Abergele, although hardly very attractive, has strong local character. The best buildings are the **Parish Church**, the biggest double-naver in Wales, restored by Arthur Baker in 1879, the admirable housing estate by Colwyn Foulkes in the N part of the town, and the big Gothic school on the Colwyn Bay road, of 1870, by G. E. Street (since much enlarged). Street also built a first-rate group of church, vicarage and school at **Towyn**, on the road between Abergele and Rhyl, in 1871–3. The church has a saddleback tower over the crossing, and excellent fittings (reredos by Earp, E window and brass coronae by Hardman). The vicarage is linked to the church by a covered passage. All three buildings are roofed with patterned slates.

Street's patron in the area was Robert Bamford Hesketh, of **Gwrych Castle**. This incredible pile, just beyond Abergele, never ceases to amaze travellers by road or rail, not for its architectural merit, which is slight, but for its sheer dramatic bravado. It is built against a steep wooded hillside, with limestone outcropping all around. The main block is straightforward, even dull, but from it great battlemented walls, with eighteen towers and bastions, run out over the hillside: they have now acquired sufficient patina of age, to say nothing of superabundant greenery, to look sublimely convincing. It would do admirably as the set for a Gothick melodrama, with a cast of giants. It was completed in 1815 by Lloyd Bamford Hesketh. His architect was C. A. Busby, a Regency man from Brighton, but Hesketh seems to have taken a large part in the design himself. Its subsequent history has been suitably dotty. An immense marble staircase was installed c. 1870 – leading nowhere. And now the whole place is the most thoroughgoing fun-park you could find, with Miniature Railway, Miniature Zoo, Chamber of Horrors, Exhibition of Works of Art, Dancing to the Resident Organist, TV celebrities, Holiday Flatlets. The stables are 'the most unique in Europe'. The park is surrounded by a huge wall, with immense gatehouses to guard the entrances.

Beyond Gwrych is **Llanddulas**, with another excellent church by Street (1867–9), and up on the hill beyond is **Llysfaen**, with a church restored by Street in 1870, and also a school by him (altered). The nice Church Hall is by H. L. North. Bungalows indicate the proximity of **Colwyn Bay**, just round the headland of Penmaenrhos – as terrifying to early travellers as Penmaenmawr (see p. 133). Colwyn Bay tends not to get a good press. The town developed only after the sale in 1865 of the estate of the big stuccoed and castellated house, Pwllycrochan, which stands above. Intense building began at once, and the result is a rather select resort, just the place for prosperous Lancashire tradesmen to retire to, where the all-pervading Ruabon brick was even brighter and shinier than their native Accrington brick. The winter climate was a great attraction: *Black's Guide* of 1897 claims that 'a consumptive patient who had been in the habit of wintering abroad informs us that after spending three successive winters at Colwyn Bay, he found them more genial than had been his experience at Pozzuoli, near Naples.' It is unfortunate that the railway runs between the town and the sea, and the building of the much-needed bypass on the same side of the town will aggravate this disadvantage. The town's main shopping streets are enlivened by gay iron and glass canopies. There are a surprising number of treats for the connoisseur of late nineteenth- and early twentieth-century architecture. The Colwyn Bay Hotel is a bleak Gothic pile of 1872 by John Douglas, not at his best, as he certainly was in the two superb churches he built here. The larger one is St Paul's 1888–1911, with a handsome tower and a wide nave (reredos 1935 by W. D. Caröe). The other, even finer, is St John's, Old Colwyn, of 1899–1903.

Colwyn Bay produced one first-rate architect of its own, and he even took his name from the town – Sidney Colwyn Foulkes (1884–1971). It is well worth seeking out the works of this remarkable man, to whom Wales owes a great deal. He began by designing a prefabricated stage for a troupe of strolling players, at the age of sixteen. Later he studied under Sir Charles Reilly at the Liverpool University School of Architecture. He became landscape consultant to the Central Electricity Generating Board, universally respected for his sensitivity and skill. His talent was amazingly versatile. He could design in strict Greek (Williams Deacon's Bank); in neo-Georgian (the Hospital); Tudor (additions to Rydal Mount School); or light-hearted classical (Woods' shop and the Wedgwood Cinema); and other styles are revealed in his work outside Colwyn. This list may make him seem like a wild eclectic, but the styles are handled with such restraint and originality that the result is always something personal. Another good twentieth-century building in Colwyn is the individualistic neo-Georgian Council Offices by Percy Worthington.

A mile inland from Old Colwyn, up in the hills, and in another world, is **Llanelian-yn-Rhos**, once the terror of North

Wales for its cursing well. Anyone wishing to put a curse on an enemy would come here, and stand near the well while its guardian read passages of scripture. Then the guardian gave him water to drink three times, while he repeated his curse. Sometimes the curse was written on a pebble, or a piece of slate or lead, and dropped in the well. The guardian could be paid (again) to 'pull you out of the well'. It sounds a lot of fooey, but Archdeacon Thomas, in his *History of the Diocese*, bears witness to the genuine ill effects of the superstition. The last guardian died in 1858, and the well (which was 600 yards N of the church) was later filled in by the Rector.

A more cheerful tale is associated with the church at **Bryn-y-maen**, two miles S of Colwyn Bay – sentimentally known as 'The Cathedral of the Hills'. It was built by a local girl, who said that if she became rich she would build a church. She went into service with the Frosts of Colwyn, married the heir, and, when he died, duly built the church, in 1897–9, in his memory. It is a splendid late work of John Douglas, with a central tower, and his usual rich woodwork. Its toughness suits the upland site. Douglas also designed the Vicarage and a house for Mrs Frost.

NW of Colwyn Bay, on the Llandudno road, is **Llandrillo-yn-Rhos**, whose church tower has stepped battlements of Irish type. Right on the edge of the shore, incongruous among the seaside suburbia, is Capel Trillo, a tiny, roughly vaulted stone cell, built over a spring. The Royal Commission scornfully suggested that it was really a comparatively modern structure, but others claim that it goes back to the Dark Ages. Nearby is Rhos Fynach weir, a fishing weir given to the monks of Aberconwy by Ednyfed Fechan, seneschal of Llywelyn the Great, who is said to have lived at Llys Euryn near by, and to be buried in the church.

Beyond Rhos, the road enters Caernarfonshire (now Gwynedd) over the shoulder of Little Orme's Head, to reveal the great sweep of **Llandudno Bay** (also called Ormes Bay), and the town occupying its isthmus site, with the much greater bulk of Great Orme's Head (carboniferous limestone) at the far end. It is a fine sight, with the brightly-painted terraces fronting the curving bay, and the pier projecting under the shelter of the Orme. **Llandudno** sprang up a little later than Rhyl. Before the 1840s there were only a few scattered houses, and the little church up on the Head, founded by St Tudno (reputed to be a son of Seithenyn, see p. 248) was almost abandoned. Land was first put up for sale in 1846, by the Hon. E. M. L. Mostyn. The site-plan was drawn up in 1848 by Williams and Jones, Welsh architects practising in Liverpool, stipulating 'uniformity of frontage and elevation'. A further project was shown at the Royal Academy of 1855 by Wehnert and Ashdown of Charing Cross. It was criticized by the Press as having 'details generally and a cement coating in the worst style of Brighton and the other south coast towns'. How much of the stuccoed terraces built is by Wehnert and Ashdown is unclear (they certainly did a lot of work in the town). They were old-fashioned for the 1850s, but today we do not share the critic's disapprobation, and Llandudno is rightly coming to be honoured as one of the finest and best-preserved Victorian towns in Britain. Its fame is not due to individual buildings. Much the best, in Mostyn Street, is post-Victorian – the National Westminster Bank, of the 1920s, by F. C. Palmer and W. F. C. Holden, a fine Beaux Arts design. The shops in the main streets have iron and glass canopies, as at Colwyn Bay.

The churches are very disappointing. They include St George's, 1840, by John Welch; Holy Trinity, 1865, by George Felton, architect to the Mostyn Estate (the tower by his assistant, Edwin Turner); and St Paul's, Craig-y-don, 1893–1901, by John Oldrid Scott – its spire never built. (St Paul's was built in memory of the Duke of Clarence, and so has been called 'Jack the Ripper's Church', but the Duke seems lately to have lost favour as a candidate for this rôle.) The Grand Hotel, by J. F. Doyle of Liverpool, is impressive in massing and skyline. Beside it is the splendid iron pier (1876–83, Brunlees and McKerrow). The Pavilion (1883, B. Nelson) has good ironwork. Birmingham architects did a lot of work in the town, including J. A. Chatwin and J. A. Cossins, who designed many of that city's best buildings. Chatwin built Gloddaeth Crescent. Cossins did one of his earliest jobs here, and was entrusted with the restoration of the little storm-wrecked church of St Tudno in 1855. The Marine Drive round the Head was made in the 1870s, and gives good views of the cliffs and caves. The Head can be climbed on foot, by road, by funicular, or by cable car. There is the Happy

Valley: 'the Happy Valley of Rasselas was a dull hole compared with this animated resort at the height of the season' (*Black's Guide*, 1897). Part is laid out as an Alice in Wonderland fantasy, to commemorate the fact that Lewis Carroll used to spend holidays here with the Liddells, at the Gogarth Abbey Hotel, on the W side of the Head (the so-called Abbey is really a ruined fourteenth-century palace of the Bishops of Bangor). Llandudno is famous for its climate – 'as mild as Ventnor yet as bracing as Eastbourne', says *Black's Guide*. 'While the main coast is shrouded in mist or rain, the friendly sun will pay private visits to Llandudno; and his too ardent advances, which might be troublesome in the absence of elderly trees to cast a shade of propriety, are tempered to agreeable modesty by the chaste sea breezes, so that the climate is remarkably equable, and you may often sit here in genial open air with the Lucretian satisfaction of observing how your mountain neighbours are shivering in mist or groaning in a feverish thunderstorm.'

A mile SW of Llandudno, in a wooded, hilly park, is **Gloddaeth**, a Mostyn house, now a girls' school. It is an exceptionally fine house, and rich in atmosphere. The sixteenth-century hall and solar wing survive intact: both have open timber roofs, elaborately decorated chimneypieces and plasterwork and wall-paintings restored in the 1870s, when a large addition was made to the house by W. E. Nesfield. His wing has a good staircase and pretty plasterwork. A further extension is dated 1889. A mile S of Gloddaeth is **Bodysgallen**, another Mostyn house, now a hotel. It is large, picturesque, and accretive: the earliest part, the Hall, is of 1620, much of the rest c. 1700. On the western side of the Creuddyn peninsula (on the A496, to Conwy) is **Degannwy**, a select residential place, with a first-rate church of 1898–9 by John Douglas, The way the low, broad spire is set against the steep hillside is admirable. On the rocky hilltop are scanty remains of the castle, with a long history, particularly stormy in the wars of the thirteenth century, from which period the ruins date. It was finally destroyed by the Welsh in 1263.

Llandudno Junction is a dreary place. The station is the junction, not only for the branch to Llandudno, but also for the line to Llanrwst and Blaenau Ffestiniog. This line came within an inch of its life in Beeching days, but was reprieved, very fortunately, as it is both useful and exceptionally beautiful – much the best way to see the Conwy and Lledr valleys. As far as Llanrwst it follows the E bank of the river, as does the A496. The Conwy valley is very different from the Vale of Clwyd: the river is wider and slower, but the valley is more sharply defined. For the first few miles upstream, the river sprawls between river-terraces and low hills. The first village (back in Denbighshire) is **Llansanffraid Glan Conwy**, where the double-naved church was turned into a single-naver by John Welch, who removed the arcade in 1839. Three miles further on is **Bodnant**, famous for its marvellous gardens (National Trust – open April–October). They were laid out originally from 1875 onwards by Henry Pochin, a rich china-clay merchant. In 1881 he built the house (architect W. J. Green), aptly described by Mark Girouard as 'dim and grim Old English'. His daughter married the first Lord Aberconway, and she and her son and grandson have further developed and improved the gardens. The magnificent site, looking over the valley towards the Carnedd range, has been superbly exploited. The gardens are most famous for their shrubs and trees. The various buildings include the charming Pin Mill, built c. 1730 at Woodchester, in Gloucestershire, as a Garden House, and brought here in 1938 to stand on the great terraces.

Beyond Bodnant is **Talycafn**, where the bridge over the river stands near the site of the Roman crossing. The perky little lodge to Penrhyd is by H. L. North. A mile SE is **Eglwysbach**, a neat, strung-out village: its church was plainly rebuilt in 1782, with stone arcades. Gothic tracery was put in in 1882.

Beyond Talycafn the valley narrows and from here to Llanrwst the flat bottom, about half a mile across, is flanked by wooded hills, steeper on the W than on the E, for here the river follows the faulted junction of the Ordovician rocks of Snowdonia and the Silurian rocks of the Denbigh moors. The escarpment above Dolgarrog marks the fault-zone (see p. 125). Five miles beyond Talycafn is **Maenan**, where, in the grounds of a house called The Abbey, are slight traces of the Cistercian monastery, founded in the late twelfth century at Conwy, and removed here by Edward I in 1283 to make way for his town and castle. Half a mile SE is a house called Maenan, built on abbey property, and partly medieval, but much added to and chiefly noteworthy for its splendid plasterwork of 1582 (probably by the same craftsmen as that at Plas Mawr, Conwy).

Llanrwst is the capital of the Conwy valley, and market town for a wide area – a lively little place, full of character. Its principal sight is the excellent three-arched stone bridge over the river, of 1636. The W arch was clumsily rebuilt in 1702. The bridge is the most celebrated, and best attested, of the numerous works in Wales attributed to Inigo Jones. He is widely thought to have been born in Llanrwst, but even Pennant knew he was born in London (in 1573), the son of a clothworker. His father's name was also Inigo, which scotches Pennant's theory that the son's name was really Ynyr, but changed to Inigo when he visited Italy. All the same, there is some evidence that Jones's father did come from Denbighshire. So perhaps Pennant was justified when he said 'our country is right to clame the son, which is done by universal tradition of the country. The turn of his countenance, and the violence of his passions, at least legitimate no distant descent.' However, of the vast number of buildings attributed to him in Wales, not one is at all likely to be his (though it is curious that the arms on a portrait of Jones are almost identical with those of the Trevors, for whom he is said to have built Plas Têg – see p. 42). Across the bridge is Tu Hwnt i'r Bont, a picturesque seventeenth-century house (National Trust – used as a restaurant).

The **Parish Church**, much rebuilt in 1882–4 by Paley and Austin, retains a magnificent rood-screen and loft, probably by the same craftsmen as that at Conwy. Attached to the S side of the chancel is the Gwydir Chapel, built by Sir Richard Wynn of Gwydir in 1633–4. It is also attributed to Jones, although it is, apart from the doorway, an entirely Gothic structure. Inside there is contemporary woodwork; a huge stone coffin, ornamented with quatrefoils, said to have come from Maenan (and to have been the tomb of Llywelyn the Great (d. 1240), founder of the abbey at Aberconwy, but it is too late to be his); and a fine stone effigy of a knight commemorating Hywel Goytmor. On the walls (formerly on the floor) are a series of seventeenth-century engraved brasses, of remarkable quality. That to Dame Mary Mostyn (d. 1653) is signed by Silvanus Crue, and others are probably by him, but much the best is the highly sophisticated one to Dame Sarah Wynne, d. 1671, signed by William Vaughan, a celebrated engraver. It is full of Baroque swagger – 'far the most beautiful piece of engraving I ever saw', said Pennant. The lady's husband, Sir Richard Wynn, attended Charles I on his trip to Spain in 1623. By the church are almshouses and school of 1610, built by Sir John Wynn (see p. 123). A second church was built S of the town in 1842 (H. Kennedy).

Tucked away in the hills, a mile NE, is the little village of **Llanddoged.** St Doged, King and martyr, was buried here, and his well, N of the church, was held to be good for the eyes. The church was rebuilt in 1839 by the Rector himself, Thomas Davies, with the help of his colleague from Eglwysbach. The result is quite delightful – double-naved, in a sort of cottage orné style, barge-boards, lattice windows, and all. Inside, the original arrangement survives (partly, no doubt, because Davies stayed here until 1873), with its tall pews (the Plas Madoc one has red baize lining and cushions) facing the three-decker pulpit on the N wall. Behind the pulpit is a plaster putto's head, flanked by oil paintings of Moses with the Commandments, and the Royal Arms. The pulpit is lit by a round skylight with coloured glass in it. Nice eighteenth-century tablets include one to Sir Thomas Kyffin, d. 1784, whose mind was 'improved by an Acquaintance with several branches of polite Literature'.

The country E of the Conwy valley, up to the Vale of Clwyd, is far less known than it should be, though this is the secret of its charm. Winding wooded valleys, between open hilltops, which give glorious views. There are few villages, but it is not by any means unpopulated. From Llanrwst, the A548 cuts diagonally across to Abergele. Five miles up is the church of **Llanddewi** (862/648), with nothing but a vicarage to keep it company. It is a surprisingly ambitious building of 1867, by John Oldrid Scott, with a fine shingled broach spire. It is now utterly derelict and ruinous.

Two miles S of Llanddewi (by the B5384), near the head of the secluded Cledwyn valley, is **Gwytherin**, a peaceful little place, with an uninteresting church of 1869 (Lloyd-Williams and Underwood). It stands in the centre of a prehistoric stone circle. By it are a house and pub, opposite each other, decorated with curious patterns in the roughcast. To this remote spot retired St Winefride, after her alarming experience at Holywell, to live in its celebrated *clas*, or college of holy men and women. Here she died, and was buried, until the English carted off her body to the Abbey of St Peter and St Paul in Shrewsbury – to its great profit. Two miles further down the Gallen valley from Llanddewi, on the A548, is **Llangernyw**, not so tiny now as it was once, but no longer famous for its stock market. The rebuilt church has a rich E window by Clutterbuck (c. 1830), and a S window by Ballantine. Half a mile W of Llangernyw is **Hafodunos**, one of the finest country houses by Sir Gilbert Scott, beautifully sited above steeply-sloping gardens. It was built in 1861–6 for H. R. Sandbach, son of a Liverpool West India merchant. In red brick and stone, it is one of the most convincing demonstrations of Scott's ability to use fourteenth-century Gothic for a workable Victorian house – better even than Kelham. The garden front is really picturesque, with its elaborate conservatory, its gabled bays, its octagonal billiard room, and the great clock tower, which rises above the entrance porch to dramatic effect. Sandbach's wife was a Roscoe: her family were patrons of Gibson, some of whose sculptures remain in the house, which is now a college for training accountants.

Three miles from Hafodunos – as the crow flies – there is a tiny church by Scott, at **Trofarth** (at 857/718 – accessible from Llangernyw by way of a maze of lanes). Built in 1873, with chancel and fittings of 1899 by Douglas, it is worth a visit more for its site, on a hillside overlooking the lovely Dulas valley, than for the simple building. Further down this valley is the idyllic park of **Coed Coch** (just off the B5381). The estate is chiefly famous for the stud of Welsh Mountain Ponies, started here by the late Miss Brodrick. The house is now a prep school. The elegant Grecian villa of 1795 by Henry Hakewill (architect of St Peter's, Eaton Square) was sympathetically improved by Clough Williams-Ellis c. 1930. Later, however, it was sadly altered. Originally the corner was cut off, and a grand diagonally-placed portico led straight in to the top-lit circular staircase, but the corner has been filled in and a new entrance made on the side. The B5381 is a delightful road, from St Asaph to Llandudno Junction, which one sincerely hopes will not be discovered by too many people, as it is a useful way of by-passing the hectic coast road. On it, a mile E, is **Betws-yn-Rhos**, with a comic little church of 1838 by John Welch. Its twin spires are dottily underscaled. Ffarm (now a hotel) is a castellated house of c. 1840 with extra castellations tacked on to increase the effect (a mini-Gwrych), and later alterations in spicy Venetian Gothic.

Two miles SE of Betws, back on the A548, is **Llanfair Talhaearn.** W of the village is **Garthewin** (not open), a Wynne house. It is a comfortable eighteenth-century building, probably by Joseph Turner. In recent years it was celebrated for its Welsh theatre: the plays were performed in a barn skilfully converted by T. S. Tait (partner of Sir John Burnet). Llanfair itself, a fishing centre, is best known as birthplace of John Jones (1810–70), the poet, whose bardic name was 'Talhaiarn'. He was apprenticed to an architect, and worked on bridge-building under Thomas Penson. Later he was involved in the building of the Crystal Palace. His best works are his lyric poems. The strength of local literary tradition is attested by a monument (white stone, with a gilded girl holding a garland) in the village of **Llansannan**, three miles down the A544. It commemorates five great writers, all born here – Tudur Aled (c. 1470–1526) the great poetic craftsman; William Salesbury (c. 1520–1599), translator of the New Testament into Welsh; Henry Rees (1797–1869), and his brother William ('Gwilym Hiraethog' – 1802–1883), poet, editor of the journal *Yr Amserau*, supporter of Mazzini, Garibaldi, and Kossuth, a popular novelist and lecturer; and Iorwerth Glanaled (1819–67). The church, over-restored in 1879 by Lloyd-Williams and Underwood, contains a splendid eighteenth-century pulpit, from St Luke's, Liverpool. The village is comfortably placed down by the Aled, but the uplands round about are bleak – buzzards abound, and the postmen use Land-Rovers.

The Aled is a tributary of the Elwy, and its valley is exceptionally lovely – steep hillsides, and plenty of trees. A minor road follows it S from Llansannan. At the top are two large reservoirs, Llyn Aled and Aled Isaf: just below the latter is Rhaeadr-y-Bedd, impressive, with the water falling down rock steps into a sombre gorge, but rather spoilt by the hideous dam and a quarry. Llyn Aled is used for sailing. The lakes are up on the wild, bare moorland of **Mynydd Hiraethog**, a fine place in summer when the heather is out, and the views can be enjoyed. The A543, from Denbigh to Pentrefoelas (on the A5), runs across it. Alas, it is great reservoir-country. Across the road from Llyn Aled is the huge Alwen Reservoir, lined with conifer woods, and a couple of miles N of that is the **Brenig** valley, soon to be flooded for yet another. Meanwhile rescue excavations are being conducted to study the important group of Bronze Age burial monuments at the head of the valley. It seems probable that in the Early Bronze Age there was a considerable settlement here: it is known that the climate was different then.

A conspicuous landmark for miles is a building, with lots of chimneys, set on the highest point of all (1627 feet). Astonishingly this turns out to be a shooting lodge, called Gwylfa Hiraethog, built in 1913 for Lord Devonport (of the firm of Kearley and Tonge). It is an effective gabled house in seventeenth-century style with good plasterwork. Now it is utterly ruinous and notices warn TRESPASSES WILL BE PROSECUTED (forgive us ours . . .). This is a pity, as it is, of course, the best viewpoint of all, taking in the mountains of Snowdonia (at their most dramatic), the Arennigs, the Berwyns, the Clwydians, and the sea. E of the Brenig valley, at 990/564, is a square enclosure, with ramparts, probably of medieval origin: it is mistakenly called Hen Ddinbych.

At the junction of the A544, from Llansannan, and the A543, is the bleak little village of **Bylchau**, with an excellent little church of 1857, in dark grey stone, by Sir Gilbert Scott. Two miles E (by the B5435) is the charming village of **Nantglyn**, climbing down the side of the hill into the valley, with the church near the bottom. Rebuilt in the 1860s, it has an E window of 1861 by O'Connor, with soldiers wearing trendy purple tights. In the churchyard are buried several notable literary figures.

From Llansannan, the B5382 goes towards Denbigh by way of **Henllan**, another village which steeply climbs a hill. For this reason the church has a detached bell-tower, set higher up so that the bells could be heard further away. This is a good way to approach Denbigh, the Castle standing out well. But it is worth diverging northwards for a final exploration. Two miles NW is **Berain**, a sixteenth-century house probably built by the famous Katheryn herself (1534/5–91). She was known as Mam Cymru (Mother of Wales) from her four marriages. Her first husband was John Salusbury of Lleweni, her second Sir Richard Clough (see p. 46), her third Maurice Wynn, and her fourth Edward Thelwall. The story is that Thelwall asked her to marry him on the way back from Clough's funeral: she replied that unfortunately she had already accepted Wynn's proposal on the way to the funeral, but would marry Thelwall if Wynn died before her. She was buried at **Llannefydd**, one and a half miles NW of Berain, whose double-naved Perp church, light and airy, is closed for lack of custom. N of Henllan and E of Llannefydd, the Meirchion and the Elwy flow through beautiful wooded valleys, beneath limestone outcrops in which are numerous caves. The most famous are **Cefn Caves**, near Dolben, where prehistoric remains (including mammoth) were found. At the SE end of the ridge called Cefn Meiriadog is a little church built in 1864 by the Williams-Wynns (who own Plas-yn-Cefn). The architect was, of course, Benjamin Ferrey (see p. 80). It is apsidal, built of crisp hard limestone, and cleverly sited so as to enjoy huge views over the Vale of Clwyd. The font, of Carrara marble, represents a kneeling angel holding a scallop-shell: it is a copy of a work of Thorwaldsen by his pupil Stein.

Less than a mile from Cefn is **Ffynnon Fair** (Mary's Well), marked on the one-inch map as 'Chapel' (029/711), and accessible by way of a lane past cottages a quarter of a mile E (private – ask permission). It is still, as in Gerard Manley Hopkins' time, 'a beautiful spot'. The path follows the shallow tree-lined Elwy along a meadow, above which rises a steep wooded hillside. Above the trees can be seen Wigfair, a large red house by Douglas. The ruined chapel, much overgrown, lies right up against the side of the hill. Probably built c. 1500, the main part is a T-shaped chapel. Against the site of its western wall the clear water rises within a stone enclosure, in the shape of a five-pointed star – as at Holywell. Hopkins wrote: 'the five points are perhaps to recall the five porches of Bethesda and their symbolism'. A strange feature is that on the stones of the well-surround are incised the outlines of shoes, apparently old (square-toed), some with initials on them. Could these date from the time when the chapel was used for clandestine marriages?

CHAPTER FOUR

Corwen to Conwy

(*By* A5 *and the River Conwy's Left Bank*)

Just across the Dee valley from Corwen (p. 89), the A5 is joined by the A494 (from Ruthin). The junction is beside the park of **Rug** (not open), an elegant house of c. 1800, with a fine portico. The garden front has a bow, and looks across a lake and an old motte. The grounds were laid out by Humphrey Repton, who deliberately created an enclosed effect, without extensive views, because of the mountainous situation. In them, beside the A494, stands the Chapel. It is a great pity that this wonderful building is no longer open to the public. It was built in 1634 by William Salusbury, who started his career as a pirate, but was later known as 'Hen Hosanau Gleision' – 'Old Blue Stockings'. He stubbornly defended Denbigh Castle for the King. It was restored in 1854, when new windows were inserted: the work of the two periods blends admirably. The chapel was visited by the young Edwin Lutyens and Herbert Baker on a walking tour in 1888. In a letter of 1942 to Baker, Lutyens recalled the woodwork 'painted by some Jacobean – red and blue – even the timbers of the roof painted with blue, white and red roses' and the 'delicious old chandelier, all made of wood painted green'. He wrote that memories of it had influenced his later work, including Viceroy's House at Delhi. The bench ends are curiously carved, and are linked by beams running along the floor (apparently imitated by Lutyens at Campion Hall Chapel, Oxford, in 1936). The gate of the Rug Estate Office, opposite the drive to the house, is one of Telford's original toll-gates, with ingeniously interlaced ironwork (for others see p. 209).

Two miles further on, the A5 enters Denbighshire at Maerdy (or Dinmael), in a narrow, wooded valley, which opens out onto mountainous upland as it approaches **Cerrigydrudion**, a bypassed village, whose name has nothing to do with Druids (it means 'the stones of the daring ones'). Three miles beyond, on what was once bare moorland (now mostly cultivated), is **Cernioge**, not much of a place now – just a handsome stone house set back behind trees – but once a well-known and much-appreciated coaching-inn, which explains why it appears on the milestones. One and a half miles W (at 883/498) is **Giler**. The charming little gatehouse of 1623 (open by appointment), with a gable on each side, and a plaster overmantel in the upper room, leads into a rectangular enclosure surrounded by a stout stone wall known as the 'Wolf Wall'. A cobbled path leads between grass to the whitewashed house. Near by is **Plas Iolyn**, home of Thomas Prys (1564?–1634), poet and pirate. Part of his house survives.

Pentre Foelas is a neat estate village of stone cottages, the estate being that of Voelas, a mile beyond, home of the Wynne-Finches. On either side of the crossroads are a fountain and a grand commemorative lamp-standard. The church, of 1857, is by Sir Gilbert Scott. Rather dull EE, it has been hideously rendered. The interior is much better. There is a splendid stone font, and some good glass (E window by F. W. Olliphant; W windows Clayton and Bell; two by J. N. Comper, a Nativity of 1912, and a Virgin and Child of 1935). The chancel fittings, in Jacobean style, are of 1906. Monuments include one with a female figure to John Griffiths, d. 1794, and some superb Victorian marble tablets to Wynne-Finches. The Victorian Voelas, at which John Hungerford Pollen did some work (he was related to the family – see p. 37) was replaced c. 1950 by Clough Williams-Ellis.

From Voelas the B4407 follows the Conwy to **Ysbyty Ifan**, a delightful stone village set on either side of the river. The name (Hospitium Iohannis) indicates that this was the site of a Hospice of St John of Jerusalem. When the order was suppressed, their church became parochial. It was rebuilt in 1861 by George Benmore of Llandygai, but retains three battered medieval effigies, said to represent Rhys ap Meredydd, a standard-bearer to Henry VII at Bosworth, his wife, and his son Robert, chaplain to Wolsey and an agent of Cromwell. This remote village was one of the first places in Wales to enjoy a public electricity supply, from a water-powered dynamo. Much of the surrounding moorland belongs to the

National Trust (Penrhyn Estate). Beyond Ysbyty Ifan, the road climbs towards the Merioneth border. It crosses the Conwy a mile below its source, the large **Llyn Conwy**, set in a flat boggy basin. The border is at the summit (1590 ft.). Just before it, a road goes N to Cwm Penmachno (p. 120): at the junction is Ffynnon Eidda, rebuilt 1846 and inscribed 'Yf a bydd Ddiolchgar' (drink and be grateful). The road is even better when taken in the reverse direction, especially on a fine evening. Three miles beyond the border is Ffestiniog (p. 230).

Beyond Voelas, the A5 follows the winding Conwy valley. A road leads N to **Capel Garmon**, where a large burial chamber of c. 1800 BC, in the form of a figure of eight, commands glorious views of Snowdonia. Opposite the Capel Garmon turning, the river is crossed by the handsome single arch of **Pont Rhyd-Llanfair**, built in 1780 by Robert Griffiths, a local man. His first two attempts failed (William Edwards had needed four goes at Pontypridd, Glamorgan – see *South Wales*). The river marks the county boundary.

The B4406 leads across it into Caernarfonshire by the Conwy Falls Hotel, a cheerful work of Clough Williams-Ellis. From it can be visited (best out of season) the famous **Conwy Falls** and **Fairy Glen**. Do not be put off by the name of this superb defile through which the river threads below the falls. It is better approached from below (sharp left onto A496: take farm road just before bridge). A lovely stroll through oak-studded meadows with old stone farm buildings, miraculously uncommercialized. Nearby, the Conwy is joined by the Machno, on which there are more Falls. Just above them (beside the B4406) is a woollen mill, still going strong. The 'Roman Bridge' near the mill, a rough single arch, is probably sixteenth or seventeenth century.

The B4406 follows the Machno up to **Penmachno**, where the river is crossed by a crude five-arched bridge: an inscription records that it was built in 1785 by I. Hughes and Harry Parry of Caernarfon (see p. 150). The stone also bears a Welsh poem, and two roughly-drawn faces of men with pipes. This quiet place was an important Early Christian centre. The churchyard originally contained two churches, dedicated to SS. Enclydwyn and Tudclud. The former has disappeared, the latter was rebuilt in 1862 by Lloyd-Williams and Underwood.

Its future is now uncertain, and the inscribed stones of the fifth–sixth centuries have been taken to the National Museum. The parish includes an unusually large number of good sixteenth–seventeenth-century houses, for example, Bennar, to the N, and Hafod-dwyryd, to the S. Beyond the village, the road follows the river, winding over its pebbly bed, to the much barer head of the valley, dominated by the vast slate quarries. The village, feeling very remote under the steep hills, is an evocative place, with its slate fences, slate kerbs, and slate-hung chapels and terraced houses.

From Penmachno, a good road, signposted Ty Mawr, climbs steeply through the Gwydir Forest. This is the easiest way to reach Wybrnant (Gwibernant), though rather depressing with its endless Christmas trees. **Ty Mawr** was the birthplace of William Morgan (c. 1545–1604), translator of the Bible into Welsh. He was vicar of Llanrhaeadr-ym-Mochnant from 1578 (see p. 269), and became Bishop of Llandaff in 1601, and of St Asaph in 1604. His Bible, published in 1588, has been called 'probably the most important book in the history of the language and literature of Wales', since it set a new standard for the language at a time when it was threatened with decay. The simple stone cottage revered as his birthplace now belongs to the National Trust. Probably built in the seventeenth century, it is a good example of its type. It is a pity that its lovely setting at the head of the valley is spoilt by conifers. The house can also be reached by a road from Pont ar Ledr, on the A496 (at 797/542): the road is rough, with numerous gates, and very steep, but more attractive than the one from Penmachno. It follows the little river, and provides spectacular views.

From near Pont ar Ledr it is also possible to drive up forestry roads (with permission) to **Fedw Deg**, a remarkable sixteenth-century house, set high up on the mountain-side (difficult to find, so best to enquire – key at the new farmhouse next door). Restored by the D. o. E., it has a doorway whose arched head is made out of a single huge block of stone, unglazed wooden windows with diagonally-set mullions, and a wooden screen inside with ogival doorways. A previous house on the site was the home of Gruffydd ap Dafydd Goch, whose effigy is in Betws-y-Coed church (see p. 122). Pont ar Ledr itself is attributed to 'Howell Saer' (see p. 123). **Pont yr**

Afanc, by which the A496 crosses the Conwy, is of c. 1800. Both road and railway follow the lovely valley of the Lledr – the train getting much better views of the rocky river. The railway crosses the road by an impressive stone viaduct, rough and castellated.

Two miles further on, the valley opens out at **Dolwyddelan**. This fair-sized village has two churches, the new one of no interest (1884, E. B. Ferrey), the old one of great interest. It stands on the side-road that goes S to the station. Very small, it was built in the sixteenth century to replace an earlier one on a different site. The S chapel was added by Robert Wynne, the builder of Plas Mawr, Conwy. It is separated from the church by two arches supported on a classical column. The rest of the church is very primitive, the windowheads cut from great slabs of stone. There is a contemporary rood-screen, with an eighteenth-century balustrade on top; a bronze hand-bell of the ninth or tenth century; a brass to Maredudd ab Ieuan, builder of the church, and great-grandfather of Sir John Wynn (it was he who bought Gwydir); a large heraldic wall-monument, also to Maredudd, and other members of his family; and numerous fragments of medieval glass. Near the station is a sombre Methodist Chapel of 1835, with half-hipped roof. Southwards runs **Cwm Penamnen**, where Maredudd's home was. Almost nothing is left of it – the slates were used to reroof the church c. 1850. The valley was recently threatened with flooding for a pumped-storage scheme, but Dinorwic was chosen instead (see p. 151).

Beyond the village, the **Castle** (D. o. E.) suddenly comes into view, its splendid keep, apparently perfectly preserved, perched dramatically on a rock bluff above the road. The old road ran north of the castle. Traditionally it is said to have been the birth-place, in 1173, of Llywelyn the Great: his father was lord of Nant Conwy. It was the residence of Llywelyn the Last during his war with the English, and was taken in 1283, but later abandoned. It was reoccupied in the late fifteenth century by Maredudd ab Ieuan. The keep is basically late twelfth century, but was much rebuilt in the late fifteenth century, when the second floor was added (originally there was a steep-pitched roof), and repaired in the nineteenth.

Beyond the castle, the road climbs towards the **Crimea Pass** (1263 ft.), where it enters Merioneth, and goes over to Blaenau

Ffestiniog (p. 231). The railway keeps by the river. **Roman Bridge** station is named after a rough stone bridge, of eight spans crossed by huge slabs. The date is uncertain (certainly not Roman). Further on, it enters the tunnel, over two miles long, by which it too reaches Blaenau Ffestiniog.

Back on the A5 is **Betws-y-Coed**, one of the most disappointing places in Wales. The hills all around are covered in conifers. Worse still is the all-pervading air of a tourist centre, submerging its pleasant nineteenth-century houses. One reason for living there might have been the fact that it had the lowest rates in the British Isles (owing to the immense revenues brought in by the Swallow Falls), but even that has ended with local government reorganization. All the same, there are some things worth seeing. The first is the Waterloo Bridge, which carries the A5 over the Conwy. It is so called because, as the big inscription states, it was built in 1815 – designed by Thomas Telford, and made by William Hazeldine. The spandrels of the elegant arch contain huge roses, thistles, leeks and shamrocks – all made of iron, and brightly painted. Over the bridge is a string of hotels, the doyen of which is the Royal Oak. The sign painted for it by David Cox – who played a big rôle in bringing Snowdonia to the attention of other artists – is now kept inside. Opposite are the hotel's grand stables, and the bridge also leads to the old church, surrounded by old yews. Built in the fourteenth or fifteenth century, it was enlarged in 1843 with a shallow transept, the seats in which face the two-decker pulpit, made up of bits of sixteenth–seventeenth-century carving. There is a well-preserved stone effigy of Gruffydd ap Dafydd Goch, great-nephew of Llywelyn the Last, who fought under the Black Prince. Near the church is a charming little suspension bridge over the Conwy: it is painted white, and very narrow. Surprisingly, it dates from 1930. Back on the main road is the new church, a splendid building by Paley and Austin of Lancaster (1873). Tall and solid, in EE style, it is built of well-contrasted grey and red stone. The central tower has a stair-turret like an Irish round tower. The interior has a French Cistercian feeling. The chancel and tower are vaulted, and the chancel arch has highly original corbelling. The floor is of buff unglazed tiles from Ancaster.

The B5106 to Llanrwst crosses the river Llugwy by **Pont-y-Pair,** a rough stone bridge of five arches, of uncertain date (ascribed to a mysterious fifteenth-century 'Howell Saer'). It then follows the left bank of the Conwy beneath steep coniferous slopes. Three miles from Betws is **Gwydir Castle** (open Easter–October). From about 1500 until 1674 this was the seat of the great Wynn family, the most famous of whom was Sir John Wynn, Bt (1553–1627)). Detested locally as an oppressor, he dominated the politics of North Wales, was a pioneer industrialist, and wrote a lively *History of the Gwydir Family*. The large and sprawling house, originally built on the unit system (see p. 367) in the sixteenth–seventeenth centuries, but much altered in the nineteenth century, gutted by fire in 1912 and 1922, and subsequently restored, is not of great interest. It is most celebrated for its peacocks, which startle passing motorists.

Much more worth a visit is **Gwydir Uchaf Chapel** (D. o. E.), up on the hillside opposite the Castle. (Not to be confused with the Gwydir Chapel at Llanrwst, see p. 111). Gwydir Uchaf itself was built in 1604 by Sir John Wynn, and in the seventeenth century was more favoured by the family than the lower house, but later fell into decay. Subsequently rebuilt, it is now a Youth Hostel. The Chapel was built in 1673 by Sir Richard Wynn (nephew of the builder of the Llanrwst chapel). It is a small Gothic building, with simplified tracery. The interior has not preserved its original form quite so perfectly as appears at first glance, but retains its atmosphere, with a rather miscellaneous assortment of woodwork – gallery, pulpit, pews, chairs, panelling, altar table, etc. Carved cherubs' heads attached to the panelling are of exceptional quality. The most interesting feature is the remarkable painted ceiling: although crudely executed it has rustic appeal, and the iconography is fascinating. Sir Richard Wynn was in touch with high Anglicans and also with Roman Catholics: he is known to have asked the Jesuit Fr Petre, confessor to James II, to get a cross for the window. This explains the representation of the Trinity, of numerous adoring angels, and of the angels of the Day of Judgment, and the use of sacred symbols and Latin texts. Flat cut-out angels are attached to the bases of the trusses, looking as if they came off cereal packets.

Trefriw is a sizable Victorian village, whose expansion was due largely to the small spa, whose crow-stepped building of 1873 stands beside the road a mile N. There are two springs – one iron oxide (for bathing), and one sulphur (for drinking). The iron oxide water was claimed to be the strongest in Europe. The spa was particularly frequented by Welsh Nonconformist ministers, a fact which disgusted A. G. Bradley – 'It may seem strange that men who lead temperate, well nourished, well occupied, but not laborious lives, amid the fresh breezes of the Welsh hills, should be so fond of filling their insides from these nauseous fountains.' The waters were particularly specified for chronic dyspepsia. The church is said to have been built by Llywelyn the Great c. 1230, but the present building is fifteenth–sixteenth centuries, much rebuilt in the nineteenth. It has a lavish pulpit of 1633. Two distinguished men born in the village were David Jones (?1708–85), poet, collector of MSS, publisher, and printer, and Ieuan Glan Geirionydd (Evan Evans, 1795–1855), a much finer poet, best known for his hymns. He was educated at Llanrwst School, about which he wrote one of his best poems – here is a stanza:

Sound of the bell is silent,
  No multitude leaves the town,
The bolts of your strong doors,
  Unused, are rusted brown;
Weaving their way of an evening
  Bats fly with silent beat,
Where rang the poems of Homer
  And Virgil, elegant-sweet.

(Translated by Anthony Conran, *Penguin Book of Welsh Verse*, 1967.) His home was Ty'n-y-Celyn, a seventeenth-century house in the S part of the village.

According to tradition, the church at Trefriw was built by Llywelyn in order to save himself the journey to 'Llywelyn's Old Church' at **Llanrhychwyn**, a mile SSW, reached by a winding hill-road. Entered through a stone lych-gate of 1762, it is a double-naved building, partly twelfth century, but mostly fifteenth–sixteenth. Attractively solid and simple, it possesses strong atmosphere. The seventeenth-century S door works on the same principle as Roman doors, the door itself being hung from a pole which pivots between lintel and threshold. Like Roman doors (as, for example, in Plautus) it groans horribly. The naves are separated by rough square piers. Fragments of old glass; seventeenth-century wooden communion rails, pulpit, and candelabrum. W of Llanrhychwyn are two lakes, Llyn Geirionydd, with a monument to Taliesin (dubiously reputed to have lived here, or even to have been buried here), and Llyn Crafnant, now a reservoir.

Back on the B5106, **Dolgarrog** is the site of a big aluminium works, established here in order to make use of the hydro-electric power which could easily be generated owing to the great quantities of water available from Llyn Eigiau and Llyn Cowlyd, and the very steep drop caused by the fault-zone escarpment (see p. 110). Both lakes are dammed and enlarged, and the lower slopes of the Carneddau are contoured by leets and pierced by tunnels to regulate the water supply. In 1925 the dam on Llyn Eigiau broke, and a flood swept down over the village, causing the loss of sixteen lives. The waterworks have spoilt the waterfalls for which Dolgarrog was once noted. The huge Llyn Cowlyd also supplies Colwyn Bay with water. NW of Llyn Eigiau is **Dulyn**, the 'black lake', aptly named. At a height of about 2000 ft, it occupies a splendid example of a glacial cirque. Its sides are so steep that at one point it is 55 ft deep only a yard from the shore. Above rises the rocky cliff of Craig Dulyn. Below the lake are traces of an extensive Bronze Age settlement, including huts and cairns (at 708/666). The area is full of botanical interest. Furthermore, the lake is rich in legend. It was said to contain ugly fish with big heads and small bodies. No birds would alight on it. 'And there is a causeway of stones leading into this lake; and if anyone goes along this causeway, even in hot sunshine, and throws water so as to wet the farthest stone, which is called the Red Altar, it is a chance if it do not rain before night.' With such thoughts in mind, it is a sore disappointment to slog up to the lake, only to be greeted by a sign, erected by the Llandudno Borough Council, announcing that the water belongs to them. The lake is dammed, the level raised, the magic gone. There are now tragically few lakes in Snowdonia that have not been tampered with, and many of those are faced with some kind of threat. Every effort should be made to save them.

Up above **Llanbedr-y-Cennin** (L off the B5106 a mile beyond Dolgarrog) is **Pen-y-Gaer**, a splendid hill-fort, at a height of 1200 ft, with strong stone walls, remains of huts, and a marvellous view. More remarkable still are the chevaux-de-frise, on the W and S – closely-set rocks one to three feet tall, intended to deter attackers. Further along the B5106 is **Caerhun**, where the church and Roman fort (Kanovium) lie in the park of a large house of 1892 by T. M. Lockwood – Jacobean, in stone and half-timber. The church stands in the NE corner of the fort, whose ramparts are clearly visible. The original fort was probably established by Agricola in 78 AD, at a site of great strategical importance, on the Chester–Caernarfon road, and at the upper tidal limit of the Conwy. It was re-built in stone, on the usual plan, in the second century. It was excavated in 1926–9. The site of the bath-house, outside the E gate, and of the dock beside the river, to the NE, can be recognized. The long narrow church was thatched until Kennedy restored it in 1850. It has a transept of 1591. A wonderful design for a new church for the parish was made in 1898 by H. L. North. Unfortunately it was never executed, but he did build a Parish Hall, which stands by a junction between Caerhun and Ty'n-y-groes. It is of a most original shape, covered in white roughcast.

A mile W of Ty'n-y-groes (best reached by the next turning L after Caerhun) is **Ro-wen**, a pretty tourist village. Capel Siloam, now the Women's Institute, is a nice little building of 1841, with its original pews. From Ro-wen, the Roman road from Kanovium to Segontium goes due W over the hills, and makes a fine walk. Just over a mile along it (at 741/718) is a well-preserved cromlech called **Maen-y-Bardd**. Beyond the cromlech, on the S side of the road, is a thin standing (or rather leaning) stone, called Ffon-y-cawr (the giant's stick) or Picell Arthur (Arthur's spear). In the vicinity are several other standing stones, the biggest of which give the name to the pass through which the road goes – **Bwlch y Ddeufaen** (the pass of the two stones). They stand near the highest point (at 1350 ft): one is ten feet high, the other six. The twentieth century contribution to the scene is a line of pylons. The Roman road came down to the coast between Llanfairfechan and Aber. This route is a convenient way to approach the western summits of the Carnedd range – not very exciting as mountains, as they are rounded and grassy, but easy going.

From Ro Wen, a minor road leads northwards (at 772/736)

back to the B5106 via the new church of **Llangelynnin**, nicely set among trees. Built in 1840 by Thomas Jones, it has a battlemented octagonal tower. The plain interior is a model of sympathetic improvement, for it was decorated and furnished by H. L. North. The walls are white, the roof blue with white beams, the doors dark red. The tiles, set in ingenious patterns, are red, green, and white. The wood furnishings are very original, and there is an 'English' altar. Elegant eighteenth-century marble font. The old church, founded in the seventh century, is one and a quarter miles W (at 751/737), 900 ft up, all alone on the bare hillside. Key at Garneddwen Farm. It is simple and unrestored, and gives a good idea of what most of the local churches must once have been like. The timber porch and large N transept (called 'Capel y Meibion' – men's chapel) are sixteenth century: the transept retains its earth floor. Seventeenth-century communion table and altar rails, and Welsh texts painted on the walls. In the SW corner of the churchyard is Ffynnon Gelynnin, a well with a stone enclosure, once roofed in. It was said to be good for sick children.

The B5106 joins the A5110 (from Tal-y-cafn – see p. 110), which leads to Gyffin (p. 130) and Conwy (p. 128).

CHAPTER FIVE

The North Coast – Conwy to Caernarfon

(*By the Coast*, A55 *and* A499)

The estuary of the river Conwy is crossed by an embankment carrying both the A55 and the railway. At its W end are the three bridges. The earliest is the suspension bridge built in 1822 by Telford to carry the road. It has castellated piers, to match the Castle. Threatened with demolition when its successor was built, it was fortunately saved and given to the National Trust. Both appropriate and pretty, it yields nothing to the clumsy new bridge which now hides it. This ugly structure was given semicircular bastions, presumably also intended to match the Castle, but sadly coarse. The third bridge is also hardly a thing of beauty, although it is of great interest – Stephenson's railway bridge, constructed in 1846–8 on the tubular system (each track enclosed within a rectangular iron casing) that he was to use again in the Britannia Bridge across the Menai Straits (see p. 211). Since the tragic destruction of that bridge, the Conwy one is all the more significant. It too has castellated ends.

Conwy, a stunning walled town, looks its very best from the river when its towers and turrets are lit by the early morning sun. It has recently officially reverted to the Welsh spelling of its name, after the folk-singer Dafydd Iwan was prosecuted for painting out the A on signs, and acquitted. The town and castle were built by Edward I in 1283–92: he moved the Cistercian abbey of Aberconwy up the valley to Maenan (see p. 110). The **Castle** (D. o. E.) is magnificently sited on a promontory formed by the confluence of the river Gyffin with the Conwy: long and narrow, it has water on three sides. It was designed by James of St George (see p. 357): there is a roughly rectangular Outer Ward, with six round towers, linked to the Town Walls at the NE and SW corners, and a square Inner Ward attached to the E end, with a further

On the pier at Llandudno, built in 1876-83, with splendid ironwork.

Caernarfon Castle from across the Menai Straits, with the mountains of Snowdonia behind—a watercolour by Peter de Wint (c. 1820).

Penrhyn Castle is 'an early Victorian house in the style of a Norman castle'. Built by Thomas Hopper in 1827-47, it now belongs to the National Trust.

pair of round towers. There was a barbican at each end, guarding the approaches from town and river. The whole exterior was originally limewashed, and the towers probably had conical roofs. Many of the architectural details are of remarkable elegance, including the richly vaulted chapel in the NE tower, and the strainer arch which alone survives of the eight put into the Great Hall in 1346–7. The splendid view from the towers clearly shows the whole extent of the walled town – roughly triangular in shape, and sloping up towards the W. The **Walls** are almost perfectly preserved, together with their three double-towered gates and twenty-one round towers – the finest walled town in the British Isles. The walls have been under repair by the D. o. E. for some years, and parts of the wall-walk are open. Modern openings have been made for the traffic and for the railway.

The little town within the walls, although choked with traffic, is a pleasant place and full of good buildings. As the street-names on the nice cast-iron plates suggest, the town was another of Edward I's English settlements (see p. 23). The **Church**, though right in the middle of the town, is nicely withdrawn, and reached by paths. It was originally the church of the abbey, but at the time when Edward moved the monks and gave it to the townspeople it was still unfinished. The oldest parts are the E and W walls: the three lancets in the tower lit the nave. The fine moulded doorway below, of c. 1235, probably came from the Chapter House. The rest of the church is of various dates: it was restored in 1872 by Sir Gilbert Scott. It contains a magnificent rood-screen of c. 1500, perhaps made in Ludlow: the loft is supported by fan-vaulting on either side. The contemporary stalls have carved ends. Numerous monuments include one in the chancel to Nicholas Hookes, d. 1627, himself a 41st child, and father of 27; and one on the E wall – a nicely carved tablet – to Anna, wife of Thomas Apthorp, d. 1786, recording that it was erected by her American husband, proscribed because of his loyalty to the King. In the S aisle is a fine bust of the great sculptor John Gibson, a native of the town. It was carved at Rome in 1852 by his pupil W. Theed. On the S side of the church is a tomb covered by an odd iron guard: this is (mistakenly) reputed to be the grave which inspired Wordsworth's 'We are seven'.

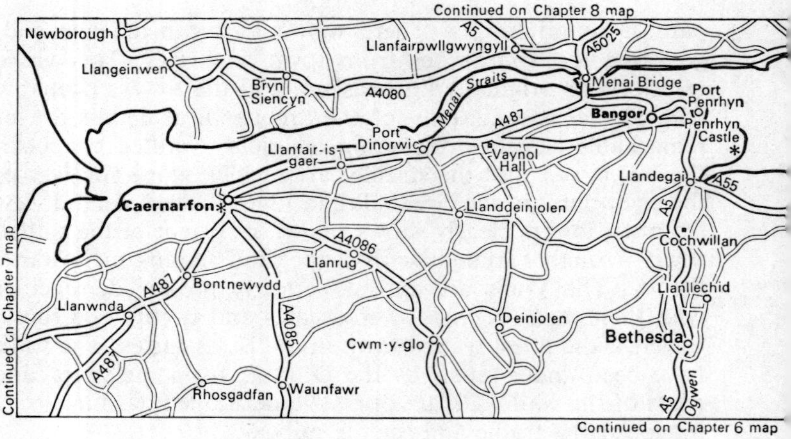

In Castle Street, at the corner of High Street is **Aberconway** (National Trust – now an antique shop), a house of c. 1500, with oversailing upper floor. In High Street is the Castle Hotel, refronted by John Douglas in 1885, in Jacobean style: the materials (Ruabon brick and small black stones) are not too sympathetic. Opposite is a strongly original cinema, in red sandstone, by Colwyn Foulkes. Further up is **Plas Mawr** (open: headquarters of the Royal Cambrian Academy of Art), the finest town house in North Wales. It was built in 1576–95 by Robert Wynne. This proper town house, on a fairly narrow street frontage, is surprisingly grand, being planned around two courtyards separated by the main hall. It is of stone, with crow-stepped gables, mullioned windows surmounted by pediments, some projecting slightly, and octagonal stair-turrets. Inside there is carved woodwork and, better still, lots of vigorous and inventive plasterwork, mostly of heraldic devices within geometrical patterns. Lancaster Square is a comparatively modern creation. Conwy is famous for its honey, and a honey market is held in September.

Just NW of the town, in extensive grounds, is **Bodlondeb**, now the Council offices: it is a rather grim house by T. M. Lockwood. The quay along the river is used, not only by numerous pleasure boats, but by the local fishermen. Mussels are collected from the estuary. Just to the S of Conwy is **Gyffin**, now swamped in suburbia, but once a separate village. Its

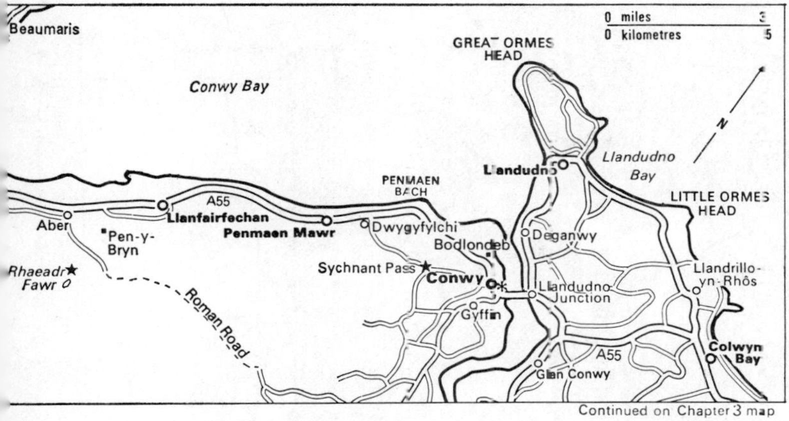

Continued on Chapter 3 map

church is pleasantly situated by the wooded valley. Masses of sweet peas grow over the churchyard wall from the market garden beside it. In spite of restoration by Kennedy in 1866, it retains its fifteenth-century chancel roof, painted with figures of saints and evangelists' symbols, and screens on either side, one sixteenth century, the other seventeenth. Opposite the church is the School, c. 1910, a characteristic work of H. L. North, very original, of white roughcast with slate-hung gables.

Conwy is faced by great problems. The first is posed by the traffic: obviously a bypass is essential, but it is not easy to see where it should go. If it comes round to the S, it will ruin the close relationship between castle and countryside which still exists. But this relationship is also threatened by the second problem – the expansion of the town, and demand for houses. Already too many houses have been built S of the Castle: no further development here should be allowed, and the wooded hill above Gyffin should be sacrosanct.

Conwy's problems are, of course, due to its site. Conwy Mountain (Mynydd y Dref) rises steeply to the NW, and W of the town is the celebrated **Sychnant Pass**, both inhibiting its spread. The Pass (reached by a minor road – the old main road – leading from outside the SW gate of Conwy) is thronged with tourists in summer. Along it are a number of big houses, the most amazing the former hotel (now a private mental

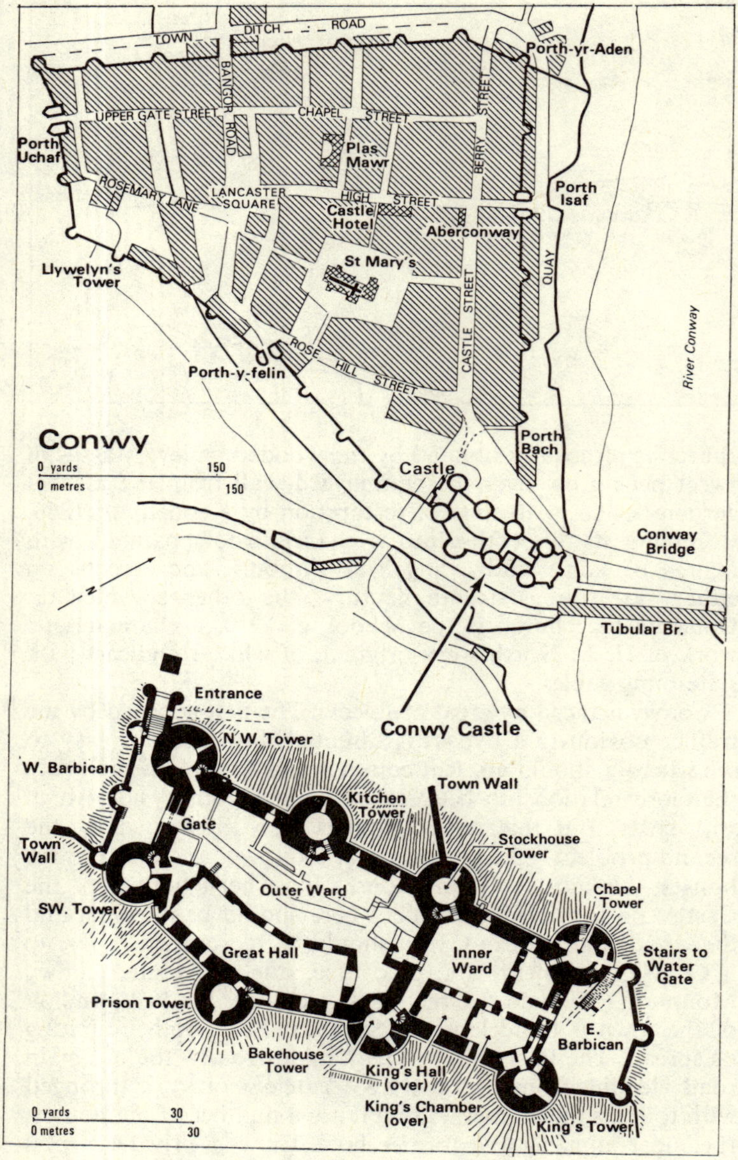
Conwy
0 yards 150
0 metres 150
N
TOWN DITCH ROAD
Porth-yr-Aden
BANGOR ROAD
UPPER GATE STREET
CHAPEL STREET
BERRY STREET
Porth Uchaf
Plas Mawr
ROSEMARY LANE
LANCASTER SQUARE
HIGH STREET
Castle Hotel
Aberconway
Porth Isaf
QUAY
St Mary's
Llywelyn's Tower
CASTLE STREET
ROSE HILL STREET
Porth-y-felin
River Conway
Porth Bach
Castle
Conway Bridge
Tubular Br.
Conwy Castle
Entrance
N.W. Tower
W. Barbican
Kitchen Tower
Town Wall
Gate
Stockhouse Tower
Town Wall
Outer Ward
SW. Tower
Chapel Tower
Great Hall
Inner Ward
Stairs to Water Gate
Prison Tower
E. Barbican
Bakehouse Tower
King's Hall (over)
King's Chamber (over)
King's Tower
0 yards 30
0 metres 30

home), with a vast array of half-timbered gables, red roofs, red chimneys, and a tower with red battlements. Even the gate-piers are painted to imitate half-timber and have gabled tiled roofs. Odd gate-piers seem to have been popular with residents along here. Over the top of the pass, a spectacular gorge opens up on the right, below the bare slope of Allt Wen. The road comes down to **Dwygyfylchi**, a tea-shoppy place which is unfortunate enough to have the only church in North Wales by E. M. Bruce Vaughan (1889): like most of his work it looks twenty years out of date.

The main road and railway go round by Penmaen-bach, piercing the steep headland in tunnels. **Penmaenmawr** takes its name from the even bigger headland beyond it, which formed a fearful hazard for travellers until 1772: here there was no Sychnant Pass to provide an alternative route, and the cliff road was notoriously unsafe. The problems of living in this part of the world are illustrated by a story told by Pennant: early in the seventeenth century, Sion Humphries of Penmaenmawr was courting Anne Thomas of Creuddyn, and they had arranged to meet at Conwy fair. On their way he fell over Penmaenmawr, but survived, while her ferryboat capsized, and she was the only person saved out of more than eighty. They married; she died at the age of 116, but he outlived her by five years. Even after the improvements made in 1772, Johnson was dreadfully scared. Now, as at Penmaen-bach, there are tunnels.

The summit of the headland is a strange shape: this is due to the unfortunate fact that the material of which it is made, quartz dolerite, is one of the best road-making stones, so that both the headland and the adjoining hillside have been quarried extensively. A model in the National Museum shows the enormous chunk which has been removed, lying beside the remaining part of the hill. The famous hill-fort on the top, **Braich-y-dinas,** has been entirely destroyed: its massive ramparts enclosed more than ninety huts. The district is full of prehistoric remains. The most celebrated is the Graig Lwyd 'factory', where the stone was used for making axe-heads which have been found all over Wales and as far away as Wiltshire and Derbyshire. Up on the slopes of Moelfre, a mile due S of the town (at 723/746), is a stone circle known as the 'Druids' Circle'. Penmaenmawr is a resort, though without much to recommend it as such: it may well have been more attractive when Gladstone used to go there – an association commemorated by a bronze bust on a column. The town is all higgledy-piggledy, squashed into its narrow site. The piers are not for tourists but for the conveyors to feed the quarry boats. It is worth visiting the church of **St Seiriol**, an extremely tough and uncompromising building of 1868 by Alfred Waterhouse. It has a saddleback tower. The interior is effective, with red and yellow brick, and some vigorous detailing. Much later woodwork, including a roodscreen by Caröe (1930).

Round the headland is **Llanfairfechan**, a more relaxed place, neater and nicer. Christ Church, with a spire, is by C. and J. Shaw of Saddleworth (1864), who also built Bryn-y-Neuadd, a huge Gothic house in a large park between the main road and the railway which was recently burnt down deliberately to provide a site for a new hospital. For the architectural connoisseur, Llanfairfechan is a place of pilgrimage, not for the crude work of the Shaws, but for the work of its own Herbert Luck North (1871–1941), who lived and practised here for most of his life. He was a pupil of Henry Wilson, Beresford Pite, and Sir Edwin Lutyens. He developed a private estate of his own, in the north part of the town, from about 1910. Entered past a sign saying NORTH & PADMORE, it is beautifully laid out. The simple, roughcast houses are excellent examples of the quiet domestic architecture associated with men like Voysey, but North also makes sensitive use of local techniques such as slate fencing (here combined with neat hedges), and roofs made with the small thick slates known as *cerrig mwsog*. These had fallen into disuse with the production of the big thin slates which William Morris (with whom North agreed) called 'one of the greatest curses of the age'. We like both. His own house, Rosebriars, is one of the best, on a very ingenious plan. His finest work, the chapel at St Winifred's School, has been recently demolished, and on the site some very poor new houses are going up, showing how rare the sensitivity of a man like North is. Even the older part of the estate has been disfigured by ugly pavements. Other works of his in the town include the Church Institute, also ingeniously planned, and cottages along the lane by the station (again with slate fencing). A road climbs up E of the town on to the hill, past various small buildings by North, easily recognizable: it gives huge views over Anglesey.

Beyond Llanfairfechan, there is a wide strip of coast between hills and sea. Just before you reach Aber, up on the left is **Pen-y-Bryn**, an interesting seventeenth-century house with a most remarkable, roughly circular tower, with a big window in the top storey and a funny Chinaman's hat roof on top. In the early thirteenth century, the princes of Gwynedd, including Llywelyn the Great, had a palace at **Aber**. Traditionally it was here that William de Braose was entertained and had an affair with Llywelyn's wife Joan (daughter of King John).

'Lovely princess' said Llywelyn,
'What will you give to see your William?'
'Wales, and England, and Llywelyn
I'd freely give to see my William'.

Her husband threw open the window to reveal the unfortunate de Braose hanging in the courtyard outside. Its site may have been Pen-y-Mwd, the castle mound, by the river just above the main road, or conceivably Pen-y-Bryn. The famous waterfall, **Rhaeadr Fawr**, is well worth a visit. It is two miles from the village, most of which has to be walked (leave the car at Bontnewydd). It is an enjoyable walk, up above the wooded stream, with the fall audible and visible from far off. The small stream falls in feathery cascades down a rocky cliff 170 feet high. Above the top is another fall with a big pool below, and a gorge through which the water boils. This is a favourite haunt of Welsh ponies, of which considerable numbers graze the Carneddau: they are small and agile, with long manes. Further up the stream, about a quarter and half a mile above the fall, are a number of irregular enclosures containing huts, all built of rough stones. The broad valley is surrounded by a great circle of mountains. The return can be made via the less spectacular but pretty **Rhaeadr Bach**, gaining fine oblique views of Rhaeadr Fawr.

From beyond Aber an astonishing sight appears over to the right – a colossal Norman castle rising from a splendidly wooded park. It looks even more improbable when the river valley in front of it is filled with mist. This is Penrhyn Castle, built not by an English king or Welsh prince, but by a slate-owner. **Llandygai** is very much its estate village, with neat pairs of gabled Tudor cottages. The rather grand church, cruciform and with a central tower, is mostly sixteenth century, but rebuilt and lengthened in 1852–3 by H. Kennedy. It contains three fine monuments. A fifteenth-century alabaster table tomb may commemorate Sir William Griffith of Penrhyn (d. 1490) and his wife. A marble wall-monument shows Archbishop John Williams (1582–1650) kneeling in prayer. He was descended from the Williamses of Cochwillan and the Griffiths of Penrhyn, and related to the Wynns of Gwydir. Born at Conwy, he was once playing on the walls with some other boys when he fell: as Pennant nicely puts it, 'the fall was on so critical a part, as ever to secure him from all reproaches of unchastity'. In the course of his career he became Dean of Salisbury, Dean of Westminster, Lord Keeper of the Great Seal, Bishop of Lincoln, and Archbishop of York. He supported the Stuarts, but opposed their excessive claims. He was a bitter enemy of Laud, but when Charles I made him Archbishop of York in 1640, to appease the moderates, Laud was already in prison, and Williams was in practice head of the church. As such he withstood Parliamentarian attacks on the episcopacy. In the Civil War he garrisoned Conwy for Charles, but was driven out by his fellow-Royalist Sir John Owen of Clenennau. He transferred his allegiance to Parliament, urging Cromwell to moderation, and died at Gloddaeth. Beside the monument are the Archbishop's helm and spurs. The third and finest monument is the one by R. Westmacott to Richard Pennant, 1st Lord Penrhyn (see p. 148), and his wife, erected in 1821. Large figures of a quarryman and a female *en déshabille* mourn at a sarcophagus decorated with four exquisite reliefs of putti, which represent a pastoral scene, industry, education and improved agriculture.

The organ, with a richly Norman case, was made for the Castle Chapel. In the churchyard, a slate pyramid commemorates Benjamin Wyatt (1744–1818), for over thirty years agent to Lord Penrhyn, for whom he did a great deal of architectural work in the district. As the inscription proudly relates, he was an elder brother of James Wyatt. His son Lewis William (1777–1853), a more versatile architect, helped him on many of his jobs.

Penrhyn Castle (National Trust) was designed by Thomas

Hopper, and built in 1827–47. It incorporates parts of the earlier castellated house by Samuel Wyatt (elder brother of Benjamin and James), which itself incorporated parts of the medieval house. Built by the second Lord Penrhyn, to symbolize his status as owner of the vastly profitable Bethesda slate quarries, it cost half a million pounds. On the whole it is an extraordinarily successful effort, granted the sheer impracticability of building an early Victorian house in the style of a Norman castle. Somehow Hopper manages to combine a real sense of Norman solidity and convincing detail with picturesque outline and a remarkable degree of comfort. The vast Keep is undeniably impressive. Inside, some of the interiors are far from historically correct, but they come off astonishingly – the immense vaulted hall, the lofty staircase with its profusion of ornament, the library with its all-over dogtooth. Appropriately furnished, and rich in atmosphere. A great bedstead of slate was made for a visit by Queen Victoria: disappointingly, she funked it and slept more conventionally. In the stables is a museum of engines used on the quarry railways and of objects made of slate (with incredible ingenuity).

A mile S of Llandygai (turn R at Talybont, further back on the A55), is **Cochwillan** (open on written application), probably built by William ap Gruffydd, who fought for Henry VII at Bosworth. The Great Hall, with its magnificent carved hammer-beam roof, has survived remarkably intact, and after being used as a barn for years has now been restored.

At the colossal entrance gate of Penrhyn, the A55 joins the A5, and follows its imposing park wall. At the NW corner of the park is **Port Penrhyn**, built by the 1st Lord Penrhyn in 1790, and linked to the quarries by a horse tramway built in 1800. The handsome Port Office is by Benjamin Wyatt. Other buildings are not notable except the jaunty round multiseater public lavatory, conveniently sited in the middle of the quay.

Bangor is a disappointing town. The Cathedral is even less inspiring than St Asaph, and the place was ruined when the A5 was driven through the park of the Bishop's Palace. Admittedly this relieves the main street of through traffic, but somehow the town fails to hang together. The part up on the hill and towards the Menai Straits is much more attractive, with its views across the Straits to the wooded grounds of houses such as Rhianfa (see p. 199).

The **Cathedral** is the oldest foundation in the British Isles, except for Whithorn in Galloway: the founder of the monastery here, St Deiniol, became Bishop of Gwynedd in 546. He came from Strathclyde. Its situation, near the sea but sheltered by hills, is typical of early Celtic monastic sites (compare St Davids, for example). The earliest parts of the present buildings are of c. 1130, but most of it is thirteenth–sixteenth century. The W tower, built in 1532 by Bishop Skeffington, is good but much too small. The Cathedral was restored in 1868–70 by Sir Gilbert Scott, and in 1879–80 by John Oldrid Scott (following his father's plan). Scott rebuilt the transepts on the basis of fragments of c. 1300. He intended to build a fine spire, which would have greatly improved the building, but neither this nor A. D. R. Caröe's design of 1945 were executed. The interior is dark and gloomy, and the contrast between the poor nave and the large choir and transepts disconcerting. Most of the fittings are by J. O. Scott and Alban Caröe. The E window is by Clayton and Bell: parts of their painted decoration have recently been restored. The finest thing in the church (on the nave pier by the N door) is the 'Mostyn Christ', a large wooden figure of Christ at Calvary, probably c. 1500, of great delicacy and pathos. It is lent by Lord Mostyn, and may have come from Rhuddlan Priory. Other features include glass by David Evans in the W windows; the tombstone of one Eva, exquisitely carved in low relief (14th century); and the early 14th-century Bishop Anian's Pontifical.

The Cathedral's setting is discouraging, but the Canonry houses a fascinating museum. The former Bishop's Palace is now the Town Hall, and looks municipal: it is basically a sixteenth-century house, with some eighteenth-century interiors. High Street contains some entertaining buildings, such as Lloyd's Bank, 1859, by Weightman, Hadfield and Goldie, in the Elizabethan style, and the National Westminster, which has round-headed windows with iron tracery. The clumsy Clock Tower is by A. Neill of Leeds (1886–7). The railway station is by Francis Thompson (1848), but much altered. Up on the hill, dominating the town much more dramatically than the cathedral, is the **University College**

of North Wales. Here at last is a building of the highest quality, the work of a great architect at the height of his powers. The College opened in 1884, in the old Penrhyn Arms Hotel, E of the town. Subscriptions were collected all over North Wales – for example, men at the Penrhyn and Dinorwic quarries contributed a fixed sum docked from their earnings, and at Pentraeth, a small Anglesey village, every family contributed. The new buildings, designed by H. T. Hare (architect of Westminster College, Cambridge; Oxford Town Hall, etc.), were begun in 1907 and opened in 1911. They are in an individual version of the Jacobean style, with simple, solid lines, but plenty of inventive carved decoration. The stout, plain tower is splendid. The light interiors have good plasterwork. It is a pity that the new building added on the W is so unsympathetic in proportions and materials. Most of the recent buildings are by Sir Percy Thomas's firm, but the best is Plas Gwyn, out in Menai Avenue, by David Roberts (1962–3). The War Memorial gateway, towards the town, is by Dan Wynne-Thomas. Near the U.C. is the **Normal College** (for teachers), a rather dour Tudor building of 1858–62 by J. Barnett of London. The College has a Hall of Residence further along College Road of 1908–10 by H. T. Hare – very different from his U.C., but equally fine, in a quiet, simplified Tudor, rendered. Also up on the hill, in Prince's Road, is the **Church Hostel** (Anglican Chaplaincy), whose chapel, built in the 1930s, is one of the best works of H. L North. The exterior is of grey roughcast, and it has a pyramidal roof over the chancel, tall narrow windows, a simple rood-screen, and pretty painted decoration in green and red. Down below the hill, on the N tip of the town, is the Pier, a jolly late-Victorian affair, from which a ferry used to cross to Anglesey (good for views). Nearby, a plain white house with bay windows is said to have been where Telford lived while working on the A5.

SW of the town is the **Friars Grammar School**, in John Douglas's Jacobean (1899–1900). Of the numerous churches and chapels, the best is **St David's, Glanadda** (on the A4087), a big solemn building by Sir Arthur Blomfield (1888). Beyond Bangor, the A5 goes over to Anglesey by the Menai Bridge (see p. 197), while the A4087 (and A499) make for Caernarfon. They pass the huge wall of **Vaynol** (not open) which enclosed a nineteenth-century collection of wild animals in the large, wooded park, where the old Hall, a well-preserved Elizabethan house, and the Chapel of the same date, stand close to the new Hall, a big stuccoed building of the eighteenth–nineteenth centuries. The road comes back to the Straits at **Port Dinorwic**, the port for the Dinorwic slate quarries at Llanberis, built soon after 1800 by their owner, Mr Assheton-Smith of Vaynol. A railway was built to provide the link in 1824–5. The town's character changes completely near the pub, halfway, where the railway cuts the road. To the N an estate village; beyond, best nineteenth-century industrial with little grey terraces overlooking the Straits. The unexpected church as you enter from the Vaynol end takes up two-thirds of a semi-rustic verandahed villa (recognize it by the bellcote). A neighbour explained that it was built 'for game-keepers and the like'. It stands with similar detached houses with lacy bargeboards and lattice windows and slate fences. The railway line drops by a steep incline from the mountain above and emerges near the port office with its multi-coloured slate roof. The little port is now a marina. New holiday housing, instead of being knit in with the existing development, spills out along the wooded bank of the Straits.

In the old town, fine slate slabs and steps abound and some of the cottages have crazy-paving-like masonry instead of the usual coursed rubble. Moriah (1862) is a big apricot-coloured chapel on the main road. From the road above there are fine views of Anglesey.

Two miles further on, the oil-lit church of **Llanfairisgaer** stands down by the Straits (at 502/660), rebuilt by Scott in 1865. Nice tablets.

CAERNARFON

The A4087 is definitely not the most romantic way to approach **Caernarfon**. The best way would be from Snowdon, as it is described in the wonderful Dream of Macsen Wledig, in the *Mabinogion*:

> 'He saw how he came to an island, the fairest in the whole world, and after he had traversed the island from sea to answering sea, even to the uttermost bound of the island, he could see valleys and steeps and towering rocks, and a

harsh rugged terrain whose like he had never seen. And from there he saw in the sea, facing that rugged land, an island. And between him and that island he saw a country whose plain was the length of its sea, its mountain the length of its woodland. And from that mountain he saw a river flow through the land, making towards the sea. And at the river mouth he could see a great castle, the fairest that mortal had ever seen.'

'Macsen' is Magnus Maximus, who crossed from Britain to Gaul in 383, and defeated Gratian, so becoming emperor himself. According to the story, he himself came to Caernarfon, and married the king's daughter Elen. As her maiden fee, she asked for the Isle of Britain, and for three strongholds to be built – Caer Llion (Caerleon), Caer Fyrddin (Carmarthen), and the chief one at Caernarfon – 'and soil from Rome was brought there so that it might be healthier for the emperor to sleep and sit and move about'. Elen also built roads (hence the name 'Sarn Helen'). The emperor was seven years in Britain, and meanwhile a usurper seized Rome. Macsen was unable to reconquer it, until Elen's brothers, Cynan and Gadeon, came to his assistance. This latter part of the story no doubt embodies a real folk-memory of the contribution made by British soldiers to Rome's armies. Striking confirmation of the legend comes from a source of c. 395 which refers to the 'Segontienses', clearly the former garrison of Caernarfon (Latin *Segontium*), among the troops of the *comes Illyrici* (modern Jugoslavia).

The association in mythology of Caernarfon with the Romans is, of course, no accident, and it is historically appropriate to approach the town by the A487, past the excavated Roman fort of **Segontium** (D. o. E.), the original 'Gaer yn Arfon'. It was probably founded in AD 78, when the governor Frontinus was succeeded by Agricola, who completed the defeat of the Ordovices in N. Wales. Rebuilt in the second century, it remained an important garrison (of an auxiliary cohort) for three centuries. The name derives from the Celtic *sego* = strong, and probably comes from the river Saint (or Seiont), on which the town stands. The main road runs across the fort, and not much is visible apart from foundations, but it is possible to get a clear idea of most of the lay-out, and there is a small museum. The pine trees here under a blue sky recall

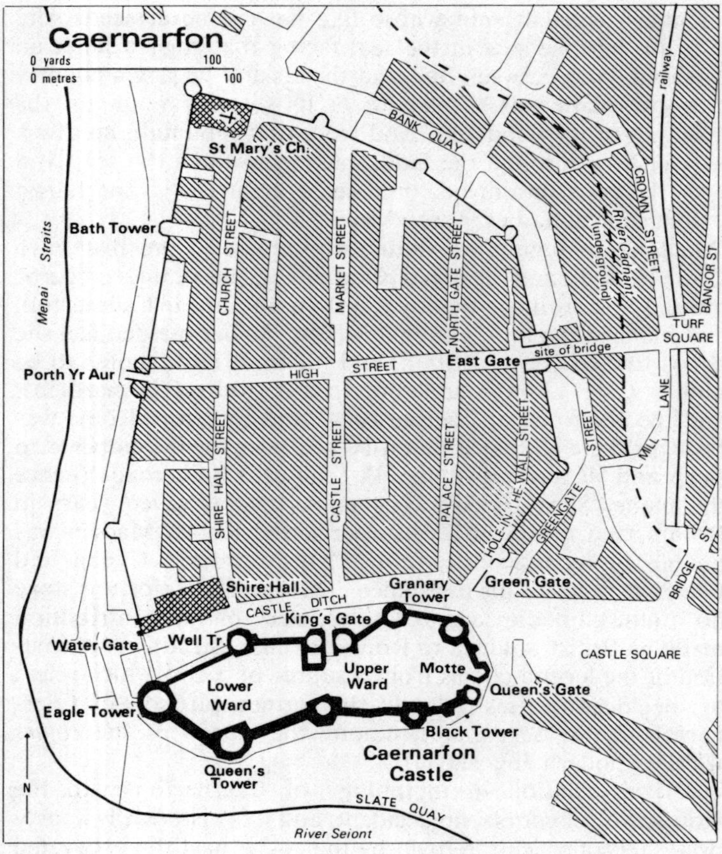

the Mediterranean. 150 yards W of the fort is 'Hên Waliau' (Old Walls), a big enclosure with walls over six feet thick, reaching a height of sixteen feet (visible from the carpark of the Dept. of Health and Social Security, on the Pwllheli road). It was built c. 200, probably as a stores compound. 150 yards E of the fort a Mithraeum was discovered.

Close to the fort (its proximity is surely no accident) stands the church of **Llanbeblig**, mother church of Caernarfon. It is probably a Celtic foundation: Peblig (Publicius) was said to be a son of Maximus, like the Constantine whose tomb was moved by Edward I, presumably to this church. The oldest part is thirteenth-century. The tower, with its crow-stepped battlements, is fourteenth-century (compare Llandrillo-yn-Rhos, p. 107), and the rest is mostly fifteenth–sixteenth centuries, heavily restored in 1894 by R. G. Thomas of Menai Bridge. It contains a grand alabaster altar-tomb, with effigies, erected in 1593, to a Gruffydd.

The **Castle** and walled borough were built by Edward I from 1283. The site he chose – already a Welsh town and seat of Welsh princes – was stronger than the Roman one. The castle, which incorporated a Norman motte of c. 1090, was defended on three and a half sides by water – on the S by the river Saint, on the W by the Menai Straits, and on the N and NE by the tidal inlet of the river Cadnant (now covered up).

In spite of the strategic importance of the site, one might well wonder why Caernarfon should have been built more grandly and splendidly than the other castles – even Conwy – and why it differs from them in having polygonal towers decorated with bands of coloured stone. Edward's other Welsh castles were built chiefly of coursed rubble and are believed often to have been plastered and limewashed (e.g. Conwy). It has been convincingly suggested by A. J. Taylor that Edward was deliberately intending to evoke both the story of Macsen Wledig (another part of the vision describes 'many great towers of various colours on the castle': this is actually the castle in Italy from which the journey to Wales begins, but that does not rule out the possibility), and the old mythical association between Caernarfon and the emperor Constantine. The Castle does in fact strikingly resemble the walls of his capital, Constantinople, with their polygonal towers, and the courses of tiles typical of late Roman work (compare e.g. the Visigothic towers of Carcassonne). Dr Taylor also suggests that the eagles which surmounted the triple turrets on the Eagle Tower were intended to recall Roman legionary standards, and that the name of the western gate, preserved in Welsh as *Porth yr Aur* (Golden Gate), was also taken from Constantinople. Presumably these links with native myths were designed to stress the fact that Caernarfon was to be the fortress-palace of the (English) Princes of Wales. Nevertheless, it must be realized that Edward's son was not born in the present castle, which was only just begun in 1284, and it was probably not here that he was presented to the Welsh nobles, but at Rhuddlan (see p. 36). Caernarfon remained the capital of the Principality of Wales until 1536. So the Investiture of the Prince of Wales here in 1911 and 1969 was not historically, but only symbolically appropriate.

Begun in 1283, the Castle was still unfinished when work stopped in about 1330. Its exterior was complete, and it is its exterior that is so fine. It looked even finer before the Slate Quay was built up along the river front to accommodate vessels. Across the river is the wooded hill of Coed Helen, with hardly a single building, except for a pretty Gothick summer-house. The old swing bridge over the river has been removed, and a new footbridge is being built. The Castle is of a long, irregular shape; at the W end is the biggest tower, the Eagle Tower, at the E the massively impressive Queen's Gate. The main entrance is through the King's Gate on the N, beneath a statue of Edward II put up in 1320. The walls and towers are pierced by numerous passages and stairs, making so much use of shouldered arches that this type – mass-produced around 1300 – has come to be known as the 'Caernarfon arch'. The Town Walls, with their eight towers, and two double-towered gates, one towards the sea, the other towards the land, were built simultaneously with the castle and are remarkably well preserved. Like those of Conwy they have been gradually opened up by the D. o. E. Sometimes this has had dubious results – the Victorian town hall built over the E gate was of little merit, but the present parapet is even worse.

The Borough received its Charter in 1284. Within the irregular outline of the walls (irregular because of the site), the streets are laid out on a grid pattern. They are well worth exploration, for they contain good buildings of all periods and kinds, mostly in painted terraces, with occasional medieval fragments – one has a niche with an angel holding a shield. Another has a little sundial dated 1616.

The Market Hall, of 1832, is by John Lloyd, with a stone front and an iron and timber roof. The County Buildings of 1863 have a grand portico. In the NW corner is **St Mary's**

Tryfan (3010 feet) gets its name from its distinctive triple peak. It stands out from the Glyder range towards the upper Llugwy valley.

Capel Peniel at Tremadoc, built by William Madocks, is remarkable for the cheerful naiveté of its portico. A watercolour by Kenneth Rowntree (1941).

A flooded section of the vast Dinorwic Slate Quarries at Llanberis, whose sublime grandeur would have delighted eighteenth-century travellers.

Church, known as the Garrison Chapel. It was built in the fourteenth century, utilizing the town walls on the N and W, and the base of the corner tower as its vestry. It was rebuilt by Benjamin Wyatt in 1809–10. On the W side is the 'Bath Tower', used as a bathing pavilion in the nineteenth century, then as a house. It now belongs to the Landmark Trust and can be rented for holidays. The proximity of the walls to the straits sometimes produces curious effects; the mist may roll over them into the town, or conversely the light from the town spills over them towards the sea.

Outside the E gate, the medieval bridge over the Cadnant still survives below the street. Turf Square is built over the line of the disused railway. The town outside the walls is more Victorian, with many characterful buildings.

Castle Square has a very varied assortment (including Georgian-looking brown brick as well as plaster), and also the striking statue of Lloyd George, MP for the Carnarvon Boroughs from 1890 until he received his earldom in the year of his death in 1945, by W. Goscombe John. The lighted grilles around it are not for its nocturnal ornamentation, but for the lavatories underneath.

Up S Penrallt is **Moriah Welsh Calvinistic Methodist Chapel** of 1826, by Robert Jones: its good Tuscan portico was added in 1867, but the fine interior is original. Up N Penrallt is Twthill (for the name, see Rhuddlan, p. 35), an excellent viewpoint. The streets running SE from the town contain handsome terraces and villas. To the N is **Christ Church**, a depressing work of 1862–4 by Antony Salvin (who worked on the restoration of the Castle in 1840–8). The tower and spire were added in 1888. There are more stuccoed houses (names like Pretoria Terrace suggest a surprisingly late date). Caernarfon is now something of an industrial town, the big Ferodo works being the chief employer. This has brought new jobs, much needed, particularly in view of the running down of the slate quarries (in January 1972 unemployment figures were said to be 10%), but has also brought development problems.

CHAPTER SIX

Snowdonia

The English name 'Snowdon' goes back to the thirteenth century, in the form 'Snaudon'. 'Snowdonia' is a modern confection, which is here used for convenience. The Welsh name for the area is 'Eryri', and for the mountain 'Yr Wyddfa'.

BETWS-Y-COED TO BANGOR – A5

From Betws-y-Coed (p. 122), the A5 follows the winding, coniferous valley of the Llugwy. Half a mile out, the river is crossed by a footbridge, called the **Miners' Bridge**, because it was used by men working at the lead and zinc mines, of which there were about twenty in the hills to the N, operating between 1850 and 1913. The remains of the mines – one called 'New Pandora' – include engine houses, inclines, reservoirs and so on, and are best reached by the road running up from **Ty Hyll**, the Ugly House, a well-known landmark just by the bridge over the Llugwy. It owes its name to the fact that it is built of immense rough blocks of stone, in a kind of parody of traditional techniques of stone building. To modern eyes it looks rather pretty. A minor road keeps to the S side of the river: half a mile along it, in a bend of the river, is Caer Llugwy, the site of a Roman fort. Occupied in the early second century, it covers four acres, with an annexe covering a further three. This road rejoins the A5 at Pont Cyfyng, which has good waterfalls below it.

Capel Curig is a straggly place, a great centre for the mountains, splendidly sited with superb views. Victorian hotels – one with the nice old-fashioned name 'Cobden's Snowdonia' – start the straggle, the main concentration of which is naturally round the junction with the A4086. Above stands the dull church of 1883, by Goronwy Owen (architect to the Penrhyn Estates): it was built to replace the humble little church down by the river. Built in the thirteenth or fourteenth century, with a S chapel of c. 1500, it was rebuilt and refitted in 1839, and has remained unaltered since. Originally dedicated to St Curig (see p. 305), he was supplanted later, like so many Celtic patrons, by a non-Celtic saint with whom his name was confused – Cyricus, a Cilician infant martyr, together with his mother Julitta. Up above the church, on the A4086, is **Plas-y-Brenin**, now belonging to the Central Council for Physical Recreation, but built by Lord Penrhyn (see p. 148) as an inn at the time when he opened up the road through Nant Ffrancon (c. 1791). It was designed by his agent, Benjamin Wyatt, and soon had to be enlarged to accommodate the great numbers of tourists and travellers. It is now rather a jumble – partly Gothick, partly slate-hung. From the foot-bridge below it, at the head of Llynnau Mymbyr, you get one of the classic views of Snowdon. Best seen at sunrise, and best of all on a clear winter morning when the mountains are covered in snow, and the sun lights up the whole scene with *couleur de rose*, the still lakes reflecting it in their dark waters.

Lord Penrhyn's road followed the S side of the upper Llugwy valley, and the W side of Nant Ffrancon itself. Telford's road, which succeeded it in 1805, follows the N and E sides. The old road makes a much better route for walking. The upper Llugwy valley is unforgettable. The vast masses of the Carnedd range rise to the N, and the much rockier and steeper Glyders on the S. The dominant peak is Tryfan (3010 ft), standing right out towards the valley. It gets its name from its distinctive triple peak. There are more climbers' huts than farms, although on one farm, Wern Gof Uchaf, below Tryfan, a 'farm trail' has been laid out, drawing attention to various aspects of mountain farming and of geological interest. One notice refers to the test-planes from the RAF Station at Valley (Anglesey). They race up and down the valleys, keeping well below the peaks, and leaving their ear-splitting din way behind them. The summit of the pass (1030 ft) is just beyond where the Llugwy comes down from its source under Pen-yr-helgi-du. Over the other side is **Llyn Ogwen**, a large but shallow lake. Even this is now threatened with interference by the local Water Board. At the far end is the Mountain Rescue Post, and the A5 crosses the river as it

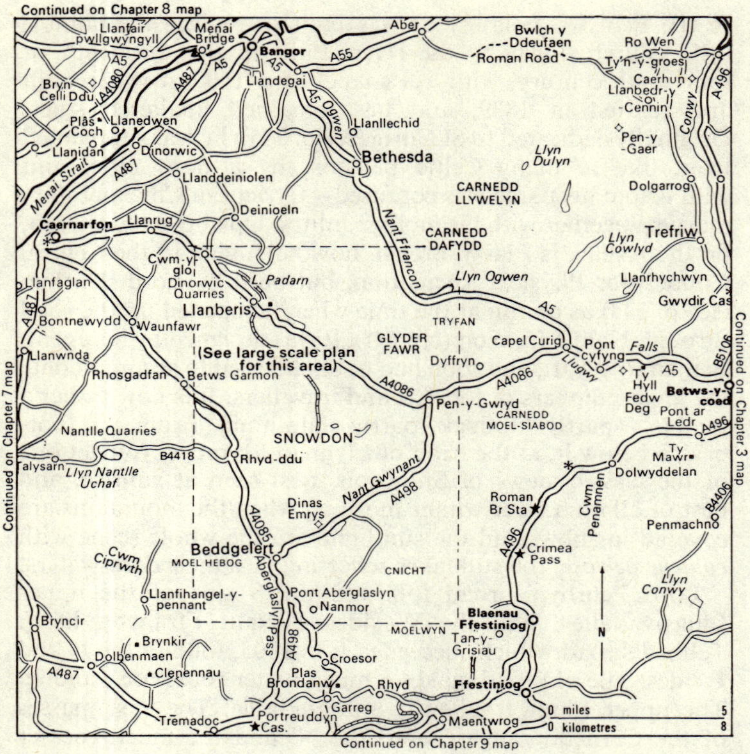

leaves the lake, below the splendid steep peak of Pen-yr-olewen (3211 ft). Part of the old bridge survives beneath the new one, above waterfalls. Nant Ffrancon itself is less spectacular, but the scooped-out sides of the N part of the Glyder range still make a fine show.

The furthermost end of this range has been completely eaten away by the huge Penrhyn Quarries, at **Bethesda**. These were developed on a grand scale by Richard Pennant (1737?–1808), who had married the heiress of half the Penrhyn estate in 1765, and bought the rest in 1785. In 1783 he was created Lord Penrhyn. He was a capable entrepreneur, and prudent in his choice of agents. He acquired a monopoly in the manufacture of writing-slates. Eventually the quarry – developed in galleries along the hillside – became 'the biggest man-made hole in the world', 1140 ft deep. Before it spread quite so far W, the Ogwen valley was a beauty spot, and at Penisa'rnant Lady Penrhyn had a dairy, which still survives among trees near the road (now a private house); designed by Benjamin Wyatt, it is a charming little Gothick building, faced with slabs of slate, painted cream, with a loggia all round. Wyatt also designed an elaborate Gothick villa called Ogwen Bank, half a mile further on, but its site is now occupied by a caravan park. Bethesda took its name from a quarrymen's chapel built in 1820. The village grew rapidly and by about 1865 the population was 5–6,000. Although not at all prepossessing architecturally, it is a place of great character, even though much of the life has inevitably gone out of it with the virtual running-down of the quarries and consequent unemployment. In the nineteenth century the community had a culture and independence of its own. The many chapels include Bethesda itself (rebuilt 1840), and the grand Siloam (1872), hung with blue and green patterned slates. Lord Penrhyn built a church in 1813, but it got swallowed up in debris, and was replaced in 1865 by St Ann's, up at Bryn Eglwys, a dull effort, with a spire, by Goronwy Owen. Down in the town is Christ Church (Glanogwen), a bad church of 1856 by T. H. Wyatt.

The A5 follows the Ogwen through pleasant country down to Llandygai, where it is joined by the A55 (see p. 137). A mile N of Bethesda, up on the hillside, is Llanllechid, with a hilarious church of 1846 by Henry Kennedy. He is one of those architects who is always at his best in his worst buildings. Here he had not yet seen the light of Ecclesiology, and his attempt at Norman is wonderfully ignorant – the windows have intersecting tracery, and the capitals are carved with all sorts of dotty symbols. The critic of the *Ecclesiologist* was not amused: 'The western bellcote is Italian, not Norman. This comes of the same architects essaying church architecture who deal in the revived-pagan.' The one thing about the church which really is Norman is its granite solidity.

CAERNARFON TO CAPEL CURIG – A4086

The first village, three miles out from Caernarfon, is **Llanrug.** The church, SW of the village (at 527/631) was restored in 1856 by Kennedy, but retains a good fifteenth-century roof. N.E. of the village is Pont Rhythallt: in 1804 the Revd. J. Evans referred to 'a stone bridge of no striking appearance', but bearing a tablet to say that it was built by 'the modern Inigo, Harry Parry'. The present bridge seems to be modern, but to judge from Parry's bridge at Penmachno (see p. 119), he had little right to his proud title (even if it was Llanrwst bridge – see p. 111 – that suggested the comparison). To the S is **Bryn Bras Castle**, an eighteenth-century farmhouse which was dolled up in the early nineteenth century with lots of Norman detail, cement-rendered, in the style of a twelfth-century castle. The result is dull.

Beyond Cwm-y-glo (Coal Valley) the road goes along the S side of **Llyn Padarn**, the biggest lake in Snowdonia, and one of the most beautiful. The view of Snowdon from the N side often appears on calendars. From the S side, the eye is chiefly held by the fantastic **Dinorwic Quarries**, rising in huge dark tiers from the lake right up the side of Elidir Fach, reaching a height of 2000 ft. Roads run into the upper terraces from the north end of Llyn Padarn. It is difficult to comprehend how some people fail to appreciate the sublime grandeur of this view and wish to 'landscape' or otherwise obliterate the quarries. Eighteenth-century travellers would have been ecstatic over their 'awfulness'.

Llanberis is a rather characterless Victorian town, owing its existence mainly to the Snowdon tourist trade. Its one sight is the church of St Padarn, a large and dignified EE building of 1885 by Arthur Baker (completed 1914–15 by Harold Hughes). It was highly praised by the French critic Paul Sédille, when he came to see what British architects were up to a few years later. The interior is particularly impressive. The clerk of works was the architect's young cousin, Herbert Baker – later of New Dehli and Bank of England fame. Opposite the Snowdon Railway Station, a road crosses the valley to the quarries developed by the Assheton-Smiths of Vaynol in the early nineteenth century. Export of slate was then a major problem, which was later solved by the construction of Port Dinorwic (p. 140) and the railway which connected it to the quarries. Production reached its peak in the 1890s when 3000 men were employed, and finally ceased in 1969.

Then the big maintenance workshops (below the dam, now under construction) were taken into guardianship by the D. o. E. and opened as the **North Wales Quarrying Museum** by the National Museum of Wales. This imposing structure was built in 1870 rather on the lines of an outpost-of-empire fort planned round a large courtyard. The illusion that the workmen have only just walked out is fostered by the pencilled calculations on the walls and the pin-ups still adorning the canteen. A more self-sufficient enterprise could hardly be imagined. Everything that was needed in the quarries (and to some extent on the company's ships) was made in the foundry here or repaired in the maintenance workshops and smithies. Objects that had become redundant were melted down. Hundreds of wooden patterns (also made here) survive like ghosts. (You can see, for instance, those from which the windows of this building were made; the small panes and heavy iron glazing bars were designed with the effects of blasting in mind.) All machinery was driven from the 80 h.p. 50 ft 5 in. dia. water wheel (housed in the high structure to the N of the building) until it was replaced by the Pelton wheel in 1925. Some slate dressing tables and a mock-up ward from the quarry hospital (the little house with the enviable view above Llyn Padarn to the left of the quarries) have also been included. Mr Hugh Jones, who himself worked here for much of his life, is in charge of the museum. The lakeside railway, the first part of the Dinorwic line, has been relaid as a narrow-gauge line by a private company, which runs passenger services for visitors. It uses engines from the old feeder tracks, the oldest dating from 1899.

Unfortunately the Dinorwic Quarries have been chosen, despite fierce opposition, as the site of North Wales' second pumped-storage hydro-electric scheme, to be worked on the same principle as that at Tanygrisiau (see p. 233). Llyn Peris will be used as the lower reservoir: its level will be raised, and embankments 43 feet high will be built at each end. The upper reservoir will be Marchlyn Mawr, beneath Mynydd

Perfedd: this will suffer an embankment 130 feet high. The power station will be underground, in the quarries, but a power line will connect it with Pentir, six miles N. The scheme will cost £75m., and will produce 1,400,000 Kw. The Central Electricity Generating Board claim that they 'are confident that the new works would be wholly compatible with their surroundings' (CEGB leaflet, July 1972). This sort of preposterous statement would be better unmade: it would be more honest to admit that no scheme on this scale could be compatible with some of the finest mountain scenery in Britain. Admittedly less damage will be done than had Croesor or Penamnen been chosen, but the fact remains that demands for electricity (possibly short-term) and employment (though the latter will be temporary and comparatively slight) are over-ruling considerations of amenity.

At the foot of Llyn Peris is **Dolbadarn Castle** (D. o. E.), so beloved of painters such as Turner, so often represented as if it were some vast towering edifice rather than the plain round stump which it actually is. It was probably built by Llywelyn the Great. His grandson Llywelyn the Last kept his brother Owain Goch a prisoner here. After the English conquest, it was partly dismantled: some of the timber was sent to Caernarfon in 1284. The keep is the oldest part. The curtain wall and other buildings, of which only foundations survive, were added later in the thirteenth century.

Half a mile above the head of the lake is **Nant Peris**, the old village of Llanberis, with the old church of St Peris. It has an odd plan, for transepts and chancel were added to the old church in the sixteenth century, and then chapels added on either side of the chancel in the seventeenth, producing a T-shape. It was severely restored in 1848 by Kennedy – including the roodscreen of c. 1500. The upper part of the pass is wonderfully impressive with the huge rocky mountains pressing in closely on either side. This is the mecca of rock-climbers, whose brightly-coloured tents make a cheerful contrast with the dark rock – a sight which did not, however, gladden the heart of one Alderman on the Caernarfonshire Planning Committee, who has gone on record as saying, 'Some of your climbers are not satisfied with having access to climb the rocks, they must use them like harlots and sleep on them.'

At the top is Pen-y-pass, where a large stone Youth Hostel has been built (the first to be open to non-members), with a café discreetly concealed at the back. However, the huge public car park dominates the scene.

The A4086 meets the A498 at **Pen-y-Gwryd**, where the hotel is a mountaineers' centre. It stands within a Roman marching-camp, parts of the ramparts of which can be seen. There was probably a Roman road from Caer Llugwy (see p. 146) to Caernarfon down the Llanberis Pass. From here the road goes to Capel Curig by way of Dyffryn Mymbyr, the broad valley between the Glyders and Moel Siabod. The farm described in *I Bought a Mountain*, by Thomas Firbank, is N of the road, two miles from Pen-y-Gwryd.

PEN-Y-GWRYD TO TREMADOC – A498

From Pen-y-Gwryd, the A498 goes down into **Nant Gwynant.** The view across to Snowdon, seen at its best within the complete horseshoe, is breathtaking, and possibly lethal to motorists, who should keep their eyes on the road and use a parking-place. On the S side of the road, just E of the head of the lake (at 653/522) is **Hafod Llwyfog**, a house rebuilt in 1638, using materials from the earlier house which was the birthplace of John Williams, goldsmith to James I, banker, and patron of John Owen (see p. 189) and Michael Drayton, who addresses him in a preface to *Polyolbion.* **Llyn Gwynant** is situated beneath steep hills, the lower slopes wooded. Below it is the village, from which a minor road crosses the river and climbs steeply, before turning SW to follow the lovely **Nanmor Valley**, with the foothills of Cnicht on the E, rocky and heathery, and dotted with little lakes, and Moel y Dyniewyd (1254 ft) on the W – a good short climb, worth doing for the views. The village of Nanmor is just off the A487 E of Pont Aberglaslyn: it gave its name to one of the finest poets of medieval Wales, Dafydd Nanmor. He was banished from the district, c. 1450, for writing poems to a married woman, Gwen o'r Ddol (Dolfriog), and went to the south, where he enjoyed the patronage of Rhys ap Meredudd, of Tywyn on the Teifi. A strong supporter of the Tudors, he was fond of puzzles, astronomy, and grammar. At the bottom of the Nanmor valley, S of the A487, at Hafod Garegog, lived another famous poet, a contemporary of Dafydd – Rhys Goch Eryri. The present house is of c. 1600, with later additions.

Below Nantgwynant, back on the A498, is **Llyn Dinas,** possibly even more beautiful, if less spectacular, especially on a summer's evening, when the still water reflects the green and brown hills. It takes its name from **Dinas Emrys**, a fort built on a small wooded hill just W of the lower end of the lake. The remains include stone ramparts, parts of a twelfth-century tower, and cultivation terraces. It was occupied from the Early Iron Age until the Dark Ages. The site is rich in legend. Vortigern is supposed to have tried to build a palace here, above a spring, but was prevented by two dragons, one white and one red, who caused the materials to disappear – as Merlin (Myrddin Emrys) explained to him. It was also chosen by King Lludd, as the safest place in his kingdom, for the burial of (the same?) two dragons, one of which let out a fearful scream every May-eve that caused havoc. His brother Llefelys had advised him to set a tub of mead in the very centre of his dominions, which turned out to be Oxford. (T. E. Lawrence maintained that the tub must have been placed at Carfax, since that is the centre of Oxford.) The two dragons met there and fought, and fell into the tub, in the shape of two little pigs, where they drank the mead and fell asleep, so that Lludd was able to put them in a stone coffer and bury them here. (See *Lludd and Llefelys*, in the *Mabinogion*.)

Beddgelert is a very handsome little village, grouped around the bridge near the confluence of the Glaslyn and the Colwyn. Sober stone houses, some with bargeboards, and one pretty Regency villa. The situation, with Yr Aran to the N, Moel y Dyniewyd to the E, and Moel Hebog to the W, is splendid. The name of the village means 'the burial place of Gelert' (or Celert): who this was is unknown. An explanation was ingeniously supplied by an eighteenth-century landlord of the Royal Goat Hotel. Not only did he use the well-known folk-tale about the faithful hound left to guard his master's baby, who saves it from a wolf, only to be killed by his master when he returns to find blood and chaos, and explain that Gelert was the dog and Llywelyn the master, but he even provided a grave, which is still a place of pilgrimage for the gullible (in the fields S of the church). The story was well chosen to appeal to a nation of dog-lovers.

The **Church** possesses medieval features much finer than are common in North Wales, namely a group of three tall lancets in the E wall, and a richly moulded two-bay arcade on the N, all of c. 1230. The explanation for this is that it was the church of a celebrated Augustinian Priory, itself the successor of a Celtic monastery founded in the sixth century. It had an unfortunate history, and the rest of the building is of little interest. It is a pity that the E windows are obscured, from within the Church, by the fussy roodscreen of 1921. The font bears two inscriptions, one, on the base, in the 'Nennius' alphabet, devised c. 800 (the Doxology in Welsh), the other, on the top, in the Bardic alphabet invented by Iolo Morganwg (recording the 'restoration' of the font in 1882). Both date from 1882. The church possesses an elegant silver chalice and paten, engraved with figures of the three Marys, presented in 1610 by John Williams (see above, p. 153).

The A487, S of Beddgelert, follows the line of the ill-fated **Welsh Highland Railway**. This started as a narrow-gauge railway from Dinas (S of Caernarfon) to Rhyd-ddu, but after the First World War it was extended to Beddgelert and into Portmadoc by way of the Croesor Tramway. The whole scheme was disastrously impractical, and it closed down within a short time. Surprisingly, efforts are now being made to reopen the line. Although the line of the railway runs along the W side of the road, there is a bridge over the road, and stone supports for another one in the field to the E. The explanation is that the route was changed after the bridges were built – the whole project had taken years to complete.

The railway finally crossed the river further S, and ran through a series of tunnels on the E side of the narrow **Aberglaslyn Pass**. This apparent desecration aroused furious protests, including a petition in 1898 signed by Ruskin. This is one of the celebrated beauty spots of Wales, and the rugged pass does look good, but the great quantity of trees – mostly firs – planted in the nineteenth century are somewhat alien to the real Snowdonia. The famous bridge, by which the A487 goes off towards Penrhyndeudraeth, is probably seventeenth century, and was widened in 1795–6 by James Defferd. Until the Portmadoc embankment was built, the Glaslyn was tidal up to this point, and boats were built at Aberglaslyn. Eighteenth-century tourists enjoyed watching the salmon leap here.

The A498 keeps to the W side of the reclaimed estuary, beneath the steep slopes of Moel Ddu. Splendid views of Cnicht, looking really sharp from here, and the Moelwyns. The road turns sharply W below Portreuddyn Castle: the cliffs along here are popular with climbers. From Aberglaslyn it is five miles to Tremadoc (p. 192).

BEDDGELERT TO CAERNARFON – A4085

From Beddgelert the A4085 (called on older maps the A487) follows the E side of the Colwyn, while the old railway track keeps to the W – just out of the village it does a great loop to gain height. The E slopes of the Hebog range are covered with the coniferous Beddgelert Forest. Beyond the forest, the railway goes under the road just before a large glacial boulder, L of the road, called Pitt's Rock because of its similarity to that statesman's profile (when seen from the right angle). Further on is Llyn y Gadair, near **Rhyd-ddu**, a little place well-known as a starting-place for walks and as the junction with the B4418, which goes over to Penygroes.

A mile from Rhyd-ddu, the B4418 passes **Llyn y Dywarchen,** once famous for its floating island. Giraldus Cambrensis first noted it, but it is difficult to see what all the fuss was about, if it was only a broken-off piece of the peaty bank. In Pennant's time it was nine yards long. Giraldus said that cattle sometimes found themselves taken on a voyage on it. Just over the pass of Drws-y-coed, with the craggy cliff and vast black scree slopes of Mynydd Mawr on the N, and the rocky cwms of Mynydd Drws-y-coed on the S, there was a copper mine, opened by Cornish miners in 1761 (though the Romans may have exploited it). It operated until c. 1918. Remains of a reservoir, waterwheel housings, other structures, and shafts can still be seen.

Further down is the broad and peaceful Llyn Nantlle Uchaf. From the far end Richard Wilson painted a magnificent view of Snowdon (now in the Walker Art Gallery, Liverpool). From Nantlle village a road runs W into the thrilling **Nantlle Quarries**. Here the slate outcropped on the valley bottom, so that the method of mining was by means of deep pits, now mostly filled with water. Around them are slate-built tramways, inclines, dressing-sheds, and tunnels. The biggest pit of all, Dorothea (best reached from the B4418 at 494/527) is stunning in its immensity. Pinnacles of rock stand up out of the blue water, and winding-gear is bracketed out giddily at the top of the sheer grey sides. Beside it are enormous platforms, built of waste slate slabs to support more winding-gear, looking, with their huge inclines, like sets for an Aztec film. One's sense of scale is baffled. Over one side a handsome Regency mansion stands derelict among trees, looking tiny in comparison with the cliffs beneath it. The engine-house (1904) still contains the gigantic beam-engine which pumped water out of the quarry, as well as a big clock. The quarries were connected with the harbour at Caernarfon by a narrow-gauge railway (long gone). It began operating on steam in 1848 (fifteen years sooner than the Festiniog).

The quarries can also be reached from **Talysarn**, at the W end. The village consists of neat terraces of quarrymen's houses, and handsome chapels. In the middle, one house has an ornate first-floor loggia, its iron columns and entablature painted green. It is now proposed to clear up the dereliction and create some kind of holiday centre here: it is to be hoped that the ruggedness of the scene and the grandeur of the quarries will not be impaired. Talysarn was the home of John Jones (1796–1857), a great Calvinistic Methodist preacher and composer of hymn tunes. Born at Dolwyddelan, he worked on Telford's road along Nant Ffrancon, as a quarryman, and as a shopkeeper, but later devoted his whole time to preaching, touring widely throughout Wales. He was said to be unusually forceful. For a number of years he was general manager of the Dorothea quarry.

A mile further on, the road joins the A4085 (Caernarfon–Portmadoc) at Penygroes (p. 167).

Beyond Rhyd-ddu, the A4085 comes down to **Llyn Cwellyn,** a large and beautiful lake, but with rather too many conifers on the far side, and now subject to a threat to extract vast quantities of water from it, which would drastically alter its level. On the N side is the Snowdon Ranger Youth Hostel, a nice Victorian house on the site of the cottage where the 'Snowdon Ranger' lived – a well-known early mountain guide. Over the other side of the foot of the lake rises Castell Cidwm, Wolf Castle, a great rocky knob standing out from the precipitous face of Mynydd Mawr. Although marked on the map in

Snowdonia
0 mile 1
0 kilometres 3
N
Llyn Padarn
A4086
Llanberis
Dinorwic
Mus
Quarries
Dolbadarn Castle
Llyn-Peris
Nant-Peris
MYNYDD PERFEDD
Marchlyn Mawr
ELIDIR FAWR
FOEL GOCH
CARNEDD DAFYDD
A5
Nant Ffrancon
Llyn Ogwen
A5
TRYFAN
Y GARN
Llyn Idwal
Llyn-y-Cwn
Twll Du
GLYDER FAWR
GLYDER FACH
Bettws-Garmon
A4085
Clogwyn Sta
Cwmglas
L. Dur Arddu
A498
Pen-y-Pass
Pen-y-Gwryd
GRIB-GOCH
A4086
YR WYDDFA
SNOWDON
Glaslyn
Llyn Llydaw
Llyn Cwellyn
MYNYDD MAWR
Drws-y-coed
Llyn-y-Dywarchen
Pen-y-groes
Llechog
Bwlch Main
Y LLIWEDD
Y GARN
Rhyd-Ddu
B4418
Llyn-y-Gadir
Hafod Llwyfog
Cwm-y-Llan
YR ARAN
L. Gwynant
A498
Nantgwynant
Llyn Dinas
A4085
MOEL LEFN
Beddgelert
MOEL Y DYNIEWYD
Aberglaslyn Pass
Glaslyn River
Cwmcloch
Nanmor Valley
MOEL HEBOG
CNICHT
BEDDGELERT FOREST
Nanmor
A4085
A498
Croesor
MOELWYN MAWR
MOEL DDU
Llyn Stwlan

antique letters, it is a natural feature: a mass of tumbled rocks and heather, it is a fine place to be on a summer's day. Beyond the lake is **Betws Garmon**, with a stubby little Romanesque church of 1841, by George Alexander, crude, but not ill-suited to its situation in the bare valley below the massive mountains. The bridge near it is by Harry Parry, 1777 (see p. 150). The road climbs through the strung-out industrial village of Waunfawr and over to Caernarfon (p. 140).

SNOWDONIA – THE MOUNTAINS

In this section, the mountains are described clockwise, starting with Snowdon and ending with Mynydd Mawr. It makes no claim to originality, which would be out of place, for the best routes have been settled long ago, and it is safer as well as more comfortable to keep to them. It should perhaps be made clear, since some people find it surprising, that one is unlikely to be alone on the better-known peaks, even in winter or in bad weather. The summit of Snowdon is, of course, notorious – though why anyone should be surprised at its being like a railway station, when it is one, is hard to understand. However, even when the railway is not running, one is likely to find anything up to thirty or forty people on top. Even Tryfan, a comparatively difficult peak, can be so crowded on a fine day that it is hard to find a quiet place to eat lunch. We say this neither to discourage, nor to complain: it would be worthy only of a dog in a manger to wish to keep such marvellous experiences to oneself. For peace and quiet, one only has to go a little off the beaten track, and the less celebrated hills are correspondingly emptier. Litter is, however a problem. It is amazing how long it remains up on such exposed places, and the gulls which infest them (particularly in bad weather) are unfortunately too choosy to be effective scavengers.

Although none of the walks suggested is beyond the capacity of a reasonably fit person with a head for heights, some experience is definitely advisable, so that it is better to start with easier climbs – don't try the Snowdon Horseshoe straightaway. Safety is a vital consideration. The number of accidents that occur in Snowdonia is far greater than most people realize: only the most spectacular reach the national Press. Even when accidents are not serious, immense trouble can be caused to overworked rescue teams. The answer is, not to be frightened off, but to take sensible precautions – wear adequate clothing, bearing in mind both the change of temperature at high altitudes and the swiftness with which the weather can alter, wear proper footwear (real climbing boots are best), take map and compass, food, and a torch, inform others of your intended route. None of the suggested climbs requires rope, in normal conditions, but in snow and ice both rope and an ice axe may be necessary.

On consideration, it seemed best not to estimate the time required for each walk: this might be seriously misleading, as different people go at different paces. All the walks can be done within even a winter's day, many can be done in a summer's afternoon. In general, it is pleasanter, and also safer, to leave plenty of time. Within the limitations of space, it is impossible to give detailed descriptions of routes. The best sources for these are W. A. Poucher's *The Welsh Peaks* (4th edition, 1970), complete with maps and excellent photographs; or (much cheaper) E. G. Rowland's *Hill Walking in Snowdonia* (1958, much reprinted).

Snowdonia – Yr Wyddfa

Snowdon (3560 ft) deserves its fame: it is very satisfactory that the highest mountain in Wales and England should also be the finest. It has a properly sharp peak, from which a series of sharp, rocky ridges run out, enclosing a fine series of steep-sided cwms, most sheltering lakes. However, to avoid disappointment, it is essential to remember that the top will almost certainly be thronged with high-spirited humans, and that it is not the romantic place one might hope for – the summit cairn is more of an immense viewing platform, the railway station is an unsightly barrack of concrete and rusted iron, and bits of brick wall disfigure the scene. Proposals to erect fences and build rock gardens would have made it even more preposterous. This is not a modern phenomenon: nineteenth-century engravings show huge flagstaffs and miscellaneous shacks for selling tea, brandy etc.

Two further warnings: Snowdon is more often in cloud than out of it, so it is as well to have a look at the summit before you start to make sure it is visible – though cloud may still descend before you get there. Even if it is clear, fabulous accounts of the view need to be taken with a pinch of salt. All the same, the nearer views are easily exciting enough to reward the climb. Secondly, don't forget that unless the trains are running the refreshment room will be shut. Even on a sunny April day, the top of the line may be buried in snow.

The easiest, but longest and dullest, ascent is by the **Llanberis Path**, which keeps close to the track of the Snowdon Mountain Railway. Of course, it is easier still to go up by the railway, but that would be cheating, and the price deters most (the return fare varies – 1973 – between £2.15 and £1.25, depending on the season). The railway operates on the rack principle, and still uses the original steam engines made at Winterthur in Switzerland in 1896. On the opening day a dramatic accident occurred, and the landlord of the Padarn Villa Hotel lost his life. Since then working has been less exciting. The only really precipitous part of the route is the last.

From Pen-y-Pass, three routes are possible. The first is the **Pyg Track** (P.Y.G. = Pen-y-Gwryd), which climbs up over the shoulder, then clings to the precipitous side of Crib Goch before going up steeply to join the Llanberis path. Not too difficult, except in snow and ice, when the upper part is tricky, and it gives splendid views of the lakes, Llyn Llydaw, below, and Glaslyn, in a fine glacial cirque, above. The **Miners' Track** is so called because it was used to reach the copper mines, of which extensive remains are visible. The main workings are up by Glaslyn. The copper explains the blueness of the water in Llyn Llydaw. The track curves round the hill from Pen-y-pass, crosses the lake by a purpose-built causeway (sometimes submerged), goes up to Glaslyn, and then climbs steeply to join the Pyg Track. The third route is the first half of the famous **Horseshoe**, the classic and unbeatable way of seeing Snowdon. It is one of the best ridge-walks anywhere, but it is not for the beginner. The route follows the Pyg Track as far as the shoulder, then goes straight up the steep, rocky face of Crib Goch (3023 ft). The ridge between here and Crib-y-ddysgl is splendidly sharp and bristly, and the Pinnacles have caused many a heart to flutter. From Crib-y-ddysgl to the summit is easy. Descent is by the Watkin Zigzags (see below) to Bwlchysaethau, the Pass of the Arrows, where, according to legend, King Arthur and his knights are sleeping, awaiting the hour when they are needed. From there, the ridge of Lliwedd is followed, narrow, but less alarming than the Pinnacles, and satisfyingly different in form, texture and colour from Crib Goch. From Lliwedd the Miners' Track is reached.

The **Watkin Path** starts from Nantgwynant, where Sir Edward Watkin, the late nineteenth-century railway tycoon, had a house ('The Chalet', now ruined). The path goes up Cwm-y-llan, following the stream as it comes over a series of waterfalls. Some way up is Gladstone's Rock, beyond the ruins of Plas Cwmllan. A plaque commemorates the fact that Gladstone, when Prime Minister for the fourth time and 83 years old, stood on the rock and addressed 'the people of Eryri' on 'Justice to Wales': 'the multitude sang Cymric hymns'. This was when he opened the Path, in 1892. Further on are the mines, beyond which the path climbs more steeply. This part was made for Sir Edward Watkin. The last part of the ascent is by means of zigzags up loose scree – much nicer to go up than down. The route can be varied by taking in *Yr Aran* (2451 ft), quite a fine peak in itself, and with an impressively steep N face, and going up the ridge to Bwlch Main. This makes a good mini-Horseshoe.

The **Rhyd-ddu** path goes up to Llechog, which has a steep N face, and then also goes along Bwlch Main. A good quick route, but the last part of the ridge is extremely narrow and can be alarming in snow and ice. The **Snowdon Ranger** path is perhaps best used as a descent, combined with the Rhyd-ddu path. It involves following the Llanberis path for half a mile, then going down over Clogwyn du'r Arddu, a nice easy spur with small lakes on either side, and by a not very exciting path down to the Snowdon Ranger (see p. 157).

Finally, a little-used but very worthwhile route is the one from the Llanberis Pass, up **Cwm-glas** and then on to Crib-y-ddysgl: it is steep and rocky, but the shortest of all, and the moment when you get on to the ridge and see the whole Horseshoe before you is really exciting.

The Glyders

The classic ascent is from Ogwen. First **Tryfan** is climbed – straight up its rocky flank to the summit at 3010 ft, the triple peaks from which it gets its name. On the top are two vertical stones known as Adam and Eve, and it is a popular test of nerve to jump from one to the other. From Tryfan scramble up Bristly Ridge, aptly named, to the summit of **Glyder Fach** (3262 ft), remarkable for being almost entirely covered in an immense jumble of great lumps of stone. The most striking feature of all is the Castle of the Winds, a huge, pinnacled outcrop, on the route to **Glyder Fawr** (3279 ft). It is also possible to come up more directly by the fine ridge Y Gribin. From Glyder Fawr steep scree leads down to the little Llyn-y-Cwn. The stream from this lake is followed by a path leading down to Cwm Idwal, past the bottom of Twll Du (The Devil's Kitchen), a sheer and sombre cleft.

Cwm Idwal is well worth seeing for itself, and is easily reached from Ogwen even by non-mountaineers. Now a Nature Reserve, it is one of the most interesting examples of glacial action in Britain. Darwin told how he went there with Sedgwick in 1831, and how neither of them noticed 'the plainly scored rocks, the perched boulders, the lateral and terminal moraines . . . phenomena . . . so conspicuous that . . . a house burnt down by fire did not tell its story more plainly than did this valley'. For at that time no one believed that Britain had had an Ice Age. Apart from these signs, Cwm Idwal also retains rare arctic flora. The great slabs of rock at the SE end of the cwm are usually crawling with climbers. Idwal was said to have been a son of Owain Gwynedd, murdered by his foster-father in this spot. Shepherds claimed that, as at Lake Avernus, no birds would fly over the water.

The mountains N of the Glyders – Y Garn (3104 ft), Foel Goch (2727 ft), Mynydd Perfedd (2665 ft), and Carnedd y Filiast (2695 ft), together with Elidir Fawr to the W (3030 ft), are less exciting, but also less frequented, and well worth an expedition.

The Carnedds (*Carneddau*)

Less popular than the Glyders, because less dramatic, these mountains are nevertheless not as dull as their rounded summits might suggest: there are fine cliffs and precipices, and the comparatively easy going makes a welcome change after their more arduous neighbours. The names of the two peaks, Carnedd Llywelyn and Carnedd Dafydd, clearly refer to Llywelyn the Last and his hostile brother.

For the best ascent, follow the river Llugwy from Pont Rhyd-gôch, on the A5 a mile E of Llyn Ogwen, to Ffynnon Llugwy, which is connected by leets with Llyn Cowlyd (see p. 125). The leets produce odd optical effects: in places they appear to go uphill. A good track (not on the one-inch map) leads up to the lake, and from there a stiff climb brings you to the crags of Craig-yr-ysfa, with the view over to Cwm Eigiau. (It is also possible to reach this point by way of Pen-yr-helgi-du, but the long slow ascent is unrewarding.) From there it is easy going to the flat top of **Carnedd Llywelyn** (3485 ft). Beyond it is Yr Elen, 3152 ft, rarely visited. From Carnedd Llywelyn you round the head of the deserted Cwm Llafar, and go along the top of magnificent N-facing cliffs to **Carnedd Dafydd** (3427 ft). Below the summit are fragments of an aeroplane which failed to clear it. The descent to Ogwen can be made either via Pen-yr-ole-wen (3211 ft), and a steep rough path, or, more easily, by way of Ffynnon Lloer (the well of the moon).

Moel Siabod

A much more interesting mountain than it looks from a distance, and especially good for views of the other hills. The best route starts from Pont Cyfyng, a mile SE of Capel Curig: a quarry track leads up from the road, and the long rocky ridge is easily reached. From the summit (2860 ft), a rough spur runs down to Llyn y Foel, dramatically sited under the cliffs. A path leads back by way of interesting slate quarries, past an awesomely deep pit with sheer sides, to the track by which one began. A small lake has been enlarged by means of a beautifully built stone dam.

Cnicht and the Moelwyns

Although the Moelwyns and most of Cnicht are actually in Merioneth, it would be perverse not to include them with the mountains of Snowdonia.

Cnicht is not particularly high – 2265 ft – but is exceptionally beautiful. Viewed from the SW, it appears to be sharply pointed, and has even (rather idiotically) been called 'the Matterhorn of Wales'. In fact, it has a long sharp ridge. Not at all difficult to climb, it makes a good beginner's ascent. It can be reached from Nanmor (see p. 153), but is best approached from Cwm Croesor (p. 237). From Croesor village, follow the Roman road right up on to the ridge, and then keep as near the top of the ridge as is convenient. The descent can be made by way of the head of the valley, littered with small lakes, both natural and artificial, and remains of quarries (inclines, tramways, huts, and so on), or else the walk can be prolonged right round the top, in which case the track from the old quarries can be used. These quarries, reached by tunnels piercing deep into Moelwyn Mawr, were used in the war for storing the pictures from the National Gallery in London, and are now used for storing explosives made at Penrhyndeudraeth.

Only the super-energetic will combine Cnicht with the Moelwyns. Most will tackle them separately, starting from Croesor village, or (more lazily) from further up the Roman road. Make for **Moelwyn Mawr** first, past numerous quarry workings with tramways contouring around to them. From the top (2527 ft) Llyn Stwlan is too close for comfort (p. 233). The rocks are strongly streaked with quartz. The ridge to **Moelwyn Bach** (2334 ft) is not difficult: its summit is very slaty.

Moel Hebog

This well-rounded but stony hill (2566 ft) can be climbed direct from Beddgelert, by way of Cwmcloch. A longer walk can be made by starting from Rhyd-ddu, and following the old track which goes over to Cwm Pennant by way of Bwlch y Ddwy-elor. This name – the pass of the two biers – must go back to the days when such mountain routes were used to take corpses for burial to remote parish churches. From the head of the pass the ridge is followed over Moel Lefn (2094 ft). A diversion can be made to visit Ogof Owain Glyn Dŵr, the cave where Owen and his men are said to have taken refuge. It would have been a good place to choose. The rocky mountain-side is riven into numerous clefts, but this slot, not very big, can only be approached by a narrow path along the cliff. Definitely not for sufferers from vertigo.

The Nantlle Ridge

Rightly celebrated as one of the best ridge-walks in Snowdonia – probably next best after the Horseshoe. From Rhyd-ddu, one climbs steeply up to Y Garn (2080 ft), and then follows the sharp ridge round by Mynydd Drws-y-coed and Trum y Ddysgl. Forestry on the slopes below, but this is left behind on the exciting needle-sharp ridge to Mynydd Tal-y-mignedd (2148 ft). A rather disconcerting down-and-up is needed to reach Craig Cwm-Silyn, overlooking the superb cirque containing the two Llynau Cwm-Silyn, and Garnedd Goch. The best way down from here is to Garn Dolbenmaen (take care to avoid Gors Graianog, a first-rate bog), but if your car is still at Rhyd-ddu, it will be necessary to retrace your steps.

Mynydd Mawr

A good short climb, easy but rewarding. From near the bridge just above the head of Llyn Cwellyn, a path goes up through forestry and leads up on to Craig-y-bera, with fine rocks and a view over Drws-y-coed. The summit (2290 ft) is rather dull. The return can be made via Craig Cwmbychan and Castell Cidwm, then steeply down to the river and over stepping-stones. Best not done when the heather is at its thickest.

CAERNARFON TO TREMADOC

N.B. The old A499–A4085 (Caernarfon–Penygroes–Tremadoc) is now the A487, and the old A487 (Caernarfon–Rhyd-ddu–Beddgelert) is now the A4085.

Fine views of the Straits can be had from the minor road which runs along the very edge of the water from the mouth of the River Saint, opposite the Castle. It can be reached by a new footbridge. Alternatively, leave Caernarfon on the A487 and bear right for Llanfaglan immediately after the road crosses the river. Continue through the village and then fork right. Foryd Bay, a big lagoon which almost dries out at low tide – waders and wildfowl gather here in large numbers – is at your feet. It is sheltered by the long spit of Morfa Dinlle which forms the narrow entrance to the Straits, guarded by Fort Belan (not open, see p. 174). It must have been somewhere here that St Beuno dropped his book of sermons. Every Sunday he came up from Clynnog (p. 175) and crossed the Straits at low tide to preach in Anglesey. When he discovered his loss, the precious manuscript was already on a sandbank cut off by the tide but a friendly curlew picked it up and laid it on a rock at the saint's feet. He prayed that night that the curlew should be blessed and in answer the Creator has made her nest particularly difficult to find.

The old church of **Llanfaglan** (sadly, in a poor state of repair) stands in a field half a mile from the spot where the road meets the water. Its big square stone lychgate was built by a churchwarden of 1722. A chancel was added to the little medieval building c. 1800 and the interior of the church is unrestored, with its eighteenth-century furniture: plain benches, box pews, pulpit with sounding board, and reading desk. The key is kept at Llanwnda vicarage near the main road, but quite a lot can be seen through a window.

Across A499 roads run E up to the much quarried foothills of Mynydd Mawr. The small fields have been cleared of stones by generations of quarrying small-holders who built the close network of big stone walls and small stone farms. It is the country described so vividly in the novels of Kate Roberts, who was born in 1891 at **Rhosgadfan** three and a half miles SE of Caernarfon. The cottage, cherished and most successfully presented as a ruin, is open to the public. Despite the encroachment of new housing it is a moving place. To find it take the minor road E off the A487 half a mile S of Bontnewydd. *Tea in the Heather*, regarded by the author as her best work, has been translated into English. It is a collection of stories set in this country, in which the relationships between the characters are seen through a child's eyes: her growing awareness is subtly indicated.

An unfenced road through the hills takes you on to the A4085, just S of Waunfawr (p. 159) or you can return to the A487, the Portmadoc road. This road leaves the A499 (the Pwllheli road) at Llanwnda. Three miles S, it is joined by the B4418 (coming over from Rhyd-ddu via Nantlle – p. 157) at **Penygroes**, a substantial quarrying township with terraced houses punctuated by brightly painted chapels. It has outgrown the old village of Llanllyfni, strung out along the road further S. Four miles beyond, just before the village of Bryncir, a Roman fort was discovered in 1954. Within ten years it had been almost completely destroyed by gravel-digging.

After another two and a half miles the little church of

Dolbenmaen stands by the road: mostly fifteenth-century, its best feature is its contemporary roof. There is also a funny little wooden font, on legs (c.1800). Here the road crosses the river Dwyfor, and a minor road follows the river (L) up the lovely and remote **Cwm Pennant**. The often-quoted words of Eifion Wyn must be quoted again – 'O God, why didst Thou make Cwm Pennant so beautiful and the life of an old shepherd so short?' A mile up the river is another bridge: over the other side a grassy hillock is surmounted by a wood, out of which rises a charming Gothick tower, substantially built of stone in 1821. It has battlements, and fake arrow-slits. The five rooms, one above the other, are reached by a staircase within the walls – still climbable by the brave, although floors and roof have gone, and leading to wonderful views. Someone should restore it. When Bertrand Russell was looking for a house in the district, Sir Clough Williams-Ellis suggested this, but the sage was unconvinced.

The tower stands on the estate of Brynkir mansion: the story of the house has been amusingly told by Sir Clough in his autobiography. A clause in a will required that each inheritor should add to it. As the family were in chronic financial difficulties, largely due to ill-advised mining operations in the valley, this meant that a new wing would be built while the older parts fell into decay (a real-life *Gormenghast*). Now the whole place is ruinous and sunk in impenetrable jungle. The mysterious letters 'LBH' on signs pointing to the stables stand for 'London Borough of Hillingdon' – one of the innumerable local authorities, schools, and youth organizations of all sorts to have found themselves a base in Snowdonia.

About a mile above Brynkir mansion, the valley is dramatically blocked by a great rocky barrier: both river and road have to wind round under its western flank. Just before reaching it, the road passes the plain little church of **Llanfihangel-y-Pennant**, rebuilt in 1850, but looking more like 1830. Its simple homeliness suits the rugged scene. A little beyond, a bridge crosses the river. A notice on a gate warns you that you enter at your own risk, but it is well worth asking the farmer's permission to explore the fascinating remains of the slate quarries over the other side. The remains of the dressing-mill are clearly visible, including the tall stone supports for the leet which feeds an overshot waterwheel. Further up the hill, a leet still follows a channel beautifully made out of slate. Near it, a tunnel enters the rock. Unwise to enter, for it emerges in the side of a vast chasm, into which a stream falls dramatically. Further N is another huge pit, with a pool at the bottom.

Returning to the road up the Pennant valley, it winds around until, after it has again crossed the river, the valley widens out. Its upper part is flanked on the W by the Nantlle Ridge, and on the E by Moel Hebog. The valley-bottom itself is strikingly flat. A mile up from the bridge, a hanging valley, **Cwm Ciprwth**, goes up W. The stream comes down by a series of rocky falls: if it is followed up to a height of 800 feet, a remarkable object will be seen beside it – a cast-iron water-wheel, 24 feet in diameter. It bears the name of its maker – 'Dingey and Son, Truro'. Part of the machinery which linked the wheel to the pumping-shaft, 150 feet away, is still there. The function of the wheel was to drain the Gilfach copper-mine. A diorama in the National Museum illustrates its operation. It is amazing to think of this huge wheel being brought all the way from Cornwall up on to this remote Welsh mountainside. And all, apparently, to little avail, for the mine does not seem to have been a success. The head of Cwm Pennant, closed in by mountains, is movingly lonely, especially as the farmhouse is now abandoned. From a little way back, a track goes over to Rhyd-ddu by way of Bwlch y Ddwy-elor (see p. 165).

Going back down the valley to the bridge below Brynkir Tower, the road which crosses it leads to the Afon Cwmystradllyn, a tributary of the Dwyfor. On it is the celebrated Brynkir Woollen Mill, which welcomes visitors. Just N of the river from here is Clenennau, the home of the Royalist Sir John Owen (see pp. 136, 192). The seventeenth-century house has been much rebuilt. A few hundred yards beyond the Mill, a road goes off up Cwmystradllyn. More open, barer, and less attractive than Cwm Pennant, it is worth visiting, if only for the sake of the impressive ruin which towers above the road one and a half miles up. So impressive is it that a local land-owner used to pack off his guests with a picnic to visit 'the ruined abbey in Cwmystradllyn' – and then waited to see what they would say on their return. It was in fact the Ynys-pandy Slate Mill, built in 1864. The huge gabled structure is pierced with rows of arches, one above the other. The slate was brought down on tramways from the Gorseddau quarries, up in the side of Moel Hebog, and entered the mill at the upper level by means of a vast curving stone embankment. Water power, assured by the big dammed lake at the head of the valley, was used to work the slate-dressing machines. The enterprise was too ambitious, and soon failed. But the ruin remains, strongly, even elegantly built, its archways framing views of foaming stream and bare mountain – a photographer's paradise. From the Cwmystradllyn turning, it is less than a mile (S) to the A487, and less than two miles from there to Tremadoc (p. 192).

CHAPTER SEVEN

The Lleyn Peninsula

LLEYN (LLŶN) AND COUNTRY TO THE WEST OF A487* TO PORTMADOC

The name **Lleyn** incorporates the same element as **Leinster,** suggesting close connections with Ireland towards which the peninsula thrusts, forming the northern arm of Cardigan Bay, as Pembrokeshire does the southern.

Lleyn has long been a stronghold of Welsh language and culture. Its popularity as a place for holidays has been growing throughout this century. This has now led to conflict, especially over the 'second homes' issue (a problem not unique to Caernarfonshire, or for that matter to Wales). It is easy to understand the feelings of local people who see more and more village cottages being bought by people from outside for holiday occupation. Something which once preserved unwanted stone cottages is now creating ghost villages out of season; a situation no one wants, and one which has been denounced, not only by nationalist sympathizers, both here and in other parts of Britain. Lleyn has a sensitive nationalist history. It was near Pwllheli in 1936 that three Welsh Nationalists (a minister of religion, a university lecturer and a schoolteacher) set fire to an RAF depot to protest against the setting up of a bombing school in Wales.

Lleyn ends in a purposeful point with Bardsey Island off its tip and, as soon as you enter the country, a strange compulsion draws you westwards, as it must have drawn the Christian pilgrims to the famous island monastery. The pilgrims' road to that remote sanctuary out in the sea near the setting sun was busy with traffic from the sixth century on. Long before, Neolithic and Bronze Age men had settled here as they had

* Until recently A4085

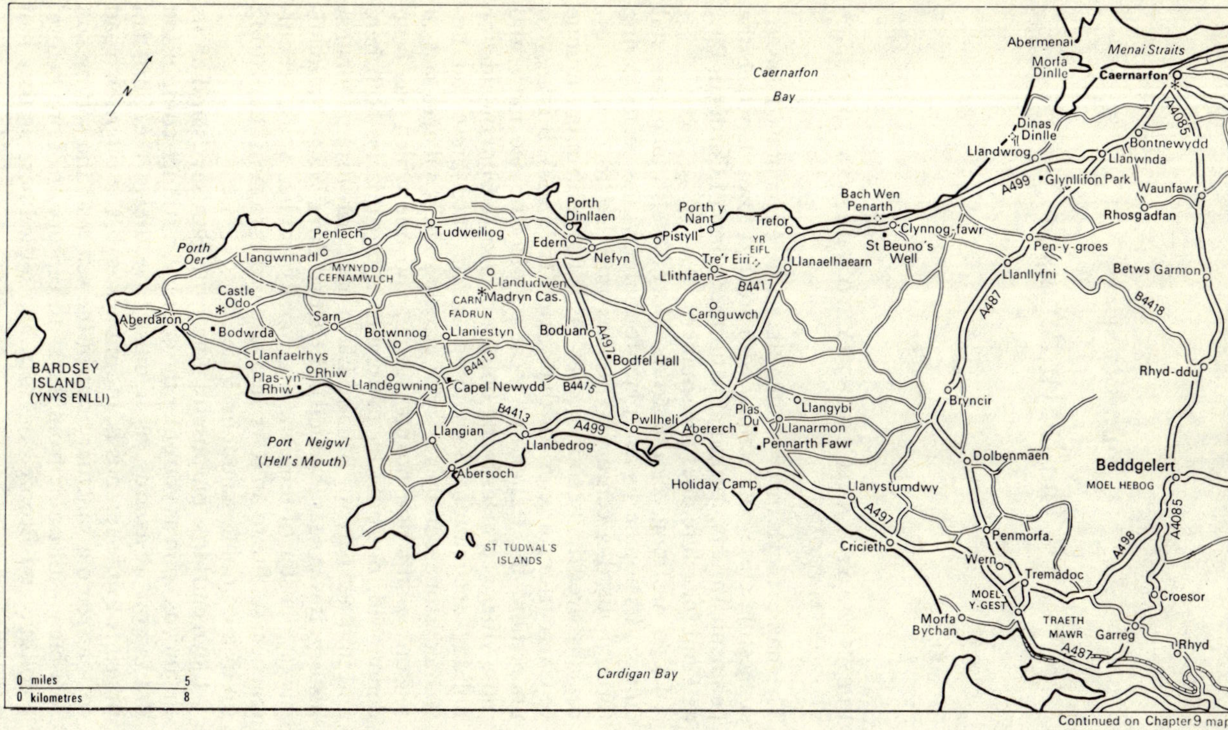
Caernarfon Bay
Cardigan Bay
Menai Straits
Abermenai
Morfa Dinlle
Caernarfon
Dinas Dinlle
Llandwrog
Bontnewydd
Llanwnda
Glynllifon Park
Waunfawr
Rhosgadfan
Bach Wen Penarth
Clynnog-fawr
St Beuno's Well
Pen-y-groes
Llanllyfni
Betws Garmon
Rhyd-ddu
Beddgelert
MOEL HEBOG
Porth Dinllaen
Porth y Nant
Trefor
Pistyll
YR EIFL
Tre'r Eiri
Llanaelhaearn
Llithfaen
Carnguwch
Porth Oer
Penlech
Tudweiliog
Llangwnnadl
MYNYDD CEFNAMWLCH
Edern
Nefyn
Llandudwen
CARN FADRUN
Madryn Cas.
Castle Odo
Aberdaron
Bodwrda
Sarn
Botwnnog
Llaniestyn
Boduan
Bodfel Hall
Llanfaelrhys
Plas-yn Rhiw
Rhiw
Llandegwning
Capel Newydd
BARDSEY ISLAND (YNYS ENLLI)
Port Neigwl (Hell's Mouth)
Llangian
Abersoch
Llanbedrog
Pwllheli
Abererch
Plas Du
Llangybi
Llanarmon
Pennarth Fawr
Holiday Camp
Llanystumdwy
Cricieth
Bryncir
Dolbenmaen
Penmorfa.
Wern
Tremadoc
MOEL Y-GEST
Morfa Bychan
TRAETH MAWR
Garreg
Croesor
Rhyd
ST TUDWAL'S ISLANDS
A4085
A499
A487
A497
A498
B4418
B4417
B4415
B4413
N
0 miles 5
0 kilometres 8
Continued on Chapter 6 map
Continued on Chapter 9 map

in Anglesey (and again in Pembrokeshire). There are striking similarities between all the peninsulas and islands which are washed by the Irish Sea, and Cornwall, Brittany and the Iberian Peninsula from which so many of their people came. They are rugged and bare where exposed to the gales; covered with luxuriant growth where sheltered. Christianity in Lleyn, although it now boasts no great monument such as St Michael's Mount or St Davids Cathedral, seems to have been powerfully integrated with the old religions. There are scores of small churches, on and off the main routes, often lost in the tiny mesh of steep-banked lanes, and most are worth finding for one reason or another.

Perhaps the easiest way to start an exploration of Lleyn is as so many of the pilgrims did, following the road from Caernarfon down the north coast. In doing this we will include what is strictly part of the Cantref of Arfon since this makes an easier boundary for the motorist: that is to say all the country west of the Portmadoc road, A487.

THE NORTH COAST

Take instead the Pwllheli road (A499). Two miles south of the junction the spire of **Llandwrog** church off the main road to the west, marks the nineteenth-century estate village of Glynllifon Park whose huge wall flanks the highway. Such villages are so rare in Wales that it is worthwhile delaying your first taste of Lleyn proper. The attractive stone cottages, some of which still have their Gothicky glazing, are grouped round Henry Kennedy's remarkable little church (1860), with its unexpected interior: a period piece from the depths of England it seems, although its architect had left Kensington for Bangor twenty years before. Cruciform in plan, it has a stone gallery across the west end, and is furnished with stalls arranged like those of a college chapel. The south chapel has Wynn monuments of the eighteenth and nineteenth centuries. The Harp Inn, a stucco, regency-looking verandahed and bay-windowed pub, carries a slate inscription extolling its hospitality but warning against drunkenness. Another inscription on a white non-estate looking cottage nearby commemorates the achievements of Wings for Victory Week, 1943, in a Welsh poem. Mary Lewis who was post-mistress at that time, is a preacher.

Dinas Dinlle, whose splendid silhouette can be seen from the main road, lies a mile below the village. It is a coastal fort of c. 100 BC. Much of its romance vanishes on closer acquaintance: unprepossessing modern holiday development below; the whole cut by a wire fence; continuous erosion suggests that a large slice might soon slide into the sea, trig. point and all. But on a clear day there are splendid views of Anglesey across the water and at dusk, in the lingering light, it is easy to people its double ramparts once again and to see below the creeks it once defended, now submerged beneath the sea.

Back on the main road the long wall of **Glynllifon Park** tantalizes but only enthusiasts will find it worth their while to ask permission of the College of Further Education which it houses to explore within. The lion and eagles surmounting the gates suggest more cheerful days. The classical house, which was rebuilt between 1836–48 after a fire, is disappointing but the (converted) stables are pleasant and the early-nineteenth-century garden with the canalized Llifon descending in a series of minute falls must once have been very attractive. It may have been designed by Thomas Wynn, the first Lord Newborough, who married as his second wife an Italian girl, Maria Stella. The story that she was really the daughter of Égalité, Duke of Orléans, having been exchanged as a baby with Louis Philippe who later became King of France (1830–48), seems quite possible when the details and family portraits are examined. If it were so, the Newboroughs would be the true heirs to the house of Orleans.

Fort Williamsburg, also within the park, was built in 1761 as a base for Lord Newborough's military and social activities. He raised several companies of militia. Although the strategically sited Fort Belan at the entrance to the Menai Straits (never open) which he also built might have been a serious military obstacle to an invader, Williamsburg can hardly have fooled even its creator. The barracks are now cottages, the walled and moated enclosure overgrown and the HQ pavilion within is falling into decay. The tower looks later than the main Fort. The Newborough Mausoleum, begun in 1826, was intended to be crowned by a chapel, but work was abandoned long before. It is now an overgrown pile.

Head again SW. Four miles on the huge-seeming tower of **Clynnog Fawr** takes one by surprise. It is astonishing to discover this great church here. The vast east window is now so close under the road that one feels invited to sail through it. Outside, apart from the sturdy tower, all is glassy, pinnacled and battlemented. It is a generous, spreading building; even the vestry has three storeys and the porch two. Inside, it is high, wide, spacious and light, spare and empty but cheerful. The present church is a perpendicular rebuilding of cruciform plan; the earlier parts are the c. 1480 transepts and chancel; the nave and porch are c. 1500; the tower and St Beuno's Chapel early sixteenth century; connecting passage early seventeenth. This is the traditional burial place of St Beuno and, lying as it does on the direct route to Bardsey, it was a very important shrine for the pilgrims bound there, hence the riches of the church. In Pennant's day the tomb of the saint, 'plain and altar-shaped' was in the middle of the chapel. It was strewn with rushes and those that spent the night lying on it might be cured of all manner of diseases. The offering of calves and lambs who happened to be born with St Beuno's mark, a natural slit or dent on the ear, also survived in the eighteenth century. Money thus raised was stored in the impregnable-looking chest (now in the nave). Pennant described its strength and records the saying 'you may as well try to break up St Beuno's chest'. St Beuno's stone, traditionally associated with the saint, stands in the chapel.

The nave, over thirty feet wide, has a handsome oak roof, carved and panelled. The chancel is cut off by a screen (unfortunately usually locked); restored in 1940, it has Tudor stalls with misericords, a double-headed eagle bench-end c. 1500, and very attractive sedilia c. 1480. On a wall memorial of 1609, ten daughters and two sons kneel behind the deceased.

St Beuno's Well lies beside the road just beyond the attractive house with the monkey-puzzle tree; a rectangular pool in a walled enclosure with stone benches down each side. Those who intended to spend the night on the tomb were supposed to dip here first. The structure is probably contemporary with the rebuilding of the church: it was touched up in the eighteenth century. A lovely site with the sea a quarter of a mile away to the west.

A field away from the sea (and visible from the main road) is the **Bach Wen Penarth** burial chamber, a small but well-shaped cromlech with a capstone on four uprights tidily enclosed in a park-like fence. It can be reached by the farm road to Bach Wen beside the church; fork left up the green track near the farm. The fields have grand stone walls.

Continuing west one gets a true sense of the wildness of the north coast. Ahead are the Rivals (an anglicization of Yr Eifl). The highest of these three peaks is only 1849 feet but they rise straight from the sea. Gaunt quarrying above the cliffs contrasts with the neatly-walled green fields above Trefor. Immediately above the road are the sheer quarried slopes of Gurn Ddu, blanketed with bracken and scree. The road climbs inland. Bear off on B4417, the Nefyn road, unless you want to explore **Llanaelhaearn**. The church, basically medieval with sixteenth- and seventeenth-century transepts and chancel added in 1892, when all was restored, has very attractive and unusual box pews whose sides are panelled in turned balusters. St Aelhaearn's well is now used for the modern water supply.

Rejoin the Nefyn road (B4417) and look out on the right for the footpath sign which marks the track up to **Tre'r Ceiri,** the Town of the Giants, that most splendid Iron Age fortification which crowns the most easterly peak of the Rivals. On a clear day the views from here are incredibly beautiful. A place to stand apart and dream over North Wales; across Caernarfon Bay to Anglesey or into the heart of Snowdonia; or right down the peninsula towards Bardsey, or across it and Cardigan Bay far to the south. But even if the wind is in the east and all this is lost in haze it is well worth the half-hour stroll which will bring you to the top. Follow the field wall, through the sheep fold and out on to the open hill. The path then gently traverses the contours. Black cattle; ravens; pale grass; heather. The path leads to the south-west entrance cutting a much denuded outer wall some fifty yards below, through the great wall and into the long irregular-shaped enclosure, 950 × 340 feet which slopes up to the cairn at its apex. It sheltered about 150 huts (maybe more; foundations to that number have been found) which get maximum warmth from the sun since the ground is tilted towards it. The wall varies in strength according to the natural defensiveness of the ground it is covering. It is best preserved on the N and W where it stands up to thirteen feet on the outer face. A parapet rising above the wall walk survives in parts. Along the north and west an outer wall runs parallel to the main defence. Both are cut by entrances whose track leads to a spring. The huts vary in plan from circular to nearly rectangular. Excavation suggests that they date mostly from AD 150–400. The town may only have been occupied in summer: the time for shepherding on the high pastures and war. The cairn is Bronze Age.

A very different deserted village clings to the skirts of the Rivals at the foot of Nant Gwrtheyrn to the W (350/448). **Porth y Nant** saw its heyday over the turn of the century when the quarries were in full swing; it was not abandoned until the 1950s. Now it is desolate apart from sporadic hippy invaders, but fascinating in its desolation. Turn off in the village of Llithfaen and leave the car at the top of the track which leads down the cwm. This road was never made up for wheeled traffic as supplies arrived by sea (the pier survives); the doctor came by sled. It would be as well to go there soon before conifers transform this lonely little valley where that unattractive-seeming villain Vortigern is said to have met his end. The small farm on the way down is empty and reeds and bracken encroach on its little fields; giant abandoned quarries loom above.

The village consists of two terraces of twelve cottages at right angles, a chapel and manager's house, all with their slate roofs but no windows. This seems to make them the more destitute. A letter box survives. It is a bleak spot, shielded in winter from all but the west sun but protected by its clumps of sycamore. There are a few older outlying cottages and quarry buildings. The last inhabitant, an elderly woman, is said to have lived here alone for five years.

A detour might be made from Llithfaen for **Carnguwch Church** which has an idyllic site at the foot of the southern slopes of Mynydd Carnguwch (374/418). A meeting place of trackways, it can be approached on foot from the north along the mountain track, or by driving through two farms and then walking from the south. The church stands alone above a rushing stream in its tree-sheltered oval enclosure. It was rebuilt in 1882 by Henry Kennedy, on holiday from his correct pointed style. A very sturdy barn with a massive bellcote and square-headed windows, except for the east, which is perpendicular, presumably from the earlier church. A two-tier pulpit of the early nineteenth century and some interesting pews survive. The key is kept in Llithfaen.

Pistyll church is a couple of miles short of Nefyn. It seems the more diminutive when contrasted with the large house once known as Goddard's Plate Palace (now a hotel) and the nearby caravan site. It is also dedicated to St Beuno; a pilgrims' church on the Bardsey route. Decked for Christmas with huge branches of evergreen, not prim sprays, and scores of white candles (ingeniously placed, for safety, in cup-cake tin foil) it silently proclaimed the eternal importance of the winter solstice and its marvellous integration in the Christmas festival. This single-cell medieval building is entered through a more or less round-headed door in the severely plain west gable; its only features are the two comparatively recent buttresses and bellcote, in keeping in their plainness. The building may be twelfth century up to the third bay of the arch-braced medieval roof; beyond, fifteenth. Windows are modern. Unfortunately the plaster has been scraped from the walls but this has revealed a sketchy mural. The late twelfth-century font is decorated with a chain pattern.

Nefyn is a sizable village with a holiday atmosphere. Pennant describes how 'Here, Edward I, in 1284, held his triumph on the conquest of Wales; and perhaps to conciliate the affections of his new subjects, in imitation of our hero Arthur, held a round table, and celebrated it with dance and tournament' (see p. 349). Cae Iorwerth (Edward's field) is also known locally as the herring-field on account of its shape. It lies just to the east of the village below Mynydd Nefyn which doubtless made a grandstand for the festivities. Nefyn became a borough at about this time. The toy church (1825) with endearingly comic west tower and most of its original fittings has, alas, long been declared redundant and is in very bad repair. Its weather-vane (a vessel in full sail) has recently been restored; a reminder of the seafaring character of Nefyn's citizens. The only other building of note is a nineteenth-century watch-tower, hard by the public lavatories near the 'new' church in the middle of the village. Nefyn has immense sandy beaches. **Porth Nefyn** is simply a cluster of cottages and boathouses sheltering under the westerly arm of the bay.

Two miles west through Morfa Nefyn (bungalows), sheltering under a big north-thrusting promontory is **Porth Dinllaen**, the only good anchorage sheltered from south-westerlies on the whole coastline. It was here that William Madocks (see p. 192) and later the GWR hoped to establish the harbour for the London–Dublin route. This idea had to give way to Holyhead but Porth Dinllaen was a serious contender: the route was claimed to be thirty miles shorter and it avoided the bridging of both the Menai Straits and the River Conwy. The embankment of Traeth Mawr (see p. 193), which Madocks was soon to achieve, was the only major work of that kind necessary. The straight roads that run ruler-like across Lleyn from the golf club house, branching for Pwllheli and Cricieth two and a half miles south-east at Tan-y-graig, are the work of the Porth Dinllaen Turnpike Trust: the beginning (or end) of the great highway to London. Porth Dinllaen now consists of a pub and a few cottages sheltering under the headland which is crowned by a strategically sited promontory fort. The new town, planned round a vast circus with optimistic disregard for topography, remained on paper only.

The fine coastline to the west of Porth Dinllaen and right down to the spectacular tip of the peninsula, is not much visible from the road. It is well worth exploring and has some sandy bays for keen bathers, but these you cannot hope to have to yourselves in the summer unless they are a long walk from a motor car. Plenty of seals in season.

Beyond Porth Dinllaen are two villages with nice simple little Victorian churches, **Edern** (Richard Coad, 1868), and **Tudweiliog** (Sir Gilbert Scott, 1850).

A little inland from Tudweiliog the Lleyn changes its character completely. Round the skirts of Carn Fadrun, crowned by its camp, are sheltered wooded valleys linked by tiny banked lanes. This odd conical hump, and Carn Boduan to the NE, are strange features in the landscape. In addition to the country's own fascination there are several buildings of interest.

Llandudwen church (274/368) lies down a farm road, two miles to the east. St Tudwen, who was St David's great-aunt, has an enticing approach to her unusual little church. A straight path leads to the door in the west gable which is capped by a bell-cote with a jaunty bell, all slightly off centre. Halfway down the path a massive lychgate (probably eighteenth century) leads into the sheltered churchyard (sycamore and daffodils). The plan is a T with now no chancel. The nave is thought to be a rebuilding on medieval foundations in 1595, the north and south transepts being seventeenth-century additions. There are eighteenth-century benches with backs in the nave and the oil lamps have been converted to gas.

Just below the northerly slopes of Carn Fadrun is the site of **Madryn Castle**, now a static caravan park, well concealed in the woodland. Only the attractive but roofless early seventeenth-century gatehouse survives; in winter the dried heads of buddleia which has seeded itself in the parapet stand exotically against the sky.

(This diversion has taken you some distance inland and you may want to take in Llaniestyn, p. 186, on the south side of the mountain.)

Back on the coast road, B4417, **Mynydd Cefnamwlch** rises steeply on your left. There is a good cromlech in a field below its N slope, and the house of that name with its simple 1607 gatehouse and extensive seventeenth- and eighteenth-century outbuildings is in the woodland opposite.

Penllech Church (220/344) above a farmyard duck-pond with breezy views, is movingly simple and has no architectural pretensions. Its early nineteenth-century furniture survives complete, painted traditional pale mushroom. The key is kept in the farmhouse. To find: turn off towards the sea, two miles south of Tudweiliog.

Llangwnnadl (209/333), one mile south-west, could hardly be a greater contrast, and is a mecca for anyone even remotely interested in churches. It takes one by surprise in a sheltered lane, but still greater is the surprise on entering. Only then is it evident that the church is actually wider than it is long. What appeared to be a small perpendicular building turns out to have three broad aisles separated by airy three-bay arcades. That to the north was added to the medieval structure in 1520 (dated) and the south about ten years later. Windows in the north wall date from Henry Kennedy's sensitive restoration of 1850. The inscriptions on the arcade pier record the erection of this aisle over the burial place of the patron saint,

St Gwynhoydl. The east windows are all contemporary (compare with Llanengan and Carnguwch). The octagonal font with its unusual carvings probably dates from the 1520 restoration. A lovely relaxed building, and the last church on the north side of the peninsula which has now tapered to barely five miles across.

The rocky coast with occasional little bays continues SW. **Porth Oer** is famous for its whistling sands which squeak when you run over them (tiny quartz granules rub together); similar sands occur on Eigg in the Hebrides.

The unclassified road skirts Mynydd Anelog and Mynydd Mawr, eventually climbing to the tip of the peninsula. Scattered farms spatter the headland and two hamlets with their chapels lie on the more gentle southerly slopes. The north and west are sheer and desolate. Fortunately this magnificent coastline has been given to the National Trust. Those who cannot walk far will find the road leading up to the coastguard look-out very helpful. Choughs near the car park seem remarkably unconcerned by human visitors. Braich-y-pwll is perhaps the most spectacular of the cliffs but the whole of this headland is splendid and gives tantalizing views of Bardsey. Scarcely anything survives of St Mary's Church, right out on the promontory, a seafarers' shrine used by pilgrims who could not make the crossing by reason of wind and weather. Near it is a spring. There are, surprisingly, no spectacular remains of Neolithic or Iron Age man on the headland as there are on St Davids Head or on Holy Island, Anglesey. Hut ruins survive on Mynydd Anelog (150/276) one and a half miles to the north and, to the east of Aberdaron, Castell Odo (187/284) probably dates from the fourth century BC. But this remote land's end or landfall, whichever way you take it, is today much as it was 5000 years ago and, like all coastal scenes, is made perfect by an island in place of an empty horizon.

BARDSEY ISLAND (YNYS ENLLI)

Bardsey Sound is narrow and often furious. Ynys Enlli means Island of the Current, and the wrong mixture of wind, current and tide can be very awkward indeed even in relatively calm weather. The crossing is from Aberdaron, about five miles, and even now, with modern engines, boats can be held up for several days. The first Christian settlers are recorded in the early seventh century when in 615 the surviving monks of Bangor Is-coed (see p. 74) came to found the monastery. It remained Celtic, unattached to any monastic order of the Church of Rome, at least until the end of the twelfth century. Little remains now of the Abbey except the stump of the thirteenth-century tower, but whether or not 20,000 saints are buried here the island does indeed seem to be a holy place. Pennant's boatmen evidently felt so 'for they had not rowed far, before they made a full stop, pulled off their hats, and offered up a short prayer'. And one may still feel as they did, particularly on those summer evenings as the sun disappears below a cloudless horizon and the blades of the lighthouse beam take over, scything the sea and the small fields and withy beds below the banked road which links the farms strung along the western skirt of the mountain. Mynydd Enlli (heather and gorse and rock) drops straight down into the Sound shielding the farms from the east. Shearwaters burrow near the summit and storm petrels nest in the crevices of its rock.

It would be hard to design an island of more satisfactory form and shape. The anchorage is sheltered by the isthmus which links the main northerly part of the island and the short springy turf of its south tail. Here the lighthouse stands among the thrift and oyster catchers and mushrooms. It first shone on Christmas Eve 1821, a 'handsome square structure' designed by Joseph Nelson. The lantern was renewed in 1856 and additions were made in 1909.

In the sixteenth century the island was said to be a nest of pirates. Samuel Lewis records 84 inhabitants on Bardsey in 1833. In 1955 there were thirteen, excluding the migrant population of the bird observatory which was then being set up. The observatory now uses the old school and has one of the farms on the island. The island has recently been sold by Lord Newborough and its future is not known. It was the Lord Newborough of the 1870s who rebuilt the farms: most are in semi-detached pairs sharing yards. These have huge walls for shelter from the gales. The houses are not interesting but the yards have great character: big arched entrances like fortresses; immense slate slabs for partitions in the sties (presumably from the Newborough quarries at Blaenau Ffestiniog), and tiny cobbles. The inhabitants made a living from fishing and farming the very windswept but fertile land.

SOUTH-WEST LLEYN: ABERDARON TO LLANBEDROG BY UNCLASSIFIED ROADS

Aberdaron was the last place of rest for the pilgrims. St Hywyn, who first worked on Bardsey, no doubt founded his church with this in mind. It is believed to date from about the same time as the founding of the island monastery, say 600, and was soon to become an important *clas* church.

Here the people gathered in the austere building above the great shingly bay waiting for the wind and tide to allow a safe crossing. One imagines them crowding in for warmth and shelter as the westerly gales tore through the sound. The only opening in the unrelenting masonry of the twin westerly gables is the simple late Norman doorway: it conveys the sense of refuge and sanctuary which the church gave not only to those seeking their Creator but to others fleeing to Ireland. Gruffydd ap Rhys ap Tewdwr, escaping the soldiers of Henry I, was one such. Inside the church seems huge by contrast; two simple barns linked by an airy five-bayed arcade. The north aisle is twelfth-century with a fourteenth-century addition to the east; the south was added in the sixteenth.

In 1841 the church was abandoned on the grounds that a new seawall, which was essential to prevent it being washed away, would cost more than a new building. John Welch's ungainly romanesque barn (behind the attractive purple-slate-hung rectory above the village) which replaced it caused an outcry. *Archaeologia Cambrensis* described it as of 'the most atrociously barbarous and even ludicrous design', and it was also inconveniently sited. In 1860, Henry Kennedy, who must have known the tip of Lleyn through his expeditions to supervise Llangwnnadl, took on the restoration of the old parish church and Welch's edifice was abandoned. If it is demolished its (original) furniture could be used elsewhere.

The village is snug in the hollow: stone cottages and pubs; a post-office by Clough Williams-Ellis; pebble-dashed cottages made perky by white plaster trim. **Y gegin fawr** is said to get its name from a communal kitchen for the pilgrims but the present building is seventeenth century; a nicely carved slate tablet commemorates the Coronation of 1953.

Turning back eastwards an unclassified road runs within a mile of the sea to Rhiw. **Bodwrda** stands to your left a mile from Aberdaron. This sturdy mansion house was given a new N front in the early seventeenth century when projecting wings were added unexpectedly in brick; its mullioned windows also date from this renovation. The coast between Aberdaron Bay and the aptly named Hell's Mouth (Porth Neigwl) is particularly beautiful and less fierce than the north. Puffins breed on the rocky islands offshore and flowers carpet the cliffs. Fortunately, thanks to the generosity of the Misses Keating, some of the best of this coast now belongs to the National Trust including that immediately south of **Llanfaelrhys Church** (210/268) which has a lovely site only a couple of fields from the sea. This is a long, narrow medieval building to which a chancel has been added, making it even longer. Recent windows are modestly domestic and the door has been charmingly grained in brown paint, metal key-hole guard along with the timber. Box pews survive and summer services are held. It is well worth walking down to the farm and on to the beach near the waterfall.

Plas-yn-Rhiw (National Trust) is a mecca for all who love this part of Lleyn for this is where the famous Misses Keating live. It stands high above the road overlooking the sea beyond the scattered hamlet of Rhiw. This small stone house of about 1634 was enlarged in the early eighteenth century and the whole thoroughly modernized in Regency times when it was given its pleasant shallow-pitched roof and verandah. It is a house of immense charm with a wonderful setting overlooking the whole sweep of Cardigan Bay to Cadair Idris, its garden dropping in a series of little terraces down the hillside below. It is the kind of almost wild garden that could only be created and cared for by the same minds and this has been its good fortune. Discovered abandoned by the widowed Mrs Keating and her three daughters between the wars, it verges magically on the brink of sweet disorder never becoming jungle. You enter through a fuchsia cavern; old-fashioned roses are pruned back just before they run riot; snowdrops have seeded themselves and carpet the woods in true drifts. This mild, dreamlike paradise is knit together by sheltering trees and is lapped by the sound of falling water and the sea.

Above, the land rises steeply to the windy tops of Mynydd Rhiw and its scattered village, **Rhiw**. St Aelrhiw's Church stands by a stone farm. This eighteenth-century building has an unusual plan, rather like an early aeroplane with big square wings (the transepts) and a very short nave and almost no chancel. The congregation are thus concentrated near the altar.

Back on the coast road just inland of Hell's Mouth, bear L at the Junction (towards Botwnnog), if you have time for John Welch's most engaging toy church of **Llandegwning** (1840), with its comic west turret (with slate sundial) and spire. Inside all is painted white (even the tiled floor) except for the box pews which are beautifully grained in green. There is a gothicky communion rail and a fine 1721 tablet to Jane Jones.

Returning to the junction, make for Abersoch. Llangian is the well-cared-for stone village, two miles on; the church is relatively dull, but a detour to **Llanengan**, one and a half miles south again, is well worth making since the church here is one of the finest in Lleyn (it is at present being restored). The earlier church was rebuilt and enlarged with a new south aisle 1520–30, and the tower was added in 1534. It has a graceful nave arcade and fine screens, the loft surviving over that to the south aisle. The roofs are contemporary and have sturdy open trusses. The font (fifteenth or early sixteenth century) is octagonal, decorated with quatrefoils and rosettes. The high land above the village was once worked for lead; some of the tall chimneys survive. It runs on to Mynydd Cilan, the easterly jaw of Hell's Mouth. **St Tudwal's Islands**, now uninhabited except for the lighthouse on the westerly island, lie off the eastern headland. St Tudwal himself probably lived in the sixth century but there is no evidence of a settlement of that time. Excavations, 1959–61, revealed an ecclesiastical settlement dating from the thirteenth and fourteenth centuries which included a hall on the E island where there is a spring. After being deserted for many years it was occupied again in the late nineteenth century when an attempt was made to establish a monastery.

The islands help to shelter St Tudwal's Road from the south and it has long been an important anchorage. **Abersoch,** a popular holiday village knit well into the mouth of its little estuary, is in some danger of spilling out and altering its character. At present it retains its Betjemanesque-Cornish-holiday character: white seaside houses, pine trees and sand in the sandwiches. It is popular with dinghy sailors and holiday yachtsmen.

Llanbedrog, half-way between Abersoch and Pwllheli on A499, is divided by the main road: holiday houses in the sheltered wooded lee of the headland, pebbly beach, and a windier working village above with several chapels. **Rehoboth,** 1871, is particularly attractive: small with Gothic windows lovingly detailed; yellow stone with grey stone dressings; hard mortar trim to the verges with pebble-dash between; the west end has a round window with petal-like glazing. The Parish Church juts out from the wooded hillside above the sea, so it has an exceptionally tall east end. This sixteenth-century chancel was added to a medieval nave. It has a sturdy, heavily-varnished screen. The ruined tower on the hill above the village is that of an old mill: a good landmark now owned by the National Trust.

Here B4413, the main Aberdaron road (see p. 183) joins A499 which continues by the coast to Pwllheli.

ABERDARON EASTWARD ON B4413, B4415 AND A497 TO PWLLHELI

This is the best road from Aberdaron for those who do not want to explore the coast; many tempting lanes lead off it, and there are few proper villages. **Sarn** is an attractive exception, its buildings knit together by its deep valley setting. Those on the hillside include a pub with INN painted in white right across its roof and a brilliant yellow ochre chapel with black trim.

A diversion north can be made here for **Llaniestyn Church,** another double-naved building in which the thirteenth-century lancets of the original have been reproduced in the sixteenth-century addition; it has a nice font of that date and good memorial tablets.

Back on B4413 and half a mile beyond its junction with B4415, look out on the right for the sign for **Capel Newydd** which, despite its name, is the oldest surviving nonconformist chapel in North Wales. It lies up a green lane and the key is kept in the twin-gabled house on the corner. It is a simple domestic-seeming building, built in 1769 by the Congregationalists who had broken away from those at Pwllheli; movement of population caused its use to cease in 1872. It was carefully restored, 1956, by T. Alwyn Lloyd and Gordon, and M. T. Pritchard, and retains its mud floor (like green velvet), box pews with raised wood floors, candelabra and coat pegs. Originally the door was central, where the pulpit now stands, but the present modifications to the plan were made early.

Mrs Edwards of Nanhoron joined the Congregationalists here after her husband's death, an unusual step for the gentry. Her house, now Regency, with low-pitched slate roof and verandah, is seen from the unclassified road to the east in sheltered parkland remote from south-westerly gales. Nant, 1877, is an upstanding well-cared for chapel, with rich brown paint on its ironwork. Not special within.

B4415 follows the wooded valley of the Horon and joins A497, the Pwllheli–Nefyn road, which cuts across the peninsula. Half-way to Boduan it passes **Bodfel Hall**, a tall seventeenth-century house, built as a gate-house. Its doorway is flanked by Doric columns. Originally home of the Gwynne (Bodvel) family, which produced two recusant priests, it was, in 1741, the birthplace of Hester Lynch Salusbury (Mrs Thrale). **Boduan** has an extraordinary great Romanesque church of 1894 by H. Kennedy and P. S. Gregory, cruciform, with central tower, and an impressive interior. An odd thing to find in Lleyn. It replaced a church of 1765, from which elegant monuments to the Wynns of Boduan Hall survive.

Pwllheli is a proper town and was possibly created a borough by one of the Welsh princes following the Anglo-Norman pattern. It is, perhaps, now at its best in winter on market day (Wednesday; cattle market, Monday) when its un-precious High Street is thronged with Lleyn shoppers.

The town is divided, old from new, snug from breezy, by the railway, and it is greatly to be hoped that both the service and the pleasant timber and iron, GWR cream and brown, railway station will survive. The line was constructed on land reclaimed from the large natural harbour, hence the name Penlan (head of the shore), on a street now stranded inland. Extensive reclamation was also made in 1811. In the High

Street (which has a Woolworths) David Williams, Men's Outfitters, with the life-like sheep suspended over the door, was established in 1841 by a farming family from Pwlldefaid (the sheep's pool). It was then a drapers-cum-grocery selling shawls, merinos, sugar, treacle, toffee from Liverpool, and tea from London. A few good well-lettered glass fascias survive like that of Cornelius Roberts, Butcher (near the car park). The Georgian Market Hall has been sensibly turned into a shopping arcade and the shiny red Edwardian edifice which has taken its place near the old Penlan public house in Penlan Street bills a variety of functions – *The Creation*, a *cofi* morning and *The Yeomen of the Guard* – (February 1972). Perhaps Pwllheli's most attractive building is **Penlan Chapel**, 1863, in Gaol Street. It is set up a flight of steps, pedimented, cream and mushroom, behind an iron railing with a graceful weeping ash.

A ride in the horse-drawn tram, with open toast-rack wagons, from the railway station to the bay-windowed stuccoed terraces out on the dunes, once crowned the excitement of arriving for a holiday at Pwllheli. These, with the rather less grand yellow-brick terraces not quite on the front, made Victorian/Edwardian Pwllheli. Little has been added except the dull council houses, the Gorsedd circle and the attractive holiday houses, zigzag in plan, near the yacht club. The harbour, large and tidal, is well sheltered. Some residents still remember the excitement when a grand pyrotechnic display was to be launched from the small island in the middle to celebrate the Coronation of King George V. Alas! the fireworks were damp.

At the east end of the town there is a pleasant whitewashed stone factory, but the first building of note is **Penmount Methodist Chapel**, 1781, but considerably altered in the last century. A big pale stucco building is grouped with its two vestries and two terraces of good plain stone cottages to form a private courtyard with brick stable-paviors and cobbles. It is worth going inside to admire the spacious galleried chapel; good nineteenth-century joinery in the balcony front (arcaded pattern) and the front of the big pew. The pulpit has a particularly nice curving stair. When the Chapel was redecorated in 1967, the ladies raised a further £60 for the completion of the gold work of the very decorative plastered ceiling. The sea once came right up to the east end of the chapel (where the organ extension now stands).

EAST OF PWLLHELI AND NORTH FROM A497

Abererch, just off the main road two miles east of Pwllheli, is a proper village with a double-naved medieval church. Arched roof trusses are supported on big corbels. Sixteenth-century stalls survive and there is a medieval cross-slab in the chancel floor.

One mile N of A497 **Pennarth Fawr**, a handsome fifteenth-century hall house whose seventeenth-century alterations include generous windows and grand fireplaces, stands in its own green-walled enclosure close to a comfortable farmyard at 420/377 (D. o. E.).

The other place thoroughly worth the trouble of seeking out is St Cybi's Well at Llangybi, a little over two miles N as the crow flies, but considerably further as the lanes wind.

On the way you may like to take in **Llanarmon Church**, which lies across B4354. It is twin-aisled with an attractive arcade, c. 1500, but not a must. You can also make a diversion one mile NW to **Plas Du** (412/403), a small early sixteenth-century house which was the home of the recusant Owen family. Hugh Owen was involved in the Ridolfi and Gunpowder Plots. He disinherited his Protestant nephew, John, the most famous member of the family, because his works had been put on the Index. John Owen (c. 1564–1628), Fellow of New College and later Headmaster of Warwick School, wrote Latin epigrams which achieved a European reputation. He called himself 'Cambro-Britannus'.

Leave the house to your left and bear R at the next junction for Llangybi. **St Cybi's Well** (Ffynnon Gybi) is reached by the path behind the church (medieval, restored 1879 and locked). It leads to an enchanting valley where a causeway crosses a reedy field to what seems to be a ruined cottage, snug below the ash and beech-clad hillside. This ancient well became an eighteenth-century spa thanks to the enterprise of William Price Esq. of Rhiwlas. He added a caretaker's room (or dressing-room) to the two dateless well chambers. The main chamber is constructed of huge blocks of stone and has walls four feet thick. The roofs (gone) were intended to be vaulted.

The satisfactory **Alms-houses** in the village were built in 1760 by the same benefactor (refaced in the nineteenth century); their windows are ingeniously arranged.

You can now return to the straight B4354, which is part of the turnpike constructed for the Irish traffic in the days when Porthdinllaen's hopes were high in that respect, and so to Llanystumdwy. If, however, you go straight back to A497 from Pennarth Fawr you will shortly pass the huge **Butlin's Camp** which provides happy holidays for thousands, while considerably reducing pressure on the roads, since it is not only served by its own railway station but also provides lavish entertainment within its perimeter. It has an interesting history. Shortly after the fall of France in 1940 the Admiralty found itself in urgent need of training camps in safe areas. Butlin's already had a site earmarked and standard plans ready for a holiday camp up here. They were asked to rush it up for the Admiralty (no planning permission of course was necessary), the understanding being that Butlin's would run it after the war. Peace brought problems. Local amenity societies were hotly against such a plan and an Inquiry was held. Clough Williams-Ellis, who was both chairman of the Council for the Preservation of Rural Wales and Planning Consultant to the County Council, was asked to give evidence. When asked by the Inspector whether he was representing both bodies he replied 'Strictly speaking I would rather say that I am *mis*representing them. I myself flatly disagree with their attitudes, and am one hundred per cent in favour of the camp'. He went on to explain exactly why and won the day for Butlin's.

Y Lôn Goed (or Ffordd Môn, a corruption of its builder's name) is a most astonishing feature to find in Lleyn. This curious 4½ mile long road, in places still a beautiful tree-lined avenue, was constructed by John Maughan, a Northumbrian, soon after he became agent to the Talhenbont estate in 1817. Its object was to link various farms. It starts just beyond Pontffriddlwyd (439/376), half a mile E of Butlin's, and runs N to Hendre Cenin (459/438).

Llanystumdwy, where a fine, mainly eighteenth-century bridge takes the main road over the Dwyfor, is renowned as the early home of Lloyd George (a plain terrace cottage). Lloyd George (1863–1945) was born in Manchester but brought up here by his uncle, Richard Lloyd, since his father died when he was two. In 1890 he became Liberal MP for Carnarvon Boroughs and in 1908 Chancellor of the Exchequer, when he was responsible for the Old Age Pension Act, something for which he was never forgotten, even though others like Hitler were to remember him as 'the prime minister who won the [1914] war'. He was one of the great orators of the century and was deeply loved and hated. Mention of this controversial character will add heat to any conversation in Wales, either a warm glow or sudden fireworks. The mossy stones of his memorial (by Clough Williams-Ellis) stand above the little river not far from the Lloyd George Museum. Llanystumdwy is the birthplace of the famous self-taught Robert Jones, Rhoslan (1745–1829), who did so much for education in North Wales as well as for religion and literature.

Cricieth is a small Victorian resort of great character grafted on to a medieval town of considerable importance, which became an English borough under Edward I. The castle crowns a short headland. It is a rarity, having been built by the thirteenth-century princes of Gwynedd, and not greatly altered by Edward I who had his usual small garrison here (thirty men including the chaplain). The inner gate-house is now its most upstanding ruin; two big rounded towers guard a narrow gate on the landward side of the inner ward (c. 1230) round which outer defences were later wrapped. Shut your eyes up here, even on a comparatively calm day, and listen to the surf crashing on the breakwater below. Cricieth later fell to Owen Glendower but he does not seem to have occupied it.

The Green slopes uphill and is bordered by pleasant houses and cottages (now rendered) which become smaller in scale and cosy towards the top. Cricieth Fair, held here on St Peter's Day (June 29th), is particularly strong in clothes and cloth. St Catherine's Church off the Green is double-naved (probably c. 1300 and c. 1500); it has late medieval-type roof trusses and late-eighteenth-century communion rails have survived the 1870 restoration. St Deiniol's (1887–9) is by John Douglas (its tower was never built). Eglwys Seion is a grand chapel in Mona Terrace; elaborate and pale blue stuccoed. Wellington Terrace, of sturdy stone cottages with gabled dormers, is probably typical of Cricieth before it got its seaside Victorian charm. Capel Uchaf, 1791, a Baptist Chapel with steps leading down to the stream, has its early-mid-nineteenth-century pews and fittings.

East of Cricieth, the lonely little church of **Ynyscynhaearn** stands on the edge of the marsh at 526/388. It is of 1830, with its fittings almost intact: three-decker pulpit, and box pews and benches painted with family and house names. The harpist David Owen (1712–41), better known as Dafydd y Garreg Wen (David of the White Rock), composer of the lovely song of that name and of others including *Codiad yr Ehedydd* (*The Rising of the Lark*), is buried here.

The sands at Black Rock on the coast one mile south are particularly prized by bathers. **Morfa Bychan** is a popular holiday place (the dunes here were the scene of the Tremadoc Races; see below) and, at the mouth of the estuary, **Ynys Cyngar** is the tiny anchorage which was the harbour for Tremadoc before Portmadoc had been created.

Inland, A497 passes **Wern**, a rebuilding by John Douglas (1892) for R. M. Greaves, owner of the Llechwedd Quarries (p. 232) and now an Old People's Home. T. H. Mawson designed the gardens. **Penmorfa Church**, restored by Douglas (1899), is immediately north. It has a monument to Sir John Owen of Clenennau, c. 1666 (see p. 169), by Robert Wynne of Ruthin.

Penmorfa means head of the marsh, and so it was until three successive embankments built by William Madocks (1773–1828) transformed the region. Madocks was a younger son of a Vale of Clwyd/London family, with little inheritance but all the expensive instincts of the eighteenth-century improver and the early nineteenth-century romantic. He bought a small property of poor land on the edge of the marsh here in 1797. First he enclosed a small tract on which he built the model town of **Tremadoc** (1805–12); this was to be a coaching town on his proposed London–Dublin route (note the street names); packets were to sail from Porth Dinllaen (p. 179). The well-proportioned Square, with the handsome little market hall and hotel, gains immeasurably by its siting under the huge crag, once the edge of the estuary. The lower part of the arcaded market hall (1809) was used as an auditorium during Tremadoc's theatrical season; the proscenium arch (blocked) can be seen in the end wall, the adjacent cottage

'he ancient St. Cybi's Well at
.langybi in Lleyn: the main
hamber is constructed from
uge blocks of undressed
tone, as often in North Wales.

A typical slate headstone:
his one is in the churchyard
f Llangristiolus, Anglesey.

Menai Bridge, built by Telford in 1818-26, was the world's first big iron suspension bridge. The wrought iron was replaced by steel in 1938.

being the stage. The room above was used for dances. (Note the Cambrian Pill Depot's nice nineteenth-century sign opposite.)

Tanyrallt, the charming small verandahed Regency house looking out from the trees above the town, is the cottage which Madocks converted for himself (the beginning of this style in N Wales). This is the house which Shelley rented when fired with the idea of saving the great embankment (below), and where the strange incident of his 'attempted murder' took place. Madocks's big woollen factory and mill are just below.

The church (less successful) was one of the first Gothic revival churches in Wales. **Capel Peniel**, opposite, is remarkable in all respects. The cheerful naiveté of its portico, and dramatic character of its interior (it has been mistaken for the theatre) are as unusual as its history. At that period it was very rare for a member of the land-owning gentry to take an interest in non-conformism, but Madocks, a churchman, encouraged all denominations. Religious toleration, freedom in education and parliamentary reform were among the causes espoused by this radical MP (for Boston, Lincs), but the great physical landmark he left was the huge embankment nearly a mile long across **Traeth Mawr** (which now carries the A497; toll 2½p). This great enterprise had daunted both professionals and rich men since the seventeenth century when Sir Hugh Myddelton (famed for London's New River) had declined Sir John Wynn of Gwydir's (page 123) invitation to propose a scheme. Madocks, already encumbered by debt and without an engineer, but supported by his wonderful agent, John Williams (who had previously been a garden boy at Plas Newydd, Anglesey), embarked on the Cob (Welsh for Embankment) in 1808. It was not finished until 1811. In 1812 a winter gale breached it but the gap was eventually closed by almost superhuman efforts. However Madocks was reduced to dire poverty and the great land reclamation scheme he planned was never carried out. In 1817 his prospects brightened. He married Eliza Gwynne, a rich young widow from Tregunter, Breconshire (now demolished). Although her estates were entailed he was able to live in comfort. New plans poured forth. They resulted in **Portmadoc** (Porthmadog) and the Festiniog Railway (one of the first in Britain) although his death in 1828 meant that Madocks had little personal hand in either.

The Port Madoc Harbour Act was passed in 1824. The harbour, which was a direct result of the diversion of the river Glaslyn through sluices built at Ynys Towyn, meant that this remote part of Wales was at last to have an outlet for its goods, chiefly slate from the new quarries at Blaenau Ffestiniog, with which it was soon connected by the railway. Rival quarrying and railway speculators (including the banker Nathan Meyer Rothschild) and their surveyors descended on the country in the 1820s, cheered on by Madocks, too sick himself to take an active part. The **Festiniog Railway** at last opened in 1836 and had a tremendous effect on the prosperity of the area. Originally the empty slate trucks were drawn up by horses and returned laden by gravity, the horses having a ride in the end truck. Steam engines were introduced in 1863.

The recent revival of the Festiniog Railway to carry passengers instead of slate has been such a success that it can no longer be run by amateurs, but the present professionals are all enthusiasts. Trains run from the Harbour Station. It is a lovely journey of about two hours up and down which includes time to stretch your legs at Dduallt, the present terminus (inaccessible by road). Work goes on to reconstruct the line, which was destroyed by a hydro-electric scheme, to Blaenau Ffestiniog. There is also a footpath across the Cob to Boston Lodge (see p. 236) – a very pleasant evening's walk with grand views, remote from the traffic which grinds across it below. The small cairn in the middle of the Cob was built in 1973 to mark William Madocks' bicentenary.

Most traces of Portmadoc's heyday, when the harbour was a forest of masts of the vessels engaged in the slate trade, have vanished. Ballast Island, just outside the mouth, is formed of stone from all parts of the world brought as ballast in the homebound ships. One quay has been developed with housing which achieves a certain port feel (close, and with plenty of hard surfaces instead of the too usual dejected grass). The town is a bustling friendly place; mostly stone and stucco with numerous chapels, it climbs from the flat reclaimed land up the slopes of Moel y Gest. Despite some modern horrors evidence of nineteenth-century prosperity survives in some shop fronts: for instance in the grandly lettered LONDON TEA WAREHOUSE and BEE-HIVE ESTABLISHMENT in Lombard Street.

CHAPTER EIGHT

Anglesey

The Isle of Anglesey is separated from Caernarfonshire by the Menai Straits, a lovely sinuous arm of the sea which seems more like a tidal river in its wooded middle reaches. For centuries it was a means of communication as well as a barrier. Until recent years five ferries plied across; Caernarfon (now twenty miles away by road) was the principal town for the south-west of the island and, until the building of the Holyhead Road and the new route to Ireland in the early nineteenth century, Beaumaris, now a charming backwater, was the chief port, at the main crossing for traffic from Chester and London.

Sea communications are the key to the island's development so most of the building works and monuments of interest are near the coast. In Neolithic times, through the Iron Age and the Age of Saints, when Ireland was an important centre of Western civilization, Anglesey was close to that hub. The wealth of cromlechs and promontory forts reflect this as do the numerous churches dedicated to Celtic saints, remote from any settlement.

The coastline is immensely varied and beautiful and, where accessible, understandably popular. It is most easily reached from the main road which rings the island and often touches the sea in its circuit. Recent development has made this drive dispiriting to say the least; modern housing and 'improvement' are the main offenders. Short cuts across Anglesey on the close network of lanes are slow and frustrating if arrival somewhere is the object. If, however, your aim is to travel hopefully, this is the island's heart; miles of tiny fields enclosed by turf banks; brown reedy bogs flecked by cotton grass; outcropping rock; blazing gorse; few trees. Occasionally you may come across a small lime-washed cottage with a slurried roof (a mixture of lime and sand spread on top of the small slates to prevent them

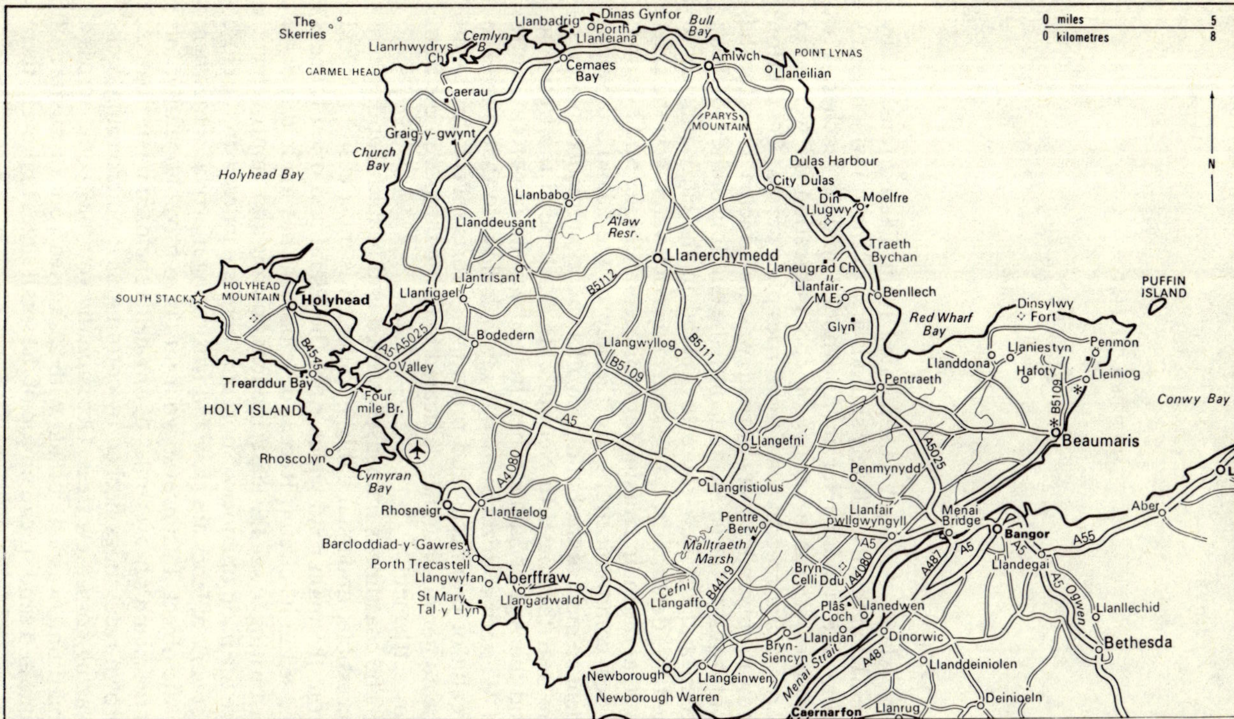

Continued on Chapter 5 map

Continued on Chapter 6 map

being blown away) which has survived improvement. Until 1939 they were everywhere (also in Lleyn and Pembrokeshire). On clear days the flattish foreground is backed by the dramatic backcloth of Snowdonia, ever changing in the shifting light. The country is now pastoral but Anglesey's corn was once vital to the hungry mountain interior. Edward I starved Llywelyn's army out of Snowdonia by cutting off this supply, thus finally subduing the Welsh.

Everyone coming by road to the island must cross Telford's splendid suspension bridge (1826), the most difficult feat in the great Holyhead Road scheme which he had engineered to link Dublin and London. It was the world's first big iron suspension bridge (span 500 ft) and made pioneer use of wrought iron, replaced by steel in 1938. The first petition to Parliament for a bridge here had been made in 1785 but each attempt had met with strong opposition both from those who feared loss of trade locally and on account of the interference it might cause with navigation in the Straits. Both John Rennie and later Telford, when he was working on his Holyhead Road Survey, produced designs for cast-iron arched bridges, but these did not satisfy the Admiralty and money was short because of the war. Eventually, in 1818, the Commissioners saw Telford's designs for the huge Runcorn suspension bridge (which was never built) and asked him to design a similar bridge for Menai. Work got under way but even the piers were a vast job. In 1820 the masonry contractors threw in their hand and John Wilson, who was supervising work on the Gotha Canal for Telford, was recalled to supervise the masonry. In 1823 it reached road level and tunnels were blasted in the rock to take the suspension chains which were anchored on enormous cast iron frames. Their design and checking was a huge task which gave Telford many sleepless nights. The chains were finally treated with linseed oil (not boiled in wine, as Lewis Carroll's White Knight claimed to have specified).

At last they were ready. 26 April 1825 dawned fine and still. The Straits were closed to shipping but thronged with boatloads of spectators and their banks dark with sightseers. The first chain lay on a raft 450 feet long, moored to the Caernarfon shore. This unwieldy craft had to be manoeuvred across the Straits (beset by currents on the calmest day) and moored while the chain was slowly hoisted to the top of the Anglesey pier to be linked to the land chain which ended there. There was dead silence among the vast crowd as the raft moved across. The men working the capstans then went into action accompanied by a fife band. The chain began to rise in a low arc over the water and a huge cheer rose from the waiting crowds. Telford and Provis, his resident engineer, were waiting on top to drive home the pin fixing the last link (two hours twenty minutes after the raft had cast off). The engineers, tiny figures on the huge structure, raised their hats as a signal that all was secure and a yet mightier cheer echoed through the Straits, the capstan's crews were liberally refreshed with *cwrw da* (good ale) and three of them celebrated by running across the curving nine-inch wide chain which they had just hoisted, to the Caernarfon shore. The bridge was open to traffic on a wild wet night the following January. Next day there was a jam of coaches, carriages, gigs and traps waiting to cross. There is every likelihood of a jam when you make the crossing if you choose a busy holiday period. The long queues may give ample time to enjoy its fine lines, and laybys up A5 allow good distant views but particularly dramatic is that from the by-road near water level in Menai Bridge town.

Telford's road, now the A5, goes straight as a die across to Holyhead and the Irish boat ferry (see p. 213). But before following this, or the ring road, the east corner of the island is well worth exploring. If you are to spend only half a day on the island and like buildings, aim for Beaumaris and Penmon.

A545 MENAI BRIDGE, BEAUMARIS AND PENMON

Turn right off A5 on to A545 in **Menai Bridge**. This unpretentious small Victorian town has a fascinating **Museum of Childhood** in Water Street. It is crammed with nostalgic delight and its musical boxes and early gramophones may be worked specially by the proprietor, Mr Robert Brown, to whom enquiries about winter opening should be made. Another family of Browns runs the Tregfryn Gallery (at the Beaumaris end of the town) which shows N. Wales's painters including Kyffin Williams, the pride of the island and far beyond. His recent autobiography *Across the Straits* gives a spirited picture of

Anglesey life. See local announcements for steamer trips from the pier and the October fair.

A superb solitary *meinhir* stands in a field near the Llandegfan road a mile north of Menai Bridge at 553/740, off A5025. It commands a most dramatic view of Snowdonia and is particularly worth the diversion from your route on a day of shifting light and cloud shadows.

The Beaumaris road was made in the 1820s to link the new bridge with the main town, Beaumaris. It still has something of a carriage drive character. Big Victorian houses were built on the choice sites that were suddenly accessible along the Straits. The most conspicuous is Rhianfa, a François Premier château built c. 1850 by two daughters of Sir John Hay Williams of Bodelwyddan. Their architect was Charles Reed (Verelst), but they helped to design it, and painted the ceilings. Unexpected trees and shrubs thrive in these gardens as elsewhere along the sheltered straits.

Beaumaris was built and settled by Edward I following his conquest of Wales. It was the chief town in Anglesey until the building of the nineteenth-century bridges, and an important port. It still feels English with its urbane terraces and sea-side-Brighton air, but there is nothing grandiose about this little town which has a relaxed charm all its own and a setting which might be the envy of any English resort.

The **Castle**, begun 1295, is on flat land at the E of the town. This site robs it of the drama of other Welsh castles built by Master James of St George, but Beaumaris is the one of which he may have been most proud. The flat site allowed him to design one of the most perfectly planned concentric castles in Europe, and a lifetime's experience of castle building has gone into it. The plan is most easily appreciated in an aerial view (see picture postcards). It is very simple and almost symmetrical: the wall guarding the square inner bailey is protected by N and S gatehouses and six towers. A great hall survives right across the N gatehouse and a delightful little vaulted chapel is built into the E tower. The outer bailey is enclosed by an octagonal curtain wall, crossfire from whose turrets covers every inch of the curtain. The moat, which still holds water, was originally connected to the sea, and the castle had its own dock and mill. Although the building was never finished (hence its rather stunted appearance), the stonework

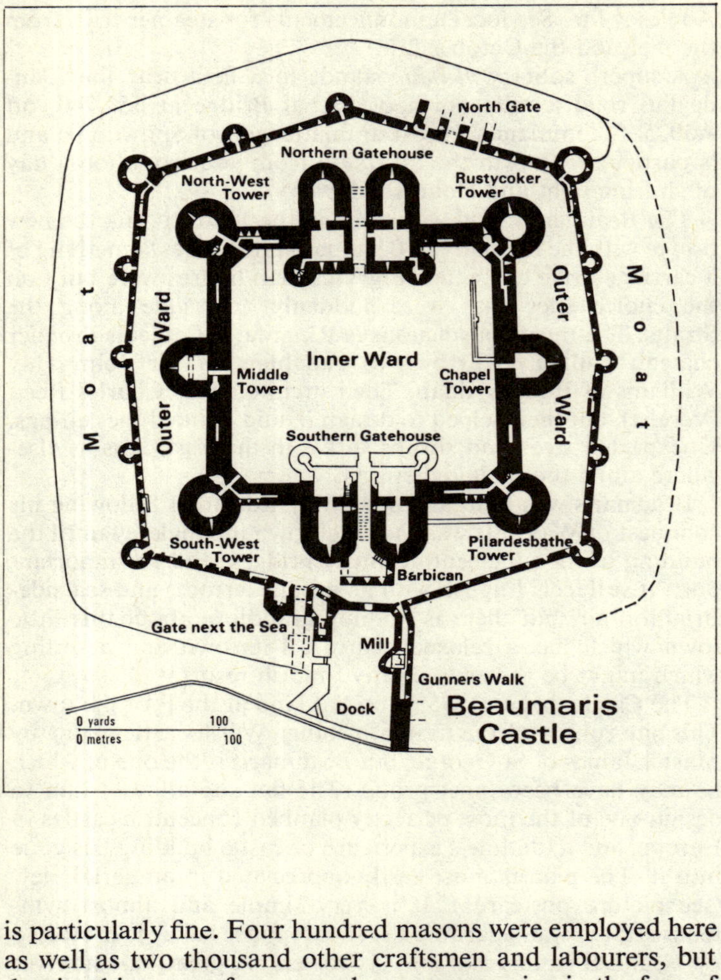

is particularly fine. Four hundred masons were employed here as well as two thousand other craftsmen and labourers, but despite this army of men, work was progressing in the face of considerable difficulties. A letter from James of St George to the Barons of the Exchequer written at Conwy on 27 February 1296 ends 'As to how things are in the land of Wales, we still cannot be any too sure. But as you well know, Welshmen are Welshmen, and you need to understand them properly; if, which God forbid, there is a war with France and Scotland, we shall need to watch them all the more closely . . . P.S. And, Sirs, for God's sake be quick with the money for the work, as much as ever our lord the king wills: otherwise everything done till now will have been of no avail.' With Caernarfon, Beaumaris was to control the Straits and thus the corn supply of any future prince in the stronghold of Snowdonia.

The **Court House** opposite the castle dates from 1614. The hammer-beam roof in the Court Room is original and many of the fittings were nicely reconstructed in the early nineteenth century when the Gothic windows were fitted and the three-sided bay added to the Grand Jury Room. The island's social life revolved round Beaumaris and the gentry had their town houses here. Many, like the Liverpool Arms Hotel (c. 1700), were refaced in the early nineteenth century when the town took on its new life as an attractive resort, doubtless encouraged by the steam paddle-boats from Merseyside. It was at this period (1835) that the Bulkeley Arms and Victoria Terrace, a grand classical block, both designed by Hansom and Welch, took pride of place next to Edge of Green Terrace (John Hall of Bangor, 1834–5). Hansom and Welch also designed the Gaol (1829; open on application at the Council offices) in Steeple Street. Hansom is better known for the cab named after him and as first editor of *The Builder*.

The early fourteenth-century **Parish Church** was one of the first buildings in the new town. Around 1500 the chancel was added and aisle walls raised and battlemented, their E windows being added soon after. Bench ends and misericords survive from that date. The N clerestory is c. 1600. G. F. Bodley restored the church in 1902. The fine alabaster fifteenth-century Bulkeley altar tomb came from Llanfaes Friary (see also that in Penmynydd church) as did the sarcophagus in the porch. This held the body of Princess Joan, wife of Llywelyn the Great and daughter of King John (see p. 135). The early-nineteenth-century watchman's box, now in the porch, was used when the graveyard had to be guarded against body-snatchers.

The Bulkeleys, for generations the leading landowners on the island, lived at Baron Hill which stands, a ruin, in the fine park designed by William Emes just above the town. The Bulkeley Memorial, 1875, is the tall obelisk in the fields one mile NW.

From Beaumaris take the road N along the shoreline for Penmon (B5109). **Castell Aber Lleiniog**, the Norman motte and bailey castle which was the fore-runner to Beaumaris, is surprisingly well preserved but buried in trees at 616/793, inland from the hamlet of Lleiniog. It was built by Hugh of Avranches, Earl of Chester, 1088–90. Stone walls have replaced the original timber. It was garrisoned as late as the Civil War.

Penmon Priory is a couple of miles on. It is perfectly sited with wide views across the Straits but sheltered from the open sea by the big limestone headland. Traditionally founded by St Cynlas, who gave it to his brother St Seiriol in the sixth century, it was inevitably harried and burnt by raiders. It was rebuilt in 1120–70 as a cruciform building with low central tower topped by a humble but very effective pyramidal slab roof. A much-weathered dragon in the tympanum of the Norman south door still guards the entrance. Inside, the nave and transepts of this diminutive building instantly convey the strength and mystery of the medieval church. The light filters through tiny windows in huge walls and the outside world is forgotten. As your eyes become accustomed to the change, the robust carving on the arches at the crossing and the interlaced arcading in the transepts emerge. The grand Celtic cross in the south transept is c. 1000 and the font is a Celtic cross base. The big chancel is an anti-climax. It is a papery rebuilding by Weightman and Hadfield of Sheffield of the thirteenth-century chancel which had been added when the *clas* monastery was granted to the Prior of Priestholm (Puffin Island) and reorganized as a body of Austin Canons.

The Prior's House (still a dwelling) adjoining the south transept has been much altered but the fact that it is lived in gives a valuable sense of continuity. The thirteenth-century refectory with a dormitory above occupies the south range of the cloister court; the warming-house and kitchen were added in the sixteenth century.

The grand domed **Dovecot** was built c. 1600 by Sir Richard Bulkeley of Baron Hill; its central pillar carried a ladder which gave access to the pigeon holes (nearly 1000). **St Seiriol's Well** is in the cool stone-benched cell (the upper part is eighteenth-century work) under the low cliff opposite. The remains of the oval cell beside it probably mark his dwelling and the well his church. The deer park wall, two and a half miles of which still stand, was built by the Bulkeleys in the seventeenth or early eighteenth century. Just inside it is another cross, c. 1000, perhaps set up then to replace one devastated in the Viking raids. Its carving represents the temptation of St Anthony.

Limestone was quarried at Penmon for Beaumaris Castle and both Telford and Stephenson opened big quarries here for the bridges. Stone for dockyards is still exported by sea from the north side of the headland and trucks carrying chippings will be met on the road. You can drive to **Penmon Point** where Anglesey juts out towards the Great Orme and listen to the lonely clanging of the bell in the unmanned light. The neat 1839 coastguard cottages here have a benevolent 'built for the British Empire' character. **Puffin Island**, off the point, so long a Christian settlement (ruins of the twelfth century church survive) is now taken over by seabirds, but puffins are sadly on the decline.

Anglesey abounds in pleasant Georgian-looking mansion houses and farmhouses, unpretentious and unopen. Some have very attractive plain panelling and pretty staircases. Most are much older than they look and have simply been given an up-to-date face. In this corner of the island Tros-y-marian, overlooking the north coast, with its extensive farmbuildings and dovecot, has a last-outpost character.

Following the winding by-road that runs nearest to the sea, **Dinsylwy Hill Fort** (586/815) gives grand views of Red Wharf Bay and far beyond and has a lovely limestone lawn of wild flowers. First–fourth century AD. The little church, under its eastern shoulder, dedicated to St Michael, has a seventeenth-century pulpit but **Llaniestyn** with its humble, whitewashed interior, set in open country east of Llanddona (585/796) is more likely to be open. Fourteenth-century with a big south chapel added in the fifteenth, in which is set the impressive low relief carving of the saint (see also that of St Pabo, at Llanbabo, 378/868, in the north/middle of the island). Hafoty (563/783), two miles SW is a small hall house of fourteenth-century origins, last improved in the sixteenth century when fireplaces were installed and a floor put into the hall.

You may now want to return to Beaumaris, which makes a very pleasant although quite uncentral base, or to continue northwards on A5025, the island's 'ring road'.

ANGLESEY, EAST: RED WHARF BAY – MYNYDD EILIAN

Pentraeth, at your junction with A5025, means 'head of the sands'. It was once at the limit of Red Wharf Bay (Traeth Coch) until land reclamation stranded it a mile inland. **Glyn,** a sturdy seventeenth-century farmhouse, hidden in trees two miles north (516/814) has most unusual and vigorous plasterwork in its seventeenth-century overmantels and friezes. A slate chimney-piece decorated with naive potted plants might be the work of a former owner. The house is open on written application.

This country to the north of Red Wharf Bay is undulating and wooded and absorbs a generous share of caravan and bungalow development. The coastline makes very popular holiday-making country, and Benllech is its main centre. **Llanfair Mathafarn Eithaf** (Llanfair M E if you are asking the way) was the birthplace of the scholar and poet, Goronwy Owen (1723–69), who was also curate here for his short-lived ministry in Wales. He scorned most of his contemporaries and yearned for a revival of the strict metres of the Welsh classicists. This unfortunate and difficult man died an exile in America but Welsh exiles from all over the world have contributed to the pulpit which was installed in the church on the occasion of the bi-centenary of his death. His cottage is at Brynteg.

Also inland, on the well-wooded Parciau estate, a sturdy early seventeenth-century dovecot, to be seen from the drive to **Llaneugrad Church** (496/842), has been little altered and is of honey-coloured gritstone, square with four gables surmounted by a little cupola of the same plan. The tiny medieval church has been much restored; it contains a well weathered but very moving crucifixion which may date from the thirteenth century. Across the main road, **Traeth Bychan**, now cheerful with caravans and dinghies, is where the ill-fated submarine *Thetis* was beached in 1939 after her disastrous trials when she failed to surface and nearly all aboard perished. Another tragedy was the wreck of the *Royal Charter* off the coast near Moelfre (famous for its lifeboat) in 1859 – see Dickens's *Uncommercial Traveller*. Four hundred and four passengers were returning from Australia with, it was reported, 'an enormous quantity of gold'.

Din Llugwy (496/862), the Iron Age village on the wooded hill to the north of the main road one mile W of Moelfre, should not be missed. The enclosure wall, thought to have been built in the fourth century AD, is faced with limestone slabs and is 4–5 ft thick. Inside are rectangular and circular huts, some with walls standing higher than a man; wild geranium creeps in the crevices. Close by is **Capel Llugwy**, a roofless ruin in good order with lovely lichened walls, rebuilt in the fourteenth century, and enlarged in the sixteenth. A fine site looking to the sea. The **Llugwy burial chamber** (501/860) is just south, close to the lane. Its colossal capstone on stumpy (partly buried) supports, dates from 3000–2500 BC, in other words it is more distant in time from Din Llugwy than we are.

Inland the heathery outcrop of **Mynydd Bodafan** with its small lake is recommended out of season. Beside the main road, before it drops down to City Dulas, the **Morris Brothers Memorial** (478/873) commemorates the remarkable eighteenth-century brothers, founders of the Cymmrodorion Society and patrons of the arts, who were brought up on Pentre Eiriannell farm just below. Lewis, the eldest, 'this useful and scientific man', combined scholarship with the practical skills of a surveyor, mining engineer and printer. He made and published a famous hydrographic survey of the Welsh coast. A gentle stroll up the path here gives a pretty view.

Dulas Harbour is now almost landlocked but still lovely. Old quays survive and it was once smelly with limekilns and brickworks. The tower on Ynys Dulas, off the mouth, was a mark for mariners. Food and clothing were left inside for those stranded, at the behest of the lady of Llysdulas. This now derelict Venetian Gothic pile was built in 1856 by Benjamin Woodward, architect of the Oxford Museum. It abounds in Ruskinian carving, presumably by the O'Sheas (see p. 37). The exceptionally dull-looking church of **Llanwenllwyfo** (spiky spire) is well worth seeing for its remarkable fifteenth and sixteenth-century Flemish glass brought here by the owner of Llysdulas in 1887.

Remote country runs up to **Mynydd Eilian**, now topped by wireless masts and once part of the Holyhead–Liverpool telegraph system (see p. 208).

ANGLESEY, NORTH AND WEST: POINT LYNAS – CARMEL HEAD – VALLEY

Off **Point Lynas**, the north-west tip of the island, ships bound for Liverpool pick up their pilots and, when delayed by weather or strikes, numbers of vessels can be seen waiting off-shore. The Lighthouse, owned by the Mersey Docks and Harbour Board, not Trinity House, may be seen on written application. Its light first shone in 1781.

Llaneilian Church, three-quarters of a mile W on the coast road, is one of the most interesting on the island. Do not be deterred from exploration by the rather horrid rendering on the twelfth-century pyramidal-topped tower. The broad nave and square chancel were rebuilt in the late fifteenth century with low-pitched roofs and battlemented parapets. There are splendid fittings mostly c. 1500: the sturdy rood screen and loft (a rare survival in these parts) and chancel stalls, and musicians carved on the corbels of the roof beams. St Eilian's chapel, a fourteenth-century rebuilding of the Sanctuary which occupied the site of the saint's cell, is set at 45° to the chancel and linked to it by a sunny passage. St Eilian, who lived in the mid fifth century, was exceptionally holy and his well (near the sea) famous for its cures. Cyff Eilian, the tremendously strong chest (1667) for pilgrims' offerings, is still in the church. A well-preserved parishioner remembers the dog-tongs (1748) being used to separate disputing dogs.

It is hard to imagine that the little creek at **Amlwch** was the world's greatest copper port in the late eighteenth cntury. It is a memorable place. The quay walls are beautifully built of big but thin slabs placed on edge, but it all seems diminutive when one remembers the shipping it sheltered. **Parys Mountain**, two miles to the south, had been mined on and off since Roman times, but in 1768 a wonderfully rich seam was struck. Then the town boomed and soon the mountain was to become a feature of the Welsh Tour; the activity of the miners swinging over the cliff face became a favourite of the topographical painters. Today the mountain, though accessible, is privately owned and dangerous. Its lunar landscape is topped by the ruined windmill which assisted a steam engine in winding and pumping operations. The precipitating pools are now the only flashes of life in the rocky desolation. Some sense of scale can be gauged from the toy-like cars now abandoned here.

The classic **Parish Church** by 'Mr Wyatt of London', erected rather belatedly by the Company in 1800, was unfortunately Gothicized in 1867. Its gravestones tell the story of the town and make for very good browsing. By the time this is printed who knows what may have happened to Amlwch, for in 1973 the Shell Oil Company, despite strong opposition, obtained permission for an off-shore single buoy mooring and a tank farm from which oil will be piped to Stanlow on the Mersey. Risks of spillage cause grave concern.

The north coast is chiefly rocky with magnificent cliff scenery. **Bull Bay**, just west of Amlwch, is a long-established holiday centre. The next big bite is the remote, cliff-bound **Porth Wen** which is reached on foot by the farm track which leaves the unclassified coast road half a mile N of its junction with A5025. Those with a liking for industrial ruins should not miss the brickworks on the west of the bay (402/945), or the strange remains at **Porth Llanlleiana** (388/951), one mile as the gull flies further W: a boiler-house and chimney, and curved sea walls to prevent the flooding of the little valley. This short-lived venture may have been a copper mine. To find it either walk round the coast from Porth Wen (a lovely walk) or leave the car by the National Trust sign and follow the path towards the grand promontory fort of **Dinas Gynfor,** but bear left towards the sea. There are tall, pale reed beds in the marshy valley. Above, the Iron Age promontory fort, whose defences are drowned in bracken in the summer, is a splendid viewpoint. The huge bulk of Wylfa nuclear power station (which can be viewed on appointment) looms up to the west on the far headland of Cemaes Bay and pylons stride towards the mainland, but there is fine coastline between. From **Llanbadrig Church** to Cemaes Bay village (cheerful, holiday) it is National Trust, so accessible. The cliff-side medieval church, restored by Bertrand Russell's Muslim uncle, Lord Stanley of Alderley, is less surprising once you know who did it. He was that determined man who married the same lady four times by different rites only to discover she had a husband living.

Cemlyn Bay is a great place for birds, particularly in winter when thousands of wildfowl gather in the almost landlocked lagoon (NT). The strange house and walled garden which is the sanctuary of thousands of small migrants was owned by another unusual character, Captain Vivian Hewitt, the 'Modest Millionaire', who besides being a keen ornithologist was a pioneer aviator, collector and racing driver.

Llanrhwydrys Church, 322/932, is remote among fields near the sea to the W of Cemlyn Bay. Leave the car by the field gate and follow the old causeway across the little marsh. Brilliant lichen brightens the small arched gateway. Cherished, cheerful and not overdesigned, as you will see. A very likable diminutive twelfth-century building with a bigger chancel added in the thirteenth (fifteenth-century east window), and west gallery (beam dated 1776). The N Chapel is of uncertain date and its free-standing cruck a definite surprise. **Caerau** (321/918), a mile S, is a fine farmhouse in the best Anglesey tradition of the seventeenth and early eighteenth centuries (open on written application).

Carmel Head is the NW bastion of Anglesey and off it lie the **Skerries** where a light first shone in 1730. The present lamp is four million candlepower. Between these two is an extraordinary story of financial failure and success. The growth of Liverpool changed the fortunes of the lighthouse so that its nineteenth-century owners were only persuaded to part with it in 1841 for a sum approaching £½m. It was the last privately owned lighthouse in the country.

On the way back to the main road, **Craig-y-gwynt** (325/898) is an old station of the Holyhead–Liverpool telegraph, as the 1841 slab set in the wall of the cottage testifies. In the days of clippers, racing home from the other side of the world, Liverpool merchants waited agog for news of their coming. A message from Holyhead took five or six minutes in clear weather going via this station, Mynydd Eilian, Puffin Island, the Great Orme and Hilbre Island.

The west coast, Carmel to Valley, has more good cliff scenery and popular beaches wherever there is sand (Porth Swtan, Church Bay, Porth Trwyn, Porth Trefadog . . .) which are easy to find, but the middle of the island is far more elusive.

ANGLESEY, INLAND TO THE NORTH OF A5

Lack of strong topographical features makes the heart of

Characteristic whitewashed cottages at Llanddona, Anglesey.

Looking across Newborough Warren and Forest to the fine outline of the Rivals, on the other side of Caernarfon Bay.

A beautifully made stairway down a slate tip in the Oakeley Quarries, Blaenau Ffestiniog.

Anglesey even more confusing to explore than other parts of rural Wales. Enthusiasts should refer to the excellent Inventory of the Royal Commission on Historic Monuments which contains good photographs of many of the unexpected delights buried here. Those who enjoy the services of a good map reader in their car might sally forth armed with the OS map. Others may find it quicker, though duller, to return to the ring road and make sorties from it. Other roads of consequence are the old Holyhead road, B5109, and the Amlwch – Llanerchymedd road which goes on to join B5109. Others radiate from Llangefni, the county town (p. 210).

The new Alaw reservoir now floods three miles of the pastoral middle of the N of the island (trout fishing by permit). Half a mile due W the little medieval church of **Llanbabo** stands near a stream beside the road. Its most remarkable feature is the splendid low relief of St Pabo; a fourteenth-century carving of great delicacy and strength. Pabo is thought to have been a North British chief who sought asylum here. The sculptor is almost certainly the same as that of St Iestyn (see p. 203). West again at **Llanddeusant** a crumbling windmill contains its machinery. This is one of the few of the many Anglesey windmills to survive: the island must have been a brave sight on a windy day when all their sails were whirring. A family watermill still grinds at Cellar to the S of the village on the way to **Llantrisant Church**, up a farm road at 349/841. This late fourteenth-century building with seventeenth-century S chapel has a very pretty late-seventeenth-century memorial and early-nineteenth fittings. It was recently open to the sky and almost buried by overgrowth, but has been restored (1972) by the initiative of the Friends of Friendless Churches. **Llanfigael**, one and a half miles SW beside the road at 328/828, looks nothing, but has excellent and complete fittings of the early nineteenth century.

One and a half miles due S, **Bodedern** was once an imporatnt village on the old Holyhead road. A mile towards Llangefni you can see one of Telford's toll-gates re-used at the entrance to a drive: a logical design of radial iron straps which seems to have been the forerunner of many suburban gates. (See also those beside Menai Bridge, Caernarfon side.) B5112 branches left to **Llanerchymedd**, for long the main centre for the north of the island. It is a proper village with a town air, medieval church and good chapels. Snuff and boots were among its products; 250 cobblers worked here in 1833.

Llangwyllog Church, just off B5111, the Llanerchymedd-Llangefni road, has a lovely marshy stream-side site, good memorials and fittings, notably the 1769 pulpit and reading desk, and eighteenth-century pews. A separate room was added to the west in the sixteenth century and the windows and doors in the church are of that date and late fifteenth-century.

Llangefni, the county town since the 1880s, is well sited in the middle of the island. It was on the old main road to Ireland but was never then of much importance, and Telford's new Holyhead road (A5) bypassed the town. Market days (Wednesday and Thursday) bring the heart of Llangefni to life; new housing and light industry thrive on its immediate outskirts. Little is known of the unusual 1824 church (among trees near the river a couple of hundred yards north of the Square). The aisleless nave appears to be supported by shallow timber arched beams decorated with cusped openwork, and the restrained west gallery is supported by tapering octagonal columns. There is iron tracery in the windows and the painted pews are nicely grained in putty green. Unfortunately the east end was altered in 1898 and again in the 1930s. The Cefni was once navigable right up to the town.

Before **Penmynydd**, Plas Penmynydd, two miles east of Llangefni, a sturdy Elizabethan and seventeenth-century farmhouse, was once the home of Henry VII's grandfather. A sixteenth-century Tudor arms and a Saracen's head have been reset in the front wall. Attractive seventeenth-century almshouses of tiny scale have been restored (at 514/742) and there is a grand alabaster late-fourteenth-century altar tomb in the church (once in Llanfaes Friary). This is to Gronw Fychan and his wife. Tudor arms have been faintly scratched on the shields.

A5, MENAI BRIDGE – HOLYHEAD AND HOLY ISLAND

Before leaving Menai Bridge (see also p. 198), the **Belgian Promenade** and **St Tysilio's Church** make a delightful diversion. Turn left off A5 as for the Tea Gardens in the pine trees shortly after the Beaumaris turning. The walk along the shores of the Strait and the causeway to the tiny church were built by

Belgian refugees during the 1914–18 war. The early fifteenth-century church still has its medieval roof trusses, and although much restored has a timeless atmosphere reinforced by the touching memorial slabs and an unexpected sense of seclusion so close to the interminable A5 traffic.

Two lay-bys a mile out of Menai Bridge give fine views of the bridges and Snowdonia. Just above the upper one a footpath through the wood takes you down to the shores of the Strait. Here, at low tide, the walled enclosures of the fishtraps which once provided thriving industry on Menai can be clearly seen. There is also a complex system of weirs and traps on the island opposite.

For a closer view of George Stephenson's mighty **Britannia Bridge** (1845–50) turn left half a mile on for Llanfairpwll church. The monumental wrought iron beams through which the trains ran were irreparably damaged by fire on the night of 23 May 1970 and have been replaced by light steel arches (the most economic solution). Unfortunately these inevitably look flimsy and make the masonry pylons seem absurd. A road may be added to the structure. The lions which guard the bridge are by John Thomas (who did the sculpture for the Houses of Parliament). An obelisk commemorating men who died during the construction of the bridge (and Emma Greaves, aged five) stands at the top of the churchyard, and beside the shore below there is a robust monument of Lord Nelson, in fact a navigation mark, by Lord Clarence Paget, himself a sailor and son of the first Marquess of Anglesey.

The **Anglesey Column** (1816) is a grand landmark and view point and very well worth the climb up 115 steps on a clear day. It was designed by Thomas Harrison of Chester and commemorates the first Marquess of Anglesey – who led the Allied cavalry and was second in command at Waterloo where he lost his leg, hence his nick-name, One-Leg. His statue was not added until 1860 and is by Matthew Noble, who had recently caused a stir by winning a competition for the Wellington memorial in Manchester. The present Marquess is appropriately immersed in a definitive *History of the British Cavalry* (1816–1919) at Plas Newydd (see p. 215), the house you can see from up here resting in a lovely curve of the Strait to the south.

Llanfair Pwllgwyngyll(gogerychwyrndrobwllllandysiliogogo-

goch), was so named by the village tailor sometime in the last century in an attempt to get the place to stick in people's minds. He certainly succeeded in distinguishing it from the twenty-two other Llanfairs (named from churches dedicated to St Mary).

The Holyhead road was the last surviving turnpike in Britain (it was freed from tolls in 1895). Four of Telford's attractive little verandahed octagonal toll-houses survive and that in the village still has the list of tolls. The villages on A5 are, naturally enough, nineteenth century. Remains of coal-mines survive at Pentre Berw on the edge of Malltraeth Marsh and **Plas Berw** (open on written application) is an astonishing and secretive house: an early-seventeenth-century addition to a hall house of 1480 on to which a tower had already been added. (Take the Llangaffo road, B4419, at the Holland Arms. The rocky drive down to the marsh is half a mile on.)

Llangristiolus Church stands well above the marsh, left of A5. It has a fine thirteenth-century chancel arch and twelfth-century font; restored by Henry Kennedy, 1852, and re-decorated very vigorously recently. The big limekiln on the opposite side of A5 is a reminder of the days when the Cefni was navigable. Indeed the island was once almost cut in two here (see Pentraeth, p. 204).

The Holyhead road goes relentlessly on, modern traffic giving little inclination or chance to pause. Some of the original iron mile markers as well as toll-houses have survived and on a bright windy day great skies blow over the green-grey country and Holyhead Mountain lures you on. **Valley Airfield** lies to the left and here plane-spotting can make a change from the usual seaside activities. During wartime excavations a mechanical grab chanced on a fantastic Iron Age hoard of bronze weapons and horse trappings, thought to be votive offerings (this is the Llyn Cerrig Bach hoard, now in the National Museum).

Valley is the recent village with the traffic lights where A5025, the north coast road, joins A5. Just beyond, Telford had to tackle the last great obstacle on the Irish route, the three-quarters of a mile crossing to Holy Island. The **Stanley Embankment** (1822) gives lovely views north, but those of the inland sea are cut off by the railway. The Telford toll-house here has been moved back to allow for road widening. The

Embankment is named after the Lord Stanley of Alderley who married the heiress of **Penrhos** (c. 1800 by James Defferd). Its Gothicky ruins can still be seen where Telford's road has been diverted round the huge aluminium smelter which now dominates this part of the island. It is powered by Wylfa as the lines joining the two amply demonstrate.

Holyhead is the port for the Irish crossing, terminal of Stephenson's railway and Telford's road. Quite the most painless way to leave Wales is by night-sleeper from Holyhead. The railway station (from 1845) gleams brilliantly: yellow light reflects off the black water. White decks glow above the black hull of the steamer moored alongside and the red funnel is bright against the navy-blue sky. The curving white station canopy and the decorated cast-iron clock which commemorates the extension of the inner harbour (1880) are equally spick and span. The new container terminal next door, with its giant yellow cranes, is almost more exciting.

By day Holyhead tends to be rather greyer but it is a likeable town with lots to see, which people tend to miss unless held up, as was George IV. Stuck here for five days in 1821 waiting to hear whether the Queen, as he hoped, had died, he eventually resorted to a newly invented steam paddler. The 1824 Doric Memorial Arch by Thomas Harrison commemorates this visit. The architect of the restrained little classical Custom House and Harbour Office is unknown. The Admiralty Pier is by John Rennie, 1821. The grand new breakwater which was to convert Holyhead into one of the 'most splendid refuge harbours in the universe' (*Parry's Railway Guide*, 1848) was not started until 1845. A mid-Victorian writer recommended that 'a morning or evening walk on the parapet . . . will have the tendency to enliven the spirits and brace the nerves'. This is still so. The light on the tip has its original brass clockwork motor (1873). The long new pier was constructed for the aluminium smelter in the 1960s.

Permission is usually forthcoming to view the **Trinity House Depot** (near the yacht club to the west of the town). The shapes of the buoys, here for repainting, are as splendid as their names are dramatically unromantic: Patches, Chester Flat, Coal Rock . . . The Lifeboat Station on Salt Island is also often open.

The Romans built a small coastal fort in Holyhead, Caer

Gybi, in the late third or early fourth century, to meet the new threat from sea-raiders. The **Parish Church** is within its walls (immediately seaward of the High Street). St Cybi founded a monastery here in 550. The medieval church was rebuilt 1480–1520 (the thirteenth-century chancel only partly). The tower is sixteenth century. The result is a light arcaded building, with a low-pitched, battlemented and pinnacled roof and some intricate carving particularly on the south parapet. It was restored by Sir Gilbert Scott and later by Arthur Baker (1877–9), who added the S aisle. The glowing pomegranate window is by William Morris, and Burne Jones designed the Pre-Raphaelite figures. The organ is from Eaton Hall Library and the Stanley tomb is by Hamo Thornycroft. **Capel-y-bedd** (near the S gate) is the remains of an eighteenth-century school made out of the nave of a medieval chapel.

The north coast of Holy Island has particularly spectacular cliff scenery. **Holyhead Mountain** drops steeply down to the sea; to the NE are extensive limestone quarries (it was from here that the stone for the breakwater came). Paths lead up to the summit both from the quarries and from the SW. It is crowned by a big Iron Age fort (never excavated) whose huge walls stand ten feet high in places. The view from up here can be breathtaking.

For the southerly approach to Holyhead Mountain, return to Holyhead and take the road which leads to the South Stack Lighthouse. Half a mile before the end of the road, look out for the D. o. E. sign on your right for the **Holyhead Mountain Hut Circles**. The remarkable remains of a village of second–fourth centuries AD lie on the sunny slopes to the SW of the mountain. Circular and rectangular huts survive, some with central hearths and the remains of benches. A path beyond leads up the mountain.

The **South Stack Lighthouse** (open usually on weekday afternoons until one hour before sunset) was built by Daniel Alexander in 1808. (This versatile man was also responsible for Princetown prison, Dartmoor, and the flanking blocks and colonnades to the Queen's House, Greenwich.) The cliffs here are renowned for their seabirds and the path down to the lighthouse can give excellent views. Lovely and less fierce cliffs run right round the SW of Holy Island; where there is sand there are people. **Porth Dafarch** is the nearest sandy bay to Holyhead; remains survive of attempted harbour works of 1820 which were to be used by sailing ships as an alternative to Holyhead.

Trearddur Bay has been a popular resort throughout this century, many English families taking holiday houses here. **Rhoscolyn**, with its two sandy bays, has been much less developed and has the advantage of being on the road to nowhere else. **St Gwenfaen's Well** (259/754) is an outpost of civilization on a lonely headland (follow the path past Plas). Lovely cliffs continue forming the north arm of the huge sweep of Cymyran Bay and this leads into the mysterious winding inland sea which separates Holy Island from Anglesey. It almost dries out at low tide and is a wonderful haunt of waders and wildfowl. Four Mile Bridge, which carries B4545 back to Valley, was used at high tide by travellers to Holyhead before the construction of Telford's embankment.

SOUTH-WEST ANGLESEY: A4080 LLANFAIR PWLLGWYNGYLL – A5

Turn left on to A4080 at Telford's toll-house in Llanfairpwll. The road passes the gates of Plas Newydd (p. 211), seat of the Marquess of Anglesey (open on written application) which was rebuilt by James Wyatt and Joseph Potter, 1800–1810, partly in the Gothick style (the battlements and turrets have now gone). It has one of the most marvellous sites in Britain with the Straits immediately below and Snowdonia beyond. In 1936–40 Rex Whistler painted his famous mural in a newly created dining-room. The house is partly occupied by Cheshire County Council Education Department. So are Wyatt's Gothick stables and new buildings in the grounds.

There are two Neolithic/Early Bronze burial chambers in the Park: one, with a giant capstone, opposite Wyatt's stables and the other, less spectacular, under a tree between the walled garden (now a Garden Centre) and the Straits. This part of Anglesey is a great place for such burials besides having been the 'Sorbonne' of the Druids of NW Europe. The two are easily mixed, but it was c. 2000 years after these burials that the Druids were established here. The description by Tacitus of their confrontation with the Roman Army in 60 AD is well known.

Turn right on the Llanddaniel-fab road where the Plas Newydd wall bends towards the Straits for **Bryn Celli Ddu**, an exceptionally fine burial chamber (Neolithic/Early Bronze). It has been excavated and re-covered with earth as when it was first constructed, except that the mound would then have been bigger and covered most of the area within the modern fence. The burial stands within four concentric circles and may have been some sort of temple. Experts note the rare carved pattern, which is not easy to pick out, on the famous central stone (a replica here, the original is now in the National Museum); the smooth pillar stone standing in the passage is most impressive.

The opposite turning towards the Straits leads past **Plas Coch**, a sixteenth-century house with nineteenth-century modifications, now a caravan centre, and **Llanedwen Church** (H. Kennedy of Bangor, 1856). Candlelight transforms this plain little building. The reading desk incorporates carving from a fourteenth-century screen including a very vigorous lion and griffin. In the graveyard, John Rowlands, 'a Gardiner' who died in 1829 warns

'Stop a foot and cast an eye
As you are now so once was I
As I am now so must you be
Prepare yourself and follow me'.

From Moel-y-don, just below, a useful ferry once plied to Port Dinorwic. New housing there spills out unnecessarily into the rare green stretch of the Strait and brings home the fact that it is always the opposite bank of any river that matters in the view.

Back on A4080 look out for the turning L a little before the Victorian church (John Welch) for **Llanidan (old) Church.** It was mostly demolished in 1844 but its fifteenth-century arcade makes a lovely ruin romantically emerging from a sea of leaves. The fourteenth-century west end was sealed off to form a small church; water in the stoup in the south porch never fails. Beyond Brynsiencyn other lanes down to the Strait give marvellous views of Caernarfon with the medieval town walls running along the water's edge from the Castle.

Three miles on, the humble medieval church of **Llangeinwen** with its endearing little 1839 tower and big N chapel of the same date stands at the sharp bend of the road. Ninth- and eleventh-century grave slabs have been set in a buttress to the N. It has a thirteenth-century font with an attractive fleur de lys and palmette pattern, and an early nineteenth-century chandelier.

The southerly tip of the island is made up of **Newborough Warren** which ends in Abermenai point. One of the main routes shown on the late-eighteenth-century maps crossed the Straits here at its southerly tip. This is believed by Dr R. M. Ogilvie to have been the ford used by Suetonius Paulinus's troops in 60 AD, and by Agricola's in 78 AD: he maintains that the Strait cannot be forded at Porthaml, as has been traditionally supposed, and has forded it here himself. Newborough Warren is a National Nature Reserve (entrance by permit only except on the rights of way – see notice boards). The general impression left by a summer afternoon here is of great dunes of silvery sand and brilliant blue anchusa, against an unforgettable backcloth of blue mountains with vast blue skies above.

Newborough was settled by Edward I after the conquest. It was long important for its fairs and markets and until recently it was the centre of a thriving mat, cord, and net-making industry from the marram grass on the dunes (conserved for this purpose by Queen Elizabeth I). The village is a cheerful breezy place with fine views down the street to the mountains of the mainland. St Peter's Church stands high beside the road to Llanddwyn Island; probably early fourteenth century, extended c. 1600 and like a long tunnel inside. Good twelfth-century font, and fourteenth-century carved grave slabs in the chancel.

A road leads through Newborough Forest to **Llanddwyn Bay** where a big car park has been sensibly hidden in the trees. The sands are immense and it is easy to be on your own. The views across to the Lleyn Peninsula and the fine outline of the Rivals make a perfect backdrop to the vast low-tide expanse. A mile up the coast is **Llanddwyn Island**, accessible except at the highest tides. Here St Dwynen lived in the fifth century and her well became a great place of pilgrimage, particularly for anxious lovers. Her concern was that they would not deceive each other. The ruins of the sixteenth-century chancel of the later church still stand. A modern Celtic cross commemorates all those buried here, and the Latin cross the saint herself. The lighthouse dates from 1845 (now automatic) and there was a lifeboat here from 1840. The gun which summoned the crew from Newborough survives on Gun Cliff near the delightful Pilot Cottages which housed the Caernarfon pilots. It is a lovely little island with rocky coast and sandy coves. The Nature Conservancy asks you to stick to the paths.

The Cefni estuary bounds the other side of Newborough Forest: a great place for waders and duck, of which a very good view can be had from the public footpath on the embankment. This was completed in 1818 and the river canalized and marsh drained. **Malltraeth Marsh** is a remote, sharp landscape with the straight lines of ditches and enclosure tracks softened by the windblown reeds and meadow sweet. The Protectors of Paradws, a hamlet on the edge of the marsh, have recently won a battle to save themselves from the effects of quarrying.

Llangadwaladr Church, close to the main road, is dedicated to Cadwaladr, saint and king, whose grandfather Cadfan's grave slab has been reset in the nave. Cadfan, who died c. 625, is described as the wisest and most illustrious of kings. The church, under its royal patronage, was a meeting place of chieftains. The present nave dates from the twelfth century, and chancel fourteenth. The fine east window (reset) is late fifteenth-century: a crucifixion, the bones of Christ's body showing as in an X-ray, and the saint, complete with sceptre and orb; the eyes have vertical pupils like a cat's. The church is lit by lovely brass chandeliers. The north chapel has a full-blooded Gothic memorial of 1857, and the south, a charming mid-seventeenth-century Gothic extension, is separated from the nave by a daringly flat arch. It contains the classic memorial of Colonel Hugh Owen of Bodowen – the ruined gates of its courtyard still stand above the Cefni estuary. This is on the Bodorgan estate (private). **Bodorgan House** (late eighteenth century), built by James Defferd, has a lovely site sheltered by trees above the river. Very similar to the Bishop's Palace at St Asaph, it may have been designed by Samuel Wyatt. The right hand headland has a good promontory fort.

Aberffraw, seat of the court of the Princes of North Wales who bore sway from Mold to Aberdovey, is mentioned in the Mabinogion as a place of royal feasting (see p. 244). No architectural evidence of its royal status survives. The village is attractively sited on one side only of the river, giving an open view of the warren beyond and the attractive round arched bridge (1731) which crosses it. St Beuno's Church, much restored but basically a double-naved structure of the twelfth and sixteenth centuries, has a reset Norman doorway decorated with spooky hounds' (?) faces.

A mile up the coast is 'the island church'. **Llangwyfan** is on a proper island in a sheltered bay where you can find cowries as you wait for the tide to drop. Mostly dating from the fourteenth century, it was once double-naved, but the sixteenth-century north aisle has been demolished and its arcade filled up. A wonderfully peaceful spot; you just have to disregard the intrusion of the M. o. D. establishment on the north headland. (Annual service, late June.)

Two and a half miles inland from the village at 368/729, the medieval chapel of **St Mary Tal-y-llyn** is well worth seeing. This diminutive humble building with eighteenth-century plank pews and other furniture intact and a twelfth-century font (full description inside the chapel) was restored in 1969 by the Friends of Friendless Churches and the County Council.

Back on A4080 **Porth Trecastell** (Cable Bay) is where the telegraph line crossed to Ireland. The famous burial chamber, **Barcloddiad-y-gawres** (the Giantess' Apronful) is on the right headland. A splendid site, it was excavated in 1953 and then covered over by the D. o. E. with a vast new mound – like an air raid shelter inside. Spiral patterns on the stones resemble those found at New Grange in Ireland.

Llyn Maelog is the attractive lake just inland and **Rhosneigr** is a 1900-ish holiday village with sandy bays, sea-shells, little rocky headlands and flowery dunes and caravans. The huge sweep of **Cwmyran Bay** beyond is backed by **Valley Airfield** (see p. 212), but A4080 returns via the much older village of Llanfaelog inland to A5, where you can turn left for Holy Island and Holyhead (p. 213), or right for the mainland, or cross the trunk road to explore the elusive country in the island's heart (p. 208) which lies straight ahead.

CHAPTER NINE

Merioneth

The old county of Merioneth is the second most sparsely populated in Wales (after Radnorshire). It has only 35,000 people to 422,000 acres. It consists mostly of mountains and moorland, and communications are poor, though current road 'improvements' (often carried out with sad insensitivity) are changing this. The only major industry was slate, and that has virtually died. Hill-farming and tourism are now supreme. The fact that Merioneth contains some of the most wonderful country in Wales means that the pressures of holiday-making, for second homes, and for houses to retire to, are intense. Yet it remains one of the most strongly Welsh areas: in 1974 it elected its first Nationalist MP.

CORWEN TO DOLGELLAU – A494

Two miles beyond Corwen (p. 89), the A494 goes off to the SW. At **Glan-yr-Afon** the road passes a simple EE church by Sir Gilbert Scott, of 1861–4 (the name of the parish is Llawr-y-Betws). It has a splendid reredos of Minton tiles. Hilly, pastoral country brings you to **Llanfor**, just outside Bala. The dull church, with saddleback tower, is by E. B. Ferrey (1875). In the churchyard is the mausoleum of Richard John Lloyd Price, built in 1887 and inscribed:

As to my latter end I go
To win my Jubilee,
I bless the good horse, Bendigo,
Who built this tomb for me.

Bendigo was a successful racehorse. Price was a famous sportsman and a dreadful punster, author of *Dogs' Tales Wagged* by R. J. Lloyd Price, etc., and founder of the Welsh Whiskey Distillery (see p. 229), the Rhiwlas Brush Works, and other enterprises. The family live at **Rhiwlas**, reached through a big castellated archway just before the bridge which leads into Bala. Their house, a fine building of 1574, was remodelled in the Gothic taste in 1809, and demolished in 1951. The new house, by Clough Williams-Ellis, incorporates inscribed beams from the old one, but the painted screen is now at St Fagan's.

It is also possible to reach Bala from Corwen by the B4401, along the E side of the Dee Valley. It is not such a fast road, but more worthwhile. Just over half a mile from the junction with the A5, a track leads down to the right to the church of **Llangar** (064/424), beautifully situated in a sloping churchyard, overlooking the water-meadows at the confluence of Dee and Alwen. At present the church is hard to appreciate, as it is entirely encased in corrugated iron: this is because, after falling into decay, it is being restored by the D. o. E. It is a small medieval building, retaining its seventeenth- and eighteenth-century fittings, including box pews and a three-decker pulpit. It was superseded by a new church at **Cynwyd**, a dull EE job of 1855 by Rhode Hawkins, with a frightful E window of 1870 by J. B. Capronnier of Brussels. Pretty painted decoration in the chancel, and some good tablets from Llangar. The attractive village is tightly grouped round the lofty stone bridge over the Trystion. Half a mile up the river are the Trystion Falls: follow the road running N of the river for a quarter of a mile, then branch right through a gate along a track leading to a ruined mill (a delightful group of stone buildings). Cross the river by the iron bridge and the falls are just above – three separate straight spouts, in a richly wooded valley. Pretty if unexciting. The bridge over the Dee is of medieval type, four arches with refuges and cutwaters. Across it are narrow winding lanes with big hedges, peaceful and prosperous country. A mile N of the bridge, at 053/427, is **Plas Uchaf**, a remarkable survival of a hall-house of c. 1400, now being restored by the Landmark Trust.

Two miles S of Cynwyd, opposite the magnificent avenue that leads to Hendwr (now a caravan park), starts the track which leads over the Berwyns to Glyn Ceiriog (see p. 94). **Llandrillo** is a neat village, with terraces of eighteenth-century cottages. The church stands near the bridge over the Ceidiog. It was rebuilt in 1877 by S. Pountney Smith, and is quite pleasing, with a short spire and a lofty, rather bare interior. Excellent Clayton & Bell glass. Outside the S wall is the tomb,

with arched canopy, of Katherine Wynne of Branes, d. 1706. A big chapel outside the village has been painted a startling pink. The road winds beneath steep wooded hills. It crosses the Dee below **Pale** (pronounced 'palais'), a large Jacobean house built in 1875, by S. Pountney Smith, for Henry Robertson, MP, the railway engineer. On the porch is carved a railway engine, and the inscription EX FUMO DARE LUCEM (to produce light from smoke). Across the river is **Llandderfel**, a pretty village beneath a wooded hill. The small Perp church was rebuilt in 1870 by S. Pountney Smith: the grotesque heads on the window-hoods must be the work of a Victorian carver who entered into the medieval spirit with gusto. It has a rich medieval rood-screen and loft. An odder relic is a large but mutilated wooden animal, kept in the porch. This is known as Ceffyl Derfel, Derfel's horse. Derfel is supposed to have been a sixth-century warrior who became a bishop. His shrine was a great place of pilgrimage, to which cattle, oxen and horses were brought to be cured and blessed. His image showed him on horseback. There was a prophecy that it would set a forest on fire which was fulfilled when it was taken up to London, as a superstitious relic, and burnt on the same fire, in 1538, as Friar Forest, who had been condemned to death for denying the supremacy of Henry VIII. Obviously, then, the animal still at Llandderfel cannot be the horse: it is in fact a red stag. It was kept near the Communion Table until 1730, and was taken out every Easter Tuesday, attached to poles, and used to give rides to the village children. However, in 1730 the Rural Dean ordered it to be decapitated. By the stag is kept a wooden staff of painted wood, called Ffon Dderfel (Derfel's staff).

From Llandderfel, the B4401 follows the N side of Dee to Llanfor (see above). Beyond Pale, the B4391 climbs steeply up the Berwyns, entering Montgomeryshire at the top and coming down to Llangynog (see p. 271). The same road follows the S side of the Dee valley, crossing the river to enter Bala from the S. Just before the bridge, a mountain road goes up Cwm Hirnant, through forestry, and over to Lake Vyrnwy (p. 272).

Bala is a busy little town, market for a wide area of hill farms, and also an important tourist centre, but it manages to combine all this with a strong character of its own and a decent appearance. Many of the tourists are drawn by **Llyn Tegid** (Bala Lake), the biggest natural lake in Wales. Over three miles long, it occupies part of the immensely long fault-guided valley which stretches right up from Tywyn on the coast, through Tal-y-llyn, to the Bryneglwys valley in Denbighshire – a distance of over fifty miles. The lake contains, among numerous other varieties of fish, one species found nowhere else in Britain – the whitefish or *gwyniad*. A popular place for sailing. The town is spread out along the tree-lined main street and the roads parallel to it. Chapels with brightly painted and varnished interiors, fish and chip shops, pubs with Welsh singing, sheep-dog trials. The church at the N end is a dignified but dull EE edifice, with a spire, by Benjamin Ferrey (1856). S of the main street is Tomen y Bala, a Norman motte, and near it is the School, nicely rebuilt in 1851 by Jesus College, Oxford. The pretty little stone chapel with a stubby spire was built as a Chapel of Ease in 1810, but superseded by the new church.

In the main street is a melodramatic statue of Thomas Edward Ellis, of 1902, by W. Goscombe John. Ellis (1859–99) was born at Cynlas, three miles NE of Bala, and educated at Bala School. In 1886 he became Liberal MP for Merioneth, in 1892 Junior Lord of the Treasury, and in 1894 Chief Whip. He fought tirelessly in the interests of Wales – for disestablishment, home rule, education. As son of a tenant-farmer, he concerned himself greatly with land reform. Also in the main street is the handsome Town Hall, with round arches along the ground floor and a clock tower. Down Tegid Street is the spired Welsh Presbyterian Chapel, outside which stands the statue (1895) of Thomas Charles, by W. Davies of London. Charles (1755–1814) was born near St Clears, in Carmarthenshire. He settled at Bala on marrying the daughter of a local shopkeeper, and became curate of Llanymawddwy, but joined the Methodists in 1784. He was a great preacher: tens of thousands flocked to hear him and others at the famous Bala meetings in the latter part of the eighteenth century. He is also remembered for his work in connection with Sunday Schools, that essential feature of nineteenth-century Welsh Nonconformity. On the Ffestiniog Road stands the former Calvinistic Methodist College, founded in 1837 by Lewis Edwards (who married Charles' grand-daughter), for the training of Ministers. The Gothic building of c. 1870 is now a Youth Centre.

A mile SW of Bala is the old parish church, at **Llanycil** down by the lake. It is where Charles is buried. The Ferrey church suggests Williams-Wynn influence: sure enough, they had a house here – Glanllyn, a handsome early nineteenth-century villa at the top of the lake. They kept a splendid steam yacht. The house now belongs to Urdd Gobaith Cymru (the Welsh League of Youth). Beyond it, N of the road, is **Caer Gai**, where, on the site of a Roman fort, stands the house rebuilt (after it was burnt in the Civil War) by Rowland Vaughan, Royalist translator and poet, some of whose verses are carved on stone slabs on the house. By the bridge over the Lliw a road goes up the beautiful valley: it has now been made up all the way over to Trawsfynydd (p. 239). Alas, at the top the reason for its being made up becomes all too clear: the bare hills are covered with baby conifers. Lots of gates.

Llanuwchllyn is something of an estate village (to Glanllyn). The church was rebuilt in 1873 by E. B. Ferrey. A Coalbrookdale fountain commemorates the birth of the Williams-Wynn heir in 1891. Of more recent significance is the memorial by the road junction, to Sir Owen Morgan Edwards (1858–1920), and his son, Sir Ifan ab Owen Edwards (1895–1970). Sir Owen, born on a Llanuwchllyn farm, was a historian, first Chief Inspector under the new Welsh Education Department (1907), and an indefatigable champion of the Welsh language and literature, concerned with ensuring their spread throughout the whole Welsh people, of whatever status. Sir Ifan was founder of the Urdd Gobaith Cymru (see p. 224). It is difficult to regard the memorial as worthy of its subjects. It consists of two life-sized statues – the father urging the son on with a gesture from behind – set in a somewhat twee enclosure.

Llanuwchllyn was also the birthplace of Michael D. Jones (1822–98), a fierce nationalist, who succeeded his father as Principal of the Bala Independent College. He was one of the chief supporters of the Welsh colony in Patagonia, whose story is one of the most remarkable, and moving, in the history of Wales. In the mid-nineteenth-century large numbers of Welshmen emigrated, particularly to America, as a result of agricultural evictions, political and religious oppression, and, above all, poverty. A vision grew up of a 'New Wales', where the language, the religious convictions, and the radical political ideas of the Welsh could flourish in freedom. The dream came true in 1865 when a small sailing-ship left Liverpool with 153 men, women, and children. Many came from the Bala district. They settled on a plain in the southern part of the Argentine, inhabited only by wandering Indians, with whom they quickly made friends. Life was harsh, but the unshakable courage of the settlers enabled them to survive. Eventually their wheat won gold medals at Paris and Chicago exhibitions. Chapels were built, and eisteddfods were held, with their own gorsedd of bards. The constitution was outstandingly democratic – for example, men and women had the vote from the age of eighteen. Disaster struck in 1899, when a flood washed away their fields, but they at once set about repairing the damage. The settlement retains a certain amount of Welshness, and close ties are still maintained, but inevitably, since complete political independence was an impossibility, the settlers have become more and more assimilated with the Argentinians. Porth Madryn, named after the Lleyn estate of Love Jones-Parry, who went out to inspect the country in 1862, is now Puerto Madryn.

From Bala, another road (B4403) follows the E side of the lake. Near the S end, three miles from Bala, is **Llangywer**: its tiny church, by a lake delta, was rebuilt in 1780–82 and restored in 1871. It preserves a horse bier (*elor feirch*), and was one of the last places where such a bier continued in use. They were once common in mountainous districts. The bier was slung between two horses, one at each end. From near Llanuwchllyn, a mountain road goes over to Llanymawddwy, with a branch to Lake Vyrnwy. It climbs up the side of the lovely **Cwm Cynllwyd**, with marvellous views from the top. The pass, Bwlch y Groes, is at a height of 1790 ft.

Beyond Llanuwchllyn, the A494 follows a straight valley between the mountains of Dduallt (2155 ft) and Rhobell Fawr (2408 ft) on the N, and Aran Benllyn (2901 ft) and Aran Fawddwy (2970 ft) on the S. The Arans are best climbed from Cwm Cywarch (p. 225): their E flanks are much more dramatic. Three miles from Llanuwchllyn, the Dee (Dyfrdwy) comes down from its source, the great boggy expanse above which rise the sheer black cliffs of Dduallt. The same bog is the source of the Wnion, which the road follows down to Dolgellau. The SW end of the Rhobell range forms a triangle, with the Wnion along the S, and the Mawddach on the W. Within this triangle there is a maze of little roads, winding around the surprisingly steep hills and through woods.

Most of this forms the estate of **Nannau**, until recently the home of the Vaughans, one of the chief families of Merioneth. The house stands at a height of 700 ft, and has been claimed to be the highest mansion in the country. Its chief glory was once 'the spirits' blasted tree', as Scott called it in *Marmion* – the hollow oak in which Owen Glendower was said to have hidden the body of his host, Hywel Sele, whom he had killed to avenge an attempt on his own life. The story is untrue. The tree fell down on the day after Sir Richard Colt Hoare drew it, in 1813. The present house, a severe Grecian block, of dark stone, was built in 1795 (possibly to designs by Joseph Bromfield) by Sir Robert Williames Vaughan, Bart (1768–1843). He was MP for Merioneth 1792–1836, and a great improver of his lands. He used to be carried around to inspect them in a carved oak chair. His most conspicuous monument is the delightful series of cottages, farms, arches, and so on, which he built in what came to be known as the 'Nannau style' – of rough stone, with hoodmoulds over the windows, some Gothic detailing, little loggias, and often highly picturesque plans. He also made use of the huge slabs found locally for lintels, and in one case, SE of Llanfachreth village, for an arch spanning the road.

Llanfachreth contains good examples of the style, and the octagonal spire of the church (1822) is another. Sir Robert also added transepts in 1820 to commemorate the death of George III, but these disappeared when the body of the church was rebuilt – nastily – in 1873, by E. B. Ferrey. The slate tablet, now on the lychgate, recorded their erection, eulogizing the Farmer King – 'Intended to Promote the Religion which he loved and practised And To preserve which in its Purity was the constant object of his Endeavours Through a Reign of Unexampled Length.' It calls him the people's 'Father and Friend'. Inside the church is a fine monument to Catherine Vaughan, d. 1733, wife of the last Nanney of Nannau: on a marble curtain float putti holding an oval portrait in high relief.

Near the road junction just N of Nannau is a car park, and signs to the **Precipice Walk**, one of the finest short walks (a couple of hours) imaginable. Notices warn off the elderly and sufferers from vertigo, but there is no real danger. The path contours round the genuinely precipitous side of Foel Cynwch, high above the Mawddach valley. The views over the Coed-y-Brenin forest are exchanged for the magnificent panorama of the Mawddach estuary, with Cadair Idris in all its grandeur to the S. The steep moorland hillside contrasts with the flat green valley-bottom. The path is laid out (by the National Park Service) as a landscape trail – the intrusive notices are rather absurdly didactic and patronizing. Round the SW point, the foreground consists of hummocky grassy hills and groups of trees. Finally, the path goes beside Llyn Gynwch, which, although used as a reservoir, is exceptionally lovely, the steep E side clothed in scrub oak. S of Nannau, at the road junction, is an entertaining castellated lodge, which, like some of the estate cottages, is derelict and labelled NOT FOR SALE.

Dolgellau is a town which arouses strong emotions: some love it, some hate it. To eighteenth-century travellers it was a joke:

If you ever go to Dolgelley,
Don't stay at the Lion Hotel,
There's nothing to put in your belly,
And no one to answer the bell.

No one, however, could deny the beauty of its site, on the southern side of the broad Wnion valley, tucked under the slopes of green hills which rise more and more steeply and craggily into the dramatic outline of Cadair Idris. What puts some people off is the fact that the town is built almost entirely out of the dark local stone, quarried in large blocks, and roofed in dark slate. To others this is the source of its attraction: sturdy plain houses, human in scale, Georgian in character. Henry Wilson, architect of the marvellous church at Brithdir (p. 256) nearby, wrote in 1895, 'What is so beautiful in Dolgelley seen from the hill on the station side of the river is the sense of appropriateness, of rightness in the arrangement of slate roofs and grey and white walls. When the eye passes from the town to Cader Idris or the surrounding hills and slopes, one feels there is a sort of family likeness, a relationship between the works of man and his maker.'

It is a pity that the town's narrow, crooked streets are crowded with through traffic. It is wonderfully higgledy-piggledy, all except the quite grand main square. The **Parish Church** is, in its simple way, a virtuoso performance in the use of local stone: built in 1716, Georgian details such as quoins are translated into gigantic proportions, but carried out with considerable finesse. There is a handsome tower and a Norman apse of 1854. The very wide nave has an extraordinary curved roof supported on wooden columns. The only medieval survival is the fourteenth-century effigy of Meurig Fychan, grandson of the founder of the Nannau family. The huge windows contain a most remarkable assemblage of Victorian glass – first-rate Clayton and Bell on the S, and on the N two amazing ones by unknown makers, showing the Crucifixion and Resurrection, old-fashioned but extremely vigorous and rich. Two of the apse windows are also striking. The churchyard gates were made at Coalbrookdale.

Dolgellau is the administrative capital of Merioneth: the old Shire Hall (E. Haycock, 1825) is by the bridge, and up above on the other side are the County Offices, 1938, by Sir Giles Scott – uncharacteristically 'modern'-looking. Dolgellau would be a good place to fall ill, as you might end up in the Hospital, a delightful building by H. L. North (1928). The informal group, covered in pebbledash, has an ingeniously-planned entrance porch, and, as usual with North, a fascinating interplay of gables and simplified Gothic doorways. Inside, each little ward has a pretty fireplace of purple brick inset with a variety of patterned tiles. The Catholic Church is a strikingly elaborate Norman edifice, in granite, largely designed by the Maltese parish priest, and built over many years (consecrated 1967).

BALA TO PORTMADOC

From Bala, the A4212 follows the Tryweryn valley northwards. The road has been vastly 'improved' since the construction of Llyn Celyn. At **Fron Goch** there is a nice little church of 1857–8 by T. M. Penson, perched above the river. This is where R. J. Lloyd Price (see p. 220) founded his short-lived Welsh Whiskey Distillery. A mile beyond is the vast dam of **Llyn Celyn**. This enormous reservoir, built in the 1960s, supplies water to Liverpool. It makes an interesting contrast with Lake Vyrnwy. Here no conifers have been planted, and the dam is covered with grass. Sir Frederick Gibberd was called in to advise on landscaping, and did an excellent job. The straining tower is inconspicuous. Yet here too a village was drowned – only a tiny one, perhaps, with a chapel and a Post Office, but a community nevertheless. And the lake will never look right: the flat surface of water is too big in proportion to the mountains which enclose it.

The memory of the village has been kept alive by Liverpool Corporation, who have built a new chapel, on the NW shore of the lake, to replace the drowned one. It is a sensitive piece of design, by R. L. Gapper of Aberystwyth. It is supposed to have some resemblance to a beached ship, and to represent the coming ashore of the drowned religion, but the symbolism seems superfluous. The tall simple building is constructed of stones from an old farmhouse. The interior, floored in slate, contains slate tablets bearing the names of those buried in the drowned graveyard. It is rather bare, and feels completely unused. Nearby is a walled graveyard containing the grave-stones from the old chapel.

Beyond Llyn Celyn, the road passes between two grand mountains, **Arennig Fach** (2259 ft) to the N, and **Arennig Fawr** (2800 ft) to the S. Each has a craggy E face, overhanging a lake. Arennig Fawr is much the finer and well worth going up. The best starting-point is from the minor road the other side of the river, near the limestone quarries. On the summit is a memorial stone to the eight crew-members of an American Flying Fortress, which just failed to clear the summit in 1943. The hole made by the crash still contains fragments of the plane. The view is splendid, as usual from mountains like this one which stand in comparative isolation. The descent can be made via the spur on the S side of the lake and then by the track from the lake itself, beautifully situated against a background of tumbled rocks and heather. The A4212 makes for Trawsfynydd (p. 239) by way of Cwm Prysor. Just beyond the small Llyn Tryweryn, there is a wonderful view down the deep valley, with the old Bala-Ffestiniog railway contouring around the steep precipices on the N. It crossed a side-valley by means of a splendid stone viaduct. Lower down the valley is Castell Prysor, a natural outcrop which was the site of a small castle.

The B4391 climbs over bare moorland to its junction with the B4407 (from Ysbyty Ifan – see p. 119). Just beyond the junction is **Rhaeadr-y-Cwm**. The valley suddenly opens out dramatically, and the river drops down a steep, rocky fall. A car park has been provided for viewing. All the uplands round here are full of small lakes. Up above the road to the N is **Llyn-y-Morynion**, the lake of the maidens. One story behind the name is that the men of Ardudwy, the coast-lands S of Harlech, went over to the Vale of Clwyd in search of wives, but on their way back were caught up by the girls' male relatives near Ffestiniog and slaughtered. Whereupon the girls, who obviously had romantic notions, leapt with one accord into this lake and drowned. For a different story, see p. 239. The stretch of road between here and Ffestiniog is marvellously beautiful on a summer evening, winding among outcropping rocks, and enjoying the view of Manod Mawr (2166 ft) with its great black cliffs.

It comes as quite a surprise to drop straight off the mountains into **Ffestiniog**, a substantial, townish village with terraces of stone houses and a large pub. Its church is perched on a prominent site at the W end of the village. It looks tiny from far off, but at close quarters it turns out to be a grossly over-scaled neo-Norman nightmare – the work of Henry Kennedy at his wildest (compare Llanllechid, p. 149). Built in 1844–5, it has a horse-shoe shaped chancel arch, a weird roof, and dotty carvings including gargoyles probably meant to be lions, but more like spaniels. The joining of nave and chancel was clearly a knotty problem for poor Kennedy. From near the old railway station, a track leads to Rhaeadr Cynfal, not particularly spectacular but beautifully situated among woods. Near it is a tall rock, rising out of the river, called **Huw Llwyd's Pulpit**. Huw Llwyd (c. 1568–1630) lived at Cynfal Fawr nearby. He fought in France and Holland, in a Welsh regiment raised to help drive the Spanish out of the Netherlands. The story of his return is told by Peacock in a ballad in *Headlong Hall*. (Peacock married a local girl.) He was well-known as a poet and sportsman, but the 'Pulpit' is connected with his more dubious repute as a wizard. His grandson, Morgan Llwyd (1619–59), was a founding-father of Dissent in Wales, a Parliamentarian, and also a poet. His most famous work was the *Llyfr y Tri Aderyn* (*The Book of the Three Birds*). This was a prose dialogue between an eagle (Cromwell), a dove (a Puritan), and a raven (an Episcopalian). Cynfal Fawr, built by Huw in 1630, has been altered.

Ffestiniog is now a much less important place than **Blaenau Ffestiniog**, up at the head of the valley (*blaen*). The slate quarries here were developed from about 1800, and, under the direction of men like Samuel Holland (a cousin of Mrs Gaskell) and John Whitehead Greaves, soon rivalled those of Caernarfonshire. The town grew up rapidly from the mid-nineteenth century, during the slate boom, leaping from 1000 to 12,000 in less than forty years, and so did the vast heaps of slate spoil which overshadow it. To some, these tips are (as at

Llanberis and Bethesda) a horrible legacy of the past, which should be covered up or destroyed as soon as possible. (They can certainly be very dangerous, especially if an avalanche is set off.) To others, they possess a fascination and a beauty all their own, particularly when wetted by the rain which falls so liberally here – the roof of the little church (Thomas Jones, 1842) has been painted blue to compensate for the rarity of blue sky. The only other building of architectural note in the town is the pleasant Hospital by Clough Williams-Ellis, perched dramatically over a cliff. But for individuality, Blaenau is hard to beat, with its rows of small terraced houses, its countless chapels (many now converted for other purposes), its bedraggled sheep, straying through the collapsing slate fences from the fields into the town, and, towering above everything, the steep hillsides and vast quarries. The plastered reveals of the windows of the houses give them a brightness and precision all the more pleasing for their Georgian proportions. With the running down of the quarries, which now employ a bare handful, unemployment is a chronic problem, but it is not surprising that people are unwilling to leave and seek work elsewhere, for the town has a friendliness and community spirit which are unimpaired. There is a grand male voice choir, and a silver band. The novelist John Cowper Powys (1872–1963), whose pride in his Welsh ancestry led him to settle in Wales in 1935, spent the last eight years of his life in Blaenau.

In 1972 one of the great quarries, **Llechwedd**, was opened to the public, and has been a colossal success. Almost entirely underground, this was opened in 1846 by J. W. Greaves. Horizontal tunnels, one above the other, connect the vast chambers from which the slate was mined. A battery-powered train takes visitors along one of the tunnels, and ex-miners explain how the quarry worked. You can also watch men splitting and dressing slate, with astonishing skill, and buy objects made of it (though the quality of design is sadly low). A visit is strongly recommended for anyone wishing to get a feel of this fascinating industry, once so vital to North Wales. On the opposite side of the road from Llechwedd are the **Oakeley Quarries**, once owned by the Oakeleys of Tan-y-Bwlch (p. 234), and still working, on a small scale. They too are highly dramatic, with their inclines, tramways, beautifully made slate stairways, and the huge yawning pit, where the lorries at the bottom look like toys. They too are now open to the public.

Beyond the quarries, the A496 goes over to Dolwyddelan (p. 121). The railway to Llandudno Junction runs from Blaenau, but the Festiniog Railway is still building its new route between Dduallt and the town (see p. 194). SW of Blaenau is **Tanygrisiau**. From here a road goes up NW into Cwmorthin, a spooky place on a misty day, with its ruined quarry-men's houses and chapel, and slate-tips, round the lake. Tanygrisiau is now a tourist place, as bus-loads flock to see the hydro-electric pumped-storage scheme. Both Llyn Ystradau, below, and Llyn Stwlan, high up above beneath Moelwyn Mawr, have been dammed and enlarged. Surplus off-peak electricity is used to pump water up from the lower lake to the higher one, and then used to generate more electricity during peak hours. So the same water is used again and again. The system has been so successful that another scheme is being carried out at Dinorwic (see p. 151).

The B4414, S of Tanygrisiau, is being widened (1973) and losing all its character, but the scenery of the valley is still strikingly beautiful, and forms a sharp contrast to the bleakness of the town. The **Vale of Ffestiniog** has long been regarded as one of the classic Welsh beauty spots, and rightly so. The river winds along flat water-meadows with the thickly-wooded sides of the valley rising steeply on either side. The rich beauty of the deciduous woods is almost unequalled in Wales.

The estate village of **Maentwrog**, set a little way round the hill from the important road junction, fits the picture admirably, with its terraces and handsome larger houses ranked up and down the slope, almost all made of the brownish-grey slatey stone of the district. Equally appropriate is the dear little church, down on the valley floor, reached from the village by way of a timber lychgate, the timbers infilled with stone slabs. This is by John Douglas, who completely remodelled the church in 1896. From the lychgate – or from the opposite side of the valley – it makes a lovely sight, with its low shingled spire rising above thick yews. Before Douglas got at it, it was a barn-like Gothic building of 1814: he put tracery in the windows, inserted timber arcades to form aisles, and added the chancel and the tower and spire. Lots of superb woodwork, and prettily decorated panels above the arcades. Memorials to the Oakeleys, who paid for Douglas's work. Maen Twrog (St Twrog's stone) is outside the church at the W end. Twrog was a sixth-century companion of Beuno. It is said that he angrily hurled the stone (a glacial erratic) from the mountain down on to a heathen altar and that it bears the marks of his fingers and thumb. 'Maen Tyriawg' is mentioned in the *Mabinogion*, as burial-place of Pryderi, son of Pwyll, treacherously slain by Gwydion when he came up from the south to recover his swine. The Rector here from 1572 until his death was Edmund Prys (1544–1623), poet and author of the most singable metrical version of the Psalms in Welsh.

The Oakeleys lived across the valley at **Tan-y-bwlch**, altered by Douglas in 1890, and now the National Park Centre: it is a rather dull castellated house on a splendid site, and with splendid grounds. In them is Llyn Mair, the beautifully wooded lake beside the B4410: this road leaves the A487 beside the **Oakeley Arms**, a very handsome early nineteenth-century hotel with twin canted bays, comfortably broad. The inn was well known to early tourists – at any rate, those who looked respectable enough to be admitted (Rowlandson was not the only unlucky one). Beyond Llyn Mair is Tan-y-bwlch Station, on the Festiniog Railway, which does a great loop to get round this valley. The railway crosses the road by means of an iron bridge made at the Boston Lodge Foundry – a good example of the railway's bold do-it-yourself policy (see p. 236). The land S of the station is a Nature Reserve. Beyond the station, the Roman road from Croesor meets the B4410, which goes on by way of Rhyd, enjoying marvellous views, to Llanfrothen (p. 237).

Below Tan-y-bwlch, on the A487, are a series of excellent stone estate buildings of the early nineteenth century: some are supported on posts which one assumes to be timber, but which turn out to be stone. The next couple of miles of road are a gruesome example of bad road-widening. **Penrhyndeudraeth** is one of those places which to the casual traveller seem to be just another unpronounceable name, an important traffic junction where you may be held up, either by the Festiniog Railway level crossing up at the top, or on the wonderfully Heath Robinson toll-bridge by which the Cambrian Coast Line and the road cross the Dwyryd (traffic lights;

toll 5p return; no caravans). In fact it is a tidy little place, with quite a townish feel around the main cross-roads. This part was laid out on reclaimed land, after the model of Tremadoc, by David Williams, the brother of Madocks' agent John Williams. The earlier village is represented by the terraces climbing steeply up the Beddgelert road. You may feel a foreigner in the shops, where far more Welsh is spoken than English, but you will certainly not be made to feel unwelcome. The main source of employment is the explosives factory by the toll-bridge. The nice little church is by T. M. Penson (1857).

Beyond Penrhyndeudraeth, at Minffordd, is the entrance to **Portmeirion.** Portmeirion has been so inimitably written up by its creator, Sir Clough Williams-Ellis, that it is difficult to elaborate. First, the reader must be recommended to read both Sir Clough's book *Portmeirion: The Place and its Meaning* (1963), and his autobiography *Architect Errant* (1971), or at least the guide-book – which contains appreciations by James Morris and Lewis Mumford. Second, practical details: a toll is charged, to keep the number of visitors to a manageable size, and for the upkeep of the place. At present it is 50p in high season, otherwise 40p or 30p. Those patronizing the Hotel or Salutation Restaurant do not have to pay the toll. Third, some history and facts. Sir Clough bought the estate in 1926: it then consisted of a pleasant early Victorian house down by a romantic little bay, on the beautiful Dwyryd estuary, where earlier there had been a little village called Aber Ia, with a shipyard and foundry. Earlier still, in the twelfth century, a castle had been built on the rocky hill above the bay by Gruffydd ap Cynan, but what little was left of it was destroyed c. 1869. The house was surrounded by wooded grounds, and Sir Clough also bought two properties which had belonged to Caton Haig, an expert on rhododendrons and azaleas. The extensive grounds, stretching right across the headland, are full of unusual trees and shrubs and well worth exploring. Sir Clough began by converting the house into a hotel, and building more cottages: since then, building has gone on more or less continuously, with numerous buildings or parts of buildings brought from elsewhere. The result is explicitly based on Italian coastal villages such as Portofino, and is a mixture of different architectural styles and elements, only in small part depending on the Welsh vernacular tradition, more Mediterranean than Celtic. Numerous ingenious tricks of scale and siting are played. Re-erected buildings include a delightful Gothic colonnade, built at Arnos Court in Bristol c. 1760; the Gothic porte-cochère from Nercwys Hall (see p. 43); the upper half of the Music Room chimney-piece from Norman Shaw's Dawpool (1883), used as the frontispiece of the domed Pantheon; the ballroom from Emral Hall (see p. 75), with its rich plaster ceiling showing the labours of Hercules, now in the 'Town Hall'; and columns from Samuel Wyatt's Hooton Hall, used for the 'Gloriette'. Most of the buildings serve as outposts of the Hotel, or for staff occupation. As well as the Hotel and restaurant, there are several shops. The Hotel has almost the atmosphere of a country house, with excellent service.

Portmeirion is impossible to evaluate – either you are bowled over by it, as we are, or you are not. Inevitably there are criticisms, and some are hard to answer – that an Italianate village is not suited to the coast of Wales, that it is all too much of a sham, and so on. The only thing to do is to go and see it and make up one's own mind. Sir Clough would be the last person to deny that it is theatrical – it is intended to be, like his own yellow stockings. For that reason, it is bound to look best when the lighting is right, so try to go, say, on a lovely summer evening. It is certainly a most astonishing thing to have been created by one man, and a self-made monument to one who, at the age of 91, shows no sign of letting-up in his busy life as an architect, landlord, and champion of what we have now come to call 'the environment'. The term may be modern, but one only has to read what Sir Clough was writing back in the 20s and 30s to realize that the fashionable doctrines and battle-cries of today were being set out clearly and forcefully by him long ago. Had they become fashionable sooner, Britain would be a far better place to live in now.

Beyond Minffordd, the A497 comes down to the E end of the Portmadoc Embankment (the Cob). Long queues build up in summer waiting to pay the toll ($2\frac{1}{2}$p return). Near the toll-house is **Boston Lodge**, named after William Madocks's far-off constituency in Lincolnshire. There is a Halt on the Festiniog Railway, and also the Works, where the Railway used to build its own engines (including the double-ended Merddin Emrys, 1879, still going strong) and still assembles its carriages. (For the Embankment and Portmadoc, see p. 193).

From Penrhyndeudraeth the A487 goes up over the ridge, and then across Morfa Gwyllt by the straight road which, after the draining of the Traeth, replaced the old road which follows the foot of the hills further E. On this road (best reached from the B4410 three-quarters of a mile E of Garreg) is the old church of **Llanfrothen**, hidden away below a farm. It is a small, rough building, with some medieval features, including the very crude screen and rood-beam. It was re-pewed in 1844: the pews are a mixed lot. A tablet commemorates William Williams of Brondanw, d. 1778 – 'He was the first who introduced Sea banks into this part of Wales.' Some of these pre-Madocks embankments can still be seen at various places along the old coastline (especially near Y Garth). The main part of Llanfrothen village is at **Garreg**, very much the estate village for Plas Brondanw, and bearing many signs of the unmistakable Clough style – most obviously the big stone folly-cum-War Memorial, but also the cottages painted white with 'Portmeirion green' trim. Just beyond the village a road goes NE past a gatehouse, up the Croesor valley. The mature hardwoods along it, like those on the main road, were planted by Sir Clough.

A short way up is **Plas Brondanw**, his ancestral home. The simple but impressive stone house was burnt out in 1951, but restored quickly. The gardens, laid out with great imagination, have marvellous views over to Snowdon. A statue of Neptune commemorates the fact that the sea once came right up below the house. Opposite, a path goes up past various Cloughish features to the castle-ruin (with concrete sub-structure) which was the wedding present he requested from his fellow Guards Officers in 1915 (rather than the traditional silver salver).

Beyond Brondanw, the road continues above the wooded Maesgwm valley, past slate quarries, until the **Croesor Valley** opens out at the village of the same name. It is a glaciated valley, straight and narrow, with the steep rocky scree-slopes of Cnicht rising darkly on the N, and smooth grassy slopes on the S, while the head of the valley is also steep and rounded. Seen from the top, it almost looks artificial. Its regularity was no doubt why it appealed to the Electricity Board engineers, who chose it as one of three proposed sites for the new pumped-storage scheme (see p. 151). It would have been a tragedy if the valley had been flooded, for this beautiful and remote place would have been ruined, and its strongly Welsh community destroyed. According to Lewis's *Topographical Dictionary* (1845), the name Croesor 'is said to have originated in an exclamation of grief uttered by Helen, the queen of Constantine, whose only son falling into her arms after he had been shot by a poisoned arrow, she cried out "*Oh! Croesawr, Croesawr i mi*," signifying, "Alas! to me, ill-fated hour"' (or 'hour of my cross'). The name Croesor really means 'cross-roads' (see below).

The village consists of a slate-hung chapel, a few rows of cottages and a scattering of farms. Once a self-contained community, it owed its existence to the slate quarries, opened c. 1858, and closed in the 1930s after an unsuccessful history. The main quarry (or rather mine, since the slate does not outcrop) was high up on the S side of the valley (see p. 165). The Croesor Tramway was begun in 1860, and extended to Portmadoc in 1864. The line starts right at the head of the valley, to which various inclines descend: from the S end of the valley an incline took the wagons down to estuary level. The line from there to Portmadoc was later used by the Welsh Highland Railway (see p. 155). The track makes a good walk up the valley from the village. For the ascent of Cnicht and the Moelwyns, see p. 164. Croesor is on the line of the Roman road from Segontium to Tomen-y-Mur: this can be followed over to Nanmor (p. 153), as a rough track, or over to Tan-y-Bwlch – this part is now made up (very steep and numerous gates, but magnificent views).

Beyond Garreg, the main road makes another straight dash across reclaimed land, only to be brought up short at the surprising great rock knob of Garregelldrem. A mile further on it enters Caernarfonshire near Hafod Garegog (p. 153).

MAENTWROG TO DOLGELLAU BY THE A487

From Maentwrog the road climbs through woodland. Beyond the junction with the A4108 (from Ffestiniog), a side road goes off E under the old railway. A mile along it is **Tomen-y-mur**, with numerous different earthworks. One, by the road just beyond a forestry plantation, is a small amphitheatre, probably used for demonstrating drill and weapon-handling to the troops. From here the Tomen itself can be seen – a motte said to have been built by William Rufus during his campaign against Gruffydd ap Cynan in 1098. It stands within the top end of a small Roman fort, which had stone walls. Around it are remains of a remarkable series of subsidiary structures: apart from the amphitheatre, these include a bath-house and civil settlement SE of the fort, a supposed parade-ground NE, with a mound built as the *tribunal* (saluting-base), and two small practice-camps NW. The site enjoys wonderful views. The land is private, and notices warn off trespassers. It was bombed in the war, presumably because marked on maps as a fort. The place appears in the *Mabinogion*, in the story of Math son of Mathonwy: it was at 'Mur Castell' that Lleu Llaw Gyffes set up his court. He was murdered by Gronw, the lover of his wife Blodeuedd, and metamorphosed into a mouldering eagle, but was restored to human form by Gwydion, who then set out for Mur Castell. Blodeuedd and her maidens fled, but were so afraid they could only go backwards. All the maidens fell in a lake (Llyn y Morynion – p. 231) and were drowned, but Blodeuedd was turned into an owl.

The vast stretch of once bare moorland between the Rhinogs and the Arennigs, which the A487 traverses, is now dominated by the immense bulk of **Trawsfynydd Nuclear Power Station** (inaugurated 1963). The artificial lake, formerly used to work the small hydro station at Ivy Bridge, near Maentwrog, has been greatly enlarged. The power station itself is a gigantic lump. Sir Basil Spence was called in to make it more presentable, but his efforts make little difference when one sees the thing from miles away. Even from the Rhinogs it appears as a sore intrusion into the wild scene. From close to, the chief impression is of all the nasty paraphernalia that goes with electricity supply, and the landscaping (by Sylvia Crowe) cannot do much to alleviate it. Worse still are the lines of pylons radiating out from the station over some of the loveliest country in Wales. For the local people the station does at least mean more readily available electricity and about fifty jobs. The power station even caters for tourists. **Trawsfynydd** itself is a close-packed stone village, bypassed now, celebrated for its sheep-dog trials. In the main street stands a bronze statue (by L. S. Merrifield) of a shepherd – Ellis Humphrey Evans (1887–1917), whose bardic name was 'Hedd Wyn'. Born on a local farm, he was mostly self-educated, and devoted himself to poetry. His poem won him the Chair at the National Eisteddfod in 1917, but it was announced that he had been killed in France five weeks earlier, and the Chair was draped in black.

The road S of Trawsfynydd gives striking views of the E side of the Rhinog range, particularly splendid when the setting sun outlines its broken silhouette. From **Bronaber** a minor road goes E, past an old army camp which is now a second-home Noddyland of Norwegian log chalets, to a junction from which one road goes up the Gain valley and over the hills to Llanuwchllyn, recently made up (see p. 225). Between this road and the other is **Llech Idris**, a tall prehistoric monolith: the reason for the name Idris is unknown. Near here used also to stand Bedd Porus, the tombstone of a fifth-century Christian, inscribed *homo planus fuit* – 'he was an ordinary man'. It is now in the National Museum. The presence of these monuments is no doubt explained by the crossings of various ancient trackways, including the Roman road S from Tomen-y-Mur (Sarn Helen), which runs roughly parallel to the A487, on the E. The second of these two roads leads S into **Coed-y-Brenin**, a huge area of Forestry Commission woodlands. (Its name recently became notorious as the site of Rio Tinto Zinc's proposed copper-mine, now thankfully abandoned: it would have been some way to the E of the forest).

From the road near **Gwynfynydd** (2 miles from the junction) one gets a good view of the winding Gain and Mawddach valleys: the few surviving patches of deciduous woodland make a telling contrast with the infamous regiments of conifers. Gwynfynydd is the site of one of the most famous gold mines in Wales, and is also the best way of approaching **Rhaeadr Mawddach** and **Pistyll Cain**, two of the best waterfalls in Wales. Gold was first worked in the 1840s; there were some rich yields in the 1860s, the 1880s, and around the turn of the century. By the 1930s most of the mines had closed, but there is still some activity. From 736/285, a track leads down past adit levels. Some buildings remain beside the Mawddach (at

737/281) including an old strong room, for storing the gold, closed by a steel door brought from the old County Gaol at Dolgellau. Someone has optimistically broken a hole through a side wall. Near it is an adit level leading to a chamber, in which a wooden head-frame still stands above a 300 ft incline. A path follows the river (beside tramway remains) towards Rhaeadr Mawddach, below which are remains of the dressing-mill, together with the cast-iron pipe which brought the river-water to feed the turbine.

The two waterfalls are very different. The Mawddach fall is wide and comparatively low, while Pistyll Cain – the more beautiful – is much higher and narrower, and set in more romantic surroundings. The falls can also be reached by forestry tracks from Pont-ar-Eden, near Ganllwyd (on the A487, four and a half miles S of Bronaber). Another very fine fall is on the river Gamlan, which joins the Mawddach at Ganllwyd: paths lead up through beautiful woodland (National Trust) to **Rhaeadr Ddu** (the black fall), where the water drops over a rock escarpment (10 minutes from the road). Paths connect the falls with **Dolmelynllyn**: the Victorian house, now a hotel, stands on the site of the pretty *cottage orné* built by W. A. Madocks after he bought the property in the early 1790s. He later had to sell it to help finance his greater projects (p. 192). The Latin inscription (recut in slate by the NT in 1973) beside the fall was almost certainly put there by Madocks or a member of his 'chaotic' houseparties. It is from Gray's *Ode to the Deity of the Grande Chartreuse*.

Beyond Ganllwyd, the road emerges from the forest to follow a more open valley, with the Precipice Walk (p. 227) high up on the E. At **Llanelltud** the small church stands within a circular churchyard – always a sign of great antiquity. It is dedicated to the great fifth-century St Illtud: most of the churches dedicated to him are in SE Wales, and it is thought that he must have come here by way of the sea. The church is something of a hotchpotch, but an attractive one, with a medieval roof and panelling, round-headed windows which look eighteenth-century, and an E window of 1899 (when the church was restored by Hodgson Fowler of Durham). A restoration also took place in 1636. A stone, possibly twelfth-century, bears an outline of a footprint (difficult to make out), and an inscription interpreted as 'The footprint of Kenyric

(Cinwrig) is affixed to the top of the stone and he himself is bound (by his vow made) before he set out on a journey.' It is suggested that he may have been making a pilgrimage to Bardsey, Rome or even Jerusalem.

Near here were found a medieval silver gilt chalice and paten, now in the National Museum. They probably come from **Cymer Abbey** (D. o. E.), across the river, reached by a lane from the other side of the bridge. Cymer means 'confluence' – the Wnion joins the Mawddach nearby. The abbey was founded from Cwmhir (p. 314) in 1199, by Gruffydd ap Cynan and his family. It was never very prosperous, and its buildings were nothing like so grand as those of other Welsh Cistercian houses, but the ruins are fairly substantial and are given added attraction by the lovely site (though the caravans are a pity). The church was built in the early thirteenth century, and was intended to extend further E, but the English Wars prevented this. The W tower was built c. 1350. Parts of the cloister and frater are visible, but much destruction has been caused by the use of the ruins as a farmyard. Up above the road, as it winds along the Wnion, stands **Hengwrt**, a house of 1892, on an ancient site, famous as the home of Robert Vaughan (1592?–1667), who assembled the finest collection of Welsh MSS ever made by one man. In 1859 it passed to W. W. E. Wynne of Peniarth (see p. 261), and in 1909 went to the National Library, of which it forms one of the greatest glories.

MAENTWROG TO DOLGELLAU BY THE COAST – A496

A mile beyond Maentwrog is Ivy Bridge, its old power station (see p. 239) still showing traces of war-time camouflage. The lane on the Maentwrog side of the river climbs steeply above the valley, with lovely scrub oak by the river and on the N side, Economic Forestry on the S. After about three quarters of a mile, a sign indicates a path down to **Rhaeadr Ddu** (not to be confused with the one at Ganllwyd, p. 241). This is well worth a visit: the stream comes down diagonally through a rocky gorge and then falls over a precipice into a large round pool, dark but clear. Beyond Ivy Bridge, the road comes close to the river Dwyryd, exceptionally lovely at this point, with rocky hills on either side which take on marvellous colours in the sunlight, and the wide blue river below. It is best seen from the toll bridge, and makes one realize how much was lost when Traeth Mawr was drained (p. 193). Alas, pylons cross the river, and the County Council have done some appalling road-widening. The stone quays on the N side of the river were used for shipping the slates from Ffestiniog before the railway was built in 1836: they were brought down here on carts, and then loaded onto barges, and rowed out to the ships anchored at Ynys Cyngar, beyond Borth-y-Gest. The bargemen were an odd lot of men, called 'the Philistines'.

Opposite the toll-bridge road, a lane climbs steeply up to **Llandecwyn**, where the little church, rebuilt in the nineteenth century, on an ancient site, stands solitary and exposed, near the big Llyn Tecwyn-uchaf. On the N shore of the lake there is said to be a pile of white stones called Bedd Dorti (Dorothy's grave). Don't interfere with them, or Dorothy may emerge from the lake and drag you in. The bare hills are disfigured by pylons. From here the old road, used before the coast road was built, can be followed all the way down to Llanfair. It is steep, narrow and gated, but well worth exploring, for its open moorland, its magnificent views over Cardigan Bay, and its numerous antiquities, including standing stones and cairn circles. Down on the main road, **Talsarnau** is a business-like place. Shortly beyond, the A496 goes off across Morfa Harlech, forming a kind of Harlech bypass. Until the land was reclaimed from the sea, this was all a vast area of tidal sands. Rising out of them was the large island, rocky but cultivated, on which stands the windswept little church of **Llanfihangel-y-Traethau** (at 595/354) – the church of St Michael in the estuary. The dedication is explained by the situation – it is a kind of Welsh St Michael's Mount. Rebuilt in 1871, it has two inscribed stones. One is outside the W door, a long, thin stone, with a lengthy Latin inscription identifying it as the tomb of Wleder, mother of Odelau, who built the church in the time of King Owain (presumably Owain Gwynedd). The other, inside, bears a line from the Roman poet Martial, used as a Christian epitaph: once thought to be Roman, the inscription is now dated to the seventeenth century. In the graveyard is buried Mari Evans y Fantell Wen ('of the white robe', 1735–89). The members of the sect she founded did not bury her for a long time, as she had claimed that she would never die. She also claimed to be betrothed to Christ, and held a wedding ceremony in Ffestiniog Church (in fact she had left her husband and lived with another man). Her followers wore white robes on Sundays and held ceremonies on the hills. N of Llanfihangel is the small Ynys Gifftan: the river used to flow S of the island, but suddenly changed course on Christmas Eve 1876, and now flows to the N.

The B4573 winds beneath woods. Just beyond the junction with the A496, a road leads up to **Maes-y-Neuadd**, a handsome, mostly eighteenth-century house in a lovely situation, now a hotel. Near the main road is Glyn, a good house of 1616, belonging to Lord Harlech. A mile SW, well off the road, is **Y Lasynys**, a farmhouse which was the birthplace of Ellis Wynne (1671–1734). His father was of the Glyn family. He was rector of Llandanwg from 1705, and of Llanfair from 1711. He is best known as the author of *Gwledigaethau y Bardd Cwsc* (*Visions of the Sleeping Bard*), a Welsh prose classic. The three visions are of the world, death and hell. Further on, the woods below the road were given to the National Trust by Dr Percival Graves, author of the song *Father O'Flynn*, and father of Robert Graves.

The A496 provides the more dramatic approach to **Harlech**, with the castle splendidly sited up on its rocky promontory, commanding the whole coast. It looked even finer when the sea came right up to it – see numerous eighteenth-century pictures. The place, although it received its charter in 1284, and is nominally the county town, is in fact just a village, and an attractive and friendly one too. Its main street winds along the hillside, while the side streets career up and down on either side. There is no historical evidence for a castle here before the present one, but Harlech plays a prominent role in the story of Branwen, daughter of Llŷr, in the *Mabinogion*. It was when he was at his court of 'Harddlech in Ardudwy' that her brother, Bendigeidfran, the giant-king of Britain, saw the ships of Matholwch, King of Ireland, approaching. Matholwch came to ask for the hand of Branwen, the fairest maiden in the world, and their marriage-feast took place at Aberffraw in Anglesey. However, nothing but trouble came of the match, both Britain and Ireland ending up devastated as a result. The seven men who cut off Bendigeidfran's head, at his request, spent seven years feasting at Harlech, being entertained both by the birds of Rhiannon and by the severed head, which remained pleasant company. After another eighty years in Pembrokeshire, they buried it in London.

The present **Castle** was built in 1283–90, as part of Edward I's series, by James of St George (see p. 357). Its striking design (comparable to Beaumaris, p. 199) involves using the gatehouse as a keep. It has a pair of huge towers facing the outside, and a more domestic façade within. The curtain-wall which meets it on either side encloses a roughly square space with a round tower at each corner. A much lower curtain runs parallel to this one, quite close to it, and further fortifications, more irregular in outline, run round the bottom of the rock on which the castle stands. They include the Water Gate which gave access to the dock. James of St George was made constable of the castle in 1290, as a reward for his achievements, and held office until 1293. In the next year it was besieged during the insurrection of Madog ap Llywelyn, but the garrison of 37 held out. In 1401 it was attacked by Owen Glendower, who finally got possession of it in 1404. He made Harlech his capital and summoned a parliament here. But in 1408 it was taken by Gilbert and John Talbot. Among the prisoners were Owen's wife Margaret Hanmer, and his daughter and her four children. His son-in-law, Sir Edmund Mortimer (see p. 287), had already died from privation.

Harlech played a part in the Wars of the Roses. Queen Margaret fled to it after the capture of Henry VI in 1460. After she went to Scotland, Dafydd ab Ifan held it for the Lancastrians. He is famous for his boast that, having held a castle in France for so long that all the old women in Wales talked about it, he would now hold one in Wales for so long that all the old women in France would talk of it. It is not known where the castle in France was, but it is true that he held Harlech for eight years, and was the last commander to surrender to the Yorkists. Sir Richard Herbert, to whom he surrendered, is said to have saved Dafydd's life by telling Edward IV that if he refused to spare him he would put him back in the castle and leave it to someone else to get him out. The stirring *March of the Men of Harlech* is associated with Dafydd's stand. Finally, in the Civil War, it was again the last of the King's castles to surrender, even though it had already become ruinous by the reign of Elizabeth.

The view from the castle walls extends over Cardigan Bay and Snowdonia, with Snowdon grandly excelling its neighbours. The plain little **Church** was built in 1841 by Thomas Jones, to replace the old one at Llandanwg (below): Ellis Wynne had wanted to build a chapel here in 1706. It contains the fifteenth-century font from Llandanwg. Harlech is famous for the enormous sandy beach which stretches along Morfa Harlech. Part of the dunes is used as the Royal St David's Golf Club. S of the village is the large, gaunt St David's Hotel, built in 1910–11 by George Walton, but burnt in 1922 and rebuilt. Walton was an excellent architect, closely associated with C. R. Mackintosh and the Glasgow School. He was also the architect for **Wern Fawr**, just N of the hotel, built as a private house for George Davison (of Kodak) in 1908–11, and opened in 1927 as **Coleg Harlech**, a residential college for adults. It is a sombre design, its severity matching the dark massiveness of the local stone. Each side has a long low pediment extending the whole length. Large additions have been made at each end, those on the N after a recent fire. The tower block to the S is sadly inappropriate, in height and materials. The charming bridge over the road (by Walton) has been removed for road widening, but it is to be hoped that it will be replaced.

Up on the hills above the town (at 586/302) are the so-called **Muriau'r Gwyddelod** (Irishmen's walls – see p. 214), two Iron Age hut groups and associated fields and terraces. A mile S of Harlech, a lane goes down to the seaside hamlet of **Llandanwg**, very much a holiday place with chalets and caravans, and a popular beach which can be dangerous owing to the currents produced by the river Artro. The tiny church has been being increasingly swallowed up by the dunes for many years. Efforts have been made to save it, but it is an uphill job, and the sands will surely win one day. Ellis Wynne (rector 1705–11) wrote in 1720: 'We have a Tradn. abt. our Ch. of Llandanwg yt was a chapell of Rest for corpses to be transported to yt fam'd Repository at Bardsey Islad' (p. 181). The church contains an inscribed stone, probably Roman.

The main road winds through **Llanfair**, of which parish Wynne was Rector from 1711 until his death: he is buried beneath the altar of the church (rehashed by Kennedy in 1858). The underground caverns of a slate mine here have recently been opened to the public. Up above Llanfair, not easy to find, is a small cromlech built into a farmyard: an eighteenth-century traveller was disgusted that the tomb of a hero should be inhabited by pigs. Beyond Llanfair is **Pensarn**, where there used to be a small harbour, used for coastal trade. Some boats went further: the rotting timbers visible in the estuary are said to have belonged to a vessel which two men took to America with a cargo of slates. On their return, they at once made for the pub, to spend some of their profits, and got into an argument, after which one of them sneaked down and set fire to the boat.

Llanbedr is an attractive village (often Best Kept), grouped around the bridge over the Artro. The church (restored by F. R. Wilson of Alnwick in 1883) is of c. 1500, and contains an incised Bronze Age stone. Two *meini hirion* (standing stones) stand near it. W of the village, accessible by a causeway one and a half hours before or after High Tide, is Mochras (Shell Island) – with an admission fee. It is chiefly famous for the tremendous variety of shells to be found along its beach, but is also noted for its bathing and fishing. More recently it has caused a stir as an unofficial nudist resort, whose denizens fix up tin cans on strings to warn of approaching policemen.

Mochras farmhouse was the home of Siôn Phylip (1543?–1620), the first of the 'Phylipiad Ardudwy' (Phylipses of Ardudwy), a group of poet-kinsmen, who were among the last of the professional bards, trained in bardic lore and genealogy. They wrote poems to many of the great families of North Wales, often describing their houses. Siôn, who had graduated at the second Caerwys Eisteddfod in 1568 (see p. 45), was drowned in crossing from Pwllheli to Mochras, on the way back from a bardic tour. (Such deaths were common when crossing the Bay was a normal means of travel.) Siôn's brother Rhisiart and his sons Gruffydd and Phylip Siôn were also bards. The wide sandy coast S of Mochras (Morfa Dyffryn) is now covered with acres of caravans. From a point roughly SW of Llanbedr, **Sarn Badrig** runs out into the sea for some ten miles, in the same direction. The name means 'Patrick's Causeway', but Pennant thought that it should really be 'Badrhwyg', or 'ship-breaking', since many ships have gone aground on it. According to legend, it was one of the embankments which kept the sea out of Cantref y Gwaelod, the area of prosperous land now covered by Cardigan Bay. It was flooded when Seithenyn, who should have looked after the sluices, got drunk and neglected the job. The story is enchantingly told by Peacock in *The Misfortunes of Elphin*. The causeway (really, of course, a strange natural feature) is best seen from up on the mountains on a bright, sunny day.

The **Valley of the Artro**, leading up to its source in Cwm Bychan, is a famous beauty spot, and rightly so, since it is one of the most attractive in Wales. The river, occasionally spanned by rough stone bridges, flows between woods of scrub oak, the damp green turf decorated with all manner of wild flowers, and open rocky moorland. The woods are inhabited by wild goats, whose sudden appearance, with their fantastically twisted horns, staring yellow eyes, and obnoxious stink, can cause a fright. At **Cwm Bychan** the lake lies beneath the splendid crags of Carreg y Saeth; to the N are the gentler but rocky slopes of Clip. There is a remarkable echo. The farmhouse beyond was the home of the Lloyd family, who claimed to have lived here since 1100. Pennant visited the place, c. 1780, and was entertained by Evan Llwyd 'in the style of antient Briton'. Llwyd rattled off his pedigree back to Bleddyn ap Cynfyn (d. 1075) – not at all an exceptional thing for a Welshman to do. Pennant was regaled with 'potent beer, to wash down the Coch yr Wden, or hung goat', but was not expected to drink out of the ancient family cup, made from a bull's scrotum. The most celebrated member of the family was Major-General Henry Lloyd (c. 1720–83), a Jacobite who went to France, became a lay brother in a religious order, took part in the '45, and served in the Prussian, Austrian and Russian armies. Nevertheless, the British Government gave him a pension. He also wrote a *History of the Late War in Germany*: his military theory influenced Napoleon. From the farm a path leads up to the **Roman Steps**, a beautifully engineered path, with long stretches of stone steps, which leads up to the pass of Bwlch Tyddiad. It is an easy walk, and well worth taking. The steps cannot really be Roman, and are impossible to date: the suggestion that they were built by the Llwyds seems likely to be true, as they would have most occasion to use them – others would more probably use Bwlch Drws Ardudwy (below). From the top there is a good view over the bleak Migneint. It is a rough, steep climb up to Rhinog Fawr.

From the bridge over the Artro a mile up from Llanbedr another road climbs up on the S side of the river. It soon passes **Capel Salem**, a simple little eighteenth-century Baptist chapel with its fittings intact. It was made famous by the painting by Sydney Curnow Vosper, showing an old lady in traditional dress. The picture, now in the Lady Lever Art Gallery at Port Sunlight, hangs, in reproduction, in the houses of Welsh people all over the world, and has even acquired a folklore of its own. It is said that the lady was notoriously vain, and that a devil is visible in the folds of her shawl. The road goes up **Nantcol**, much more open and bare than the Artro valley, but impressively rugged, with the rocky Rhinogs towering above, and grassy ridges enclosing either side. At the top is **Maes-y-garnedd**, birthplace of Colonel John Jones (1597?–1660), the regicide. He was a signatory of the death-warrant of Charles I, and later married Cromwell's sister. He was executed at the Restoration. He was nothing like such an ogre as he was made out to be, but was a deeply religious, cultivated, and fair-minded man.

Beyond the farm, a path leads up to **Bwlch Drws Ardudwy** (the pass of the door of Ardudwy), between Rhinog Fawr and Rhinog Fach. It is a place of magnificent ruggedness, for the Rhinogs are rockier than any of the other mountains of Snowdonia, except the Glyders. Black, tumbled rocks and heather, and comparatively little grass anywhere. Their peculiarity was noted by Giraldus, who stayed at Llanfair on his recruiting campaign in 1188. He called them 'narrow, compacted, and crest-like in form'. There is, of course, a geological explanation for this: Rhinog Fawr (2362 ft) forms the centre of the Harlech Dome, a massive anticline of Cambrian rocks. The Middle Cambrian rocks of the Rhinogs are tough and resist erosion. The going on these mountains is naturally hard, but exhilarating, and they have a rough beauty all their own. The best walk is to start by the Roman steps, and follow the range down to Diffwys, the problem being, of course, that this involves the use of two cars or of accomplices. More simply, the circuit can be made from Nantcol. It requires a strenuous crossing of the pass: the descent from Rhinog Fawr, over seemingly endless shelves of rock, is particularly gruelling. Between Rhinog Fach (2333 ft) and Y Llethr (2475 ft) is Llyn Hywel, one of the most impressive in North Wales, with huge stone slabs sloping steeply into the water.

S of Llanbedr is **Dyffryn Ardudwy**: the part of the village along the road is unattractive, but the lower part, round the church (strictly **Llanenddwyn**) is more pleasant. Betjeman's well-known lines apply to the church only too neatly:

The church's restoration
In 1883
Has left for contemplation
Not what there used to be.

The culprit was Kennedy, together with the Vicar who ignored the protests of the Society for the Protection of Ancient Buildings. Behind the school, on the main road, is a large portal dolmen (D. o. E.). The two burial chambers were originally incorporated in a single long cairn. This is one of the innumerable prehistoric antiquities which are scattered over the slopes of the Dyffryn – cairns, stone circles, hut groups, forts, and so on. Clearly this area was the site of intensive settlement.

A number of these antiquities can be reached by way of the long, straight avenue which leads up to **Cors-y-Gedol**. This fine old house was the seat of the Vaughans, one of the greatest families in North Wales. They traced their pedigree from Osbwrn Wyddel (the Irishman), who married the heiress of Cors-y-Gedol in the thirteenth century. Dafydd ab Ifan ab Einion, defender of Harlech Castle (p. 245), was of this family. In later years they extended their estates over 11,000 acres, and were great patrons of literature. The house was built in 1592–3 by Griffith Vaughan, but has been much extended since: a wing with elegant Adamesque rooms was added in the late eighteenth century. Some rooms have seventeenth-century chimneypieces and panelling. The gatehouse, big and gabled, was built in 1630 by William Vaughan, a close friend of Ben Jonson. Inevitably, it is attributed to Inigo Jones. After being almost unoccupied for some time, the house is now again lived in, and is not open: unfortunately the drive past the gatehouse is private, but glimpses can be caught from the public road. Beyond the house a track continues to the E: another track leads S from it to a ruined burial chamber, its huge capstone propped on only one support. It is known as **Coeten Arthur** (Arthur's quoit), because Arthur is said to have thrown it from the summit of Moelfre, up above. A short way N of the cromlech are remains of a hut group. The track continues right up the valley to Llyn Bodlyn (now a reservoir), and Llyn Dulyn, below Crib-y-rhiw. A mile below Llyn Bodlyn another track joins it for a while, coming SE from Llanbedr: it crosses the river Ysgethin by an old pack-horse bridge, and then zigzags up the steep side of Llawlech and over to Bontddu. Before the coast road was built, this was an important route.

Opposite the drive of Cors-y-Gedol is **Llanddwywe Church**, not of great interest in itself, but the chapel added c. 1615 by Griffith Vaughan contains splendid seventeenth- and eighteenth-century monuments to the family. Those to William Vaughan (1786) and Margaret Vaughan (1772) are by Van der Hagen of Shrewsbury. Beyond Tal-y-bont, just E of the road, is **Egryn Abbey** (private): there was never an abbey here, but possibly it is the site of a hospice for poor travellers. What stands here now is a pair of houses (an example of the 'unit system' – see p. 367). One is a late-medieval hall-house, altered in the seventeenth and nineteenth centuries, the other is seventeenth-century. A mile inland from Egryn are **Carneddau Hengwm**, a pair of long cairns: the S one, better preserved, is a portal dolmen (like the one at Dyffryn, p. 250). To the NW, on a spur, is Pen-y-Dinas, a fort protected by a ditch and stone-faced rampart.

Further S, the gap between coast and hills narrows as Barmouth is approached. One and a half miles N of the town is its mother-church, at **Llanaber**, beautifully sited up above the sea, in a large churchyard packed with tombs, many of them, appropriately, of sailors. The church is most unusual for Wales, an almost perfectly preserved thirteenth-century building, with aisles and clerestory and a good-sized raised chancel. It was built by Hywel ap Gruffydd ap Cynan, a great-grandson of Owain Gwynedd, and a supporter of Llywelyn the Great. A proposal for its restoration by T. M. Penson in 1857 was severely criticized, and two years later the job was done very carefully by Philip Boyce, under the supervision of W. W. E. Wynne. All windows except one are lancets, and they are filled with a variety of good Victorian glass. The roofs are fifteenth century. There are two fifth-century inscribed stones, found on the beach.

Barmouth, although very much a holiday resort, is a most unusual and attractive town; it is built up against steep towering cliffs, and the houses climb the rocks and perch wherever they can find a foothold, reached by narrow winding steps. In early summer, the cliff blazes with yellow gorse, making a cheerful contrast with the dark stone. The picturesque qualities of the town appealed strongly to artists such as Cornelius Varley. John Ruskin was delighted that Barmouth was the site of 'the first bit of ground – noble crystalline rock, I am thankful to say – possessed by St George in the island'. He was referring to the dozen cottages up at the top, which were given to his new Guild of St George ('for the education of English peasantry') in 1875 by Mrs G. T. Talbot. This 'social experiment' has been curiously ignored by modern Ruskin scholars. In fact, it did not amount to much: the cottages were let at fixed rents to carefully chosen tenants, but diligently supervised and improved as necessary. It all sounds patronizing to us, but as part of Ruskin's policy, 'to work with the minutest possible touches – but with a steady end in view', it makes sense. The most remarkable tenant was Auguste Guyard, himself a social reformer, who left France in the Franco-Prussian War: he was a friend of Lamartine, Dumas, and Victor Hugo (who left his white Persian cat in Guyard's care when he went into exile). He was buried in the cliff-top garden which he cultivated. Also up at the top is Dinas Oleu, the first piece of land ever given to the National Trust – also by Mrs Talbot, in 1895.

Barmouth (the name is a corruption of Abermaw – Abermawddach) was, until the later nineteenth century, a small fishing port, and development of the lower part of the town came comparatively late. The oldest building, down by the harbour, is 'Y Tŷ Gwyn yn Bermo', said to have been built by a fifteenth-century Griffith Vaughan of Cors-y-Gedol 'in order to enable him to communicate more safely, relative to the invasion of England, with Jasper Tudor, Earl of Pembroke, uncle of Henry of Richmond, afterwards Henry VII' (W. W. E. Wynne). Much rebuilt. Near by is a jolly little circular lock-up of c. 1820. Barmouth's first church was **St David's**, a plain cruciform job, of 1838, by Edward Haycock

Senior. It pleased J. L. Petit (see p. 254), but A. G. Bradley held that 'as a specimen of that debased period it would for unmitigated homeliness be very hard to beat'. It is now used for Welsh services, having been superseded by the great **Church of St John**, set in a commanding position, with a backdrop of bracken-covered cliff. It was designed by Douglas and Fordham, and largely paid for by Mrs Dyson Perrins (of Worcester Sauce). It was begun in 1889, but in 1892, when it was just completed, the tower collapsed, and the church was not finally finished until 1898. The old-fashioned feel of the town's main street is fast disappearing: the wonderfully archaic Cambrian Drapery Stores, complete with iron loggia, has closed at last and is being turned into a restaurant. The big houses built by rich English businessmen in the nineteenth century are now mostly hotels: N of the town is the best, Plas Mynach, a romantic castellated house by John Douglas (this was Mrs Dyson Perrins's house). Near it is the silliest, also castellated but with a big Norman porch.

Barmouth is at the mouth of the **Mawddach Estuary**, wide and lovely, with wooded hills on both sides and Cadair Idris towering grandly above the S side. A good place to enjoy it from is the railway bridge, built by Benjamin Piercy, regarded at the time of its building as an appalling desecration, but now widely loved. A footpath crosses it (toll 3p). An even better view can be had from the charmingly Victorian **Panorama Walk**, reached from the road which climbs the hill from near the bridge. The serpentine path is dotted with serpentine benches, the seats supported on twisty cast-iron snakes. On a rocky promontory which juts out S of the road, right into the estuary, is a perky Gothic house with a grand clock-spire and elaborately carved porch. Called Coes Faen, it was enlarged in 1844 by Thomas Jones, for himself. He died here.

The A496 follows the Mawddach. Three miles along, a narrow lane goes up to the extraordinary little church of **Caerdeon**. This was built in 1862 as a result of a dispute between the Rev. W. E. Jelf, who settled here and coached undergraduates in classics, and the Rector of Llanaber, who refused to provide English services. The church was built, but the Rector quoted a law of Queen Elizabeth's time according to which services in predominantly Welsh areas had to be in Welsh. The result was the English Services in Wales Act of

1863, by which services could be held in English if ten or more parishioners requested them. It is an exceedingly odd church, and was even odder as first built, when it consisted simply of a rectangular building of rough local stone, with plain rectangular windows, and a rough loggia over the entrance, supported on square piers. The eaves are broad, and the E window (now liturgical W) is circular. The chancel and transept, together with the massive bell-cote, are sensitive later additions. A tablet over the door commemorates John Louis Petit, 'founder and benefactor'. The *Ecclesiologist* of 1863 published an amusing critique, describing the church as 'something between a large lodge gate and a lady's rustic dairy . . . The architect is the Rev. J. L. Petit, and the object of the building (its religious services apart) is to exhibit to the world the notions of picturesque appropriateness entertained by that clever amateur. Mr Petit, as everybody knows, is always drawing and denouncing Gothic, while seeking his practical model in the rustic Italian of hillside chapels on the flanks of the Southern Alps. Such a chapel, with a great dash of Cymric roughness, does he present to us in Merionethshire. There is no doubt a certain amount of quaint picturesqueness about the pile . . . but, after all, the thing is an exotic . . . its whole form is somehow alien from the idea of a church . . . Above all, the frame is not big enough for the picture. . . . In a word, the effect of the building is something like that of the Swiss chalet on the Barnet road' (i.e. Swiss Cottage). To modern eyes, the church is a refreshing change from the repetitive little Gothic chapels of the mid-nineteenth century, and it does draw on local traditions and materials – even if they be those of the barn rather than the church. It makes a fascinating comparison with Brithdir (p. 256).

Further along the crudely widened main road is **Bontddu**: up the Hirgwm valley to the N are the remains of the famous Clogau gold mines, at their peak in the 1860s (they produced gold worth £43,000 in 1863–5), and giving substantial returns during 1900–5. They have continued to be worked on and off until recently, traditionally providing the gold for royal wedding rings. A level remains open at Llechfraith (668/194). Beyond Bontddu, a causeway crosses the river-marsh to the Penmaenpool toll-bridge (p. 259). The views of Cadair Idris from this stretch of road are so glorious as to be a real hazard to motorists. Two miles further on, the A496 joins the A487 at Llanelltud (p. 241).

MALLWYD TO DOLGELLAU (A458)

After crossing the hills beyond **Foel** (see p. 289), the A458 enters Merioneth by way of the narrow, wooded Dugoed valley. Where the Clywedog comes down from the N, the road does a hairpin bend. This is said to have been the site of a gruesome incident in the sixteenth century. The district was notorious for its bandits, known as Gwylltion Cochion Mawddwy (the wild red men of Mawddwy). In 1554 one of them was caught and sentenced to death. His mother's pleas for mercy failed to move the judge, whereupon (in true tragic style) she tore open her dress, and cried out 'These yellow breasts have given suck to those who shall wash their hands in your red blood.' Sure enough, the dead man's brothers ambushed the judge at this spot, murdered him, and soaked their hands in his blood. The Brigands Inn at Mallwyd is named after them. From here the A470 runs S to Machynlleth (see p. 298).

A mile N is **Dinas Mawddwy**, set below steep conifer-clad slopes at the junction of the Cerist and Dovey (Dyfi) valleys. It has a woollen mill. A minor road follows the beautiful Dovey valley up to **Llanymawddwy**. The delightful, plain little church has a black and white interior, setting off the lovely E window (c. 1863, by Heaton, Butler and Bayne). The village rests below steep green and brown hillsides. Beyond, the road climbs up the side of a bare, dramatic valley, with surprising steepness. From the top (Bwlch y Groes, 1790 ft), you can go down either to Llyn Tegid or to Lake Vyrnwy (see p. 226).

From further back on this road, a mile from Dinas Mawddwy, another road follows the Afon Cywarch up its steep-sided valley. The head of the valley is impressive, the flat bottom dominated by the towering cliffs of Craig Cywarch. This wonderful place is also the best starting-point for the ascent of **Aran Fawddwy** and **Aran Benllyn**. A splendid shepherd's path climbs gently up the bare Hengwm, and on to the shoulder, from where it is easy going on to the rocky spur of Drws Bach. Here a cairn incorporates a piece of Old Red Sandstone which was previously the summit stone of

Pen-y-Fan, in the Brecon Beacons. The cairn was erected in memory of a member of the RAF St Athan Mountain Rescue Team who was killed by lightning here in 1960. Pen-y-Fan was the summit of their regular beat. A tin box contains visitor's books, a map, boot-laces, and money. The walk up to the top of Aran Fawddwy (2970 ft) and on to Aran Benllyn (2901 ft) is rocky, but gives dramatic views across the huge cliffs dropping away sharply on the eastern side. Below Aran Fawddwy the little Craiglyn Dyfi lies in a hollow, and below the cliff of Aran Benllyn lies Llyn Lliwbran. The most exciting way of returning is to go down to the latter, and then return to Hengwm beneath the cliffs. It is, however, hardly economical, as it involves going up and down twice. It is also possible, if transport permits, to go down over an interminable succession of rocky knobs to Llanuwchllyn. (The name 'Benllyn' means 'head of the lake' – i.e. Llyn Tegid.) The slopes of the Arans are especially rich in botanical interest, as was discovered by the great seventeenth-century botanist, Edward Lhuyd.

Beyond Dinas Mawddwy, the A470 climbs more and more steeply up to Bwlch Oerddrws. Down the other side, it joins the A487 (Machynlleth to Dolgellau) at Cross Foxes. As this road winds downwards, it gives glimpses of **Caerynwch**, a handsome stone house on the other side of the wooded valley. Built by Joseph Bromfield in 1786, and subsequently enlarged, it was the home of the Richards family. On the estate, reached from the B4416 (to Brithdir) is the Torrent Walk, where a well-built path follows the river Clywedog as it tumbles down through the woods.

Further along the same road, at **Brithdir**, is the church built in 1895–7 by Mrs Charles Tooth (who had previously been married to a Richards) in memory of her husband, founder of St Mark's Anglican Church, Florence. The Vicarage, next to it, is said to have been built in 1888, before he died, and designed by one of the finest ecclesiastical architects of the day, J. D. Sedding. It is a charming stone house. Sedding died in 1891, and the church was designed by his young partner, Henry Wilson. Wilson, best known for his metalwork, built very few complete buildings, but Brithdir is a great success. Wilson explained to Mrs Tooth that he wanted the church to look 'as if it had sprung out of the soil instead of being planted on it.' 'I am not giving you a church turned out in a mould. I

A striking view across to the east side of the Rhinog range.

A sunset view of Snowdon and Moel Hebog from the beach at Llandanwg.

Rhaeadr Ddu at Maentwrog: 'the stream comes down diagonally through a rocky gorge and then falls over a precipice into a large round pool, dark but clear'.

have built it as simply as I know how.' He said that it was essential 'that the building shall be formed of materials gathered in the neighbourhood. There is a subtle connection between the look of a scene and the geology of it.' So it is built of local granite, and roofed with local slates. It is cruciform in plan, and the striking exterior has a broad W gable, the roof sweeping down over porches with battered walls. The windows are small and narrow. The interior comes as a great surprise: the lofty cream-painted nave contrasts strongly with the barrel-vaulted, apsed chancel, which is decorated in an intensely effective scheme of dark red, pale blue, and pale green. Here again Wilson was aiming at 'simplicity and studious severity': 'I have had constantly in my mind one or two of those delightfully simple churches just south of the Alps where all the effect comes from management of the light and the proportions of the roof and walls.'

Unfortunately, this and similar remarks by Wilson have created a myth that the church is based on Italian models – or even that it is a copy of Tooth's church in Florence. Nothing could be more mistaken: Wilson took the 'opportunity of doing something quite new and simple in church work'. He looked forward to 'embellishing the interior in an individual and country manner'. Not all the fittings he designed were carried out, but those that were include the lovely altar with its beaten copper front – an enchanting Annunciation, set among roses, where the little angel has a bigger one to keep an eye on it – the beaten copper pulpit, the moulded lead font, the stalls, carved with all sorts of animals, and the doors, inlaid with mother-of-pearl. The altar was the gift of Charles Tooth's brother Arthur, who had been the first Anglican priest to be imprisoned for ritualism. It is hard to imagine that Wilson would have approved of the church's setting, amid a rather suburban grove of shrubs and ornamental trees. If you go further along the road, you can look back at the church with Cadair Idris towering beyond, and appreciate how Wilson achieved his aims.

Back on the A487, a couple of miles of winding descent bring you to Dolgellau (p. 228).

DOLGELLAU TO MACHYNLLETH VIA TALYLLYN AND CORRIS (A487)

For the route as far as Cross Foxes, see p. 256. A gentle climb of two miles reaches the pass, at 938 ft, from which the road goes down straight along the side of the dramatically steep and narrow Fawnog valley, with huge cliffs on either side, towards Tal-y-llyn. This valley runs in a straight line all the way to Tywyn on the coast, and is part of the same fault-line as the valley containing Llyn Tegid (see p. 223). At the bottom, where the A487 turns L, the B4405 goes straight on towards Tywyn. This is the starting-point for the most rewarding ascent of **Cadair Idris** – a grand mountain range, deservedly popular and much loved, even though it does fail to reach the magic 3000 feet. The route follows the stream which comes down from Llyn Cau. Gates on the B4405 are marked 'Idris & Co.', which, as Idris was a giant, is nicely suggestive (a firm of Valhalla-builders, perhaps?). The path up through the woods (a nature reserve) is marked. Nice waterfalls. Llyn Cau, which formed the subject of one of Richard Wilson's finest paintings (in the Tate), is sublimely dramatic. The small lake (which reaches a depth of 163 ft) lies in a glacial cirque beneath an almost complete ring of broken crags. A good path leads up Craig Lwyd, S of the lake, and round a fine rocky ridge, on to the summit, Penygadair (2927 ft), on a ridge excitingly set between two vast, wild cirques – that on the S containing Llyn Cau, 1500 feet below, and that on the N containing Llyn-y-Gadair. The view over the Mawddach estuary is a worthy reward. The shelter on top has been rebuilt by the National Park authority. The return can be varied by going down Cwm Amarch. (For other routes, see below.)

At the bottom of Tal-y-llyn lake (which, surprisingly, is nowhere more than 12 feet deep) is **Tal-y-llyn** church, whose guidebook contains some wonderfully unlikely tales. The font is dated to the 2nd or 3rd century, on the grounds that, since Constantine was baptized in an ornamental font, all unornamented fonts must be pre-Constantinian. More amazing still is its account of the roof-panels above the altar, which are painted with Tudor roses. It claims that they are not later than the fifth century, and of Egyptian (Coptic) origin. It finds all manner of symbolism – e.g. 'The Red Petals signify that when God looks at the Church He asserts that it is more divine than human but acknowledges that there is a human element in it all'. In the churchyard is buried Jenny Jones (1789–1884), who followed her husband to Waterloo, where she spent three days on the battlefield. The lake is the source of the Dysynni river: for its valley see p. 261.

The A487, after turning southwards, climbs up and over to **Corris**, a slate-quarrying centre. The Dulas valley comes down to here from Aberllefenni, which supplied the slates for Brithdir church. The combination of slate tips, straggly settlements, caravans and conifers is unattractive, and it is with a sense of relief that one emerges from the long twisting valley into the broad and open Dovey valley. The A487 is joined by the A493 (from Aberdovey – see p. 264) at the old bridge over the river. The grandiose railway station over the other side seems oddly out of place, until you go a bit further and realize the size of Machynlleth (see p. 299), tucked away into its cosy valley behind a lump of hill.

DOLGELLAU TO MACHYNLLETH VIA TYWYN AND ABERDOVEY (A493)

Just as the A493 leaves **Dolgellau**, a minor road goes off L: this is a much older road than the coast road, and can be followed all the way to Llanegryn (p. 261), although it is only made up as far as Llynnau Cregennen, above Arthog. Two miles from the town is Llyn Gwernan, opposite which the Foxes' Path goes off L, climbing up past Llyn-y-Gafr, then right up to Llyn-y-Gadair, in its glacial cirque, and up steep, loose scree to the summit of Cadair Idris (see p. 258). The old pony-track leaves the road three quarters of a mile further on.

On the A493, two miles from Dolgellau, is **Penmaenpool**, where the George III Hotel stands near the toll-bridge over to Bontddu (p. 254), a wonderfully rickety construction of railway sleepers. It is well worth the 5p toll to save going round by Llanelltud and Dolgellau. Beyond Penmaenpool, the road passes through woods, until a vast quarry on the L heralds the approach of **Arthog**, with its neat terraces that housed the quarrymen. Across the marshes, on the edge of the river, are two little bumps called Fegla Fawr and Fegla Fach. From

Arthog, a winding road climbs up the hill past Llynnau Cregennen. A fine walk can be made by striking straight up from here on to Tyrau Mawr (great towers), the western part of the Cadair Idris ridge, and then keeping above the impressive cliffs all the way to the summit, and going down by the Foxes' Path (see above). The railway can be used to get back to Arthog – or, if you preferred to add in the walk over the Mawddach bridge, you may have started from Barmouth.

On the southern side of the mouth of the Mawddach estuary there are huge sand dunes, on which stands the exceedingly respectable resort of **Fairbourne**. Its church (J. B. Mendham, 1926) is romantically perched on a rocky hillock. The Fairbourne Railway runs for two miles out to the Mawddach ferry. Constructed to carry building materials for the village, it was later used as a horse-drawn passenger tramway, and converted into a fifteen-inch gauge steam line in 1916. Regular services run in season. Along the edge of the vast sandy beach concrete dragons' teeth still await the arrival of the Germans. Further on, the road, and the main-line railway down below, have difficulty in squeezing themselves in between the steep bracken-covered cliffs and the stony seashore. The railway line is exposed to sea-gales and subject to landslips, and its maintenance is a challenging problem. The Cambrian Coast Line, now at last reprieved, is a marvellous journey, and especially useful for birdwatchers and walkers. Temporary breathing-space is found at Llwyngwril, before the squeeze starts again. Two miles S of Llwyngwril, a lane drops sharply down to the halt at **Llangelynnin**. Near it is the old church, semi-abandoned since the new church at Llwyngwril was built in 1842. Unassuming, and full of atmosphere, it crouches low on the ground only a short distance above the shore. A small window in the W wall dates from the twelfth century. The seating consists entirely of nice early-nineteenth-century benches, egalitarian in that all are identical, but all the same the rentpayers' names painted on them preserve a clear distinction between those labelled 'Gent.', those labelled 'Esq.', and those labelled neither. There is a horse-bier (see p. 226). In the churchyard is buried Abram Wood, founder of a dynasty of Welsh gipsies, who died in a nearby cowshed in 1799.

Beyond Llangelynnin, the road suddenly turns sharply

inland. Half a mile from the bend, a road goes off S, back towards the coast, to Tonfanau, where the old army camp was recently used to house Ugandan Asians, and so into Tywyn (below, p. 262) across the mouth of Broad Water, a great lagoon formed by the river Dysynni. Back on the A493, just over a mile further on, a road goes L to **Llanegryn**, whose church, over-restored in 1878 by E. B. Ferrey, would reward a lengthy pilgrimage, for the sake of its glorious sixteenth-century rood-screen, related to those at Llanengan and Llanbedrog in Lleyn. The eastern parapet of the loft is formed of panels pierced with intricate patterns. The western parapet originally had statues in canopied niches. The name Ferrey here does not, for once, point to Williams-Wynn influence, but to kinsmen of theirs, the Wynnes, whose home, **Peniarth**, is close by. Not open, it has a grand front of c. 1700, faced in brick – uncommon in these parts. The most famous member of the family was William Watkin Edward Wynne (1801–80), the antiquarian. The famous Hengwrt collection of manuscripts (see p. 242) was left to him: he not only catalogued it but added to it.

Between Llanegryn and Bryncrug, the A493 crosses the broad valley of the Dysynni, the head of which is grandly closed by Cadair Idris. A prominent landmark on the R side of the valley is a steep crag jutting forward from the hills behind, three miles up from the main road. Known as **Craig yr Aderyn** (Bird Rock), it is well worth climbing up the side and peering round at its vertical face, on which cormorants nest (further inland than anywhere else in Britain), and wild goats frisk about vertiginously. One and a half miles further up the valley is **Castell y Bere**, whose ruins, crowning a rocky lump were rescued from dense undergrowth by the D. o. E. in the 1950s. The castle was built by Llywelyn the Great in 1221, to command important trackways over the hills. It was captured by Edward I in 1283. He created a borough near by, as so often (see p. 23), but the whole settlement seems to have been abandoned by the end of the century (presumably because so remote). The plan includes the D-shaped towers typical of Welsh castles (e.g. Ewloe, p. 25; Dinas Bran, p. 86). These contained the best rooms, decorated with finely-carved sculpture of which fragments are preserved in the National Museum, testifying to the sophistication of Llywelyn's court. Just beyond the castle is **Llanfihangel-y-Pennant**, whose best-known building is not the plain little church, but the ruined cottage where lived a girl called Mary Jones. As an inscription records, in 1800, at the age of sixteen, she walked over the hills to Bala in order to get from the Rev. Thomas Charles (see p. 224) a Welsh bible. His admiration for her determination is said to have contributed to his leadership in the foundation of the British and Foreign Bible Society.

The river in this upper part of the valley is not the Dysynni, but the Cader. The Dysynni comes down out of Talyllyn lake (see p. 259), but two and a half miles below, at Abergynolwyn, instead of going straight down the fault-valley to Tywyn, it goes northwards through a steep valley and joins the Cader. Cae'r Bellan, near the end of this valley, is an astonishingly perfect-looking seventeenth-century house. Abergynolwyn, back on the B4405, is the eastern terminus of the **Talyllyn Railway**. Built in 1866 to convey slate from the quarries up the Gwernol valley down to the harbour at Tywyn, it was taken over by a preservation society in 1951 and has been restored. Regular summer services are run. The gauge is two feet three inches, and the route is six and a half miles long. Two of the original locomotives are still in use. Two others (one built in 1878) came from the Corris Railway.

The line follows the Fathew valley, which is steep and narrow as far as Dolgoch, where it widens. The railway keeps to the S side, going over a stream (with waterfalls) by means of a viaduct, while the road (B4405) keeps to the N, until it joins the A493 at Bryncrug. A mile before the junction is Dolau Gwyn, an attractive house of c. 1620 (open on written application). From there it is two miles to **Tywyn**, past the lodge of the sadly demolished eighteenth-century Ynysmaengwyn. This estate was sold by the Corbets in 1874 to John Corbett (no relation), MP for Droitwich, and the man who gave that quiet Worcestershire town its grandiose aspirations as a spa – not least by means of his own house, the vast Frenchy Château Impney. His effect on Tywyn was not quite so overpowering, but it is largely owing to him that it became the prosperous seaside resort which it now is. Entering the town by the main road, one is greeted by a striking succession of buildings. The Corbett (formerly Corbet) Arms Hotel faces the parish church across a square of which the central feature is the Assembly Rooms. The latter, built in 1893, steals the show, with its cast-iron balcony and its cheery colour-scheme – pale blue, with red and white trim. The hotel is vast and Italianate.

The **Church's** external appearance is grand – cruciform, with central tower – but sadly unattractive, as the stonework has been coarsely renewed. It is, however, a building of great historical interest. A *clas* was founded here in the sixth century by St Cadfan, and still had an abbot in the twelfth century. It survived, in the form of a college, until the time of Henry VIII. In the mid-twelfth century, at about the time when the wealth and hospitality of the *clas* were celebrated by the poet Llywelyn Fardd, the church was rebuilt on a cruciform plan. The nave survives from that date, with its arcades and circular clerestory windows. The rest of the church is disappointing. The tower fell in 1692, and a new one was built at the W end, cutting short the nave. Then in 1884 the W tower was demolished, and a new central tower, together with a new chancel, transepts, and W end, were built. In the church is a stone whose inscription, in half-uncials dated to c. 750, is probably the earliest example of Welsh preserved on stone. Two fourteenth-century effigies survive, of a knight and a priest. A bass viol stands inconsequentially on a ledge in the nave. Just beyond the church is the Market Hall, given by Corbett: it now contains an odd mixture of antique shop and grocer. There is not much else in the way of architecture: do not waste your time looking for the delightful eighteenth-century house illustrated in the *Shell Guide to Mid-Western Wales*, as it has been demolished. The grand esplanade along the sea-front, and Marine Terrace at the N end, are also due to Corbett. The Talyllyn Railway (see above, p. 262) starts from Wharf Station (by the A493 as it leaves the town going S). The Narrow Gauge Railway Museum there has exhibits from other railways as well as this one.

A mile out of Tywyn on the A493, a road goes off L, by way of 'Happy Valley' and 'Bearded Lake', rejoining the main road near Pennal. There are good walks off it: the old drovers' road goes N to the Fathew valley (and Talyllyn Railway) from 668/998. The A493 comes closer to the sea as it nears the Dovey estuary and enters the outskirts of **Aberdovey**, a very cheery place on a sunny day, even if there isn't much for the architectural connoisseur. It began as a little port, and a fine conglomeration of wooden jetties and boat-sheds stands out over the shingly beach. It developed into a distinctly classy resort, beloved of yachtsmen and golfers. The brightly painted houses jostle one another between the road and the hills behind, all eager to enjoy the lovely views across the estuary to Cardiganshire. The Dovey Hotel has a plaque recording that it was built by Athelstaine Owen in 1729 (much altered since): he married the heiress of Ynysmaengwyn and wrote poetry. The church has to elbow its way in among the houses. It was only built in 1837, and the bells, with which most people associate Aberdovey, have nothing to do with it. The legend is supposed to relate to the story of the submerged land, Cantref y Gwaelod (see p. 248), but the famous song was written in 1785 by Charles Dibdin – 'If to me as true thou art, As I'm true to thee, sweetheart, We'll hear one, two, three, four, five, From the bells of Aberdovey.'

Beyond Aberdovey, road and railway snake along between sandy estuary and wooded hills, the railway often piercing the rock in short cuttings and tunnels. After about four miles they part, and the road strikes inland towards **Pennal**, now a quiet little village at the mouth of the broad-shouldered Rhonwydd valley, but once a place of much greater importance. It was one of the four towns to which Owen Glendower summoned his parliaments in 1404 (along with Harlech, Dolgellau and Machynlleth). It was also the site of a Roman fort, commanding the first good river-crossing. The farm of Cefn-caer, half a mile SE of the church, has destroyed most of the remains. The church is right in the middle of the village, and the road has to wind round its churchyard. It is a handsome early-nineteenth-century structure, and contains good memorials to residents of Talgarth, an eighteenth-century house nearby which is now a hotel. One has portrait heads of Humphry Edwards (d. 1772), his wife, daughter, and son. Another is a Victorian brass to Blanche, Emily and Parker Thruston, showing one girl dying on a couch while her brother and sister look on.

Three miles beyond Pennal, the A493 joins the A487 at the bridge over the Dovey leading to Machynlleth (see p. 299).

CHAPTER TEN

Montgomeryshire

Montgomeryshire consists largely of prosperous agricultural land, very hilly but never really mountainous, except in the SW. In many ways rather un-Welsh country, in other ways it has preserved its Welshness much more strongly than one might expect in a border area whose links are more naturally with Shropshire than with the rest of Wales. Although at first it seems unexciting compared with other parts of the country, the more one gets to know it, the stronger one's affection for it. One striking feature which it shares with its English neighbour is its rich variety of timber-framed houses, ranging from small cottages to large mansions.

SOUTH-EAST DENBIGHSHIRE AND NORTH MONTGOMERYSHIRE

From Oswestry, which is five miles S of Chirk (p. 91) by the A5 and A483, the B4580 runs W, entering Wales at **Rhydycroesau**. Here it crosses the river Cynllaith near the church of 1838. This is actually Denbighshire, of which a sizable chunk rather perversely strays S of the Berwyns. The view ahead down the fertile valley would be typical of Montgomeryshire. Two and a half miles down is **Llansilin**, a neat village with terraced cottages. Its church stands in a fine churchyard, with yews, elms and views. The exterior, with its pinnacled tower of 1832, gives little promise of the riches within. The twin naves are divided by a partly thirteenth-century arcade, the responds and one capital carved with foliage (said to be identical to carving at Valle Crucis). The magnificent fifteenth-century roofs, including the elaborately carved chancel roof, were uncovered at the time of the restoration by Arthur Baker in 1890: he was attacked by the SPAB for re-

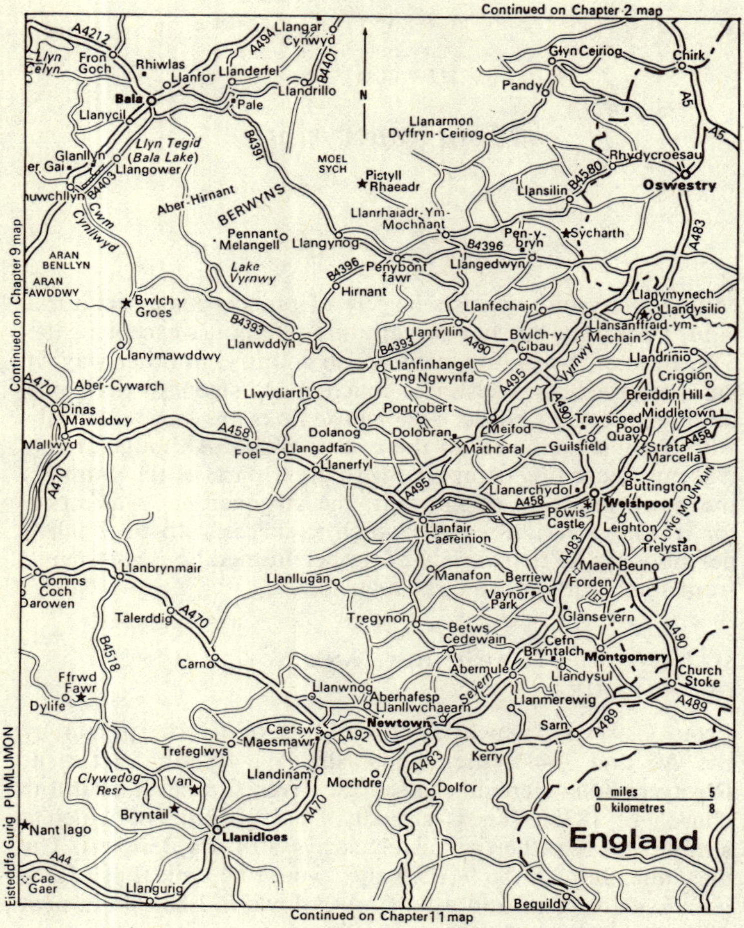

moving the old plaster ceilings, but he was justified by the result. The E window of 1866 is by Powell's: the Ascension scene was designed by E. J. Poynter. The glass was given by an Australian who claimed descent from the donor of the original medieval glass. The stalls and pews, carved by Bridgeman of Lichfield, are even better than Baker's usual standard. Fine red and yellow tiles, by J. C. Edwards of Ruabon. Eighteenth-century pulpit and panelling. The W gallery survives, and above it are the Commandments on canvas, with figures of Moses and Aaron. Seventeenth-century alms box and font cover. Royal Arms modelled in plaster – vigorous but delicate. Magnificent double chandelier of brass. In the N aisle an iron box is mysteriously suspended on a chain from an iron bracket.

In the chancel there is a large marble monument. with a long Latin inscription, to Sir William Williams Bt (1634–1700). Son of an Anglesey parson, he had an outstanding legal and political career, and became Speaker of the House of Commons in 1680 and 1681. Later he supported James II, and as Solicitor General in 1688 he prosecuted the Seven Bishops: this unpopular action got him his baronetcy. He married the heiress of the Glascoed estate, near Llansilin. He was grandfather of the Great Sir Watkin Williams-Wynn (see p. 78).

At the E end of the N aisle is a marble wall-monument to David Maurice, d. 1719, which, most unusually, has a delightfully elaborate iron grille to protect the putti at the bottom, and a wooden covered canopy above, painted blue. On the S side of the church, Huw Morus of Pontymeibion (Eos Ceiriog) was buried in 1709; a new stone was put up in 1875. (On him see page 94.) Notice was given in 1819 that all in Powys wishing to be instructed as bards should assemble at his grave: this was the beginning of the well-known Powys Eisteddfod. The parish produced several other notable writers.

A mile and a half down the Cynllaith from Llansilin, at the point where the lovely valley narrows, is **Sycharth**. All that is to be seen now is a flattish mound with big trees on it, near the bridge over the river, yet this is the site of the chief residence of Owen Glendower, described by Iolo Goch (c. 1320–98), in his famous poem. It is difficult to reconcile the elaborate description with the castle's actual form – a motte and bailey, with timber buildings – but it is best not to be too pedantic and to enter into the poet's impressionistic rapture:

. . . Lo, the form of it – a gold cirque
Of water held by earthwork;
A court with one gate and bridge
Where a hundred packs have passage. . .
. . . There are joists upon the hillside
As in a vault, side by side,
And each one, in a tightknit
Pattern, to the next is knit.
Twice nine dwellings to look up
To a wood fort on a hilltop.
Next to heaven his court towers
On four marvellous pillars.
On each thick wooden pillar
A loft tops all, built with care,
With all four lofts for friendship
Joined as one, where minstrels sleep.
These four well-lighted lofts,
Fine nestful, make eight cocklofts.
The roof's tiled on each gable,
There's a chimney that draws well.
Nine halls in true proportion
And nine wardrobes in each one.
Elegant shops, comely inside,
And stocked as full as Cheapside.
A church cross, lovely limewhite
Chapels and the windows bright . . .
. . . No one need act as gateman,
Here are gifts for every one –
No hunger, disgrace or dearth,
Or ever thirst at Sycharth!
Haply the best of Welshmen
Owns the land, of Pywer's kin;
It's a strong, lean warrior owns
This most lovable of mansions.*

From Llansilin, it is six miles by the B4580 to **Llanrhaeadr-ym-Mochnant**, which takes its name, as does the river on which it stands, from the famous waterfall four miles NW. It is quite a substantial village, and not unpleasant. The church is reached by way of a little square and a narrow street of pretty houses. It stands in a churchyard which slopes down to

* (Translated by Anthony Conran, *Penguin Book of Welsh Verse*, 1967)

the river, with a wooded hillside beyond. It has a most odd plan: a tower at the W (with an eighteenth-century top), a long narrow nave, and aisles only along the eastern part of the nave. Mostly renewed by Spaull in 1882, the nave retains its plaster barrel vault, and the sanctuary has a good medieval roof. In the S aisle stands a fragment of a great collared cross of ninth-century Mercian type. There are also an eleventh-century grave cross, and a fragment of a Romanesque shrine like that at Pennant (p. 272). These remains recall the important *clas* (religious community), still in existence here in the thirteenth century. William Morgan worked on his translation of the Bible while Vicar here (1578–88). The church is dedicated to St Dogfan, one of the many saints of the family of Brychan Brycheiniog. The Berwyn mountains are the only place in Wales where the cloudberry (something like a raspberry) grows, and these are known as *mwyar Dogfan* (Dogfan's blackberries), because he is said to have received his stipend in the form of cloudberry fruit. A tradition survived until the nineteenth century that anyone who brought a quart of ripe fruit to the parson on St Dogfan's feast-day had his ecclesiastical dues remitted for the year. As the plant fruits very sparingly it was unlikely that many people would take advantage of this offer.

From Llanrhaeadr there are two valleys leading up to the Berwyns, each ending up more or less equidistant from the summit, Moel Sych (2713 ft). The northern one, Cwm Maen Gwynedd, is unfrequented, but the southern one is crowded with tourists flocking to see **Pistyll Rhaeadr**. This is a sight not to be missed – the highest waterfall in Wales, and higher than any in England (or so it is said). The fall, of 240 ft, is broken two-thirds of the way down by a natural rock arch. Borrow likened it to 'an immense skein of silk agitated and disturbed by tempestuous blasts, or the long tail of a grey courser at furious speed'. The surroundings, tree-clad rocky cliffs, are appropriately grand. A pavilion, with a portico made of rough tree-trunks, was constructed near the bottom by a nineteenth-century Sir Watkin Williams-Wynn, who also planted the trees. It makes an odd contrast to scramble up the side and see the stream up above flowing quietly along, little knowing what a fate is in store for it. It is said that once, when a bishop was coming to view the falls, the locals were worried because the flow of water was less than usual, so they climbed up, dammed the stream, and then let it go just as his Lordship arrived.

The Berwyns, although not among Wales's grander mountains, are worth a climb if only for the views of Snowdonia. The going is generally easy, apart from the vigorous growth of heather.

The Afon Rhaeadr is a tributary of the Tanat, whose broad valley was once followed by a railway. Four miles E of Llanrhaeadr, by the B4396, is **Llangedwyn**. The Hall (not open), has belonged to the Williams-Wynns since the Great Sir Watkin inherited it from his father-in-law, Edward Vaughan, in 1718. Its pink-washed front can be seen up a fine avenue, through eighteenth-century gates, opposite the church. Originally an E-shaped Elizabethan house of brick, it was stuccoed and remodelled in the early eighteenth century. The wing containing the grand staircase has recently been demolished. In the early nineteenth century the Hall was the home of Charles Williams-Wynn, MP, described by Southey as 'my earliest friend'. It was while staying here that Southey wrote *Madoc*, and it was after hearing the old harper play the tune *Ar hyd y nos* that Bishop Heber wrote his evening hymn 'God who madest Earth and Heaven, Darkness and Light', to that famous melody.

The **Church** was rebuilt in 1869–70 by Benjamin Ferrey (inevitably), and later altered by H. L. North, who added the pretty dormers. The N porch, in Norman style with elaborate terracotta decoration, is of c. 1840. The amazing altar rails, of wood, copper, and enamels, are probably by John H. M. Bonnor, a local man, d. 1913, in whose memory they are erected. He certainly designed the War Memorial tablet in the same style. In the chancel there is a recumbent effigy of a priest, fourteenth century, known as '*Yr Athro*' (the professor). There are good eighteenth-century monuments to Edward Vaughan, and also to Katherine Vaughan, whose epitaph begins oddly:

> 'A wife much loved much famde she lived
> and died Exextrix of that worth . . .'

On the S side is a dreadful window of 1884, by Ward and Hughes, to Marie Nesta Williams-Wynn, showing a fat and ugly little girl being carried up to heaven by angels while gathering flowers. In the churchyard there is a richly elegant stone cross set up in 1886 to the memory of the 6th Baronet of Wynnstay; and also two even more remarkable monuments to two Bonnors who died in 1912 and 1913 – highly original reinterpretations of Celtic crosses. Half a mile NW of the church is **Pen-y-bryn**, a house with an ordinary exterior, but retaining inside interesting late medieval features, especially the splendid timber roof.

The upper part of the Tanat valley is in Montgomeryshire. **Penybontfawr**, seven miles W of Llangedwyn, on the B4391, has a distinguished church of 1855 by R. K. Penson: a simple, EE building of stone, it is carefully detailed, and has an admirable spire. Beside the churchyard is the pretty School, slate-hung and with lattice windows. The church was built to replace the old one at Pennant Melangell, five miles further on, almost at the very head of the valley. To reach Pennant, one leaves the B4391 at **Llangynog**, once a great lead-mining centre, whose revenue brought great wealth to the owners of Powis Castle (especially in the first half of the eighteenth century). This road goes up over the Berwyns, reaching a height of 1595 ft (marvellous views), to Bala (p. 223).

Pennant Melangell is not only a most attractive place, but it also possesses a church of outstanding interest. Its origin goes back to the eighth century. The legend tells how Brochwel, Prince of Powys, was hunting here one day. His hounds started a hare, which fled into a thicket. There he found a virgin praying, with the hare under the fold of her garments. When the hounds were urged on, they ran away. A nice extra touch adds that when the huntsman tried to blow his horn he found that it was stuck to his lips. The woman told Brochwel that she had lived there fifteen years without seeing anyone, and that she had fled from the court of her father, an Irish king, to escape marriage. Her name was Monacella (Melangell). Brochwel then gave her the lands at Pennant, and she founded a community of nuns there. St Melangell was naturally considered to be patron saint of hares, and it was said that if anyone called out to a hare that was being pursued 'God and St Monacella be with thee' it was sure to escape. Until the seventeenth century no one would kill a hare in the parish.

The **Church** is a simple building, originally twelfth century, but much rebuilt. The square tower, with a pyramidal roof surmounted by a wooden belfry, of common Montgomeryshire type, was rebuilt in 1877. It retains a fifteenth-century rood-screen: part of its loft, now at the W end of the church, is carved with scenes illustrating the legend. Attached to the E end of the church is **Cell y Bedd** (cell of the grave), rebuilt, as a school, in the seventeenth century, but on the site of the Romanesque apse within which was the saint's burial place. In 1958 the shrine put up for her relics in the late twelfth century was reconstructed from fragments embedded in the church walls. It was built of stone; the tomb-chest and gabled superstructure stood on arches, supported on six columns. The capitals, arches, and gables were ornamented with rich Romanesque carving. The tomb-chest itself was probably covered in precious metals and jewels. The whole stood about ten feet high. Although the shrine has been re-erected in **Cell y Bedd**, it stood originally not within the apse, but W of it, in the chancel of the Romanesque church. It is probable that a new shrine was made c. 1400 in an added S aisle, and that the effigy of a woman (in the church), with what are presumably intended to be two hares peeping out at her waist, was intended to represent St Melangell and was made for the shrine. The church contains an unusual chandelier of turned wood made in 1733. The porch is dated 1737.

From Penybontfawr the B4396 runs up the Hirnant valley. The church at **Hirnant** was rebuilt in 1892 by Lawrence Booth of Manchester. Shortly beyond, one enters the gloomy conifers which indicate the proximity of **Lake Vyrnwy**. Built to supply Liverpool, this huge reservoir, over four miles long, was begun in 1881, and completed c. 1910. It is a magnet for tourists, and for those who like artificial lakes surrounded by conifers it no doubt possesses charm. It tends to be used to film scenes set in Switzerland. A road runs down each side, so when the sun is low choose accordingly. The one feature which really is worth seeing is the magnificent **Straining Tower**, a mile from the dam along the eastern side. Designed by George Frederick Deacon, the engineer to the Liverpool Water Board, it is a first-rate building, worthy of Burges, and very much in his manner. It is constructed of excellent masonry, with a picturesque conical roof, and a corbelled-out stair-turret. (Deacon also designed the splendid Water Towers at Everton and at Norton in Cheshire.) The enormous

Barmouth 'is built up against steep towering cliffs, and the houses climb the rocks and perch wherever they can find a foothold'. Looking south across the Mawddach estuary

Maentwrog Church was cleverly remodelled by John Douglas in 1896, using local slate. 'It makes a lovely sight with its low shingled spire rising above thick yews'.

At Brithdir Church, built by Henry Wilson in 1895-7, 'the roof sweeps down over porches with battered walls'. The roof-projection was intended to shield a crucifix.

stone dam is less successful: it has rugged grandeur, but could hardly be called sympathetic. On the hill above stands the new church built by Liverpool Corporation in 1887 to replace the old church of **Llanwddyn**, submerged beneath the lake. Designed by F. V. Holme, it is very ugly. The W window is in memory of Deacon (d. 1909), and shows Hiram – 'He wrought all the work'. St Wddyn is said to have been 'a giant, or, more probably, an early Christian hermit'.

Southwards from the B4393, from Llanwddyn to Llanfyllin, run several roads crossing the river Vyrnwy. The first (B4395) crosses it at Pontllogail, or **Llwydiarth**, where there is a church of 1854 by Ferrey, built by Sir Watkin Williams-Wynn, who had another estate here. The churches at Dolanog and Pontrobert, further down, are both by R. K. Penson (1852–3). They are reached by way of **Llanfihangel-yng-ngwynfa** (on the B4382). The church here was rebuilt in 1862–3 by Benjamin Lay of Welshpool, and is chiefly famous as the burial-place of Ann Griffiths (1776–1805), who spent her short life at the farmhouse of Dolwar Fach, two miles SW. She underwent a profound conversion at the age of about twenty, became a Methodist, and wrote seventy-six hymns. She did not write them down, but recited them to her servant Ruth Evans: Ruth later married the Rev. John Hughes of Pontrobert, and he transcribed them. They are among the finest hymns of the Revival, for as well as being a gifted poet she was a genuine mystic, filled with an ecstatic sense of Christ's presence. The parish is also celebrated as the subject of Alwyn D. Rees' classic book, *Life in a Welsh Countryside* (1950), a penetrating study of the rural community. **Pontrobert**, beautifully sited in a wooded valley, three miles SE of Llanfihangel, has a neat little church, good Gothic with no frills, that was very up-to-date for 1852, and also suits its situation admirably. The plain but attractive school is also by Penson.

Llanfyllin is a friendly little town, and good to look at too. The church was rebuilt, in local red brick, in 1706. The tower is curiously stark, particularly when compared with the rich stone doorway on the S side. The interior is a large plain rectangle, but an effort was made to churchify it in 1863, when Walter Scott of Birkenhead inserted an elaborately Norman triple arch between chancel and nave. Rich E windows by Clutterbuck.

Opposite the church, above the chemist's shop, is a room whose walls are painted with scenes of mountains and lakes, in highly romantic style: this is the work of Captain Augeraud, a French prisoner taken in the Napoleonic Wars. Attached to the church on the N is the pretty school of 1826. Just beyond the church is the sad gap where stood, till about 1960, the charming Town Hall of 1789 by John Yenn. Around it are some delightful eighteenth-century and early-nineteenth-century buildings – two of them, alas, recently painted. The error of this is shown by the Post Office, with its warm reddish-brown brick setting off its dotty Gothick windows.

The road by the Post Office leads to a little square with two nice buildings, the handsome Manor House, brick with stone quoins, dated 1737, and the Hall, with an early-nineteenth-century front, stuccoed, with Chinoiserie glazing and a crazy Gothick porch. The old Rectory which completed the group has been replaced by a cedar bungalow. Further down the main street are gabled houses, those on the S set back behind trees. On the N is the 'Protestant Chapel', now Congregational, built in 1708, destroyed by the Jacobites in 1715, rebuilt at the Government's expense in 1717, then again in 1829, and later tarted up with Ruabon brick. It was here that Ann Griffiths was converted. Outside the town, on the main road, is the grand and extensive workhouse built in 1838 by Thomas Penson, now an Old People's Home (soon to be replaced). It is perhaps unkind to recall here the saying 'Old ale fills Llanfyllin with young widows.'

The A490 goes SE over the hill to the Meifod valley by way of **Bwlch-y-Cibau**, with an excellent little church of 1862–4 by Sir Gilbert Scott. It is a small apsed building, EE, with glass in the chancel by Wailes, and at the W end by Powell's (1877). Admirably suited to its sheltered upland site, it shows how sensitive Scott could be to the *genius loci*. Another road, however, the B4393, leaves the A490 two miles E of Llanfyllin and runs NE along the Gain valley, by way of **Llanfechain** (where the Norman church was fortunate enough to be restored in 1859 by R. K. Penson and again in 1883 by John Douglas), to **Llansanffraid-ym-Mechain**. This is a substantial village, mostly red-brick, with the church up above one end, and the eighteenth-century stone bridge at the other. Near the bridge a disused signalbox has become an extra bedroom. The church is an attractive hotch-potch, restored in 1892–3 by John Oldrid Scott: he added the nice shingled spire. There is a remarkably grand S transept, with quoins, added in 1729. The miscellaneous collection of windows includes a tiny Norman one, a dormer of 1669, and some curious earlier seventeenth-century ones (one dated 1619 with a Latin couplet). Good woodwork, Jacobean and by Scott. Interesting mid-nineteenth-century glass: the window of 1847 on the S side of the sanctuary is probably by Evans. Fine timber porch.

Two miles E of Llansanffraid, by the B4393, the Vyrnwy (now joined by the Tanat) is crossed by the **Montgomeryshire Canal** by means of an astonishingly ungainly stone aqueduct, built c. 1796 by John and Thomas Dadford. It has five small arches, which have been compared to elephant's toenails. The aqueduct began to collapse soon after it was built and had to be tied together with crude iron strengtheners. It is a far cry from this to Pontcysylltau – built only a few years later. The Montgomeryshire Canal (the Montgomeryshire Branch of the Shropshire Union Canal) enters Wales at Llanymynech, and runs down through Welshpool to Newtown. It was built between 1794 and 1821, but it has been leaking and becoming choked with weeds since its closure in 1944. Now, however, thanks to the spirited work of the volunteers of the Shropshire Union Canal Society (notably in Welshpool) and the Montgomery Waterway Restoration Group, there is every hope that it will be reopened. The towpath makes a lovely walk, punctuated by little brick bridges, abandoned locks, and modest lock-keepers' cottages.

Llanymynech (a mile NE of the aqueduct) is right on the border, which actually runs down the main street. It goes straight through the Lion Inn, which, when Montgomeryshire was 'dry', could only serve drink in the English part of its premises on Sundays. The extremely handsome stone bridge over the Vyrnwy, built by Thomas Penson in 1828, is in Wales, but not the amazing church he built in 1844, an elaborate Norman effort, of grey stone, but with all the ornamental parts made of yellow terracotta (compare his church at Welshpool, p. 281). The border runs round Llanymynech Hill (following Offa's Dyke along its W side). This steep and rocky outcrop is rich in copper and lead, which have been mined since Roman times.

A mile S of Llanymynech on the A483 is **Llandysilio**, which has a superb church of 1866–8 by G. E. Street, in a refined Dec. style, with a little circular spire. The reredos is by Earp, and the excellent E window, by Clayton and Bell, was designed by Street. On the S side there is a richly-coloured window, showing the sea giving up its dead, in memory of four sailors lost in the China Sea while trying to save a shipmate in 1876. At the W end there is an exquisite brass (from the earlier church) to Mary Eyton, d. 1674, by Silvanus Crue: The epitaph reads:

Eyton, the flower of All the Virgin Crue,
Youth's chiefest glory, bids the world Adeiu.
To heaven she now is gone there for to bee
One of those glorious Saints which ever see
Naught else but joy, and that eternallye.

E of Llandysilio the border follows the Vyrnwy for a few miles, but it then loses all reason and wanders insanely around for a while, before at last settling down and going off southwards again. On the B4393 is **Llandrinio**, with a small, partly Norman church. Beyond it the Severn is crossed by means of a very handsome bridge of 1775 with three quoined arches. On the border, four miles E of the bridge, is **Prince's Oak**, where the Prince of Wales 'was introduced into his Principality' in 1806. SW of here rises the steeply wooded mass of **Breiddin Hill**, disfigured by a huge quarry in its side. On top is a pillar commemorating Admiral Rodney's victory over the French at Dominica in 1782 – put up here by 'the Gentlemen of Montgomeryshire' because timber for the Navy came from the forests of Powys. Down below is **Criggion** (or Crugion), with an eighteenth-century brick church, retaining its pews and pulpit, but with a chancel added in the nineteenth century. S of Breiddin the main Shrewsbury–Welshpool road (A458) enters Wales beneath the tree-clad cliff of Moel y Golfa, the highest point of Breiddin (1324 ft).

SW of Llandysilio is an area of low rolling hills: near the top (two miles W of the A483) is **Penrhos**, with an unattractive church of 1845 by Sydney Smirke (architect of the British Museum Reading Room), only remarkable for being built entirely of yellow terracotta. Further SW is **Dyffryn Meifod**:

the Vyrnwy winds along its broad, flat valley between steeply wooded sides. The A495 runs down it from Llansanffraid-ym-Mechain (p. 274). It is astonishing to think that this essentially quiet and rural scene has recently been threatened with the intrusion of an enormous radio telescope, the largest in the world, which would have been worked by remote control from Jodrell Bank, and been built at Rhos-y-glascoed, up on the hill W of Meifod. It is ironical that Meifod is the HQ of the Council for the Protection of Rural Wales (Cymdeithas Diogelu Harddwch Cymru): that admirable organization fought hard against the scheme, but it is financial considerations that have caused the scheme to be modified.

Meifod was once a place of great importance, both in church and civil affairs. Within its very large churchyard there once stood three separate churches. The first was Eglwys Gwyddfarch, the oratory of a hermit of that name; the second was Eglwys Tysilio, founded by that great saint himself; and the third was Eglwys Fair (St Mary's). Two have now disappeared, although their ruins survived until the eighteenth century. The present church, although dedicated to St Mary, probably represents that of Tysilio, for at the restoration of the church by Benjamin Ferrey in 1871–2 parts of early Norman arcades were uncovered at the W end of the nave. The E window of the S aisle is by David Evans of Shrewsbury; other windows contain armorial glass of 1838–40. There is a pretty Gothick organ-case, and a finely carved Celtic gravestone (tenth century). Meifod is now only a village, with handsome Georgian houses along the main road. The bridge over the river is a tough piece of work of 1862, by J. W. Poundley, quite a contrast to his churches: stone abutments support an iron trough made by S. Woodall of Dudley. Over the other side, beautifully set among trees, is Penylan, a white-painted Regency house of rather odd design.

The Rev. Randolph Davies, vicar of Meifod 1647–97, apart from being deprived of his benefice from 1649 to 1660, was much troubled by the conversion of many of his parishioners to Quakerism: this was under the leadership of the Lloyds of Dolobran. Two miles SW of Meifod, turn R towards Pontrobert. **Dolobran** is on the R, just across the river. Here they erected a Meeting House in 1700. Charles Lloyd (1637–98) became a Quaker in 1662, and underwent much persecution.

His brother Thomas went to Pennsylvania with William Penn, and became its Deputy Governor. Charles Lloyd's son founded an iron forge at Dolobran in 1719, and it was his nephew Sampson, an ironmaster at Birmingham, who founded Lloyd's Bank in 1765. The Meeting House (at 124/124) is reached by way of a farm and a grassy track. It is a few hundred yards W of the (rebuilt) Dolobran Hall. A simple little building of brick, designed to look like a double cottage, it is hidden away among trees in a fold of the hills. The bare meeting room has a gallery, and next to it are the caretaker's quarters. The walled burial ground contains fruit trees instead of gravestones. Meifod's civic importance was due to the castle of **Mathrafal**, S of Dolobran, where a large tree-topped mound near the junction of the A495 and B4389 is all that survives of the seat of the Princes of Powys, said to have been built by Eliseg in the eighth century, and destroyed by King John. Both these roads lead to the A458.

The A490, to Welshpool, crosses the river three miles N of Meifod, and climbs Broniarth Hill. From the sharp bend near the top there is a splendid view of the valley. Further S, the road crosses the B4392: from the junction can be seen **Trawscoed Hall**, up on the hill, an elegant house of 1777 in delicate red brick. It was the dower-house to Trawscoed Hen (half a mile N), a much grander mansion built in 1771, burnt in 1858, and recently demolished. Half a mile NE of the junction is **Guilsfield** (Cegidfa), with one of the best churches in the county. It is dedicated to St Aelhaearn ('Ironbrow'), its seventh-century founder. Mostly fourteenth–fifteenth centuries, it was restored in 1879 by G. E. Street. It is a pity that he removed the line of charming seventeenth-century dormers which lit the S gallery. He also did away with the higgledy-piggledy jumble of pews, of every shape, size and description, which made the place resemble a rabbit warren (see the model and plan in the church). Magnificent panelled roof (fifteenth century). The highly original screen, with its circle-patterns, was put in by Street, as also the reredos and pulpit. The living was appropriated by Henry VII as part of the endowment of Christ Church, Oxford. Near the entrance to the churchyard is a huge yew tree, and under it the tomb of Richard Jones, d. 1707 aged ninety, with the epitaph:

Under this yew tree
  Buried would hee bee
For his father and hee
  Planted this yew tree.

Guilsfield was served by a branch of the Montgomeryshire Canal (now a nature reserve). The B4392 follows this. Just after the road crosses the canal, a minor road runs E to the A483. A mile S is **Pool Quay**, where the main Canal and the Severn flow close to either side of the road. This was the highest point to which the Severn was navigated, and there was a flannel mill here. The rather silly church of 1862 is by S. Pountney Smith of Shrewsbury: it has what Goodhart-Rendel called 'a most elaborate and hideously fantastic carpentry belfry', painted white. A mile S, between road and river, is the site of **Strata Marcella** (Ystrad Marchell): virtually nothing is left of this great Cistercian Abbey, founded from Whitland in 1170. Its church was 373 ft long. A memorial was erected beside the road in 1970, by the Powysland Club, to mark the Abbey's 8th centenary. Further S again, the A458 from Shrewsbury comes in at **Buttington**, over a bridge of latticed iron (1872, by W. N. Swettenham, County Surveyor). Beside it stands the plain church, rendered and Omo white. It has a timber belfry, a funny sloping porch of 1686, a fine medieval roof, and a most odd font, apparently formed out of a large early Gothic capital (presumably from Strata Marcella). Buttington is supposed to have been the site of a great battle in 894 at which Alfred beat the Danes, who were reduced to eating their horses.

Welshpool (Y Trallwng) is a prosperous and expanding market town. It is fortunate in its situation, tucked into a fold of the hills on the E side of the Severn valley, with the parks of three great houses around it – Powis Castle to the S, Llanerchydol to the W, and, away to the SE, Leighton Hall. It is an important road junction, the railway still runs at its grand French Renaissance station, and a recent scheme to fill in the Shropshire Union Canal, as it passes through the town, in order to build a bypass, was abandoned in face of furious opposition. On market day (Monday) the town is cram-full of people, cars, and animals. Fortunately, all this activity has not yet seriously impaired the town's architectural character – largely eighteenth–nineteenth century.

Everything focuses on the main cross-roads. N of this, up above the road, is the **Parish Church**, founded in the sixth century, only a little earlier than another church, just to the E, which survived until 1659. The tower is thirteenth century, and the chancel fourteenth, but the church was wrecked in 1401 when the town was sacked by Owen Glendower, and rebuilt at the end of the fifteenth century, and again in 1774 (except chancel and tower). It was restored in 1856–7 by John Billing, and again in 1870–1 by G. E. Street, who put in the nave roof, S windows, reredos, stalls, brass lectern, etc. In the chancel there is an elaborate monument to the 2nd Earl of Powis, d. 1848: he was chiefly responsible for ensuring that the diocese of St Asaph was not absorbed into that of Bangor. It was designed by Sir Gilbert Scott, the effigy was carved by Edward Richardson, and the arch by J. Birnie Philip. Below the nave E window is an unusual sixteenth-century Flemish triptych. The church possesses a chalice, made out of the purest Guinea gold, and weighing 30 oz.: it was presented in 1662 by Thomas Davies, Governor of the Guinea Coast. Outside the S porch is a glacial boulder, once in the church, but thrown out by the Puritan Vavasor Powell. It is said to be a wishing stone: stand on it and turn three times with the sun. Below the W tower is a pitched (cobbled) path, with the date 1846: this type of work was a local speciality. At the E end of the church is a small timbered cottage, given to Grace Evans by her mistress Lady Nithsdale as a reward for her part in helping her husband to escape from the Tower (in women's clothes), when he was condemned to death for his part in the 1715.

Further on is the aggressively yellow **Powysland Museum** (1874, David Walker), erected by the Powysland Club, the local archaeological society. Charmingly old-fashioned, it is full of interesting, mostly local, antiquities, including parts of an Iron Age shield from Moel Hiraddug, fragments from Strata Marcella, mosaic from the Temple of Diana at Smyrna, a model of a guillotine in mutton bone, and so on. There is also a bronze group 'illustrative of Welsh history', set up in 1876 to the memory of Morris Charles Jones, founder of the Club. The subject – the death of Tewdric Mawr in AD 610, comforted by Marchell, mother of Brychan, and played to by an aged bard – was suggested by Lady Llanover. It was designed by John Evan Thomas, modelled by his brother, and made by Elkingtons of Liverpool.

In the streets around the main crossroads are many handsome eighteenth- and early nineteenth-century houses, of brick or stucco. The main street climbs gently westwards. In it stands the proud, rather coarse Town Hall (1873, by Benjamin Lay of Welshpool). Its clock faces are lit up a lurid green at night. Opposite are some half-timbered houses, and a lane leading to gates into the park of Powis Castle. Another lane, further up, leads to **Christ Church**, an alarming neo-Norman elephant. It was built in 1839–44, by 'voluntary public subscription' (it is nice to know it was voluntary), to commemorate the coming-of-age of Viscount Clive, the heir of Powis. The exterior is of greyish-green local stone, but inside terracotta is extensively used to provide rich Norman ornamentation – on the nave arches, and on the rich arcading and vaulting-ribs of the apsidal chancel. The elaborate font is entirely terracotta. The architect was Thomas Penson. His use of terracotta – surely not unconnected with the fact that Ruabon, the great centre for brick and terracotta, lay between Wrexham and Oswestry, where he practised – is interesting, as it was only in the 1840s that the material was coming to be extensively used.

Beside the roundabout just W of the town are the gates of **Llanerchydol** (not open), a delightful castellated house of 1776, remodelled c. 1820 (possibly by the Reptons), in a beautiful park. To the S (reached off the A483, a mile S of the town) is **Powis Castle** (National Trust: grounds open May–September; Castle open June–September). The ungainly red bulk of the castle stands high up within a magnificently wooded park. The site of the original castle may be the 'Ladies Mount', to the W. The present castle was built in the late thirteenth century by Gruffydd ap Gwenwynwyn, Prince of Upper Powys. As a result of Gruffydd's strife with Llywelyn the Last, the previous castle had been destroyed in 1275, but Gruffydd's alliance with the victorious Edward I brought him the barony de la Pole (Pool) and new prosperity. The last Baron de la Pole died in 1551. In 1587 the castle was bought by Sir Edward Herbert, a younger son of the Earl of Pembroke. His son, William, created Baron Powis in 1629, defended it for the King in the Civil War. In 1674 the 3rd Lord

Powis was created Earl, and in 1687 Marquess. But in 1688 he had to flee into exile while his wife, a Lady of the Bedchamber, smuggled the Prince of Wales to Versailles. On his death in 1696, William III gave the estates to a Dutch nephew of his own, the Earl of Rochford. George I reinstated William, son of the first Marquess, in 1722; on his son's death in 1748 the titles became extinct. In 1784 Henrietta Herbert married Edward Clive, son of Clive of India. He was created Earl of Powis in 1804, and his son took the name Herbert in 1807. The 6th Earl still lives at Powis.

The architectural history of the castle is extremely complicated, since it has been continuously occupied and continuously altered and extended. The present appearance of the exterior is owed partly to Sir Robert Smirke, who built the E tower around 1828, and partly to G. F. Bodley, who did a great deal of sympathetic work, including the 'Elizabethan' fenestration, around 1900. The most impressive medieval feature is the fourteenth-century gateway leading from the Outer Bailey into the Inner Castle: the recessed arches between the great round towers were uncovered by Bodley, who moved the portico of 1665 which covered them to the Orangery. The W gate was rebuilt in 1688. In the Outer Bailey stands a splendid lead figure of Fame. The Ballroom and Billiard Room, N of the forecourt, contain fascinating relics of Clive of India, including Tippu Sahib's cedar bed.

The interiors of the Castle proper are in amazing contrast to the bleak exterior: they form one of the most splendid series of sixteenth-, seventeenth-, eighteenth- and nineteenth-century rooms to be seen in Britain. There is a glorious Staircase Hall of the 1670s, possibly by William Winde: the ceiling painting by Verrio, after Veronese, probably shows the glorification of Catherine of Braganza, while the wall paintings, done in 1705 by Lanscroon, are of mythological scenes. The quality may not be high, but the effect is gorgeous, as in the State Bedroom, also of the 1670s, where the ceiling painting is positively awful. But the richly hung bed in its alcove, complete with rail to keep off the crowds at the *levée* (*à la* Louis XIV), the tapestries, the profuse gilding, the silvered furniture covered in crimson Spitalfields velvet, all stifle criticism. There is a narrow but light and cheerful Long Gallery, of 1593, with jolly plasterwork. Originally it was 50 ft longer. The

Blue Drawing Room, early eighteenth-century, has another ceiling by Lanscroon. The Oak Drawing Room is almost entirely of 1902, by Bodley, with woodwork and plasterwork of great delicacy. He was also responsible for the Dining Room on the ground floor, richly dignified as the Victorians liked their eating rooms to be. The Castle contains many good pictures, mostly portraits, but far the most attractive is the famous miniature of Lord Herbert of Chirbury by Isaac Oliver, in the Library. Exquisitely rich and brilliantly coloured, it shows the poet, historian and philosopher reclining under a tree, the words MAGICA SYMPATHIAE probably referring to one of his treatises.

Powis would be worth a visit for its gardens alone. The steep drop on the SE side of the Castle was formed, in the late seventeenth century, into a series of terraces and hanging gardens which are a unique survival: they may have been designed by William Winde. The lowest stage is the Orangery, with lead figures of shepherds and shepherdesses along the balustrade. It is fortunate that Capability Brown's advice – to remove the terraces and return to bare rock – was not followed. The extensive gardens E of the Castle have been laid out comparatively recently, and are exceptionally well designed and maintained. The famous Powis woods used to contain some of the largest oaks in Britain.

A tall stone spire forms a prominent landmark on the opposite side of the valley from Welshpool. It belongs to the church at **Leighton**, which stands on the estate of Leighton Hall (reached by the B4381 E from Welshpool). Both church and house were built, and the whole estate laid out, by a Liverpool banker, John Naylor, from 1851 onwards. He spent enormous sums of money, and the result is, if not exactly on the highest aesthetic level, without doubt one of the most characterful early Victorian ensembles to survive. His architect was the obscure W. H. Gee, from Liverpool. The church is a real joy. Built of yellow stone, it is wonderfully elaborate, with flying buttresses, crocketed pinnacles, arches and lots of rich carving. The carvers clearly had a whale of a time. On one side of the tower is an oddity – a Romish-looking cleric holding the text 'Honour the King'. The churchyard is surrounded by a ha-ha, and an avenue is aligned on to it from the grounds of the house, more than a mile away. The lofty interior is strongly atmospheric, full of varnished oak pews, coloured tiles, and glass by Forrest and Bromley of Liverpool. All the doors are covered in red baize. At the SE corner an octagonal chapel is attached, containing the Naylor monuments: in the centre is a large white marble angel, with cobwebs on her nose, carved by Georgina Naylor. The Cambridge Ecclesiologists, as one might have expected, were not at all impressed: 'It belongs to a class which we fondly hoped had passed away for ever – a class of churches bearing manifest tokens of having been built for the honour and convenience of man, rather than for the glory of GOD' (*Ecclesiologist*, 1854).

The **Hall** (not open) now belongs to an American firm who have a factory in Welshpool. Also Gothic, it has an enormous octagonal tower. Much of the interior work is of far higher quality than the house itself, for it was executed by J. G. Crace (famous for his work at the Houses of Parliament), and some of it may even have been designed by A. W. N. Pugin. It includes elaborate painted ceilings, superb alabaster chimney-pieces, and richly-carved doorcases. Up in the entrance tower there is a glorious clock-cum-carillon, made by Hausburg of Liverpool: appropriate tunes could be played by means of barrels, to greet the guests as they arrived or left. The grounds were laid out by Edward Kemp, a pupil of Paxton. They contain magnificent trees, on which Naylor was an expert. A pool contains a statue of Icarus, ingeniously shown hitting the water in his fall. Naylor also drained land, and built roads, bridges, and grandiose farms. A large pool contained golden carp, and he built a funicular railway up the hill. His most extraordinary undertaking was the erection of a huge tank on top of Moel y Mab, to store liquid manure from the adjoining cow-byres: this was spread over the fields by means of two huge pumping-engines and vast lengths of piping, with brass taps to regulate the flow. It is said that when the piping was sold it made a fortune for the contractor.

Naylor's superb redwood grove and his fine sequoias are in the woods above Leighton. The redwoods, brought over in pots from California in 1857, now form the most heavily timbered area of woodland in Britain. The stand is the equivalent of 26,000 cu. ft to the acre (sitka might be 10–15,000). You can see them from the B4388, the Forden road, but for a closer view write to the Royal Forestry Society at Tring to whom they belong, or to the Leighton Woodlands forester. Beyond the grove, near the new pinetum, is an imposing nineteenth-century brick poultry house.

Through this woodland runs Offa's Dyke, which climbs along the side of the **Long Mountain** (where Henry Tudor rallied his troops before the final march to Bosworth) for several miles before coming down to the Severn. On the summit of the Mountain (1338 ft) is **Beacon Ring**, a good hill-fort, now planted with trees. Along the ridge runs the Roman road from Caersws and Forden Gaer to Wroxeter, with great views eastwards into Shropshire. It turns E as it enters England. Half a mile off the road (two miles SE of Leighton Church, at 263/039) is **Trelystan** church, delightfully set on the edge of woods, looking down a valley to a half-timbered farmhouse, and reached over fields by a track. It is a sweet little building, thickly surrounded by yews. It was recased with brick-infilled half-timbering in 1856, but retains its fine medieval roof. The highly melodramatic E window, showing the Agony in the Garden in vivid chiaroscuro, is perhaps by David Evans. A tiny Gothick barrel organ, built by S. Parsons of London in 1827, is still in excellent playing order. It has two barrels with eight hymns on each.

The Roman road runs steeply down the hill, joins the A490 for a few hundred yards, and then follows the B4388. Along the E side of the road a fine stretch of Offa's Dyke is clearly visible. **Forden** is a scattered place. The church, of 1867, by T. Nicholson of Hereford, is costly and colourful (grey stone with red and yellow trim outside, yellow with red stripes inside), but mediocre. It contains a handsome oval font of marble given in 1794, and an E window of 1873 by Morris and Co. The various scenes are from cartoons by Burne-Jones: although not well related to one another, they include some beautiful pieces, especially the Annunciation. A mile SW of the church is the big Workhouse (now a hospital): it was built in 1792-4 to house five hundred paupers, but like other workhouses it was a failure, for people preferred to be poor at home rather than be treated like convicts. Funds were, much more sensibly, applied to helping them with their rents. Another mile SW is **Forden Gaer**, site of an important Roman station.

Montgomery (Trefaldwyn) is now no more than a large village. Reached only by B-roads, not on any canal or railway, it has for years been the county town only in name – the administrative capital is Welshpool. Yet its isolation has ensured that it has remained very much as it was in about 1800, and it is a delightful place. It nestles comfortably against the E side of a steep bluff, which is crowned by a big Iron Age hill-fort, and a medieval castle, both commanding huge views. They bear witness to the strategic importance of the site, at what was once the principal approach into mid-Wales from Shrewsbury. The ford at Rhydwhiman, two miles NW, was an important crossing-place of the Severn, which is why it was there that the Romans built Forden Gaer (see above), and Earl Roger de Montgomery built his motte and bailey castle (Hen Domen). It was Roger, seigneur of Montgomery in Normandy, and a trusted henchman of the Conqueror, who gave the town its English name. The Hen Domen castle belonged, in the time of Henry I, to one Baldwin de Boulers, from whom the town gets its Welsh name. The present **Castle** was built in 1223–5 by Henry III. It passed to the powerful Marcher family of Mortimers, and later to the Herberts. Lord Herbert of Chirbury (see p. 283) surrendered it to the Parliamentarians in 1644, and after the Civil War it was demolished. Not much is left, but the ruins have been cleared recently by the D. o. E.

The town acquired its charter in 1227. It had stone walls with four gates, but only parts of the bank and ditch survive; the town is still confined more or less within their rectangular area. Below the Castle is the neat little main square, closed by the sedate brick Town Hall, built in 1748 by William Baker. A new top storey was added in 1828 by Thomas Penson, Baker's arches were filled in in the later nineteenth century, and the clock-cupola was added in 1921. The way it stands against the hillside is remarkably like Tremadoc (see p. 192).

Up a lane opposite the square is the **Parish Church**, mostly thirteenth-century, with the tower rebuilt in 1816. The church was restored by Haycock in 1861–8, and by Street in 1875–8. The nave has a splendid roof, the W part open, the E part panelled. There is a double screen, fifteenth-century, of which the E part, along with the stalls, was probably brought from the Priory Church of Chirbury at the Dissolution. The S porch (1868) was designed by George Beadnell, of Meifod, a London banker and amateur architect. The elaborate reredos was designed by R. C. Carpenter (figures by Earp; mosaics by Clayton and Bell). The S transept is known as the Lymore transept, after the magnificent half-timbered house of that name (alas, now gone), which belonged to the Herberts. It contains the canopied tomb, erected in 1600, of Richard Herbert of Montgomery Castle, d. 1596. He was father of Edward, Lord Herbert of Chirbury, and of George Herbert, the great Metaphysical poet. His wife Magdalen is also represented in effigy, although she did not die until 1627, and was not buried here: she later married Sir John Danvers, and was buried at Chelsea. John Donne preached her commemoration sermon (he also addressed the first of his Holy Sonnets to her). The eight children are shown kneeling, and beneath is a cadaver. The Latin epitaph is in hendecasyllables. There are also two much-restored medieval effigies, the smaller of which probably represents Sir Edmund Mortimer (Shakespeare's 'revolted Mortimer'), son-in-law of Owen Glendower, c. 1408/9. In the churchyard is the famous Robber's Grave (near the N gate, on the W side of the path). John Davies, hanged in 1821 on a charge of robbery, prophesied that, to prove his innocence, no grass would grow on his grave for at least a generation. To this day the grave remains a cross of bare earth.

NE of the town is the former Gaol, built c. 1832, but with a monumental gatehouse of 1866 by J. W. Poundley – showing that he could handle the classical style as powerfully as the Gothic. The town leaves an impression of sober Georgian houses, of brick, often with pretty details; the occasional half-timbered cottage; and cobbled pavements. The War Memorial, high up on Town Hill half a mile S, is a grand viewpoint.

SE of Montgomery, the border does an irrational loop, to take in Corndon Hill and **Churchstoke**, a very Shropshire-like village, at the junction of the A490 and A489. Its church has a naïve weather-boarded spire (eighteenth century). There are several fine half-timbered houses. Three miles W of Churchstoke, on the Newtown road (A489), is **Sarn**, with a spiky little church of 1859 by T. M. Penson. From Glanmule the B4368 winds up the Kerry Hills, through conifer woods, to Clun Forest in Shropshire. Just beyond is **Kerry**, a neat village, mostly off the main road, which has given its name to a well-known breed of sheep. The church was the scene of a celebrated ecclesiastical shindy in 1176. Bishop Adam of St Asaph came to rededicate it, during a vacancy in the see of St Davids. However, Giraldus Cambrensis, as Archdeacon of Brecon, was determined not to let the see of St Asaph lay claim to Powys, which for 300 years had been in the diocese of St Davids. Each turned up with a large retinue. Giraldus managed to gain possession of the church, and when Adam tried to excommunicate him, started to do likewise, in an even louder voice, having the bells tolled at the same time. The Bishop turned and ran for it, pursued by sticks, stones, and yells. As a result, Kerry remained in the diocese of St Davids for another 700 years. The present large church has a characteristic Montgomeryshire stone tower and timber belfry, of two storeys with a pyramidal roof. The restoration was begun in 1881 by G. E. Street, and continued after his death by A. W. Blomfield. An odd custom used to exist here: the sexton patrolled the church during services, and, if he found anyone asleep, rang a bell. Beside the main road is the yellow brick and stone Gothic school, of 1868. It was designed by J. W. Poundley who lived at Black Hall nearby. A couple of miles more bring you down into Newtown (see p. 293).

WELSHPOOL TO THE MERIONETH BORDER – A458

The A458 leaves Welshpool between the parks of Llanerchydol and Powis Castle, and follows the delightful Sylfaen valley. So also does the **Welshpool and Llanfair Caereinion Railway,** a narrow-gauge railway, begun in 1901, which has been re-opened recently by an amateur society. The line used to run right into the town, but it is said that the civic authorities are not so keen that it should do so again since a train once collided with the Mayoral car. Road and rail part company for a while near Castle Caereinion (whose Victorian spire is a conspicuous landmark), but reunite in the Banw valley, and enter Llanfair Caereinion side by side. Regular trips are run from here in the summer. Llanfair is quite a substantial little town. It had two flannel factories in the early nineteenth century. Its main streets are the one which runs along the other side of the river from the A458, parallel to it, and the one which climbs up to it from the bridge. In the latter are terraced brick houses, a big Gothic chapel, and, by the bridge, the Institute, built by Lord Davies in 1922. It is an odd building with half-timbering, plasterwork, and a stone tower. The church is well sited above the river, but not up to much. It was built in 1868 by Edward Haycock, and the tower added in 1884 by A. E. Lloyd Oswell. Grey and red stone – the red very red. A medieval S door, and a well-preserved effigy of an armed man survive. The effigy (c. 1400) represents Dafydd ap Gruffydd Fychan, a supporter of Owen Glendower.

Further on, the road climbs through a pass, with the steep Moel Bentyrch on the N, richly coloured in autumn: it is the harbinger of the bare mountains ahead. **Llanerfyl** has a church of 1870 by Haycock, with a medieval roof and crude Gothic shrine, and a Christian tombstone of the fifth or sixth century AD. At **Llangadfan** is the oddly named Cann Office Hotel. Abernodwydd, a thatched timber-framed farmhouse from this parish, is now at St Fagan's. A mile further on is **Foel** (really Garthbeibio), where, as the name suggests (it means 'mountain'), the road enters wilder, more mountainous country, climbing over the bleak pass to enter Merioneth by the Dugoed valley (see p. 255).

WELSHPOOL TO NEWTOWN – A483

South of Welshpool the A483 follows the west side of the broad Severn Valley, with the Montgomeryshire Canal following the foot of the hills on the right. Five miles along, a rough track goes east: beside it, half a mile down, stands a monolith with glacial markings, called **Maen Beuno**. Beuno is said to have founded a religious house here, and the church at **Berriew** (Aberrhiw), a mile west on the B4390, is dedicated to him. It was rebuilt in brick, with quoins, in 1803, but completely Gothicized in 1875 by Edward Haycock, who added the chancel, pyramidal spire etc. Reredos 1896, designed by F. R. Kempson, carved by Earp; E window by Hardman. There is a fine tablet, with portrait relief, to W. Owen of Glansevern, d. 1837, by E. H. Baily. The War Memorial cross in the churchyard is by Sir Ninian Comper (1933). The half-timbered vicarage is dated 1616. In the pretty village are numerous black-and-white cottages done up in the nineteenth-century with bargeboards, and moulded brick chimneys which have

has a round arch with Gothic decoration. Near it is a peculiar semi-dormer window. It is a tragedy that Parker's work was largely obliterated in 1892 by Aston Webb and W. H. Spaull: they shortened the tall and elaborate chimney, moving it to the vestry, and removed most of the interior decoration, which included stencil paintings, and a great deal of ornamental work, some of it in carved oak (partly medieval, partly new), some of it in cast iron. The galleries have gone – described in 1845 as 'plain as to their mouldings, but exceedingly rich in spandrils of tracery, bosses, pendants, open arches, and running borders, with inscriptions in the church text alphabet'. Parker went on from here to be Vicar of Llanyblodwel (alas, in Shropshire), and that is much the best place to study his work. (He rebuilt the church there too, giving it a strangely bulging spire, and a rich interior (recently lovingly restored), as well as building the school, and rebuilding the vicarage.) Llanmerewig Church is dedicated to St Llwchaearn, who seems to have been quite a chap: not only did he cause a troublesome hind to jump into a pool by waving his episcopal staff, but even slew a dragon single-handed. His shrine here was a place of pilgrimage.

Below Llanmerewig, the B4389 leads north towards Llanfair Caereinion. The first village is **Betws Cedewain**, whose Perp. church has a big tower with a good timber belfry. The rest was rebuilt in 1868 by W. E. Nesfield. Further along the road, before Tregynon is reached, a pair of ugly semi-detached cottages stands on the right, constructed entirely of concrete (including even the roof) c. 1870. A number of these were built on the estate of **Gregynog** by the Hon. H. Hanbury-Tracy. His father, Charles, first Lord Sudeley, had married the heiress of the Blayneys of Gregynog: he sold off much of the timber to pay for his amazing Gothic house at Toddington in Gloucestershire. Lord Sudeley also built a new house at Gregynog in 1837. Altered by his son c. 1865, it is a strange, cumbersome affair, gabled, and imitating half-timber. One room has elaborate panelling of 1636, from the earlier house. The estate was later bought by Lord Joicey, the Northumbrian miner-millionaire, and later still, in 1921, by Miss Gwendoline Davies and Miss Margaret Davies, grand-daughters of David Davies of Llandinam (see p. 301), and sisters of the first Lord Davies. They built up a marvellous collection of pictures, particularly strong in French nineteenth-century works, and established their famous private press, which produced forty-two books between 1923 and 1940. They also helped living artists, such as Paul Nash, some of whom stayed at Gregynog. They left the house, the large and splendid park, and a considerable endowment to the University of Wales, which uses it for conferences, courses, etc. The pictures were left to the National Museum. The printing press is still partly *in situ* and is to be restored.

The church at **Tregynon** was rebuilt in 1895 by William Scott Owen, Lord Joicey's agent, retaining the old wooden belfry, supported by timber-framing. There is a lavish alabaster reredos of 1902, and pretty stencilled decoration on the E wall, around the window, a fine work of Clayton and Bell originally made for Helperthorpe Church in Yorkshire. An amazing window on the south side, commemorating W. S. Owen (d. 1921), is by Leonard Walker – chunky glass, and wraith-like Expressionist figures. There is also a monument to Arthur Blayney, last of the Blayneys of Gregynog (d. 1795), by J. Bacon: it shows a mourning female holding a pelican's nest. The village school and schoolmaster's house are in Hanbury-Tracy's concrete Tudor.

Newtown (Y Drenewydd) is rapidly expanding, as it is the principal focus of efforts to attract more industry to Mid-Wales. It has a long industrial past, for it was the chief centre of the wool (later flannel) manufacture for which Montgomeryshire was celebrated. Some brick houses still survive which have a third or fourth storey with large windows to light the looms. Three of these, in Commercial Street (across the river), now house a good Museum, which concentrates on the textile industry. Until the recent river diversion schemes, the town was frequently inundated by the Severn. The three-foot tarred plinths on many of the houses are a reminder of this. The river also produced power.

In the early nineteenth century, Newtown was a stronghold of Chartism, and although in the end no disturbances occurred as serious as those at Llanidloes or Newport, it killed Newtown's aspirations to be the Leeds of Wales. Mills failed and fires were common. Capital, poured in in the middle of the century, came too late and business moved to the Teifi valley in Southwest Wales. Indeed, the big Severn Valley Mills,

chimneystack. It may date from as late as c. 1690. **Caersws** was, as the name implies, the site of a Roman fort, of considerable importance. The main road and a railway cut through it, and much of its site is occupied by the workaday village, but parts of the ramparts can be seen. The stationmaster here from 1871 until 1887, when he died, was John Ceiriog Hughes. Born at Llanarmon Dyffryn Ceiriog in 1833, he entered railway service at Manchester at the age of seventeen, but returned to Wales, as stationmaster at Llanidloes, in 1865. He was a prolific and popular lyric poet, whose work does not, generally speaking, come up to the highest level. But some of it is of touching simplicity, for example this poem:

Still do the great mountains stay,
And the winds above them roar;
There is heard at break of day
Songs of shepherds as before.
Daisies as before yet grow
Round the foot of hill and rock;
Over these old mountains, though,
A new shepherd drives his flock.

To the customs of old Wales
Changes come from year to year;
Every generation fails,
One has gone, the next is here.
After a lifetime tempest-tossed
Alun Mabon is no more,
But the language is not lost
And the old songs yet endure.*

At Caersws, Ceiriog managed the six-mile railway which had been built by David Davies in 1871 to link Caersws with the Van lead-mines (see p. 304). People came to travel on the line just to have the pleasure of talking to him. He is buried at **Llanwnog**, a mile north, on the B4568, where the church was rebuilt in 1863 by R. K. Penson. It contains a splendid fifteenth-century rood-screen and loft, and also an E window by the Evans brothers of Shrewsbury, an extraordinary Resurrection scene.

The B4568 leads back to Newtown by way of **Aberhafesp**:

* Translated bv Anthony Conran, *Penguin Book of Welsh Verse*, 1967.

the church was much rebuilt in 1857, but was still considered too unecclesiological by the Rev. J. E. Troughton when he arrived here from Pentrobin (see p. 39) in 1864. So in 1866, on a Monday, he brought in workmen, who removed the gallery and skylights, cut down the pews, took away the two-decker pulpit, and moved the font – and all was ready for the next Sunday.

Four miles W of Caersws, along the B4569, is **Trefeglwys,** in the broad valley of the Trannon: the church is by Poundley and Walker (1865). It incorporates old bits, but is otherwise a rich example of their work – note especially the fantastically stilted arches of the chancel windows, and the richly carved corbels supporting the chancel arch. In the parish are many good half-timbered houses, especially Talgarth and Rhyd-y-Carw.

In the hills S of Trefeglwys is the lovely wooded **Llyn Ebyr.** Once upon a time, the twin children of a Trefeglwys couple were stolen and replaced by imps. The parents wondered why they did not grow, and consulted a Wise Man in Llanidloes. He told them to make broth, and serve it to the reapers in egg-shells. If the infants said anything beyond the minds of children, it was certain they were changelings, and they must be thrown in the lake. The imps gave themselves away by chanting:

Acorns before oak I saw; an egg before a hen;
Never did I see an egg-shell stew, as dinner for harvest-men.

They were thrown in the lake, and the parents found their children back at home.

From Caersws the A470 follows the valley of the river Carno up into the hills, through the nicely-named Clatter and **Carno** itself. At Carno the inn is surprisingly called The Aleppo Merchant: it is said to have been named by a retired sea-captain, after his ship. Opposite it is the church, an even more startling manifestation of Poundley and Walker's *joie-de-vivre* than Trefeglwys. Built in 1863, of lumpy grey stone with red and yellow dressings, it has an amazing little tower whose funny wooden belfry is painted maroon. Carno is where Laura Ashley makes her fabrics and dresses. North of the church was the fort, probably Roman (Caer Noddfa), from which the village takes its name.

Three miles further on is **Talerddig**, where road and railway

of Plas is the so-called **Parliament House**, next to the Owen Glendower Institute. It is certainly true that Owen Glendower held a parliament in Machynlleth in 1404, but it is not really known where he held it, and even if he did hold it on this site, it was not in the present building, which cannot be older than the late fifteenth century. It was in any case much rebuilt, at the expense of Lord Davies, in 1911.

It was at Machynlleth that Owen was nearly killed, for his brother-in-law, Dafydd Gam from Breconshire, came to the Parliament with intent to assassinate him. The plot failed. Owen pardoned Dafydd, who later fought at Agincourt (see Shakespeare's *Henry V*). Further up Maengwyn Street, on the S, is a half-timbered house built by Owen Pugh in 1628, but much rebuilt since. Otherwise most of the buildings are large and stuccoed. The Parish Church is north of the Clock Tower: it is an odd and ungainly effort of 1827, by Edward Haycock Sen. The great bare interior was altered in 1864 by Poundley and Walker, and more recently decorated with red, yellow, and blue lines in folk-art style. On the main road south of the town is an entertaining former smithy, with the doorway in the form of a horseshoe, made of orange terracotta. Out to the W is the Garden Village, an excellent lay-out of 1914, for the Welsh Town Planning and Housing Trust, by T. Alwyn Lloyd.

Two miles SW of Machynlleth, on the A487, is **Derwen-las**, which was a busy port until the railway was built in 1863–4, used for shipping lead from the Dylife mines and slate from Corris. Two miles beyond, the road enters Cardiganshire (see *South Wales*).

NEWTOWN TO LLANIDLOES AND LLANGURIG – A492/A44

The road from Newtown up to the divergence of the A489 at Caersws has been described above (p. 295). Two miles further on is **Llandinam**. The element *dinan* means a small fortress-hill, and refers to the position of the church up above the village. It is dedicated to St Llonio Lawhir (Long-arm), said to have come over from Brittany in the sixth century. There was a famous *clas* (see p. 352) here, which survived until the thirteenth century. The church was rebuilt in 1864–5 by

G. E. Street, incorporating what was left of the medieval one. The massive tower has a pyramidal roof. The woodwork incorporates seventeenth-century work. On the W wall are five seventeenth-century panels which formerly decorated the piers of the old wooden arcade. The excellent E window is by Clayton and Bell. In the S aisle is an odd wooden carving showing three heads which share four eyes, brought from Trefeglwys.

There is no memorial in the church to the most famous son of Llandinam, David Davies (1818–1890), for he was a strict Calvinistic Methodist. The elaborately Gothic Chapel (1872, Szlumper and Aldwinkle) on the main road was his place of worship, and he is commemorated by the large bronze statue beside the bridge. The statue is the work of Alfred Gilbert, the greatest British sculptor of the late nineteenth century: it is a replica of the one at Barry. Davies left school at eleven to work on his father's farm. His skill and industry were remarkable, particularly as a sawyer (hence his nickname 'Top Sawyer'). His first speculation was the purchase of an oak tree from Mr Crewe-Read of Llandinam Hall for £5, which he sawed up and sold for £80. The statue is well sited, for his first public contract was for the foundations, embankment, and approach road to the bridge. The contract was given to him by Thomas Penson, County Surveyor, whose name, with that of the Hawarden Iron Works and the date 1846, appears on the charming Gothic structure. Subsequently, Davies built many roads and railways in mid-Wales. Later he was chiefly responsible for exploiting the coal of the Upper Rhondda Valley, forming the great Ocean Coal Company, and building Barry Docks as his outlet (see also *South Wales*). He sat as Liberal MP for Cardigan from 1874 to 1880. He was a deeply religious man, a true philanthropist, and solid as the oak on which his fortunes were based.

In 1864 Davies built a large house over the other side of the bridge, called Broneirion (now the Girl Guide Centre). When Captain Crewe-Read of **Plas Dinam** (just N of the village) died in 1884, Davies bought the house for his son. It was built in 1872–4 by W. E. Nesfield: the Davies family added to it later (their architect was E. S. Hall). It is now rather rambling, but strikingly picturesque, with its gables, slate-hanging, and parapet of lead rosettes. David Davies' grandson, Parlia-

capitals. The arcade was brought from Abbey Cwmhir (see p. 314) at the Dissolution. For once, this is no mere legend, but certain fact: surviving bases at Abbey Cwmhir are identical to those at Llanidloes. It must have been an appalling labour carting the carved stones all the way up from Radnorshire. The east window (now rebuilt) less probably came from there. It is also doubtful whether the magnificent oak roof of the nave came from Abbey Cwmhir: at any rate the carved angels date from 1542. The church was restored in 1880–82 by G. E. Street: he extended the chancel. The fat tower has a wooden belfry. Up on the wooded hillside north of the town, clearly seen from the main road, is **Dol-llys**, a charming stuccoed Gothick villa of c. 1820, in the Nash style, with rounded bows. It is now an Old People's Home.

Over the Long Bridge, the B4518 follows the Clywedog valley. A mile up, a road goes off R to **Van** (Y Fan). The famous lead-mines here were the richest in the county. They were at their most productive in 1869–81: in 1876 6,850 tons of lead ore were produced, and the company's profit was over £50,000. Considerable remains survive, just N of Fan Pool. They include terraced houses, chapels, great grey mounds of waste, ruined buildings, and, high up on the hillside, two yellow-brick chimneystacks (originally there were eight). The plant was sold in 1901. The new B4518 has been made up in connection with the construction of the vast **Clywedog Reservoir** (begun in 1964). A concrete dam 237 ft high (the tallest in Britain) was built so that six miles of the winding valley could be flooded, chiefly to regulate the Severn, but also to provide water for Montgomeryshire and elsewhere. Right at the foot of the dam, at **Bryntail**, the surface remains of a small leadmine are being restored by the D. o. E.

Beside the reservoir, the B4518 goes over to Llanbrynmair (p. 298), running for several miles above 1000 ft, and dipping steeply up and down through wonderful country. From a mile beyond Staylittle – so named presumably because of the inhospitable altitude – a minor road goes off W to Dylife. Less than a mile beyond the junction there is a spectacular sight. The little river Twymyn drops suddenly, just below the road, down the sheer waterfall **Ffrwd Fawr**, into a deep and rocky gorge, almost artificial-looking. The lovely valley runs northwards for several miles.

The glorious view of Cadair Idris across the River Mawddach.

The sublimely dramatic glacial cirque which encloses Llyn Cau, below the summit of Cadair Idris, forms the subject of one of Richard Wilson's finest paintings.

The State Bedroom at Powis Castle dates from the 1670's: 'the richly hung bed in its alcove, complete with rail to keep off the crowds at the *levée* (*à la* Louis XIV), the tapestries, the profuse gilding, the silvered furniture covered in crimson Spitalfields velvet, all stifle criticism'.

The road, however, soon comes into a desolate lunar landscape, grey with lead-waste from the famous Dylife lead-mines. Both John Bright and Richard Cobden had an interest in them. Cobden married a local girl, from near Machynlleth, daughter of the mine-owner, and sister of Hugh Williams (the solicitor who defended the Llanidloes Chartists, himself author of Chartist songs and defender of the Rebecca rioters). The mines were first worked in about 1770 and were abandoned in 1896. Further on, the road goes through wonderful mountain scenery, reaching a height of 1671 ft, before it starts to drop down to the Dulas valley, so reaching Machynlleth (p. 299).

Beyond Llanidloes, the A492 joins the A44, which follows the Wye valley up from Rhayader, at **Llangurig**. It is a neat little village, an oasis among bare hills, with its grand church set in a sloping churchyard below the main road. Here, as at Llandinam, there was a *clas*, and this one was particularly celebrated because of its famous founder, Curig (d. 550). The *clas* disappeared in about 1180 when the church passed to the Abbey at Strata Florida. The tower, of about 1350, has a most effective shingled spire, added at the time of the extensive restoration of 1877–8. This was carried out by Sir Gilbert Scott in association with Arthur Baker. The cost (£11,000), was paid by the 'Chevalier Lloyd', J. Y. W. Lloyd of Clochfaen, author of that amazing ragbag, *The History of Powys Fadog*. He was once Curate of Llandinam, but was converted to Rome, served in the Pontifical Zouaves, and was made a Knight of St Gregory by Pius IX. In 1875 he returned to the Church of England. He devised the rather dubious scheme of iconography for the stained glass windows, covering five themes – the Story of St Curig; SS Cyricus and Julitta (see p. 147); heroes of the Faith; princely families of North and Mid Wales; and Clochfaen heraldry 1200–1748. However bogus the subjects, the windows are superbly executed, with fine detail and excellent colouring, by the firm of Burlison and Grylls. The rood screen is based on drawings made of the original by the Rev. John Parker in 1828 (it was destroyed in 1834). Together with the stalls and the rich chancel fittings, it forms an outstanding ensemble, very much in the manner of Bodley.

From Llangurig the road follows the Wye up through bleak

mountains, their bareness spoilt by conifers on the south side. Five miles on, at Bontrhydgaled, the road leaves the river, coming down from its source up on Pumlumon. Up the valley, at 827/863, is **Nant Iago**, where lead was mined between 1846 and 1917, at a height of about 1600 ft. Not much is left to be seen, but the amazing thing is that a mine should ever have been operated at such a remote and weatherbeaten spot. Life for the miners must have been pretty grim. A mile beyond Bontrhydgaled, S of the road, is **Cae Gaer**, a Roman fort, its site left clear among the conifers. The A44 enters Cardiganshire, only two miles S of the summit of Pumlumon, at **Eisteddfa Gurig** – the resting-place of Curig. The name is supposed to indicate that he rested here on his way over the mountains from the sea, by which he reached Wales, possibly from Brittany. For the road beyond, see *South Wales*.

CHAPTER ELEVEN

Radnorshire

Radnorshire is the most consistently beautiful county in all Wales. Over half is above the thousand-foot contour but there are no spectacular peaks: '*Mon Dieu*, but the Almighty has forgotten to put the tops on them', was the reaction of Jean Charlet, Miss Emmeline Lewis Lloyd's Swiss guide, when he saw them. Radnorshire was certainly rated low in picturesque terms by English tourists, nor was the railway system in sufficiently direct communication with industrial England to boost the county's spas. Above all it is one of the few Welsh counties to have no seaside. Indeed the editor of another excellent series of guidebooks decided to retire to Radnorshire since the guide to this particular area sold less well than any others he had published.

John Speed, when making notes for his atlas (1608–10) described the soil as 'hungry, though not barren, and that in the East and South the best: the other parts are churlish, and hardly bettered by painfull labour'. Few thought it worth their while. That much quoted rhyme, the lament of a commissioner sent to collect fines from the Royalists during the Commonwealth, sums up matters nicely:

> Radnorsheer, poor Radnorsheer,
> Never a park and never a deer.
> Never a squire of five hundred a year,
> But Richard Fowler of Abbey Cwmhir.

Great houses and parks are still non-existent (although there are two or three in the richer Wye Valley which are quite grand). On the other hand small medieval castles abound, but since the country is so poor in good building stone most of these now look like splendid prehistoric earthworks, having been used as quarries for other buildings. The constant warfare between the Welsh, the Lords Marcher, and the Crown

Continued on Chapter 10 map

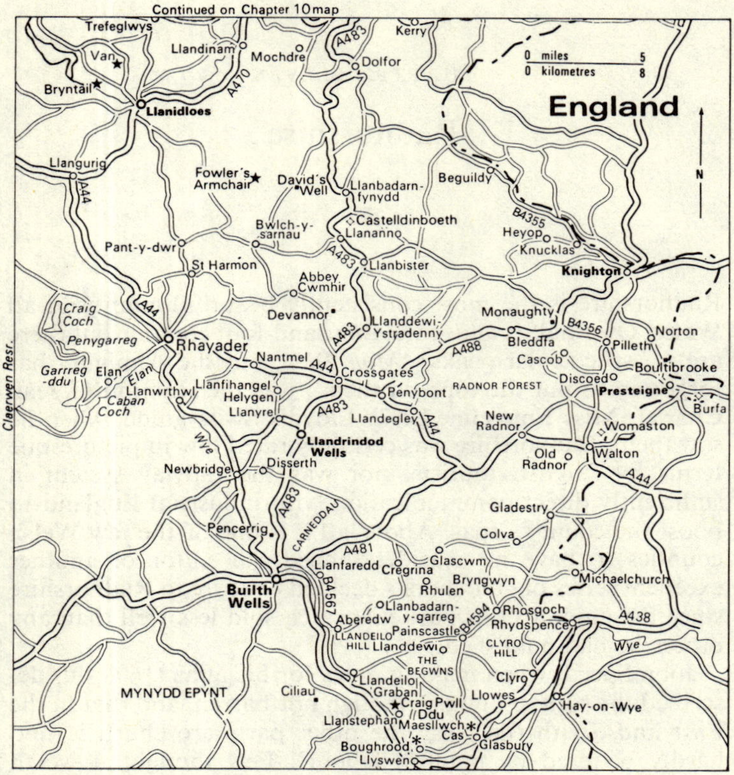

meant that these castles were constantly changing hands. In pre-Norman Conquest times too the country on each side of Offa's Dyke was notoriously ungovernable – a hideout of robbers and outlaws.

Today the Radnorshire people are special to themselves. Welsh is seldom heard except on the Cardiganshire border, but their use of English and their soft voices survived the Second World War (see, for this and much else, the late W. H. Howse's *Radnorshire*, one of the best of county guides which has just been reprinted).

Everywhere you will see and hear sheep. Welsh Mountain graze the high land; up on those bleak brown hills none other can prosper. The border hills are the home of the Clun and Kerry, and on the lower land are crosses of these and Suffolks with the mountain sheep. Everywhere shepherds are to be seen working with their dogs. They may be high up in the hills on their sturdy Welsh ponies, or cruising gently along a main road shouting instructions out of the window of the car. It is a blessed relief for most of us to be held up by sheep instead of traffic (there are no traffic lights in Radnor).

In June 1971 the Agricultural Census gave the numbers of sheep and lambs in the county as 652,971. The breeding ewes in this total accounted for 319,443, which is approaching double the 1950 figure of 174,000. It has probably now reached its peak and some would shake their heads and say that They (the Government) have encouraged overstocking by the payment of subsidies. The main markets for the lambs are Knighton and Rhayader, Builth Wells and Hay-on-Wye (just over the boundary in Brecconshire). It is well worth choosing market day to visit these towns. Those that are to be fattened as stores are sold at the great lamb sales (see the local papers: these will be at the end of July or early August). The sales of breeding ewes are held in the autumn.

It would be fascinating to know how many sheep the Cistercians ran on the great sheep walks of Abbey Cwmhir. Now much of this country, as elsewhere in Radnorshire, is under forestry. One thing is clear: scenically speaking it would seem impossible for the county to grow one more sitka spruce without destroying its unique character.

In the mind's eye it is an October country. Open grassy hills with slopes covered in bracken, deep red-brown, glowing in the low autumn sun. Yellow oak woodland, scrubby indigenous sessile, lightly covers the lower slopes where the dark green of sitka has not taken over. There are small, secret valleys, movingly humble churches, remote chapels, and everywhere the sound of sheep, even in the Wye Valley itself, that pastoral idyll and fishermen's paradise. It is small wonder that the long-haired drop-outs have discovered that Radnorshire is as near heaven as Khatmandu and with un-plumbed cottages going at £1 a week they moved in in the late 1960s.

Gurus too are settling in Wales, perhaps helping to redress the balance in a country where teachers are a major export.

RHAYADER AND THE ELAN VALLEY

The River Wye, having risen from that most elusive mountain Pumlumon, finds its way down through Llangurig (p. 305) in company with A44 into Radnorshire and so to Rhayader. This is one of the most beautiful stretches of that lovely river. Several fine foot suspension bridges have been thrown across it to allow children from remote farms to get to school. The more recent, designed in timber and wire, are by Mr Hope, carpenter and undertaker of Newbridge-on-Wye.

Rhayader is the most seasonal of towns; it changes character absolutely with the arrival of the tourists. Unlike Llandrindod Wells which gives an open-armed welcome throughout the year, Rhayader is a business-like place which tourism overwhelms seemingly despite itself; it lies on A44 between Birmingham and the sea.

In winter the town comes alive for funerals and its sheep and cattle market (Wednesday), both of which are admirably conducted, but the zenith of its season comes with the sheep sales in the spring and autumn. It is a place for people, not buildings; of these it has an unselfconscious hotch-potch.

The town has one long street (A44) lined with shops and pubs (none has an off-licence) and you will be out of it before you have stopped unless caught in a traffic jam. Park up near the market (north of the main street). A small road by the dull-looking church leads past attractive traditional cottages where cobbled paving survives and a cherished chapel to the Cwmdauddwr Arms, an attractive stone country-type pub on the main road again. All this gives a taste of pre-Victorian Rhayader.

Rhayader may be remembered for its particularly militant salmon poaching at the time of the construction of the early Elan reservoirs when the navvies joined the natives, turning out in scores with flaring torches and tridents, faces smeared with clay to avoid recognition – highly organized latter-day 'Rebecca riots' in which 200 big fish were said to be taken.

B4518, leading SW out of the town, is the only direct way to the Elan Valley and the other reservoirs which make up what the Tours advertise as 'the Lake District of Wales'. It is indeed a lake district but of a very different kind from that of England. It is an ideal mecca for motor-coaches and might have been designed for car-borne tourism (whence much of the congestion in Rhayader itself).

An alternative route is the circuit made by taking first the Devil's Bridge road off B4518 on the outskirts of Rhayader as far as the head of Craig Goch reservoir. This is a wonderful early morning road with the sun behind you. Everything is brilliant and miniature; raindrops sparkle on the small oak which lightly cover the slopes. Soon the road is unfenced and the little falls in the stream beside it fairly dance in the sun. Various paths, marked on the 1 inch OS, link the Wye Valley which lies behind the steep crags to the north with the now flooded valleys of the reservoirs. Just over the watershed on the 1500 ft contour the road is on the line of an ancient trackway which leads SW over the empty moorlands to the Cistercian Abbey of Strata Florida, (see *South Wales*) and E over to the Wye Valley. Beware of any of these hills in misty weather. B4518 goes W to Cwmystwyth (see *South Wales*). There are plans to flood this valley with water diverted from the Ystwyth which now flows W to the sea at Aberystwyth. It should then form an extension of the Craig Goch reservoir.

At Pont-ar-Elan, at the head of Craig Goch reservoir, the left fork leads south into the Birmingham Water Corporation's Lake District in the **Elan Valley.** Facts: it consists of five reservoirs with a total capacity of close on 22,000 million gallons which flow by gravity to the midlands. The gathering grounds of over seventy square miles of grassy hill country have an average rainfall of seventy inches, are grazed by 45,000 sheep and support a population of about a hundred people. Cattle are discouraged because of possible pollution to the water and no sailing or bathing is allowed on the lakes. For trout fishing permits apply to the Estate Office in Elan Village. Read, Elizabeth Clarke's *The Valley* – a brilliant book.

Long before the flooding of the valleys **Cwm Elan** was a favoured tourist haunt. Mr Thomas Groves, a Wiltshire gentleman, had created here a paradise in his '10,000 almost worthless acres' and the nineteen-year-old poet Shelley had put the place on the map by taking Nant Gwyllt for a short time with his young wife Harriet in 1810.

The first enabling Act for the Elan Valley scheme was passed in 1892 and work was completed in 1904. The Birmingham Corporation had most enlightened ideas about the social conditions of the navvies who were to construct the dam. Instead of housing them in the usual barracks a model hutted village was built. The idea was that each hut would house a hut-keeper, his wife and family, and eight lodgers who would be looked after by the wife. There was also a school with 168 scholars, a mission room, a public hall and library, a hospital with eighteen beds, and a canteen which was a municipal pub. The doss house where new workmen spent their first few nights and an infectious diseases' hospital were separate. Ironically perhaps, since it was later to be drowned, Nant Gwyllt was put in order for Mr Yourdi the resident engineer and Cwm Elan for members of the staff. No contracts were let, the whole being done by the Corporation itself.

Scenically there is little doubt that Penygarreg, Garreg Ddu and parts of Caban Coch are infinitely more successful than the recent vast Claerwen Reservoir or even Craig Goch which, although bare, has a much more interesting shore line. Steep crags like those above Caban Coch immediately give it 'anchorage' in the landscape and there is a striking difference of mood created by the trees: contrast the native oak, birch and alder and the few splendid beech which survive with the sitka spruce which creates a gloom as all pervasive as that round Lake Vyrnwy. It is well worth leaving the car to explore the side valleys where in a matter of minutes you may be among old lead mines and on timeless sheep walks utterly remote from petrol fumes.

The dams are obviously best seen with a roar of water coming over the top, but after a long drought the reservoirs have a special fascination. They are seldom as low as in the autumn of 1971 when the island in **Penygarreg** (below Craig Goch) was a conifer oasis in a brown desert and the narrow end of the reservoir was like a dried-up wadi. There is a good view of the dam from the bridge just downstream; all these turn-of-the century works are fairy-tale stuff compared with those of fifty years on. The bereft little building by the next bridge down (between Garreg Ddu and Caban Coch, really one reservoir) was built to replace the drowned Capel Nantgwyllt, a chapel of ease of Cwmdauddwr, Rhayader. The engineers are reported to have proposed concreting over its little graveyard for fear of pollution. The descendants of those buried strongly objected, demanding to know how their forebears were to rise at the last trump?

Now follow the west bank of **Caban Coch**. Some lovely beech survive in a few places along the road and there are good larch plantations. Shelley's submerged house is near the mouth of the Nant Gwyllt stream before the saw mill. After a severe drought long stretches of the garden wall can be seen. The strange unfinished dam near the head of this reservoir was built before the flooding of this valley in accordance with an earlier scheme.

The next stretch of road beside the rushing Claerwen is indeed idyllic. Scrubby birch and alder grow between the boulders; the crags above look far grander than they are. The stream dashes over little rapids and drops suddenly down miniature falls like a five-year-old out of school.

The more the shock then to see suddenly the great cliff of the **Claerwen Dam** towering across the valley ahead. Behind it lie four and a half miles of imprisoned water. At its foot (sadly detracting from its grandeur) an absurd line of evergreens encircles the stilling pool. A shepherd who runs 3000 sheep on the hills lives in the little modern villa. You can drive to the top of the dam but the reservoir beyond is too open and vast to be a likely lure for walkers. The ancient road to Strata Florida crosses the boggy hill country half a mile up from the top of the reservoir; the track along the reservoir leads to it.

On the return journey to Rhayader a short detour can be made just below the Caban Coch dam (i.e. the last one) over the suspension bridge to look at **Elan Village** (c. 1906). This model village was built for the maintenance staff: a rare example of its kind with stone cottages and a school beside the lovely but heavily shaded Elan river soon after it leaves the lowest reservoir. B4518 returns to Rhayader.

NORTH OF A44 TO A483 FROM RHAYADER

Within easy reach of Rhayader, over grassy hills four miles N up B4518 to Llanidloes, is **St Harmon**. Here the diarist Kilvert (p. 357) was vicar, 1876–7. He deplored what sounds to have been a plain church of the 1820s and would probably have delighted in its thorough remodelling in 1908. Vortigern found refuge in the surrounding hills. St Germanus, who is reputed to have founded the church, is said to have prayed for forty days for its protection from this unwelcome refugee.

West of St Harmon the country is higher and emptier but much of it is cloaked in forestry. A minor road to the S of the church goes over to **Abbeycwmhir**, once the centre of a vast Cistercian sheepwalk but now hemmed in by conifers; the indigenous oak has gone. This monastery, founded in 1143 and eventually sacked by Owen Glendower, had by far the largest church in Wales. It is reached down the lane by the Happy Union pub. You can easily pick out the huge nave between its walls, now field boundary height; it appears a good deal smaller than it actually is (as do the foundations of new houses), 242 × 70 ft, one of the biggest naves in Britain (Canterbury is about the same width but is under 200 ft long). The choir and transepts may never have been completed. An arcade is now in Llanidloes. A lovely site and tranquil in its uninformative boskyness. No one has glamorized it but a little restrained conservation is needed. Level grass; hornbeam, thorn and ash thrust through the masonry and the remains of attached columns cling to the rubble walls. The base of a great column with clustered shafts gives some idea of its glory. Llywelyn the Last was buried here. There are said to have been only three monks at the time of the Reformation when the lands went to the Fowler family (of the well-known rhyme – see p. 307).

This long remote valley still has a feeling of sanctity despite the small sewage works so inappropriately screened by macrocarpa. Abbey Farm is a pretty gothicky building with bits of column built into its gable. The origin of the inn sign (a man riding a goat) of the Happy Union is not known. The large Victorian house above the road was much admired in 1870, when it was almost finished, by Kilvert. Gabled and bargeboarded, with a striped slate roof, it is by Poundley and Walker, who also designed the church (1866). Admirers of this partnership will certainly wish to see it. Very characterful, it is built of knobbly brownish stone, in early French Gothic style. The porch is beneath a spirelet which turns octagonal. The intense Pre-Raphaelite glass in the apse, with rich browns, greens, and purples, is by Heaton, Butler and Bayne, and the W window is by Clayton and Bell.

On down the valley, one mile E on the side of the hill, is **Devannor**, a tall, cream-washed farm with high chimneys set diagonally. The Griffith family, faithful Wesleyan Methodists, have lived here for many generations and services have been held in the farm kitchen since 1818; every fourth Sunday they are now held in the church. The Clywedog Brook follows the road almost to A483. Crossgates (p. 317) is one and a quarter miles down the main road but turn L for Newtown. Two miles ahead on your right the hill is crowned by an Iron Age Fort (115/698) which has good earthworks and gives superb views. The approach from the east is much less steep; to reach it turn right in Llanddewi Ystradenny, the village to its south, and bear left. This approach brings you first to Cwm-Cefn-y-Gaer which fortifies the neighbouring hill.

Back on the main road for **Llanbister** which has a good little Wesleyan chapel cared for by a married daughter from Devannor. Turn R for the post-office where the key is kept. This unassuming brick building with roundheaded windows and Gothick glazing was built by a nineteenth-century Anglican vicar. It originally had a hipped roof. To the right of the central door the floor consists of six broad flagged steps on which the pews sit. The communion and pulpit rails look contemporary but the pulpit is a little later.

Another vicar of Llanbister sunk a pool for total immersion in the **Parish Church** during the restoration by W. D. Caröe in 1908. This most invigorating thirteenth-century building juts out of the hillside. The west gable is windowless and mysterious, and the tower is at the east end so that is windowless too. The approach is unusual: up a sloping path followed by broad steps right across the large porch which continue at right angles as you enter the building, so it is as though you were emerging from a well. A great open roof runs right through to the east end, making the church one despite the fact that the chancel is four steps up from the nave and separated from it by a sturdy, basically fifteenth-century, screen. The musicians' gallery (1716) across the west end is pleasantly light and open with turned balusters. Remnants of a wall painting of architectural promise survive on the N wall. The communion rails are of 1828 and the oil lamps have been well adapted to electricity. Giraldus Cambrensis spent the night in this church c. 1176; it is dedicated to St Cynllo and dates from the sixth century. Very attractive and unusual gravestones, designed in two panels and decorated with scrolls, cherubs, angels or urns in low relief, stand to the S and W of the church (see also Llananno churchyard). They date from the late eighteenth to the mid nineteenth centuries.

One mile north, below the road, in the ever-narrowing gap between road widening and the river, is the dull-looking church at **Llananno**, rebuilt 1877–80, in which a marvellous late fifteenth/early sixteenth-century screen survives. It is claimed (with justification) to be 'the best in Wales' and is believed to have come from the Montgomeryshire workshop which produced Llanidloes and Llanwnog. Its adaptation to the new church is skilful (two new bays and figures added). Both sides of the head beam are decorated with trails of lovely leaf patterns with intricate interweaving of stems. The bressummer beams are also finely carved on both sides, the stems issuing from serpents' jaws (the north one is the copy). On either side of Christ are patriarchs and the apostles. The church has good nineteenth-century pews, a church warden's box pew of 1681, and the babbling Ithon outside its door.

Another mile up the road on the right is the steep green track through scrub oak to **Castelldinboeth** or **Dinbaud** (090/754), one of the best viewpoints for miles. Follow the diagonal track until it meets the fence, then back along the edges of the wood to the corner, and straight up the hill which is crowned by the castle. Its impressive earthworks are as high as a house. The steep bank and ditch enclose a space of 60–70 yards' diameter and unexpectedly the fragment of a stone tower survives. Little of interest is known about this medieval castle; a prehistoric fortification also commanded the site.

The high country to the west of A483 is meshed by paths on the OS map and the lovely **Bwlch y Sarnau** road runs back into it (and S to Abbeycwmhir). This turning L is about four miles N of **Llanbadarn Fynydd** church (an 1875 rebuilding, with some older contents) which is sandwiched between the Ithon and the road. The turning is at a lovely spot where beeches shadow the clear shallows of the Ithon.

Another four miles bring you to **David's Well** (061/785) just above the tiny stream in the field near the telephone box.

It is one of the many curative springs in these hills, less widely renowned than Llandrindod but, until recently, popular locally. Mr Pritchard who lives near by, and who, besides owning 42½ acres and tending the roads, has won over forty cups for singing and conducting, explained that one must drink from the spout where the water trickles into the rectangular pool rather than the pool itself since lorry loads of mangy dogs might be brought from Newtown and dipped here. The pool is also reputed to be good for sore feet. The well for eyes, nearby, has recently been covered in.

The country around here can be depressing in bleak weather. It has an open featurelessness that demands great skies. A shining winter day with brilliant sun and a hard frost is perhaps best of all since it is also firmer under foot. **Fowler's Armchair** (a rather nondescript stone) at 041/791, one and a half miles W of David's Well, is a good place to make for. There are fine views and plenty of paths converge here.

Bwlch-y-Sarnau is three miles due S along the prehistoric ridgeway; four small roads meet here. The quickest way back to Rhayader (p. 310) is by Pant-y-dwr on B4518.

CROSSGATES TO KNIGHTON

Crossgates is an important road junction where A44 and A483 cross right in the middle of Radnorshire. You may often find yourself at this roundabout and enjoy the pleasant Regency house which has been draughtily exposed by its construction. **Penybont** is two miles E on A44. It was once famed for its fairs but is now for its trotting races. A488, the main Knighton road, leaves A44 here and runs NE through open hilly country. Radnor Forest (p. 323) is the great block of high country between the two main roads. It is cut by no public roads, but the Forestry Commission has planted the northerly slopes so there are forestry roads into it.

Bleddfa is the village on the bend where A488 drops down towards the Lugg valley. The medieval church has a fourteenth-century tower and an unusual roof made up of a mixed lot of very bold trusses (mostly a kind of sloping queen-post with a central post thrown in for good measure) and quatrefoil wind bracing. There are fine Jacobean communion rails and a carved pulpit.

Two miles on the road crosses the Lugg. On your left **Monaughty** (open on written application), the great gloomy seventeenth-century-looking house, is basically Tudor. It was re-furbished in 1636. Rea of Monaughty and his neighbour Rogers of Tyluggan were early breeders of Hereford cattle. When the famous Monaughty herd was sold in 1863 on Rea's death, a special train was run from Hereford for the sale.

Here the main road is joined by B4356, the Presteigne road, which follows the Lugg valley eastward. About one mile on, at the Battle of Pilleth on 22 June 1402, Owen Glendower vanquished Edmund Mortimer (see *Henry IV*, *Part I*), who became his ally, married his daughter and perished in the siege of Harlech. Many of those slain are buried in **Pilleth** churchyard which is up in a field on the hillside above the road (look out for the small sign on your L which shows where you can pull off, and walk up the green track).

There are lovely views from the churchyard into the edge of Radnor Forest, and if by chance followers of the Teme Valley Foxhounds are up there silhouetted against the sky, the Middle Ages spring to life. The rather grandiose steps inside the churchyard dispel this medieval mood but the little church, despite what has happened to it, somehow does not. A sturdy fourteenth century tower survives but the building was burnt, not for the first time, in 1894 and it still has its temporary felt roof. Inside it is lime-washed but stripped of almost everything, although there are two seventeenth-century seats in the chancel, and some armour that has been dug up is a sharp reminder of the battle.

From here you may want to go straight to Discoed (p. 321) or Presteigne (p. 320) but from Monaughty A488 goes over to Knighton.

THE ENGLISH BORDER

Knighton, a small town in the north corner of the county, is almost in Shropshire. It saw its heyday in the 1880's and the result is a rich mixture of brick, gabled black-and-white Victorian, and stone, with redundant mills down by the river and no undue civic pride. The streets clamber up and down the hill from the 1872 clock-tower (by Haddon of Hereford).

The handsome church with its big squat tower (rebuilt from the first storey) is towards the river, below steep conifer-clad slopes. It was restored and largely rebuilt in the nineteenth century, the nave, aisles and tower by S. Pountney Smith (1875–7) and the chancel by J. L. Pearson (1897–8). A neat factory made of sheet metal has recently been built to the east of the town and a little further on **Stanage Park** (not open) can just be claimed by Wales. It was built by Humphrey Repton in 1807 for Charles Rodgers, whose descendants still have Repton's Red Book of 1803 in which, as was his practice, he showed, with the help of cut-outs, how he would transform the property. It has been a good deal altered (J. A. Repton, 1822; dining-room by E. Haycock 1845), and rendered, but is attractive in silhouette and there are exceptional trees in the park. A Repton lodge on the Knighton road survives.

The Mid-Wales Railway and B4355 follow the lovely Teme Valley up to Knucklas. The railway, a most useful and enjoyable line (Craven Arms – Llanelli), runs right through Radnorshire. Here it heads west to cross the **Knucklas Viaduct,** three miles from Knighton: this grand stone structure is entertainingly castellated, possibly because the wooded hill just N was the site of a castle. It is threatened with demolition if the railway closes. Half a mile W down in the valley is **Heyop Church**, simply and elegantly rebuilt in 1880 by J. L. Pearson, with a shingled broach spire. It has a plain fifteenth-century screen.

The **Teme Valley** continues to be Welsh border. The pack of foxhounds of that name is kennelled at Knighton and supported by hardy farmers and border squires; a very different sport to that of the English shires. B4355 follows the valley NW into the hills. The river marks the border with Shropshire. At **Beguildy** (five miles up from Knucklas) the church stands up above the road. Restored in 1885 and 1896, with a big bell-cote, it contains a splendid screen, the coving painted with roses, a curious castellated bench-end, and other old woodwork. Across the valley, NW of the church (in England) is a pretty and well-preserved motte-and-bailey castle. The B4355 goes over to join the A483 at Dolfor (p. 295).

South from Knighton, a particularly fine stretch of Offa's Dyke (p. 360) with lovely wide views over enclosed hills cuts B4355, the Presteigne road, half a mile south of the Walton turning. This is an easily accessible stretch. The pink granite obelisk, which seems to have escaped from a cemetery, in the lovely rolling field to the S, commemorates Sir Richard Green Price (1803–87) whose untiring energy brought the railway to these parts. Hawthorne Hill (1328 ft) gives grand views.

Back on B4355 you come to **Norton**. The church was rebuilt (except tower) by G. G. Scott in 1868; attractive in its completeness. Scott renewed and added to the picturesque timber belfry. Commanding the church stands the remarkable great Victorian vicarage, with a strange roof-structure. **Boultibrooke** (not open), a very attractive cream plastered house with deep Regency eaves in the trees a mile south, was built in 1815 by Robert Smirke for Sir Harford Jones-Brydges. There is an octagonal brick library behind, added later.

Presteigne is an exceptionally attractive little town beside the swift, shallow Lugg, right on the border. The packhorse bridge survives. It was a coaching town on the London–Aberystwyth route and the withdrawal of the service meant that it has survived wonderfully intact. The Radnorshire Arms (a 1616 house turned inn in 1792) thrived on this trade, as did the Bull Hotel (present building 1820) and the much older Duke's Arms. Llywelyn the Last finally destroyed the Norman motte castle on the wooded Warden (Hill) in 1262 (a pleasant walk) and Owen Glendower burnt the town at the time of the Battle of Pilleth (*q.v.*). It is, surprisingly, the county town and assizes were held here until recently; this probably came about in the Civil War when New Radnor lost its castle. Llandrindod Wells is the administrative centre. Unpretentious shop fronts survive, often bay windowed and always domestic in scale like the houses above them. More exotic are the Victorian Gothic building at the main crossroads, and the half-timbered shop opposite, which has mosaics of broken tiles between the timbers. Down the astonishingly quiet main street is the sedately Grecian former County Hall.

There is plenty to see in **St Andrew's Church** which has Saxon work (E and N walls of N aisle) but is mainly late fourteenth century. The chancel was rebuilt in the mid fifteenth (restored 1927). All is explained on the plan inside. It was restored by J. L. Pearson c. 1890. There are lovely chandeliers, a sixteenth-century Flemish tapestry similar to one designed for Canterbury and sold to Aix-en-Provence in 1656, and a

Llandinam Hall is a characteristic example of the timber-framed houses common in the Welsh border country.

Scrub oakwood in Radnorshire, once common throughout Wales, but now rapidly disappearing.

Thomas Jones' painting (1772) of his own home at Pencerrig shows typical Radnorshire scenery, with cultivated fields giving way to bare hilltops.

The little whitewashed church at Rhulen: 'the west wall, which looks immensely sturdy and upright from the gate, is in fact thrusting out like the prow of a ship'.

1726 carillon (the wooden apparatus was restored in 1968; it plays at 09.00 and 15.00). The curfew is rung at ten past eight.

West of Presteigne the Lugg valley cuts the Dyke but there is another splendid stretch just to its south. St Michael's Church, **Discoed** (277/647), is to the east of the Dyke and easy to miss. A careful little building topped by a perky wooden belfry with a little conical spire of tiny slates, 1869, by an unknown mind.

Three miles NE, **Cascob Church** (239/664) is in remote farm country in the corner of Radnor Forest. It stands beside a snug painted cottage and a sad empty village school. It has huge thick walls but the upper part of the tower is half-timbered, as is the porch. Inside there is a simple, elegantly proportioned screen with a plain panelled loft. A most moving abracadabra prayer and incantation are among the church's relics.

B4362 leads S from Presteigne. On your R **Burfa Camp** crowns a now forested hill (285/610) just outside the Dyke but inside the modern border. The top is mostly clear and there are impressive earthworks. Just below, **Burfa Farmhouse** is a fascinating building now being restored by Mr M. J. Garner; it has sixteenth-century crucks but is probably medieval in origin.

Castle Mound, Womaston, one and a half miles W in the valley below, is wooded, pretty and overgrown with water still in its moat. Edward the Confessor (1042–66) had a castle here. To see, ask at the house. There are several ancient standing stones around here but by far the most dashing are the Four Stones, **Walton**, which went every evening to Hindwell Pool to drink. They are usually to be found in the field one and a half miles W again beside the minor road N off A44 which joins B4362 at Walton.

If you have just entered Wales here on A44, skirting the great cliffs of the Stanner Rocks (renowned to botanists), a treat is immediately in store. Right ahead is the much quarried Old Radnor Hill; there were twenty-two limekilns here in the early nineteenth century. Turn left in Walton for **Old Radnor**. The hamlet on the hillside has grand views of Radnor Forest, and the tower and beacon turret of its justly famous church, more English than Welsh in character and still belonging to the diocese of Hereford, is a sturdy landmark for miles westward. It is a perfect Victorian restoration, largely by F. Preedy of Worcester, of a fine fifteenth-century church; astonishingly fine if you arrive here from Wales; slightly less spectacular if your architectural standards are English. Unfortunately all the paintwork was stripped off. The E end was entirely rebuilt and a vast window 'uncommonly grand' with glass by Hardman put in (1882). Most of the rest of the glass is clear (but there is good late fifteenth-century, a lovely St Catherine, in the vestry), so the light floods through the aisle arcading and lights the handsome nave and its carved roof (arms of the Lords of Radnor). There is much to see. Do not miss the organ; its excitingly carved case, c. 1500, is the oldest in Britain; the intricately carved screen, once painted, is now highly polished; sturdy medieval choir stalls survive; medieval tiles have been supplemented by Godwin; the font is a huge lump of igneous rock, probably of pre-Christian religious significance; the Easter sepulchre in the north chapel; an eighteenth-century painting of Moses and Aaron which was once behind the communion table; and interesting tombs and hatchments.

Charles I is said to have complained of the food at the **Harp Inn** (restored 1971 by the Landmark Trust) on the green beside the church.

By way of contrast spare a glance for the humble little cream-washed chapel of **Yardro**, with Sankey's *Sacred Songs and Solos*, and a fine view back up the valley to Old Radnor tower if you take the back lanes to New Radnor (also on A44).

It was in **New Radnor** that Giraldus Cambrensis began his recruiting campaign for the first crusade and met The Lord Rhys (Rhys ap Gruffydd) who, having taken the Cross, was dissuaded by his fond wife (see p. 364).

The village, a borough from 1562–1833, is dominated by the Castle (take the Knighton road) probably first built in 1096 by a Norman, Philip de Breos, and last garrisoned in the Civil Wars. It was rebuilt by a descendant in the thirteenth century, square in plan with massive corner towers (two smaller to the SE). Its typically bloody history includes the beheading by Owen Glendower of the whole garrison (sixty men); heaps of skulls were excavated in 1843. Clear lines of the town wall can be seen below to the west of the village and a path leads down to the church (1843, Thomas Dashwood) which Goodhart Rendel described as 'utterly unimaginative in a misunderstood convention'. The sanctuary has recently been refitted by George Pace.

The **Lewis Memorial Cross**, 1864, by John Gibbs of Oxford, at the east entrance to the village, commemorates the owner of Harpton Court, a Nash house now demolished; parts of his outbuildings survive.

Radnor Forest is the lonely high land, immediately north, cut by no public roads. It rises to 2166 ft and is lovely open country except where the N slopes have been thickly planted (see p. 317). Steep dingles cut it from the south and paths lead on into the hills. Harley Dingle is a lovely valley one mile W of New Radnor which leads up to the Shepherd's Well, but one is warned to beware of Imperial Metal Industrial Testing. A track one mile W again on A44 leads to the dark falls of Water-break-its-neck (185/601) and the path goes on over the tops to a great network of rights-of-way (including Shepherd's Well); easy to get lost.

A44 soon swings NW following the flank of Radnor Forest. **Llandegley** was once a small spa. Here Pales Meeting House (138/641) is eminently worth seeking out. Take the minor road N and just W of the village and the farm road left as you reach the first farm. Park in the quarry through the gate. This thatched building rests on a spur of Radnor Forest well above the 1000 ft contour with great views south. It epitomises all that one understands of the Quakers: simplicity, humility, assurance. This is underlined by a wonderfully restrained use of colour both inside and out; soft greys and browns and clean whitewash. It was built in 1717 on land acquired for a Quaker graveyard in 1693 (Quakers were then refused burial on consecrated ground); the attached cottages are later. The building is divided by a shuttered partition into a schoolroom and prayer room. There is a narrow platform at one end of the prayer room with two pews facing the congregation. The plain balustrade which forms the back of one of these is about the most ornamental feature of this peaceful well-proportioned room. The school was set up in 1867.

The Quakers were strong in Radnorshire during the seventeenth century. George Fox himself preached on Penybont Common in 1657 for about three hours, some fortunates listening on horseback. However, they suffered fierce persecution and many emigrated with William Penn leaving 'almost a desolation' among those who stayed behind.

A44 goes on through Penybont and Cross Gates (p. 317). One mile beyond the roundabout you can turn L on the Llanyre road for Llanfihangel Helygen (p. 327) but this is an easy trip from Llandrindod Wells. Two miles east is **Llyn Gwyn**, a fishing preserve of Strata Florida and the home, perhaps, of Gwyn, King of the Fairies. The earthworks may be connected with the monks. This pretty sheltered lake is a short walk through the forestry from the turning S off A44 about one mile beyond Nantmel. A44 goes on to Rhayader.

A470, RHAYADER – BUILTH WELLS

South of Rhayader, A470, the main road for Builth Wells and Llandrindod Wells, follows the Wye for nearly thirteen miles. The only village, and it is on the Breconshire side, is **Llanwrthwl.** Turn right and cross the bridge about three miles out of Rhayader: there are lovely walks from here back over to the Elan valley and Caban Coch reservoir.

The main road continues down a fine stretch of the Wye, prized by salmon fishermen and canoeists, but names like the Vulcan Arms and Argoed Mills suggest busier days. Doldowlod House (not open), to your right just beyond Argoed Mills, was built partly by James Watt, son of the inventor, in 1827 with help from R. W. Mylne, and added to by his grandson and S. W. Williams in 1878. The family still live here but the railway down the valley, part of the famous Mid-Wales Line (1864), has gone. One and a half miles on, A4081 branches L for Llandrindod Wells (p. 325) and the next large village on the Builth road is **Newbridge**, which is rather raw architecturally and tends to ignore its lovely river. Llysdinam (not open) just across the bridge on your right high above the Wye, is the house to which Archdeacon Venables, Kilvert's rector at Clyro, retired. It seems that the Archdeacon may have out-Kilverted his curate: 79 volumes of his diaries came to light in 1971 (now in the National Library). The house was rebuilt in 1936.

From Newbridge A470 follows the Wye down to Builth Wells and B4358 runs R to Beulah (both in *South Wales*) and L up to Llandrindod Wells. Half a mile up this road on your right a minor road runs down to the delightful little church at Disserth (p. 328).

LLANDRINDOD WELLS AND THE ITHON

For countless people **Llandrindod Wells** is the great caravanserai of the Principality, only the wares offered are argument, eloquence or stone-walling. Any conference which hopes to be reasonably accessible from the north and south must meet here: religion, coal, forestry, education, the cultivation of dahlias and the fish content of cosmetics are all debated in this cheerful metropolis of which the largest hotel is, appropriately enough, the Metropole.

Older people will tell you that Llandrindod has a lovely setting (true) but tend to be slightly shamefaced about its buildings, which have only recently become fashionable. Certainly it is surprising to come upon this spic-and-span citadel of shiny red and yellow brick, purple slate, big white bay windows, broad streets and public parks in the small green hills of Radnorshire. It is like suddenly discovering that a respectable Edwardian aunt whom you had never actually met is endearingly open-armed and welcoming. The atmosphere is cheerful, prosperous and unhurried. The shops are good and some admirably old-fashioned. The splendid ironmonger's emporium only recently disposed of the last of its stock of nineteenth-century blacksmiths' aprons. Many shops still have good iron fronts but are let down in most cases by poor modern fascias. However, some Art Nouveau is in evidence (e.g. the Pastry Cook next to Smith's). Iron balconies, particularly when painted white, hanging baskets of geraniums, alyssum and lobelia, and awnings make it a pleasant place in which to wander, with perhaps a touch of the best North Wales seaside town about it.

Although its architecture would suggest a late start, Llandrindod was a seventeenth-century watering place. However, by the mid eighteenth it fell into disrepute. Indeed it attracted such 'an influx of such gay and dissolute visitors' that the parents of Thomas Jones the painter (p. 328) abandoned their house here for Pencerrig (R. C. B. Oliver, *Transactions of the Radnorshire Society*, 1969). Llandrindod really came into its own with the coming of the railway in 1865 which linked it as well as Llanwrtyd and Llangammarch Wells with Swansea and the mining valleys. A population of around 350 in 1870 increased nearly tenfold in forty years. Mr Pryse in his *Handbook to the Radnorshire and Breconshire Mineral Springs* could not wonder that 'so many people quit the smoke and dust of the Iron Works to spend a few days amid the invigorating breezes of Llandrindod Common'. Between three and ten glasses of the water, saline, sulphureous and chalybeate, were recommended to be taken each morning. Now it is available on reasonable terms on the National Health.

The Spa is in **Rock Park** on the lower edge of the town (everywhere is within easy walking distance). The entrance to the Park is uninviting, but persevere. Attractive sloping woodland leads down to the Ithon and the edge of the open country, and Lover's Leap, a rock in a loop of the river, is not so high that the leaper would not live to love again. The Spa buildings are disappointing except for the attractive brick Arcade Cottages, once part of a shopping arcade. There is a bowling green and tennis courts. In such a cheerful atmosphere it is hardly surprising that Mr Pryse was able to report that '. . . many a broken down old bachelor has come to Llandrindod with shattered health and buttonless shirts and returned home . . . with a beautiful bride'. The **Lake**, with its rustic shelters, may have abetted such courtships. From here there is a clear view of open country and the golf course: long may it remain so. For bad weather there is an excellent library. This and the **Museum** of local finds have recently been rehoused in Temple Street, immediately behind the Metropole Hotel. The finds are chiefly Roman.

There is not now much to see at **Castell Collen**, half a mile north of the town on the right bank of the Ithon. Its ramparts protected an enclosure 380 ft square which dates from the first century AD. Eighteen Roman practice camps, the largest group known in the Roman Empire, have been recorded on the common to the south of the town. Their construction, and the military exercises with which they were associated, must have given Llandrindod a Salisbury Plain atmosphere.

A variety of expeditions by foot or car can be made from here. **Cefnllys** and **Shaky Bridge** two miles E of Llandrindod on the ever-twisting Ithon make a good one. A small road, dotted with new houses near the town, leads down to the bridge where you leave the car. To see the fifteenth-century screen in this much restored thirteenth-century church first collect the key (it may still be kept at Bailey Einon, the attractive farm with the monkey puzzle on the Llandrindod side of the river). The church has a lovely secluded site in a field above the water, but the atmosphere may be transformed by the fumes of motor-cycle exhaust and the vigorous revving of scores of rally entrants. National championships are held here.

It is well worth climbing the steep grassy slope to **Cefnllys Castle** which crowns the hill in this strategic loop of the river. No stone remains but there is a fine view. It is said to have been defended since prehistoric times. Later it was a stronghold of the Lords Marcher (the Mortimers built here in the twelfth century) and it constantly changed hands between the Welsh and the English. By Owen Glendower's time it was so 'burned and wasted' that it was thought to be of little use.

Alpine Bridge (a modern structure, no longer Swiss), one mile but several twists N, is another lovely spot favoured by our grandparents on the little Ithon which makes the best of itself, winding for miles within a very short distance. It is a dipper, heron, trout stream with every reason to hope for kingfishers.

Llanfihangel Helygen (046/644) is a sturdy little church like a cottage in a clearing, so although close to the road it is easy to miss. It is one and a half miles N of Llanyre off A4081. Brown stone walls, brownish slate roof with green moss (and a low, white timber bellcote) make it a supremely simple little cell, which is beautifully kept and was most sympathetically restored in 1956. The vestry floor is cobbled, the main church paved and the walls limewashed; the open roof has carved braces; the windows are domestic. Furnishing is reminiscent of a chapel since all the pews (seventeenth-century box) face the three-decker pulpit, therefore some have their backs to the altar. There is no choir. There are some simple diamond-shaped slate memorials of the first half of the nineteenth century, and one oil lamp.

SOUTH FROM LLANDRINDOD WELLS TO BUILTH WELLS ON A483

Two and a half miles S, R off A483, **Disserth Church**, in a hollow by a whitewashed farm and yew trees beside the Ithon, should not be missed. The building, including its sturdy tower, is largely thirteenth century with later square-headed windows. A handsome open roof with patterned braces and the whitewashed nave with its flagged floor make a simple setting for the seventeenth-century box pews and pulpit. Many of the pews, which rise towards the back of the church, are carved with the owners' initials and dates. When a church was re-pewed it was customary to specify the overall height and size and leave it to individuals to construct their own. An unusual recess behind the altar below the four-light stone mullioned east window, which has clear glass, makes a most satisfactory substitute for a reredos. Mercifully there is no electricity.

Back on A483, the big rocky outcrops of the Carneddau climb steeply on your left (grand views but a stiff walk up from the S). **Pencerrig** on your R (look out for the hotel sign), has considerable charm but has been much altered (1831 and later) since Thomas Jones (1742–1803) inherited it in 1787 and settled down as a Radnorshire squire. This most refreshing painter had spent several years in Italy and had previously been a pupil of Richard Wilson. It is in Jones's journal that that laconic remark of the master to his high-spirited pupils was recorded, 'Gentlemen, this is no way to rival Claude.' Some of Jones's compositions are extraordinarily modern to our eyes and the country today is astonishingly like his few surviving paintings of it, for example *Penkerrig* in the City Museum and Art Gallery, Birmingham. Most are of Italy, but like several of his contemporaries he was inspired by Thomas Gray's ode, *The Bard* (1757) and the result (in the National Museum, Cardiff) is most dramatic and awesome.

One and a half miles on and you again meet the Wye and A481 comes in on the L. Bear R for Builth Wells which is across the bridge in Breconshire (and in the companion volume, *South Wales*, for this; we apologize, but the break had to come somewhere). The Royal Welsh Show has its permanent ground here on the Radnorshire side: unfortunately it presents a suburban-looking scatter of undistinguished buildings, but it is a lively place in July when the show is held.

A481, the New Radnor road, follows the Wye valley below the big Llanelwedd road-stone quarries which eat into the Carneddau, before climbing N, away from the river over to A44. B4567 follows the left bank of the Wye.

RADNORSHIRE: HILLS BETWEEN THE WYE AND A481

Downstream to the S of Builth Wells, the **Wye** cuts a deep valley ten or twelve miles south-eastwards before the hills again allow it to make for Hereford. These hills, to the E of the Wye (and S of A481), make up a remote country cut by tiny valleys. They seem to have no collective name as do the Black Mountains across the Wye to the south or the mass of the Epynt due west. This makes them the more secret – when you have been there, there is no quick way of explaining where you have been. They are eminently explorable on foot, as a glance at the one-inch OS map (Sheet 141, Brecon) shows and as the Reverend Francis Kilvert so endearingly proved in his famous diaries. Clyro, the parish of which he was curate from 1865 until 1872, is in the Wye valley on the south-east edge of this tract of country with Clyro Hill just above it.

The high valleys have few villages but churches, sometimes remote even from a farm house, still serve the scattered community. One way to begin to know the area is to explore these, leaving the car to walk as weather and whim suggest and, from this initial exploration, plan further journeys on foot. The following route suggests one of the many ways it might be made. None of the churches could be classed as great or even very good architecturally in the national sense, but all have individuality. Often it is their marvellous siting or the moving quality of their monuments that makes their exploration so rewarding.

Follow B4567 down the L bank of the Wye. Three and a half miles S, tear yourself from the idyllic valley up the road to **Aberedw**, a big thirteenth–fourteenth-century church with a bold tower, rather fiercely restored in 1888 (by S. W. Williams). Inside it is broad and high. The fifteenth-century king post roof with arched braces (ceiled as a barrel in the chancel) emphasizes this. It has a fine open fifteenth-century screen. The upper part is divided by wavy mullions which ingeniously give the impression of barley sugar, but are in fact of flat rectangular section. The cast-iron communion rails are also elegant and the Commandment boards good. In the huge porch is a nice memorial to Samuel Cartwright (d. 1722, aged 73) who had himself been a prolific memorial maker in these parts. It is worth walking to the end of the churchyard to look down on the little Edw making its eager way to the Wye.

The road climbs out of the village and winds beside the now gentle, grassy-banked stream. The valley is wooded and remote. Two miles up near a stone bridge with steps beside it (for sheep dippers) is **Llanbadarn-y-garreg Church**, a humble white-washed building standing alone in a field beside the stream; there is not even a path. This primitive church (perhaps thirteenth or fourteenth century with eighteenth-century windows) could hardly be simpler: single cell without even a porch, adorned only by its little bell-cote and a big yew tree. It is built of shallow stones reminiscent of the Lake District and has a brownish slate roof growing yellow lichen and, miraculously, it still has no gutters. It is small; the brown wren who disappeared between a joint of the masonry was exactly in scale. Inside: whitewashed walls; slab floor; seventeenth-century timber roof and communion rails. The painting, now faint, on the immense board which has been fixed to the rood beam, bears the Royal arms. There is an early font much encrusted in limewash. Sad to say it is no longer candlelit and the only discordant feature of this movingly timeless spot is the ungainly electricity pole, a recent improvement. But the sound of the rushing stream with its cheerful flotilla of ducks almost compensates for this obtuse intrusion.

Follow up the valley another couple of miles but bear right at the telephone box for **Rhulen**. This branch valley has an upland feel quite different from that of the Edw. The first view of this remote thirteenth–fourteenth-century church (at 138/498) is a splendid surprise. The backcloth is a hillside of bracken, a burning brown in late October; below it and immediately behind the brilliantly white church is black-green yew. The west gable end, which is what you see head-on, has only one opening, a small black door slightly off-centre. The west wall, which looks immensely sturdy and upright from the gate, is in fact thrusting out like the prow of a ship. The church is crowned by a black timbered bell-cote and its low south porch is generously proportioned, with stone benches. The door has a sanctuary ring and the whole place a sense of refuge. The east wall has no window (probably because of the yew hard against it) but instead a deep recess behind the altar above which a beam forms a kind of gallery. The building is beautifully lit by only two windows in the chancel (probably both eighteenth century) but the gas has recently been replaced by unpleasant electric fittings.

The cottages below the church are now deserted and the network of mountain paths which converged on this remote valley are little used. The lane leads back to the Edw and on to **Cregrina**, a stone-built hamlet with a pleasant old rectory and mission house. The church, largely thirteenth century, sensibly restored, has been rendered outside and cream-washed within. It is open-roofed with simple trusses and has a rugged fifteenth-century rood screen and a Norman font. There are faint traces of fine lettering of the Commandments on the north wall.

Follow the road east up the Clas Brook for **Glascwm**; a narrow, wooded valley, which opens out a little near the thousand-foot contour where the church stands in a banked curving churchyard with sycamore lining the road above. It is a big medieval building with a large timber bell-cote believed to have been founded by St David in the sixth century; thirteenth-century with fifteenth-century additions. The nave has a massive timber roof and the chancel is ceiled by a very flat barrel; they are separated by a big pointed chancel arch.

It is now an open mountain road to **Colva**. Here on the empty hillside protected by an oasis of four yew trees is one of the most impressive and lonely of all Radnorshire churches. A kestrel hovering above matched its primitive isolation. It is largely thirteenth-century. The deep porch and low door make a rather tunnel-like entrance to this simple cell whose deeply splayed windows make the thick walls seem even thicker. It has an open roof with ties, not trusses, and school benches for pews. It has mercifully escaped electrical improvements and is still lit by oil lamps. The Royal Arms were painted by Cartwright of Abare dow (*sic*) in 1733 and there are some nice signed eighteenth-century tablets.

You are now right in Kilvert's country and his diary is essential to one's full enjoyment, whether or not all his haunts are explored. It gives an inch by inch account of the countryside, his parishioners and his feelings (sadly, at times, of quite hopeless love). Above all it shines in conveying atmosphere and season. Then it is immaterial whether the spot is identified. Of spring, for instance, at 'the Wild Duck Pool' he writes 'To this pool the people used to come on Easter morning to see the sun dance and play in the water and the angels who were at the Resurrection playing backwards and forwards before the sun.'

It was at Blaencerdi farm, a couple of miles SW of Colva that Kilvert was shown the jug from which King Charles II had drunk milk on the hot march from Gladestry to Painscastle. Riding two abreast down the narrow lanes his horsemen stretched a mile.

From Colva you can continue N to **Gladestry**, a good village whose fiercely restored church gives antiquarian interest rather than architectural.

Alternatively return to the road junction by the telephone box and turn L for **Bryngwyn**, another church near the 1000 ft contour standing near a forbidding Victorian vicarage. The church, largely thirteenth-century with a fourteenth-century chancel arch and single light window, has good roofs and two interesting inscribed stones. That in the porch was a sepulchral slab, which later became part of the sedilia. The other with the curious cross design was in the churchyard – probably pre-Christian. Less than two miles S is **Rhosgoch** and the mill where the old man who slept in the mill trough used to hear the fairies come in at night and dance to sweet fiddles on the mill floor. Rhosgoch Common is indeed red in winter with bare twigs of scrubby birch trees; it is now a bird reserve. Kilvert's beloved **Clyro Hill** lies to the south; from it, and from all the lanes and dingles leading down to Clyro (p. 336) in the Wye valley there are magnificent views of the Black Mountains.

But to continue now in the hill country. **Painscastle**, one and a half miles SW of Rhosgoch, is an attractive stone village with a plain stone Baptist chapel (1848). The place still has an independent air. Early in the nineteenth century an advertisement for a local farm was able to boast 'No Nobleman resides within ten miles, nor any Busy Sporting Esquires in the Neighbourhood.' Matters were very different in the Middle Ages when the village was justly famed for its castle which, although now robbed of its stones, is still a spectacular, sheer-sided earthwork. It lies behind the handsome Georgian façade of Castle Farm. An important motte-and-bailey castle was built here by the Normans. It constantly changed hands between the Welsh, the Lords Marcher and the Crown. Following the execution of Welsh prisoners held at Montgomery, Llywelyn the Great made devastating attacks on the Lords Marcher. This led Henry III to rebuild Painscastle (1231) and to stay here for several months. He commanded that his subjects 'bestir themselves to destroy the wolves' which were far more numerous and destructive here than in any other part of the realm. The Painscastle postman who until recently rode fifteen miles a day on his rounds has since retired to a modern bungalow in the village. Delivery is now by van.

For **Llandewi Fach** go S out of Painscastle, across the bridge and sharp R. The little church lies snugly on the sunny edge of a little wood (145/455) below a farm called Cwm, which is the highest of the four strung along this remote valley; it is an interesting looking seventeenth-century building at the high watermark of derelict cars. Bracken-covered hills traversed by enticing grassy tracks enclose the little valley. For architecture this detour to a Prichard and Seddon church of 1866 on a very ancient site is perhaps not worth the effort but for all else, despite the insensitive work of the Electricity Board, it is. The church is virtually a single cell although it has a chancel arch. It has a flagged floor, contemporary pulpit, panelling and a fireplace. A 1692 grave slab is the doorstep. Through the clear glass of the decorated east window you see a wonderful close up pattern of green leaves, like looking into a pool.

Immediately to the south are the **Begwns** whose highest point, a fir-capped hill known as the Roundabout, has for long been a well-known viewpoint.

The parish church, **Llanbedr Painscastle**, is beside the road one and a half miles to the W of the village near a farm. Unattractive veridian green chain link fencing surrounds an unpretentious big church whose interior is impressive in its economic simplicity: whitewashed walls; round chancel arch; nave open-roofed but the light bracing of each pair of rafters gives the impression that it is ceiled. Good eighteenth- and nineteenth-century tablets in the chancel. It was restored by J. H. Evins of Hereford whose plan (framed in the nave) provides 'accommodation for 108 adults all free for ever'.

The previous church had become a ruin and its vicar, the Reverend John Price, MA, a hermit who lived on **Llanbedr Hill.** Kilvert, who was clearly sympathetic although not enamoured by the squalor in which the Solitary lived, quotes a verse which Mr Price wrote for him in his newly invented method of shorthand:

> 'A little health,
> A little wealth,
> A little house and freedom,
> And at the end
> A little friend
> And little cause to need him.'

One hopes that this gentle soul had both at his end and that the new church was not started before his death. Kilvert's call was made in 1872, that is, seven years before the building.

The road now runs south of Llanbedr and Llandeilo Hills, enticing walking country. The once romantic **Llyn Bwch-llyn** lies behind municipal fencing (veridian again). Whether this would have deterred the beautiful girl from Erwood from bathing (as it is intended it should you) or William de Breos or anyone else from carrying her off is doubtful.

St Teilo's Barn, in a field by the road one and a half miles on, a good plain dateless building marked on the OS map, seems devoid of recorded history. Worth a stroll up the hill behind for the marvellous views. These too can be glimpsed through the sheltering trees from the churchyard of **Llandeilo Graban** in its hamlet high above the Wye valley. This basically fourteenth-century church is lit by perpendicular windows with clear glass. It is majestically simple inside: broad nave, ceiled by boarded barrel vault, linked to the open-roofed chancel by a plain pointed arch in a thick wall. The only decoration in the chancel, apart from a carved timber fascia board, was the ivy trailing gracefully. The last dragon to be killed in Radnorshire slept each night in this church tower, and on the east wall (outside) is a nicely factual epitaph which begins 'diametrically opposite to this stone very much Regretted and Lamented lies . . .'

Immediately below, the lane leads back into the Wye valley, only two miles south of the Aberedw turning where you left it.

DOWN THE WYE ON THE RADNORSHIRE BANK: BUILTH WELLS TO THE ENGLISH BORDER

For the first twelve miles the valley is deep and wonderfully sheltered: a long green oasis threading the windy uplands. One mile down B4567 on your L, **Llanfaredd Church**, just above the road by a big farm, had until recently an idyllic view of the river but it is now of a large asbestos cement shed (that the shed was sheltering baled bracken was illogically consoling). The dullish church was thoroughly restored by E. V. Collier in 1890, but it has a huge yew (the biggest in the county) and its seventeenth-century communion rails and fifteenth-century font survive. The 1709 memorial to Ann Probert, aged twelve, in the porch begins 'In hopes of A joyfull Resurrection; under the Greene stone there Lyeth . . .'

A couple of miles further downstream a minor road turns L to Aberedw and into the hills (see p. 329). South of the road junction are the scanty remains of **Aberedw Castle**. (Much of what had survived was destroyed to make room for the Mid-Wales railway, 1864 – a most beautiful line, now abandoned.) Of historic rather than architectural interest, it was the final refuge of Llywelyn the Last who perished in a skirmish nearby in 1282, having revolted against Edward I with whom he had come to terms after the conquest five years earlier. Llywelyn had the most beautiful of outlooks for those last nights on earth: the Wye, soon to become a lowland river, still has a hint of wildness as it flows swiftly below the sheer Aberedw Rocks, while sheep graze its gentle lawns on the opposite bank.

A new road, not marked on the 1″ OS map, now follows the line of the old railway south along the Wye valley. After about a mile the Bach Howey (which has cut through the hills from the bog of Rhosgoch Common) joins the Wye. **Craig Pwll Ddu**, a mile up the Howey, makes a lovely sheltered valley walk up to the gorge and waterfall. Take the path beside the bridge and keep low. For a longer walk (say, six miles) take the track up on the R bank up towards Ciliau, an untouched seventeenth-century-looking farm with a great leaning chimney, and follow the valley at high level until you reach the small footbridge about three miles up. Lovely on an autumn day.

Another mile downstream turn up L for **Llanstephan Church**. It has a real Radnorshire site with wonderful views and an unusual lychgate which incorporates a stable for the parson's horse. A grassy path leads to the porch of the Victorianly restored thirteenth-century building with fourteenth-century chancel. The suspension bridge over the Wye below was constructed in 1922 by the Phillips family of Llanstephan House (demolished). Two miles downstream through the hamlet of Boughrood is **Boughrood Castle**, built by Francis Fowkes 1817–20. It was originally stuccoed and was intended to be battlemented, but there was a change of mind during construction to deep eaves and pediments. The bridge downstream over a lovely stretch of the Wye leads into Breconshire at Llyswen (see *South Wales*). A toll-house built into it survives (tolls ceased in 1934). With the cream-washed Boat Inn and some neat cottages with iron framed windows with labels over them, this makes a very attractive hamlet.

Glasbury is a big village close to an important crossing of the river where a new bridge takes A4153, the Hereford road, across the Wye. It has good houses and again a feeling of Herefordshire. **Maesllwch Castle**, above, has a fine site with grand views of the Black Mountains. Its symmetrical main block, c. 1830 by Robert Lugar, has been demolished, and what survives is of 1874 (Burnell and Legg). Maesyronnen Chapel (177/412), up the lane off A4153 one mile N of Glasbury, stands on the pastoral hillside above the Wye Valley overlooking the Black Mountains. Built in 1697, it is one of the oldest chapels in Wales still in use; a simple stone building with caretaker's cottage next door. It has blue-washed plastered walls, a whitewashed coved eighteenth-century ceiling and flagged floor, and very attractive contemporary furniture.

Llowes Church on your left two miles downstream has an ancient stone carved with an early cross. Next comes **Clyro,** where Kilvert was curate 1865–72 (see pages 313 and 357).

The snug stone cottages by the lychgate, Ashbrook House where Kilvert lived (it has a plaque), and the regency Baskerville Arms, must be much as he knew them. The church, 1853 by T. Nicholson, is not of architectural interest but the whole village, with Clyro Hill behind it, has a wonderful setting and great views south to the Black Mountains. Immediately across the river is the attractive little town of Hay-on-Wye but that is in the N tip of Breconshire.

A 4153 crosses into England at Rhydspence, three miles NE of Clyro. Here bear L up the minor road for **Michaelchurch-on-Arrow** which by some freak of the boundary happens to be in Wales. The church has a big saddlebacked tower and stone slabbed roof, well lichened. Inside the fifteenth-century screen and the early-fifteenth-century baldacchino with its carved heads are well worth seeing. Hugh Lloyd, a bone-setter who died in 1856, has a delightful epitaph:

'A talent rare by him possessed
T'adjust the bones of the distressed;
When ever called he ne'er refus'd
But cheerfully his talent used.
But now he lies beneath this tomb,
Till Jesus comes to adjust his own.'

Glossary

1. ELEMENTS USED IN WELSH PLACE-NAMES
2. SOME OTHER USEFUL WORDS AND PHRASES
3. PRONUNCIATION

1. Elements used in Welsh Place-Names

It is well worth familiarizing oneself with these, for Welsh place-names are usually descriptive, and reflect an acute perception of a place's physical character.

One essential point that must be taken into account is that many initial consonants in Welsh are mutated when used in compounds. To give a few examples: **Llan** + **Mair** (Mary) becomes **Llanfair**; **Llan** + **Pedr** (Peter) becomes **Llanbedr**; **Llan** + **Sant** + **Braid** (Saint Brigid) becomes **Llansanffraid**; similarly **moel**, but **y foel**; **ban**, but **y fan**.

The following table of mutated consonants, and the glossary of elements in Welsh place-names, and notes on pronunciation, are taken from *Rhestr o Enwau Lleoedd: A Gazetteer of Welsh Place-Names*, edited by Elwyn Davies, and published by the University of Wales Press (3rd edition, 1967), with whose permission they are here reprinted.

	Radical	p	t	c	b	d	g	m	ll	rh
Mutation	Soft	b	d	g	f	dd	—	f	l	r
	Nasal	mh	nh	ngh	m	n	ng	No change		
	Spirant	ph	th	ch	No change			No change		

aber estuary, confluence
afon river
allt hill, hillside, slope, wood
ar on, upon, over, by
arth *see* **garth**

bach (*adj.*) small, little, lesser
bach (*noun*), *pl.* **bachau** nook, corner, bend
ban, *pl.* **bannau** peak, crest, bare hill, beacon
banc bank, hill, slope
bangor consecrated land or monastery within a wattled fence
bedwen, *pl.* **bedw** birch
bedd, *pl.* **beddau** grave
betws chapel of ease
blaen, *pl.* **blaenau** head, end, source of river, upland
bod abode, dwelling
bont *see* **pont**
braich ridge, spur, arm
bro region, vale, lowland
bron hill-breast, hill-side
bryn, *pl.* **bryniau** hill
bwlch pass, gap
bychan little, small, lesser

cadair, cader seat, stronghold
cae, *pl.* **caeau** field, enclosure
caer, *pl.* **caerau** fort, stronghold
canol middle
capel chapel, meeting house
carn, *pl.* **carnau** cairn, rock, mountain
carnedd, *pl.* **carneddau, carneddi** cairn, barrow, tumulus, mountain
carreg, *pl.* **cerrig** stone, rock
cas (as in Cas-bach) castle
castell castle, stronghold
cefn ridge
celli grove, copse
cemais river bends
cerrig *see* **carreg**
ceunant ravine, gorge, brook
cil, *pl.* **ciliau** corner, retreat, nook
cilfach cove, creek, corner, nook
clawdd dyke, hedge, ditch
clogwyn precipice, crag
clun meadow, moor, brake, thicket
cnwc hillock, knoll
coch red
coed trees, wood, forest
cors bog
craig, *pl.* **creigiau** rock
crib crest, summit, arête
croes cross, cross-roads
croesffordd, croeslon cross-roads
crug, *pl.* **crugiau** knoll, tump
cwm valley, combe
cwrt court, yard
cymer, *pl.* **cymerau** confluence

dan under, below
dâr, *pl.* **deri** oak
darren *see* **tarren**
dau, *f.* **dwy** two
derwen, *pl.* **derw** oak
diffwys precipice, desolate place
din hill fortress
dinas hill fortress
diserth hermitage
dôl, *pl.* **dolau, dolydd** meadow, water meadow
domen *see* **tomen**
dre *see* **tre**
drum *see* **trum**
drws gap, narrow pass
du, *f.* **ddu** black, dark
dwfr, dŵr water
dwy *see* **dau**
dyffryn valley

eglwys church
eithin furze, gorse
erw acre
esgair ridge

fach, fechan *see* **bach, bychan**
faenor *see* **maenor**
fan *see* **ban**
faerdref *see* **maerdref**
fawr *see* **mawr**
felin *see* **melin**
foel *see* **moel**
fron *see* **bron**

ffin boundary
fforch bifurcation, fork
ffordd way, road
ffos ditch, trench
ffridd, *pl.* **ffriddoedd** rough grazing enclosed from mountain, sheepwalk, wood
ffrwd, *pl.* **ffrydiau** stream, torrent
ffynnon, *pl.* **ffynhonnau** spring, well

gaer *see* **caer**
gallt hill, slope, wood
garn *see* **carn**
garnedd *see* **carnedd**
ganol *see* **canol**
garreg *see* **carreg**
garth hill, height; enclosure
garw rough, coarse
gelli *see* **celli**
gefail smithy
gilfach *see* **cilfach**
glan river-bank, bank, hillock
glas green, blue
glas, glais (as in Dulas, Dulais) brook, stream
glyn deep valley, glen
goch *see* **coch**
goetre woodland dwelling or farm
gors *see* **cors**
graig *see* **craig**
grib *see* **crib**
groes *see* **croes**
gwaun moor, mountain pasture
gwern place where alders grow, swamp
gwyn, *f.* **gwen** white
gwyrdd green

hafod, hafoty summer-dwelling, shieling
haidd barley
haul the sun
helygen *pl.* **helyg** willow
hen old
hendre(f) winter dwelling, permanent home, *lit.* old home
heol, hewl road
hir long

is below, under
isaf lower, lowest
isel low

las *see* **glas**
lwyd *see* **llwyd**

llain, *pl.* **lleiniau** narrow strip of land
llan church, enclosure
llannerch clearing, glade
llawr flat valley bottom
llech slab, slate, stone, rock
llechwedd hillside
llety small house, shelter
llethr slope
lluest hut, cottage, shieling
llwch, *pl.* **llychau** lake
llwyd grey, brown
llwyn grove, bush
llyn lake
llys court, hall

maen, *pl.* **meini** stone
maenol, maenor residence of district chief
maerdre(f) hamlet attached to chief's court, lord's demesne
maes, *pl.* **meysydd** field, plain
mawr great, big
meini *see* **maen**
melin mill
melindre(f) mill village
melyn yellow
merthyr burial place, church
mign, *pl.* **mignedd** bog, quagmire
moel bare hill, bald
morfa marsh, sea fen
mur, *pl.* **muriau** wall
mwyn ore, mine
mynachlog monastery
mynydd mountain, moorland

nant, *pl.* **nentydd, nannau** brook
newydd new

odyn kiln
onnen, *pl.* **onn, ynn** ash tree

pandy fulling mill
pant hollow, valley
parc park, field
pen head, top, end
penrhyn promontory
pentre(f) village, homestead
pistyll spout, waterfall
plas hall, mansion
pont bridge
porth gateway, harbour
pwll pit, pool

rhaeadr waterfall
rhiw hill, slope
rhos, *pl.* **rhosydd** moorland
rhyd ford

sain, san, sant, saint saint
sarn, *pl.* **sarnau** causeway
sych dry

tafarn, *pl.* **tafarnau** tavern
tair *see* **tri**
tal end
tan end, below
tarren, *pl.* **tarenni** rocky height, precipice
teg fair
tir land, territory
tomen mound
ton grassland, lea
traeth strand, beach, shore
trallwng wet bottom land
traws cross, transverse; direction, district
tre(f) homestead, hamlet, town
tri, *f.* **tair** three
troed foot
tros over
trum ridge
trwyn point, cape (*lit.* nose)
twyn hillock, knoll
tŷ, *pl.* **tai** house
tyddyn, ty'n small farm, holding

uchaf upper, higher, highest
uchel high
uwch above, over

waun *see* **gwaun**
wen *see* **gwyn**
wern *see* **gwern**

y, yr, 'r (*definite article*) the
ych ox
yn in
ynys island, holm, water meadow
ysbyty hospital, hospice
ystrad valley floor, strath
ystum bend (in river)

2. Some other Useful Words and Phrases

Names of old (pre-1974) counties

Brycheiniog (Sir Frycheiniog)	: Breconshire
Caerfyrddin (Sir Gaerfyrddin)	: Carmarthenshire
Caernarfon (Sir Gaernarfon)	: Caernarfonshire
Dinbych (Sir Ddinbych)	: Denbighshire
Fflint (Sir Fflint)	: Flintshire
Maesyfed (Sir Faesyfed)	: Radnorshire
Meirionnydd (Sir Feirionnydd)	: Merioneth
Môn (Sir Fôn)	: Anglesey
Morgannwg (Sir Forgannwg)	: Glamorgan
Mynwy (Sir Fynwy)	: Monmouthshire
Penfro (Sir Benfro)	: Pembrokeshire
Trefaldwyn (Sir Drefaldwyn)	: Montgomeryshire

Some saints' names

Braid: Brigid (as in **Llansanffraid**)
Dafydd/Dewi: David (as in **Llanddewi**)
Mair/Mari: Mary (as in **Llanfair**)
Mihangel: Michael (as in **Llanfihangel**)
Pedr: Peter (as in **Llanbedr**)
Siôn/Ioan: John

Terms used in Chapel inscriptions

Annibynol: Independent
Cynulleidfaol: Congregational
Bedyddwyr: Baptists
Methodistaidd: Methodist

Adeiladwyd: built
Ailadeiladwyd: rebuilt
Helaethwyd: enlarged
Adnewyddwyd: renewed

Some other words and sayings

Abaty: abbey
Bore da: good morning
Chwarel: quarry
Croeso: welcome
Cyfleusterau: conveniences
Cymraeg (yr iaith Gymraeg): the Welsh language
Cymreig: Welsh
Cymru: Wales
Cymru am byth: Wales for ever
Cymru rydd: free Wales
Cymry: the people of Wales
Diolch yn fawr: thank you very much
Duw: God
Dynion: men
Y Ddraig Goch: red dragon
Fferm: farm
Heb Dduw, heb ddim: without God, without anything
Hen Wlad fy Nhadau: Land of my Fathers
Hiraeth: longing, nostalgia (German *Heimweh*)
Hwyl: ecstatic fervour
Llwybr Cyhoeddus: public footpath
Merched: women
Ogof: cave
Plwyf: parish
Nos da: goodnight
Sant: saint
Sir: shire
Tân: fire
Ysgol: school

3. Pronunciation

Welsh is not as hard to pronounce as it seems at first sight. In fact, its pronunciation is almost entirely phonetic.

CONSONANTS

Each has only one sound.

b, d, h, l, m, n, p, t as in English

c always hard, as in **cat**

ch as in Scottish **loch**

dd the same sound as **th** in **this**

f as English **v**

ff as English **f**

g always hard, as in **gate**

ll almost impossible to represent exactly, but something like **hl**

r trilled as in **merry**

s hard as in **essay**

DIPHTHONGS

ng usually as in **long**, but sometimes as in **longer**, e.g. **bangor**

ph as in **phone**

rh a trilled **r** followed by the aspirate

th as in **thin**

VOWELS

In Welsh these are **a, e, i, o, u, w, y**, and they have two values, short and long.

Long **a** as English **ah**

Short **a** a pure flat sound as in French **à la**

Long **e** a pure sound similar to **a** in **face**, **gate** in Northern pronunciation

Short **e** as in **pen**

Long **i** as in **machine**

Short **i** as in **pin**

Long **o** as in **gore**

Short **o** as in **not**

Short **u** in North Wales, not unlike the French **u**, but not rounded; in South Wales it approximates to long and short **i** as above

Long **w** the **oo** sound in **pool**

Short **w** the **oo** sound in **good**

y long and short, has two sounds, the 'clear' sound which is similar to the Welsh **i**, and the 'obscure' sound which, when long, is like **u** in **further**, and when short is like **u** in **gun.**

In general vowels are short when followed by two or more consonants or by c, ng, m, p, t, and long when followed by b, ch, d, f, ff, g, s, th.

STRESS

As a rule the stress is on the penultimate syllable. In some place-names it is thrown forward on to the last syllable, e.g. Caerdýdd, Pontyprídd, Llanrwst.

Who's Who and What's What

This section includes only characters and subjects which cannot be easily located in any particular part of Wales.

Act of Union, 1536. Brought Wales under English law and gave Welshmen the same rights as the English. It abolished the powers of the Lords Marcher.

Archaeological dating. Through the recent process known as Carbon 14 dating a revised chronology has been worked out by archaeologists. Readers may find considerable discrepancy between this and that used in older books and on signs on some ancient monuments.

Neolithic	beginning	3500 BC
Late Neolithic (Beaker people)	,,	2500/2400 BC
Bronze Age	,,	1900/1800 BC
Iron Age	,,	600/500 BC

Arthur: the early sixth-century soldier king who was more than legendary but about whom no facts emerge. A heroic figure who lived after the departure of the Romans and led the Britons against the Saxons. King Arthur is associated with Caerleon (on the Usk) as well as Cornwall. During the twelfth century a legend emerged that he would return and liberate his fellow countrymen. In 1485, the year of Henry VII's accession, Malory's *Morte D'Arthur* was printed by Caxton's press. Henry named his eldest son Arthur, who, had he lived, would have succeeded instead of Henry VIII.

Baker, Arthur, 1841–96. A pupil of Sir Gilbert Scott, and his assistant until 1878. Cousin of Sir Herbert Baker: in 1888 they published jointly a book on Plas Mawr, Conwy. He was a good architect, and a particularly skilful restorer of old churches, including many in North Wales. For a time he was in partnership with **Henry Harold Hughes**, who also married his daughter. Hughes was Diocesan Surveyor of Bangor, and author, with H. L. North, of *The Old Churches of Snowdonia* (1924).

Baldwin, Archbishop, conducted his famous recruiting campaign in Wales for the 3rd Crusade in 1188 (see also Giraldus Cambrensis). Over 3,000 Welshmen took the Cross but Henry II delayed the expedition and, by the time Richard I was ready, the Welsh were too occupied in fighting at home to join. Baldwin died in camp at Acre.

Bards. See also Eisteddfod. Bards played an important role in the courts of the princes and continued to attach themselves to the households of the gentry right up to the seventeenth century; some of their descriptions of houses and demesnes survive. The quality and intricacy of structure of their poetry is greatly prized, but a minor by-product, the keeping of law and order in the community through their use of satire, was also of great value.

Beuno, Saint. Early seventh century. (April 21). A particularly peripatetic saint who founded many monasteries and is specially associated with Clynnog Fawr. He is probably best known for miraculously restoring the head of his niece, St Winefrede.

'Bevan, Madam' (Bridget Bevan), 1698–1779, was the chief patron and adviser of Griffith Jones, founder of the Welsh Circulating Schools, which she organized after his death. She was a Vaughan of Derllys Court, Carmarthenshire, and her father was organiser of the SPCK schools in the county. She married Arthur Bevan, a barrister in Laugharne.

Buckeridge, Charles, 1832/3–73. A pupil of Sir Gilbert Scott, he practised in Oxford. A keen High Churchman, he was primarily an ecclesiastical architect. He designed Holy Trinity Convent, Oxford (1865–8, now St Antony's College) for Mother Marian Hughes, a disciple of Pusey, as well as Llanthony Abbey, for Father Ignatius. He did much work in Breconshire and Glamorgan, through the Rev. Gilbert C. F.

Harries, Rector of Llandyfaelog Fach and Rural Dean of Breconshire, and after 1862 Rector of Gelligaer.

Cadfan, Saint. Early sixth century. (November 1.) Patron saint of warriors. In the fifth century several bands of settlers left Brittany for Wales (see Padarn). Cadfan founded the church at Tywyn, Merioneth, which became a famous medieval monastery, and was later first Abbot of Bardsey. See also Llangadwaladr, p. 218 for King Cadfan.

Cambrian Archaeological Association. Founded 1846. The first President was Sir Stephen Glynne, and the Vice-Presidents were W. W. E. Wynne and Sir Samuel Rush Meyrick. The first volume of its celebrated journal, *Archaeologia Cambrensis*, was published the same year. In 1847 it held its first Annual Meeting, at Aberystwyth, and these have continued ever since. They are held in a different area each year, and combine scholarly investigation with friendly merriment.

Caractacus (d. AD 54). The last leader of the Ordovices. He put up a long fight against the Romans and, on his defeat in AD 51, was taken to Rome and exhibited in triumph by Claudius. This was the end of any organized resistance to Rome in Wales.

Caröe, William Douglas, 1857–1938. Of Danish origin. For nine years J. L. Pearson's chief assistant. A London architect, prolific and inventive, and a sensitive and skilful restorer of old buildings, he did much of his best work in Wales. His practice is carried on by his son Alban D. R. Caroe and his grandson Martin Caroe.

Celtic. Strictly a branch of the Indo-Germanic group of languages (not a race). These include Breton, Cornish, Gaelic, Irish, Manx and Welsh. However the term is widely used to describe the settlers who came to Wales from Central Europe during the Iron Age. They are always described as tall and fair (as distinct from the earlier Iberian settlers who are small and dark) and form the aristocracy of the *Mabinogion*.

Charles, Thomas (1755–1814), the great evangelical reformer, was, at the end of his life, chief leader of the Calvinistic

Methodists and was directly responsible for the formation of their separate church although he had done his utmost for many years to prevent the schism between it and the Anglicans. The final break came in 1811 when he ordained six of his leading lay preachers so that they might administer the Sacrament.

Church in Wales. The Anglican Church in Wales was disestablished in 1921. It has a governing body of bishops, clergy and laity. The archbishop is elected by an electoral college, so may be a bishop of any diocese.

Clas. A monastery of the Celtic church consisting of a body of hereditary canons, often headed by a layman (marriage was allowed). *Clasau* were outposts of scholarship and some held important schools. The Normans did their utmost to Romanize the Celtic church and the *clas* was suppressed or replaced by cathedral chapters or collegiate churches.

Council for the Protection of Rural Wales (Cymdeithas Diogelu Harddwch Cymru). Founded in 1928 'to secure the protection and improvement of rural scenery and amenities in the Welsh countryside'. This active but level-headed society does splendid work, not only in protesting against harmful developments, but also in more positive ways.

The Court of the Council of Wales and the Marches was established by Edward IV 'to restrain the wild Welchmanne'. In 1534 it became a regular court sitting at Ludlow Castle. It brought a measure of peace to the borders, often by ruthless hangings.

Crucks take the place of roof trusses in some old buildings. A pair of arched timbers spring from floor level instead of resting on the top of the wall. A surprising number survive in Wales, chiefly in houses and barns.

Cunedda Wledig (fl. 450?). A Brythonic (British) prince from Scotland (the shores of the Forth). He drove the Goidels (Irish) from NW Wales thus laying the foundations of Gwynedd at the time when the last legions had left Britain.

Most Welsh rulers have claimed descent from one of his eight sons.

Cybi, Saint. Mid sixth-century. Quarrelsome and aristocratic. Born in Cornwall, with a prince as great-grandfather and a saint as uncle. Went to Monmouthshire (Llangibby-on-Usk) then via St Davids to Arran for four years. Settled in Anglesey where Holy Island is called Ynys Gybi and Holyhead Caergybi after him. He is reputed to have said 'There is no misfortune like wickedness.'

David, Saint, d. 601 (March 1), the patron saint of Wales. Traditionally the grandson of Ceredig, king of the region centred on Cardigan and son of Sant and Non, a nun. He may have been a descendant of Cunedda which would add political strength to the tradition of his refutation of the Pelagian heresy (at Llanddewi Brefi). After spending some time as a pupil of Paulinus, David went on several preaching journeys before founding his monastery in West Pembrokeshire (now St Davids). The earliest life was written by Rhygyfarch c. 1090. He was canonized in 1120.

Double-naved churches. Churches consisting of two naves of equal size. Often called 'double-aisled', but this can cause confusion with churches like St John's, Cardiff, which have two aisles on each side of the nave. Numerous explanations have been offered for this phenomenon. The simplest is that it was the easiest way of substantially enlarging a church, as it involves least alteration to the existing structure. Those who find this dull may prefer, e.g., to see it as a reflection of the fifteenth-century popularity of the cult of the Virgin, requiring a second altar of equal prominence with the high altar. These churches are particularly common in the Vale of Clwyd.

Douglas, John, 1830–1911. Born at Sandiway in Cheshire. Pupil of E. G. Paley of Lancaster. He practised in Chester from 1855 until his death. A first-rate architect, prolific, imaginative, and practical. He built many churches and private houses, and did much estate work, especially for his chief patron, the 1st Duke of Westminster. A brilliant exponent of half-timbering, he also made extensive use of Ruabon terracotta.

Eisteddfod (meeting). A public meeting at which contests in literature and music are held, chiefly poetry and singing, both of which were of such importance in the courts of the princes. Today's ceremony of the chairing of the bard is an echo of the regard in which the medieval court poets were held (modern bardic chairs are quite often to be seen in churches or chapels, having been presented after the owner's death).

The first recorded eisteddfod is claimed by Cardigan, 1176. One of the most famous was that at Caerwys (1568) held by order of Queen Elizabeth I to test the claims of vagrants calling themselves poets and harpists who were sponging on the hospitality of the great houses.

The romantic movement of the eighteenth century saw a great revival of interest in Welsh music and literature among the gentry who promoted eisteddfodau. In London societies were formed for the study of Welsh literature. Iolo Morganwg, a young stonemason turned antiquarian, of great imagination, invented in 1792 the ceremony of the Gorsedd, which many of his contemporaries believed he had discovered in old manuscripts. The 'Gorsedd of the Bards of the Isle of Britain' is the union of all the enrolled bards. It was grafted on to the eisteddfod, and today it is responsible for administering the National Eisteddfod. The Gorsedd ceremony takes place in a stone circle, which explains why modern ones are to be found all over Wales.

Today numerous local eisteddfodau are held in towns and villages throughout Welsh speaking Wales (Cardiganshire is particularly prolific). The National Eisteddfod moves to a different town each year, alternating north and south. The International Eisteddfod is held annually in Llangollen.

Most eisteddfodau are held entirely in Welsh and are in effect celebrations of the Welsh language.

Evans, David (1793–1862), glass painter, b. Llanllwchaearn near Newtown, was apprenticed to John Betton of Shrewsbury with whom he later became a partner, and eventually took over the firm. His work is widespread in N. Wales. Its importance derives from the fact that he re-introduced medieval techniques. The results vary. He liked shrill colours which are not to everyone's taste. See Bangor Cathedral and Worthenbury.

Fenton, Richard, 1746–1821, topographical writer, antiquary and barrister. Born at St Davids where he was educated at the Cathedral School. Entered the Middle Temple. Lived and died in Fishguard.

Flower Sunday. Palm Sunday is so called in many parts of Wales because of the custom of dressing the graves. Quiet churchyards and grey cemeteries blaze yellow with daffodils. It is like a dress rehearsal for the Last Trump, or a rite of spring.

Gavelkind (partible succession). The Welsh system of inheritance by which a kingdom or property was divided equally among the children, instead of that of primogeniture, was a principal cause of lack of unity among the Welsh.

Giraldus Cambrensis (1146–1223), topographical writer and priest, was the youngest son of William de Barri, of Manorbier Castle, where he was born, and a grandson of Nest. He was a student at the University of Paris where he later lectured (very successfully, he records). Giraldus was a passionate Welshman, despite or because of his Norman blood, and it was probably this, combined with his intelligence and vigour, that caused his nominations to the See of St Davids to be repeatedly turned down by the Pope through the intervention of the Crown. He travelled three times to Rome to plead his cause. This remained his life's ambition and he would accept no other bishopric. He later campaigned to free St Davids from the archbishopric of Canterbury (achieved in 1921). He is best known for the accounts of his travels and particularly for the journey he made through Wales with Archbishop Baldwin on his recruiting campaign for the 3rd Crusade. *Itinerarium Kambriae* has been translated into English.

Goodhart-Rendel, Harry Stuart (1887–1959). Grandson of Lord Rendel, related to the Gladstones of Hawarden. He was a versatile architect and a brilliant architectural writer. His card-index of Victorian churches (copies at the National Monuments Record and at the RIBA) is the prime source for architects and dates, and often contains penetrating and witty comments on churches he had visited.

Harris, Howell (1714–73). Religious reformer and Methodist leader. See *South Wales*.

Harrison, Thomas (1744–1829). Born at Richmond, Yorkshire, the son of a joiner. In Rome 1769–76. Practised in Lancaster until 1793, when he moved to Chester. His finest works are Chester Castle, severely Greek Revival, and the Grosvenor Bridge, a superb single arch of stone. Also worked in Gothic. C. R. Cockerell called him 'undoubtedly the noblest genius in architecture we have had'. His work in Wales includes the Marquess of Anglesey's Column, the Memorial Arch at Holyhead, and the Moel Fama Tower.

Haycocks, The. Edward Haycock Sr. (1791–1870) was a pupil of Sir Jeffry Wyatville. He practised in Shrewsbury. He built numerous feeble Gothic churches, and a few splendid Greek Revival houses, notably Clytha Park, Monmouthshire, and Millichope Park, Shropshire (1835). His son, Edward (1830–82), also practised in Shrewsbury, chiefly as a church architect.

Hughes, Henry Harold. See under Arthur Baker.

Howell the Good (Hywel Dda), grandson of Rhodri Mawr, reigned 910–950 and eventually ruled most of Wales. He greatly admired King Alfred of Wessex (d. 899) and was on friendly terms with his successors. A great man whose outstanding achievement was the codification of the laws of Wales. Traditionally this work was done at his hunting lodge at Whitland, Carmarthenshire.

Illtyd, Saint, d. 505 (November 6), fought for his cousin King Arthur and was one of the three knights in charge of the Holy Grail. Left his wife to become a solitary and later founded the famous school and monastery of Llanilltyd Fawr (Llantwit Major). Also said to have founded the monastery on Caldey Island. A famous teacher who also introduced an improved method of ploughing.

Iolo Morganwg (Williams, Edward), 1747–1826, poet, antiquary, inventor and stonemason. See also Eisteddfod.

James of St George (d. c. 1309). Master of the King's Works in Wales. Came to work for Edward I from the court of his cousin Count Philip of Savoy for whom he built numerous castles. In spring 1278 he was bound for Wales 'to ordain the works of the castles there' (Flint, Rhuddlan, Builth and Aberystwyth). After the revolt of 1282, the plan for the N Wales chain of castles was conceived. He was responsible for Caernarfon, Conwy, Harlech and Beaumaris. These are undoubtedly among the finest medieval castles in Europe. In 1290–93 he was Constable of Harlech and from 1298 worked in Scotland.

Jesus College, Oxford was founded in 1571 by Queen Elizabeth I on the initiative of Dr Hugh Price, Chancellor of St Davids, who provided the money for the first buildings. The College has always had a very close association with Wales, and nearly all of its endowments have been provided by Welshmen.

Jones, Griffith (1683–1761), was the creator of the imaginative and influential Welsh Circulating Schools. (See *South Wales.*)

Jones, Thomas (c. 1794–1859). Architect. Protégé of Thomas Netherton Parker, and friend of John Parker. He practised in Chester, and was County Surveyor of Flintshire. Designed mostly in Gothic or Tudor. Died at Barmouth.

Kennedy, Henry, d. c. 1897. From London. Settled at Bangor in the 1840s, and practised there, mostly as a church architect, until he retired in 1894. He was Bangor Diocesan Surveyor. Much of his work ranges from dull to dreadful, but some is so bad as to be quite entertaining – e.g. Llanllechid, Ffestiniog.

Kilvert, Robert Francis (1840–79) is renowned for his diaries (1870–79) which give a fascinating and endearing close-up of the country and life around Clyro in the Wye valley where he was curate (1865–72), and of St Harmon, Radnorshire, where he was rector (1876–7).

The Landmark Trust was started in 1965 by John and Christain Smith with the object of protecting small buildings or sites of special value and where possible finding new uses for them so that they can be enjoyed (usually as holiday accommodation). In Wales these include cottages, a nineteenth-century fort, a tower in Caernarfon town wall, and an eighteenth-century folly. The address is Shottesbrooke, Maidenhead, Berks.

Leet. A channel taken off a stream, usually to operate a water-wheel.

Llywelyn the Great (Llywelyn ap Iorwerth) (1173–1240) was indeed a great leader. His father died about the time of his birth so he probably was brought up in Powys, his mother's home, safe from his father's half-brothers to whom he was a potential menace. He took to arms at a tender age and seems to have quickly proved this point. By 1199 he ruled the whole of Gwynedd and was clearly an able statesman as well as a successful soldier. At first he was on terms with King John, marrying his natural daughter Joan in 1205, but the royal armies took some of his territory in 1211. He then took advantage of the unrest leading up to Magna Carta, taking the key castles of Carmarthen, Cardigan and Montgomery from the king and becoming the acknowledged leader of all the Welsh princes. However, he never called himself Prince of Wales, realizing the jealousy this title would cause. He was a signatory of Magna Carta in which three clauses dealt specifically with Wales, the most important being the confirmation that disputes within Wales were to be settled by Welsh law.

In 1218 he paid homage to Henry III, the new boy-king, and his authority was not disputed seriously again. Thus Wales enjoyed a rare spell of peace.

Llywelyn the Last (Llywelyn ap Gruffydd) (d. 1282), grandson of Llywelyn the Great, seems to have veered between statesmanship and intransigence. This eventually broke the precarious unity of the Welsh princes, which he had to some extent re-established. As a prince of Gwynedd he first re-united North Wales, annexed much of mid-Wales and raided the south. He supported Simon de Montfort against Henry III and became engaged to his daughter Eleanor (the English prevented their marriage until 1278). Llywelyn was recognized as Prince of Wales after the Treaty of Montgomery (1267) provided he paid homage to Henry III. He later refused to attend the coronation of Edward I and the treaty was broken on both sides. War broke out in 1276. Neither Powys nor South Wales were on Llywelyn's side; his brother Dafydd was in Edward's army as were many Welsh soldiers from the Marches. Edward's coup was to burn the crops in Anglesey, the granary that fed Llywelyn's army in Snowdonia. By the Treaty of Conwy, 1277, Llywelyn was deprived of all lands except Gwynedd. Edward I rapidly built his grand chain of castles to control the north. War broke out again in 1282 and Llywelyn was killed by chance near Builth.

Llywelyn's life was full of contradictions: he strongly supported the monastic orders but was excommunicated by the Archbishop of Canterbury. His adoption of the style Prince of Wales caused much jealousy in his lifetime but its passing was deeply lamented by ballad writers after his death: it was the embodiment of the idea of a united Wales.

Lockwood, Thomas Meakin (1830–1900). Born in London. Went to Chester as pupil of T. M. Penson, and practised there for the rest of his life. Many of his numerous buildings make use of half-timbering, but later he turned to the Renaissance style. Work in Wales includes Bodlondeb, Conwy, and Caerhun, Caernarfonshire.

Long house. A long building in which stock was housed in the lower end and the family in the upper, with an interconnecting door. Once common in Britain, a few survive in Wales and Scotland.

Mabinogion, the. A strange and wonderful collection of heroic tales, passed down by word of mouth from the Dark Ages. The earliest surviving manuscripts are the *White Book of Rhydderch* (c. 1300–25), now in the National Library, Aberystwyth and the *Red Book of Hergest* (c. 1375–1425), now in Jesus College, Oxford. They rank with Chaucer's tales in their importance to European medieval literature. The eleven tales include the earliest Arthurian tale in Welsh (*Culhwch and Olwen*). The collection was given its name (a misnomer) by Lady Charlotte Guest as a title to her translation (1838–

49). An English version (by Gwyn Jones and Thomas Jones) is available in Dent's *Everyman's Library.*

Marcher Lordships, granted by the Norman kings to reward their earls and control the country, covered a large area of Wales, much of it remote from the Welsh border but accessible from the sea; it was mostly rich lowland. The earls could exploit the land and people as they saw fit and were not answerable to any judiciary. They had power over life or death within their territories. Throughout the Middle Ages there were thus three factions in Wales, not two: the Crown, the Welsh Princes and the Marcher Lords.

Nesfield, William Eden (1835–88). Nephew of Anthony Salvin, and son of a well-known landscape gardener. Pupil of Burn and Salvin. In the 1860s he was, with Norman Shaw (with whom he worked), a pioneer of the Domestic Revival. His Welsh country houses include Kinmel, Bodrhyddan, Gloddaeth, and Gwernyfed. Drink tended to get the better of him.

Nest, the 'Helen of Wales' (fl. 1120), daughter of Rhys ap Tewdwr, is renowned for her compelling charm and numerous offspring, one of whom was a son of Henry I. The king arranged that she should marry Gerald of Windsor who held the earldom of Pembroke. Giraldus Cambrensis (*q.v.*) was her grandson.

Offa's Dyke. King Offa of Mercia (757–796) constructed the dyke as a boundary between his kingdom and the Welsh from Prestatyn in the north to the Bristol Channel. Where possible its line follows natural boundaries – rivers and hills. There are eighty miles of earthworks. A long distance footpath has been opened along the Dyke; see *Offa's Dyke Path* by Frank Noble (a Shell book) for details. It is particularly spectacular in the uplands of Radnorshire but there are many lovely stretches in both England and Wales.

Ordovices. The Brythonic Celtic settlers who controlled North Wales c. 200 BC to AD 50. They built many border forts. See also Caractacus.

Owain Gwynedd (1137–70) was described by Giraldus Cambrensis as 'a man of distinguished wisdom and moderation'.

His aim was further to strengthen Gwynedd and extend its supremacy by resisting the Marcher Lords and making treaties with the South Wales princes, notably the Lord Rhys. When the English throne was weak he achieved great success, but Henry II (1154–89) attacked both North and South Wales and Owain and Rhys wisely paid homage. However, Becket's quarrel with Henry II encouraged them to rebel. The king's great army, sent to subdue the united princes in NE Wales, was defeated (1165) by a combination of wild weather, inhospitable hill country and a Welsh army who knew how to exploit both. Affairs elsewhere occupied Henry II and for many years Wales knew comparative peace.

Owen Glendower (Owain Glyn Dŵr) (c. 1354–1416), born a country squire in the Upper Dee valley, was descended from the princes of Powys through his father and Deheubarth through his mother. Married Margaret, daughter of Richard Hanmer, an Anglo-Welsh judge (see Maelor Saesneg). His education included a spell in the Inns of Court, and he later served in the English army on Scottish campaigns. In his late forties, a quarrel with his neighbour, Reginald, Lord Grey of Ruthin, seems to have precipitated his attack on Ruthin (1400) which was followed by fourteen years' guerrilla warfare against the English in much of which he was very successful, taking castles and laying waste the country. His aims were Welsh independence, a Church independent of Canterbury, and the establishment of a Welsh university. He wanted to replace Henry IV by a Yorkist. The Mortimer family, to whom he was allied by the marriage of his daughter Catherine, had claims to the crown through kinship with Richard II. In 1404 he established himself in West Wales by taking Aberystwyth and Harlech. He made a treaty with France and the Scots supported him.

Tantalizingly little is known of Glendower. He can have borne little resemblance to Shakespeare's character. The time was ripe for his rising and in calling himself Prince of Wales he allied to himself popular support restless under foreign rule. Eventually in 1414 he disappeared and is believed to have died in the house of his daughter, Anne Scudamore, near Hereford. Henry V sent him a special message of pardon before his death. Whether he received it is not known.

Padarn, Saint, late fifth century. (April 15). Born in Brittany and said to have sailed for Wales as a young man and to have studied at the college of St Illtyd. Founded the monastery of Llanbadarn Fawr (near Aberystwyth). A great preacher. Rhygyfarch in his life of St David says that Padarn accompanied St David and St Teilo to Jerusalem.

Penillion is the free improvisation by a voice or voices on an air which is played over and over again by an instrument, usually the harp. There is a marked contrast between the strict metre observed by the instrument and the freer vocal line. This traditional form is very popular today.

Pennant, Thomas (1726–98). Topographical writer, antiquary and zoologist, lived at Downing, Flintshire. See bibliography.

Pensons, The. Thomas Penson the elder (d. 1824), was a Wrexham mason, auctioneer, and architect. He was County Surveyor of Flint until he was dismissed after Overton Bridge collapsed, in 1814. His son **Thomas** (1791–1859) was a pupil of Thomas Harrison of Chester. He practised in Wrexham and Oswestry, and was County Surveyor of Denbighshire and Montgomeryshire. A versatile stylist, he was a practical man, interested in new materials like terracotta and iron. He married the daughter of Richard Kirk, a Wrexham ironmaster. His elder son, **Richard Kyrke Penson** (1816–86), trained in London, practised in Ferryside, Carmarthenshire, also in Swansea and (later) in Oswestry. He was County Surveyor of Carmarthenshire and Cardiganshire, and succeeded his father as Surveyor of Montgomeryshire. He was a sober and accomplished Gothicist, and his numerous ecclesiastical works nearly always have a touch of refinement. He retired in 1864, and went to live in Ludlow. His younger brother **Thomas Mainwaring Penson** (1818–64) practised in Chester, where he initiated the half-timber revival. He built all the stations etc. on the Chester and Shrewsbury Railway, c. 1848, and was County Surveyor of Flint.

Powys. The modern county has similar boundaries to the ancient kingdom of East Wales of which Shrewsbury was once the capital. The princes of Powys were often hostile to those of Gwynedd and were allies of Henry III and Edward I in their fight against the Llywelyns. The Powys lands were restored after Edward I's conquest.

Prichard, John (1817–86), son of Rev. Richard Prichard, priest-vicar of Llandaff. Pupil of Walker, who is said to have been an assistant of Pugin. Partnership with J. P. Seddon (1852–62). They were Llandaff Diocesan Architects: Prichard took the Glamorgan jobs, and Seddon those in Monmouthshire. Their greatest work was the restoration of Llandaff Cathedral.

Rebecca Riots, 1843–44. These riots, though best known in connection with the attacks on the turnpikes, came as the culmination of many grievances caused by economic depression and took place throughout South Wales. The rioters were principally farmers and small-holders. Eventually a Royal Commission was appointed to look into their grievances. See *Genesis XXIV*[60] and also *South Wales* for the origin of the name.

Rhodri Mawr ('the Great'), d. 877, succeeded as king of Gwynedd c. 844 and extended his rule over the whole of North Wales and much of the south. He was thus the first to unite Wales and became the ideal of the medieval princes; those of both N and S could claim descent from him. The terrible menace of the continuing Viking raids (beginning 850) against which he effectively led the Welsh, may have been the reason for their rare unity. His reign overlapped with that of King Alfred (871–99). On Rhodri's death Wales was divided between his six sons, one of whom paid allegiance to Alfred, who was the acknowledged protector against the Vikings. Later demands of homage from the Welsh princes by the English throne sprang from this precedent.

Rhys ap Thomas, Sir (1449–1525), head of the Dynevor family and chief Welsh supporter of Henry VII. When Henry Tudor landed in Pembrokeshire in 1485, Rhys rallied the men of South Wales and marched to join him on the Long Mountain, near Welshpool, and thence to Bosworth where tradition has it that it was he who slew Richard III. At all events Rhys was knighted on the battlefield and was rewarded by becoming virtual ruler of South Wales. He was granted numerous castles and took a mortgage on Carew, Pembrokeshire. His tomb is in St Peter's Church, Carmarthen, having been moved there on the dissolution of Greyfriars monastery.

The Lord Rhys (Rhys ap Gruffydd), (1132–97), one of Wales's great medieval rulers, was four when his father died and at thirteen was fighting alongside his elder brothers against the Normans in the SW. He succeeded as ruler of Deheubarth in 1155 and united the Welsh against the Lords Marcher in the E as well as W. He achieved peace and paid the traditional homage to Henry II, remaining consistently loyal. On Owain Gwynedd's death (1170) paramount power in Wales shifted to the S for the rest of Rhys's life. He built Dynevor (his capital) and Cardigan castles (at Cardigan he held the first-recorded Eisteddfod). On Henry's death, Richard I was indifferent to his special position *vis à vis* the throne and Rhys spent his last years fighting the Normans again. His old age was marred by quarrels with and between his eight sons. Henry VII was descended from his only daughter who married Ednyfed Fychan. According to tradition, he is buried in St Davids Cathedral.

Roman occupation of Wales. c. AD 47–400. The Romans exploited Wales's mineral wealth, and built roads so that the country could be controlled from a network of military stations, notably Deva (Chester), just outside to the NW; Segontium (Caernarfon), Isca Silurum (Caerleon, Monmouthshire) and Moridunum (Carmarthen). These four bases, one in each corner, were joined by main roads. During the Roman period Wales probably enjoyed a longer peace than at any time until the accession of Henry VII.

Rowland, Daniel (1713–90). Great evangelical preacher and Methodist leader. See *South Wales*.

Scotts, The. Sir George Gilbert Scott (1811–78) restored three cathedrals in Wales (St Davids, St Asaph, and Bangor), and many churches. He also built new churches (e.g. at Rhyl), and one of his best houses (Hafodunos). He had two architect sons. The elder, also **George Gilbert** (1839–97), was a fine architect, an associate of Bodley and Garner, but became insane. The younger son, **John Oldrid Scott** (1842–1913) carried on his father's practice. **Sir Giles Gilbert Scott** (1880–1960), the architect of Liverpool Cathedral, was the son of George Gilbert Scott Jr.

Seddon, John Pollard (1827–1906). Son of a Regency furniture designer, and brother of Thomas Seddon, a Pre-Raphaelite painter. Partner of John Prichard 1852–62, he had a London office from 1857. A friend of Street, Burges, Rossetti etc. (he designed and owned the bungalow at Birchington in which Rossetti died). From 1885 until 1904 he was in partnership with **John Coates Carter**, a highly original architect. Seddon was an extraordinarily inventive, somewhat quirky designer, as interested in the design of woodwork, ironwork, tiles, stained glass, etc., as in buildings themselves.

Seven Wonders of Wales. According to a rhyme found in several versions, presumably dating from the time of the Romantic interest in Wales, these are:

> Pistyll Rhaeadr and Wrexham Steeple,
> Snowdon's mountain, without its people;
> Overton Yewtrees, Saint Winifred Wells,
> Llangollen Bridge and Gresford Bells.

It will be noticed that they are all in the North.

Surnames. Surnames did not come into existence in Wales until comparatively recently. The old system of naming was for the son to use his father's name – so Llywelyn ap Gruffydd (*ab* or *ap* means 'son of'). The *ap* was often omitted: e.g. James Thomas' son would be John James. This practice continued until within living memory in some remote areas. Pride in pedigree, coupled with the need to know your ancestry for legal purposes, meant that most people could extend the series over numerous generations, when precision was required. When surnames did come to be used (largely as a result of pressure from English judges), they were based on the Christian names. Three possibilities existed: either the name was kept intact, e.g. John, Harry, Howell (Hywel); or the genetival – *s* was added, e.g. Jones, Harris, Howells; or the *ap* was elided, e.g. Parry (ap Harry), Powell (ap Howell), Price (ap Rhys). The result of this was inevitably too few surnames to go round. In country areas individuals could be distinguished by the names of their farms, e.g. John (Jones) Hafod, and John (Jones) Bryngwyn. Or they might be distinguished by their occupations, e.g. Jones the Milk, Evans the Coal. Alternatively, nicknames might be used. In industrial communities, neither of the first two methods would work: large numbers of people did identical jobs, and addresses were not handy (e.g. John Jones 56 Victoria Terrace). So nicknames were normal. Some were highly picturesque, e.g. Sam Half a Mo, Dic Bol Haearn (Dic Iron Stomach), Dan Bach Drifa i (Little Dan I'll drive), Twm Cwrcyn Carcus (Tom the Careful Tom Cat). A good story concerns David Jones, who went to work in the pit. The overman said that there were already seven David Joneses there, so he would have to have a nickname. The lad said he didn't mind, as long as it was something substantial. From then on, he was known as Dai Substantial. The tradition continues: a dealer in polythene bags is known as Disposable Des.

Telford, Thomas (1757–1834), the great Scottish engineer, constructed some of his finest work in North Wales. In 1787 he became surveyor of public works in Shropshire and this put him in touch with the pioneering ironmasters in Coalbrookdale. He was appointed engineer to the Ellesmere Canal (of which the Llangollen branch is a feeder); see Pont Cysylltau and Chirk aqueduct. Later he became Surveyor for the Holyhead Road; see the Menai Suspension Bridge; Conwy Bridge; the Jubilee Bridge; the Stanley Embankment.

Thirlwall, Connop (1797–1875) had considerable impact on the Anglican church, particularly in West Wales, during his thirty-four years' bishopric at St Davids, which See he was given by Melbourne after he had been forced to resign his university appointments on account of his liberal views. He was responsible for much new building in the diocese and it was during his bishopric that the restoration of the Cathedral under Scott began. He continued to take part in national affairs. He learnt Welsh and insisted on preaching in it, often, it is said, to the mystification of his Welsh congregations.

His tomb, in Westminster Abbey, is by Edward Davis of Carmarthen.

Tudor. Henry VII, the first of the Tudor dynasty, was descended from the Tudor family of Plas Penmynydd in Anglesey. His claim to the throne was through his mother Margaret Beaufort, great-grand-daughter of John of Gaunt. She married Edmund, Earl of Richmond, and was already widowed, aged fifteen, when Henry was born. The Tudor accession brought much needed peace to the country and made a great difference to the prosperity of Wales, as the numerous parish churches enriched and enlarged at this time, and many notable houses dating from this period, show.

Tysilio, Saint, d. c. 640. (8 November) Son of a prince of Powys, born in Shrewsbury, then the capital. Ran away to be a monk, first to Meifod and then, for safety from his father, to Ynys Sulian, the island in the Menai Straits where his church now stands. When he returned to Meifod the old Abbot had it in his head to go to Rome. Tysilio sensibly advised him to dream about it instead, and took him for a walk to tire him out, pointing out that the journey to Rome would be much worse. After his brother's death his sister-in-law wanted to marry Tysilio. Eventually to escape her he moved to Rance in Brittany.

The **Unit System** is a name given to describe two or more houses occupied by members of a family and built close together. Each is a complete unit in itself and is of roughly equal status, but they share the same yard or open space. It is found in various parts of Wales.

Wat's Dyke was an earlier earthwork than Offa's Dyke, made to mark the Mercian frontier in the north. It ran from the Dee at Holywell and can be picked out on the one-inch OS map in other parts of Flintshire and near Llay and Ruabon in Denbighshire.

Welsh, old English, *welisc*, from the Anglo-Saxon name for the Briton, *wealh*, a foreigner.

Welsh Black Cattle. A very ancient and gentle breed. 'Britain does not afford a more useful animal', wrote William Youatt, the renowned English authority in 1838, adding that they were 'very fair milkers with a propensity to fatten'. The drovers took thousands to the English markets.

Welsh Cob. Once pulled nearly every London milk van (whence 'vanner') and were widely popular with farmers and tradesmen because of their equable temperament, strength and sound feet. 'Few or none can equal them for the road; none stand our turnpikes like them . . .' (George Culley, *Observation on Livestock*, 1794). Having become nearly extinct the cob is enjoying a great comeback through the popularity of riding and trekking.

Welsh Hound. Pure Welsh hounds are now rare; many have been crossed with English foxhounds. They were bred from hounds imported by French monks at Margam Abbey and have some pointer and Scottish deerhound in them. They are small, mostly white and rough-coated with heads like setters and long ears set low. Some say they think for themselves too much when they should be hunting with the pack.

Welsh Mountain Sheep. Small, active, hardy animals who will prosper where few other breeds can. Long prized for sweet small joints and soft wool. Black Welsh Mountain were bred by enthusiasts in the last century, particularly those who had all black stock on their home farms, e.g. Llanover. Some flocks survive.

Welsh National Opera, founded in 1946, started with an amateur choir giving a fortnight's season. Now a full professional company based in Cardiff but touring regularly in the UK (and also performing in Europe). Enthusiasts should look out for local advertisements.

Williams, William, Pant-y-celyn, (1717–91). Great Methodist leader, hymn-writer and author. See *South Wales*.

Withers, R. J. (1823–94), a competent and imaginative London architect with a large church practice, notably in South and West Wales, 'where he imparted to many a barn-like structure some semblance of life and feeling'. (*Building News* obituary.) His most unusual and vigorous work is probably Cardigan Market Hall.

The Wyatt family. This vast tribe, of Staffordshire origin, included an extraordinary number of members of the architectural and related professions. **William Wyatt** (1701–72) was steward to Lord Uxbridge (see Plas Newydd, Anglesey). His younger brother, **Benjamin Wyatt** of Weeford (1709–72) had no less than five architect sons. The second, **Samuel** (1737–1807), worked for Lord Penrhyn, through his younger brother **Benjamin** (1744–1818), who was Lord Penrhyn's agent. In this capacity Benjamin designed new buildings as well as developing the slate quarries. Some buildings on the estate were designed by his own fourth son, **Lewis William** (1777–1853). The elder Benjamin's fifth son, **James** (1746–1813) was the most famous of all. He had a big London-based practice, both as a neo-classicist (supplanting Adam in fashion) and as a Gothicist (in which style his most famous work was Fonthill Abbey). His work in Wales includes examples of both styles – classical at Wynnstay, Erddig, etc., Gothic at Plas Newydd, Eglwys Newydd (Hafod), etc. **Jeffry Wyatt** (1766–1840), later **Sir Jeffry Wyatville**, was the son of the elder Benjamin's third architect son, Joseph. As architect to George IV, he transformed Windsor Castle. In Wales he built Golden Grove, Carmarthenshire, and the Nant-y-Belan Tower at Wynnstay. **Thomas Henry Wyatt** (1807–80) came of another branch of the family, descended from the William Wyatt mentioned above. An amazingly prolific architect, he was competent but had little aesthetic talent. His uncle, **Arthur Wyatt** (1775–1833), was agent to the Duke of Beaufort, and brought him much work in Monmouthshire. Thomas Henry also did a lot around Flintshire, as architect to the Earl of Denbigh. His younger brother was **Sir Matthew Digby Wyatt** (1820–77), buried at Usk.

Bibliography

GENERAL

This list includes only the better known and readily accessible titles – there are many obscurer works of charm and interest, particularly describing tours in the eighteenth and nineteenth centuries.

Bell, Idris: *Welsh Poetry*.

Borrow, George: *Wild Wales*.

Carter, Harold: *The Towns of Wales*.

Colvin, H. M. (ed.): *The History of the King's Works*, Vol I, Chapter VI: The King's Works in Wales, 1277–1330.

Condry, William: *Exploring Wales*.

Davies, Elwyn (ed.): *A Gazetteer of Welsh Place Names*.

Dictionary of Welsh Biography (to 1940).

Evans, Emrys: *The University of Wales: A Historical Sketch*.

Famous Welshmen. University of Wales Press (paperback).

Fenton, Richard: *Tours in Wales 1804–13*.

Fitzgibbon, Theodora: *A Taste of Wales in Food and Pictures*.

Frazer, D.: *Wales in History, I, to 1066, The Invaders*.

Frazer, D.: *Wales in History, II, 1066–1485, The Defenders*.

Giraldus Cambrensis: *Itinerary of Wales 1188*.

Griffith, Wyn: *The Welsh*.

Howe, Melvyn G. and Thomas, Peter: *Welsh Land Forms and Scenery*.

Howe, Melvyn G.: *Wales from the Air*.

Jenkins, J. Geraint: *The Welsh Woollen Industry*.

Lewis, Samuel: *Topographical Dictionary of Wales*.

Lewis, W. J.: *A History of Lead-Mining in Wales*.

Lloyd, D. M. and E. M.: *A Book of Wales* (Collins National Anthology Series).

The Mabinogion, tr. Gwyn Jones and Thomas Jones (Everyman's Library).

Nash-Williams, V. E., rev. Jarrett, M.: *The Roman Frontier in Wales*.

Noble, Frank: *The Shell Book of Offa's Dyke*.

Owen, Trefor: *Welsh Folk Customs*.

Peate, Iorwerth C.: *The Welsh House*.

The Penguin Book of Welsh Verse, trans. Anthony Conran.

Pennant, Thomas: *A Tour of Wales.*
Poucher, W. A.: *The Welsh Peaks.*
Rees, D. Morgan: *Mines, Mills and Furnaces: Industrial Archaeology in Wales.*
Rees, Wm: *Historical Atlas of Wales.*
Roderick, A. J. (ed.): *Wales through the Ages.*
Steegman, John: *A Survey of Portraits in Welsh Houses.*
Trueman, A. E.: *Geology and Scenery in England and Wales.*
Williams, Bryn R.: *The Welsh Colony in Patagonia.*
Williams, David: *A History of Modern Wales.*

NORTH WALES: GENERAL

Beazley, Elisabeth and Brett, Lionel: *Shell Guide to North Wales* (Caernarfon, Anglesey, Denbigh and Flint).
Burn, Michael: *The Age of Slate.*
Condry, William: *The Snowdonia National Park.*
Dodd, A. H.: *The Industrial Revolution in North Wales.*
Fletcher, H. L. V.: *North Wales* (The Queen's Wales).
Lewis, Mostyn: *Stained Glass in North Wales up to 1850.*
Rolt, L. T. C.: *George and Robert Stephenson.*
Rolt, L. T. C.: *Thomas Telford.*
Thomas, D. R.: *A History of the Diocese of St Asaph.*
Watson, Katherine: *North Wales* (Regional Archaeology series).
Vale, Edmund (ed.): *Snowdonia National Park Guide.*
Verey, David: *Shell Guide to Mid Wales* (Brecon, Radnor and Montgomery).

ANGLESEY

Clarke, M. L.: *Anglesey Churches in the Nineteenth Century,* Anglesey Antiquarian Society Transactions 1961.
Evans, G. Nesta: *Social Life in Mid 18th Century Anglesey.*
Glazebrook, F. F.: *Anglesey and the North Wales Coast.*
Richards, Melville, (ed.): *An Atlas of Anglesey.*
Roberts, Dew: *Mr Bulkeley and the Pirate.*
Williams, Kyffin: *Across the Straits.*

CAERNARFONSHIRE

Beazley, Elisabeth: *Madocks and the Wonder of Wales.*
Clarke, M. L.: *Bangor Cathedral.*
Clarke, M. L.: *Church Building and Church Restoration in Caernarfonshire during the Nineteenth Century,* Caernarfonshire Historical Society, 1961.
Dodd, A. H.: *A History of Caernarfonshire 1284–1900.*

DENBIGHSHIRE

Howell, Peter and Pritchard, T. W.: *Wynnstay*, Country Life, March 23 and 30, April 6, 1972.

FLINT

Bevan-Evans, M.: *The Farmhouses and Cottages of Flintshire.*
Bevan-Evans, M.: *Early Industry in Flintshire.*

MERIONETH

Bowen, E. G. and Gresham, C. (ed.): *History of Merioneth I – From the Earliest Times to the Age of the Native Princes.*
Lewis, M. J. T.: *How Ffestiniog got its Railway.*
Rees, Vyvyan: *Shell Guide to Mid-Western Wales.*

MONTGOMERYSHIRE

Rees, A. D.: *Life in a Welsh Countryside.*
Thomas, Ivor: *Top Sawyer* (biography of David Davies).

RADNORSHIRE

Clarke, Elizabeth: *The Valley.*
Howse, A. E.: *Radnorshire.*
Plomer, William, (ed.): *Kilvert's Diary.*

The Royal Commission on Historical Monuments in Wales and Monmouthshire: Inventories of Ancient Monuments

Montgomeryshire	1911
Flintshire	1912
Radnorshire	1913
Denbighshire	1914
Merioneth	1921
Anglesey	1937
Caernarfonshire	1956, 1960, 1964 (3 vols.).

Index

Note: Page numbers in *italics* indicate the principal references

Abbeycwmhir 304, 307, 309, *314*, 316
Abbey Farm, Elan Valley 314
Abbey Paper Mill, Basingwerk 29
Aber 126, *135*
Aberconway *130*; Lord 110
Abercrombie, Sir Patrick 63
Aberdaron 181, *183-6*, 184, 186; Bay 184
Aberdovey 218, 259, *263-4*
Aberedw *329-30*, 331, 335; Castle *335*
Abererch *189*
Aberffraw *218-19*, 244
Aberffrydlan 298-9
Abergele *104*, 105, 112
Aberglaslyn 155, 156; Pass *155*
Abergynolwyn 262
Aberhafesp *296-7*
Aber Ia 235
Aberllefenni 259
Abermenai Point 217
Abermule *290*, 291
Abernodwydd 289
Abersoch *185-6*, 186
Aberystwyth 23, 299, 311, 320, 351
Ablett, Joseph 49-50, 100
Act of Union 13, *349*
Acton Park *63*, 65
Adam, Bishop of St Asaph 288
Adam, Robert 79, 80, 81, 97
Admiralty Pier, Holyhead 213
Afon Cwmystradllyn 169
Afon Cywarch 255
Afon Rhaeadr 270
Agricola 126, 141, 217
Alaw Reservoir 209
Albert, Prince 88
Aled, River 114
Aled Isaf Reservoir 114
Alexander, Daniel *214*
Alexander, George 159
Alfred, King 279, 356, 363
'Alleluia Monument' 40
Allt Wen 133
Alpine Bridge *327*
Alun 39, 40, 42, 44, 47, 48, 60
Alwen 56, 221
Alwen Reservoir 115
Amlwch *206*, 207, 209
Anglesey 15, 36, 135, 139, 140, 166, 173, 174, 176, *195-219*, 215, 244, 267, 353; Column *211*, 356; Marquess of *211*, 215
Anian, Bishop 36, 138
Apperley, C. J., 72
Aqueducts 84, 85, 91, 275, 290
Aran Benllyn 226, *255-6*
Aran Fawddwy 226, *255-6*
Ardudwy 230, 247
Arennig Fach *230*
Arennig Fawr *230*
Arennigs, The 115, 239
Arfon, Cantref of 173
Argoed Mills 324
Arnos Court, Bristol 236
Arthog *259*, 260
Arthur, King 52, 90, 126, 161-2, 178, *349*
Artro 246, 247, *248*, 249
Ashbrook House, Clyro 337
Ashley, Laura 297
Assheton-Smith family 140, 150
Audsley, W. and G. 67
Augeraud, Captain 274

Bachegraig 45, *46*, 52
Bach Howey 335
Bach Wen Pennarth 176
Bachymbyd *96*
Bacon, J. 293
Bagillt *24*, 26
Bagot, Bishop 103; Lord, of Blithfield 55; Sir Walter 97; William, second Lord 56
Bailey Einon 327
Bailey Hill, Mold 39
Baily, E. H. 289
Baker family 76
Baker, Arthur 51, 55, *56*, 57, 96, 104, 150, 214, 265, 267, *349-50*; Elizabeth, 76; Sir Herbert 117, 150, 349; William 286
Bala 90, 220, 221, 223, *223-4*, 224,

Bala [*contd.*]
225, 226, 229, 262, 271; Independent College 225
Bala—Ffestiniog Railway 230
Baldwin, Archbishop 350, 355
Balfour 25
Ballantine 113
Ballast Island 194
Bangor *137-9*, 173, 350; Bishops of 109; Cathedral 137, *138*, 282, 354
Bangor Is-coed *74*, 75, 182
Bankes family 26
Bank of England 150
Banw Valley 288
Barcloddiad-y-gawres *219*
Bardsey 74, 171, 175, 176, 178, 181, *181-3*, 242, 246, 351; Sound 181, 182
Barmouth 251, *252-3*, 260
Barnett, J. 139
Baron Hill 93, *201*
Barrow, Bishop of St Asaph 103
Barry 301; Docks 301
Barry, Sir Charles 67
Basingwerk Abbey *29*
'Bath Tower', Caernarfon 146
Batoni, Pompeo 79
Beacon Ring *285*
Beadnell, George 287
'Bearded Lake', The 263
Beauclerk, Father S.J. 28
Beaufort, Lady Margaret 28
Beaumaris 23, 195, 198, *199-201*, 202, 203, 210; Castle *199-201*, 202, 203, 245
Bedd Dorti 243
Beddgelert *154*, 155, 156, 165, 166, 235; Forest 156
Bedd Porus 240
Beeston Castle 60
Beguildy *319*
Begwns, The *333*
Belgian Promenade, Menai Bridge *210*
Bendigeidfran 244
Benedictine Order 32
Benllech 204
Benlli, King 48
Benmore, George 118
Bennar 120
Berain *115*, 116
Bernini 76
Berriew *289-90*, 290
Berse Drelincourt 68
Bersham 64, *70*, 103; Works 69, 70
Berwyns, The 50, 87, 89, 95, 115, 221, 223, 265, 269, 270, 271
Bethesda 137, *148-9*, 232
Betjeman, Sir John 250
Bettisfield *76*; Park 76
Betton and Evans 75
Betton, John 354
Betws Cedewain *292*
Betws Garmon *159*
Betws Gwerful Goch *56*
Betws-y-Coed 120, *122*, 123, 146
Betws-yn-Rhos *114*
Beulah 324
Bevan, 'Madam' Bridget 350
Billing, John 280
Black Hall 288
Black Mountains 329, 332, 336, 337
Black Prince, The 122
Black Rock 192
Blaenau Ffestiniog 109, 121-2, 183, 194, *231-2*, 233
Blaencerdi Farm, Radn. 332
Blandford, Marquess of 298
Blayney, Arthur 293; family of Gregynog 292, 293
Bleddfa *317*
Bleddyn ap Cynfyn 248
Blinstone 100
Blodeuedd 239
Blomfield, Sir Arthur W. 139, 288
Blore, Edward 103
Bodedern *209*
Bodelwyddan 67, *103*, 199; Castle *103*,104
Bodfari *47*, 58
Bodfel Hall *187*
Bodley and Garner 76, 365
Bodley, G. F. 201, 282, 283, 290, 291, 305
Bodlondeb *130*
Bodnant *110*
Bodorgan *218*
Bodowen 218
Bodrhyddan Hall *33-4*, 35
Bodrhyddan mausoleum 36
Boduan *187*
Bodwrda *184*
Bodysgallen 109
Bonnor, John H.M. 270
Bontddu 251, *254*, 259
Bontnewydd 135, 167
Bontrhydgaled 306
Booth, Lawrence 272; Raphe 43
Borrow, George 269
Borth-y-Gest 243
Boscawen, George 61
Boston Lodge 194, 236; Foundry 234
Botwnnog 185

Boughrood 336; Castle *336*
Boultibrooke *320*
Boyce, Philip 251
Bradley, A. G. 124, 253
Braich-y-dinas *133*
Braich-y-pwll 181
Branes 222
Branwen 242
Brecon 288
Brecon Beacons 256
Breconshire 15, 300, 309, 328, 336, 337, 350
Breiddin Hill 276
Brenig Valley 115
Bridges (*see also* Aqueducts *and* Viaducts) 72, 77, 85, 103, 111, 119, 120, 122, 123, 128, 150, 155, 159, 190, 197, 211, 221, 253, 259, 275, 276, 279, 290, 301, 310, 336
Bridgman 267
Bright, John 305
Bristly Ridge 163
Bristol 230
Britannia Bridge 128, *211*
Brithdir 228, 254, 256, *256*-7, 259
Brithdir Mawr *48*
British Museum Reading Room 276
Brittany 15, 29, 173, 300, 306
Broadlane Hall 24
Broad Water 261
Brochwel, Prince of Powys 271
Brodrick, Miss 113
Bromfield, Joseph 227, 256, 290
Bronaber *240*, 241
Brondanw 237
Broneirion 301
Broniarth Hill 278
Bronington *76*
Bronllys 58
Broughton 24, 38
Brown, 'Capability' 79, 80, 283
Brown, Robert 198
Browning, Robert 88
Brunel, I. K. 43
Brunlees and McKerrow 108
Brychan Brycheiniog 269, 280
Brymbe *69*; Hall 65; Steelworks 42, *69*
Brynbella *46*
Bryn Bras Castle *150*
Bryn Celli Ddu *216*
Bryncir 167
Bryncrug 261, 262
Bryneglwys *51*, 66, 89, 149, 223
Brynford 29
Bryngwyn *332*
Brynkinallt 92, *93*
Brynkir 168; Tower 169; Woollen Mill 169
Brynsiencyn 216
Bryntail *304*
Brynteg 204
Bryn-y-Maen *107*
Bryn-y-Neuadd *134*
Bryn-y-pys 77
Buckeridge, Charles *350-1*
Buckler, John C. 26, 38, 55
Buckley *38*
Builder, The 201
Builth Wells 309, 324, 328, 329
Bulkeley family 201, 203; Memorial 201; Sir Richard 202; tomb 201
Bull Bay *207*
Bunker's Hill 71
Burfa Camp *321*
Burfa Farmhouse *321*
Burges, William 39, 272
Burial Chambers 115, 119, 126, 176, 180, 205, 215, 216, 219, 247, 250, 251
Burke 85
Burlison and Grylls 43, 305
Burn, William 104
Burne-Jones, Sir Edward 25, 214, 285
Burnell and Legg 336
Burnet, Sir John 114
Busby, C. A. 105
Bushnell, John 92
Butler, Lady Eleanor 85-6; John 73, 75
Butlin's Camp *190*
Buttington *279*
Bwlch Drws Ardudwy *249-50*
Bwlch Main 162
Bwlch Oerddrws 256
Bwlch Pen Barras *48*
Bwlch Tyddiad 248
Bwlchycibau 274
Bwlch y Ddeufaen *126*
Bwlch y Ddwy-elor 165, 169
Bwlch y Groes 226, 255
Bwlchysaethau 161
Bwlch y Sarnau *316*, 317
Bylchau *115*
Byres, James 80
Byron, Lord 85

Caban Coch 312, *313*, 324
Cadair Fair 42
Cadair Idris 227, 228, 253, 254, 257, *258*, 259, 260, 261
Cader 262
Cadfan, King 218
Cadnant 143, 145

Cadwaladr, King (*see* Saint Cadwaladr)
Cadwgan Hall 65
Caecilia Metella, tomb of 81
Cae Gaer *306*
Cae Iorwerth 178
Caerau *208*
Cae'r Bellan 262
Caerdeon *253-4*
Caer Drewyn *89*
Caer Gai *224-5*
Caergwrle *42*
Caer Gybi *213-4*, 353
Caerhun *126*
Caerleon 141, 349
Caer Llugwy *146*, 153
Caernarfon 23, 36, 126, 139, *140-5*, 150, 152, 153, 154, 157, 159, 166, 167, 173, 195, 197, 201, 209, 216, 218, 231; Bay 176; Castle *143-4*, 145, 166, 216
Caernarfonshire 107, 119, 152, 171, 195, 238
Caer Noddfa 297
Caersws 285, 295, *296*, 297, 300, 302
Caerwys *44*, 45, 247, 354
Caerynwch *256*
Caldey Island 32, 356
Cambrian Coast Line 234, 260
Campbell, Mrs. Patrick 54
Campion Hall Chapel, Oxford 117
Canals 84, 87, 88, 91, 275, 279, 289-90, 366
Cantref y Gwaelod 248, 264
Capel Curig 146, 153, 164; Dyffryn 58; Garmon *119*; Llugwy *205*; Nantgwyllt 312; Newydd *186-7*; Peniel *193*; Salem *249*; Siloam 126; Trillo 107; Uchaf 192
Capel-y-bedd *214*
Capronnier, J. B. 221
Caractacus *351*
Caradoc 27
Carcassonne 143
Cardiff 67
Cardigan 36, 301, 353, 354; Bay 171, 176, 184, 243, 246, 248
Cardiganshire 264, 300, 306, 308
Carmarthen 36, 141
Carmarthenshire 224, 350
Carmel 30; Head *208*
Carmelite Friary Church, Denbigh *100*
Carnarvon Boroughs 191
Carn Boduan 179
Carneddau, The 110, 125, 126, 135, 147, 163-4, 328, 329
Carneddau Hengwm *251*
Carnedd Dafydd 163, *164*
Carnedd Llywelyn 163, *164*
Carnedd y Filiast 163
Carn Fadrun 179, 180
Carnguwch Church *177*, 181
Carno *297*; River 297
Caröe, Alban D. R. 138, 351; Martin 351; William Douglas 61, 76, 106, 134, 315, *351*
Carpenter, R. C. 287
Carreg-y-big 90
Carreg y Saeth 248
Carroll, Lewis 109
Carryll, Mary 85-6
Carter, John Coates 365
Cartwright, Samuel 330, 331
Cascob Church *321*
Castell Aber Lleiniog *202*
Castell Cidwm 157-9, 166
Castell Collen *326*
Castell Dinas Bran 82, 84, *86*, 91
Castelldinboeth *316*
Castell Odo 181
Castell Prysor 230
Castell y Bere *261*
Castell yr Adwy (*see* Tomen y Rhodwydd)
Castell y Waun 92
Casterton Church 38
Castle Brick Works 91
Castle Caereinion 288
Castle Farm, Painscastle 333
Castle Mill, Ceiriog Valley 93
Castle Mill, Ruthin 54
Castle Mound, Womaston *321*
Castle of the Winds 163
Castlereagh 85; Lord 299
Castles (Medieval) 23, 24, 25, 35, 39, 42, 50, 51, 53, 72, 86, 92, 93, 97, 100, 109, 117, 121, 128, 135, 143, 152, 154, 191, 199, 202, 230, 235, 245, 261, 267, 278, 281, 286, 290, 307, 316, 319, 320, 321, 322, 327, 333, 335
Ceffyl Derfel 223
Cefn Bryntalch *290-1*
Cefn Bychan 80, *90-1*
Cefn-caer 264
Cefn Caves *116*
Cefni 210, 212, 218
Cefnllys *326-7*; Castle *327*
Cefn Mawr 82
Cefn Meiriadog 116
Cefn Park 65
Cegidog 42, 221

Ceiriog 87, 91, 92, 93, *94*, 95; Forest 95
Celestine I, Pope 74
Cellar 209
Cell y Bedd *272*
Cemaes Bay 207
Cemais Road 298
Cemlyn Bay *207-8*, 208
Ceredig 353
cerrig mwsog 134
Cerist 255
Cernioge *118*
Cerrigydrudion, 55, 56, *117*
'Chalet, The', Nantgwynant 162
Chantrey 61
Charles I, King 45, 52, 76, 88, 94, 112, 117, 136, 149, 281, 322
Charles II, King, 332
Charles Edward, Prince 78
Charles, Thomas 224, 262, *351-2*
Charlet, Jean 307
Chartism 293, *302-3*, 305
Chase of the Wild Goose, *The* 86
Chatwin, J. A. 108
Cheere, Sir Henry 39
Cheshire 63, 73, 74, 75; Plain 61
Chester 21, 24, 29, 38, 59, 60, 67, 82, 126, 195, 353, 356; Battle of 74; Earl of 202
Chester and Holyhead Railway 29
Chester and Shrewsbury Railway 91
Chester-Ruthin Railway 43
'Chevalier Lloyd', The (*see* Lloyd, J. Y. W.)
Chirbury 283, 286, 287
Chirk 71, 87, 90, *91*, 92, 93, 265; aqueduct 84, *91*; canal tunnel 91-2; Castle *92-3*; viaduct *91*
Christian, Ewan 73
Christ's Hospital, Ruthin 53
Church Bay 208
Churchill, Lady Randolph 54; Winston 88
Churchstoke *287*
Cilcain *44*, 48
Ciliau *336*
Cistercian Abbey, Maenan 110; Order 29, 87, 242, 279, 290, 309, 311, 314
City Dulas 205
Claerwen Dam *313*; Reservoir 312; River 313
Clarence, Duke of 108
Clarendon School (*see* Kinmel)
Clarke, Harry 30
clasau 113, 155, 182, 183, 263, 269, 300, 305, 352
Clas Brook 331
Clatter 297
Claudius 351
Clayton and Bell 61, 89, 118, 138, 222, 228, 276, 287, 293, 301, 315
Cledwyn 112
Clenennau 136, 169
Clip 248
Clive, Edward 282; of India 282; Viscount 281
Clocaenog *55*
Clochfaen 305
Clogau gold mines 254
Clogwyn du'r Arddu 162
Cloisters, The, Ruthin 53
Clough, Sir Richard 46, 52, 100, 116
Clun Forest 287
Clutterbuck 113, 273
Clutton, Henry 53
Clwyd 13, 21, 35, 36, 46, 52, 55, 57; Forest 48; Hills 26, 48, 50, 51, 88, 97, 115; Vale of 21, 33, 45, 46, 50, 51, 53, 54, 56, 68, 96, 110, 112, 116, 192, 230, 353
Clynnog Fawr 166, *175*, 350
Clyro 324, 329, 332, *336-7*; Hill 329, *332*, 337
Clytha Park, Monm. 356
Clywedog 57, 72, 96, 255, 256, 302, 315; Reservoir *304*; Valley 304
Cnicht 153, 156, *164-5*, 237, 238
Coad, Richard 179
Coalbrookdale 229
Coalbrookdale Ironbridge 66
Coal-mining 30, 63f., 69-70, 78, 90, 94
'Cob', The (*see* Portmadoc Embankment)
Cobden, Richard 305
Cochwillan 136, *137*
Cockerell, C. R. 81, 91, 356
Coed Coch *113*
Coed Helen 144
Coed-y-Brenin Forest 227, *240*
Coes Faen 253
Coeten Arthur *251*
Coleg Harlech *246*
Collier, E. V. 335
Colomendy Hall *47*
Colva *331*, 332
Colwyn River 154, 156
Colwyn Bay 104, *105-6*, 107, 108, 125
Comins Coch 298
Comper, J. N. 118, 289
Comyn, Heaton 100
Connah's Quay 23

Constantine, Emperor 143, 238, 258
Constantinople 35, 143
Conwy 23, 109, 110, 111, 127, *128-31*, 133, 136, 200; Castle *128*, 131, 143, 144; Falls *119*; Falls Hotel 119; Mountain 131; River 118, 119, 121, 122, 123, 126, 128, 179; Valley 96, 110, 111, 112, 119
Conwy, Sir John 35
Copper-mining and working 29, 156, 161, 169, 206, 207, 240
Corbet family 262
Corbett, John 262, 263
Corndon Hill 287
Cornwall 15, 169, 173
Cornwallis-West, George 54
Corris *259*, 300; Railway 262
Cors-y-Gedol *250*, 251, 252
Corvo, Baron 27-8
Corwen 51, 54, 55, *89*, 90, 117, 220, 221
Cossins, J. A. 108
Courtauld's 23
Court House, Beaumaris *201*
Cox, David 37, 122
Crace, J. G. 93, 284
Craig Cwmbychan 166
Craig Cwm-Silyn 166
Craig Cywarch 255
Craig Dulyn 125
Craig Goch Reservoir 311, 312
Craig Lwyd 258
Craiglyn Dyfi 256
Craig Pwll Ddu *335*
Craig-y-bera 166
Craig-y-gwynt *208*
Craig yr Aderyn *261*
Craig-yr-ysfa 164
Craven Arms 319
Cregrina *331*
Cresswell, H. B. 23
Creuddyn Peninsula 109, 133
Crewe 72
Crewe-Read, Mr. 301; Captain 301
Crib Goch 161, 162
Crib-y-ddysgl 161, 162
Crib-y-rhiw 251
Cricieth 23, 179, *191-2*, 192; Castle 191; Fair 191
Criggion *276*
Crimea Pass *121*
Croes Foel *71*
Croesnewydd Hall *69*
Croesor 152, 165, 234, *237-8*, 238; Tramway 155, *238*; Valley *237*, 238
Cromlechs (*see* Burial Chambers)
Cromwell, Oliver 118, 136, 231, 249
Crosses 31, 33, 55, 57, 87, 90, 202-3, 323
Cross Foxes 256, 258
Crossgates 315, *317*, 324
Cross Lanes 73
Crowe, Sylvia 239
Crue, Silvanus 66, 73, 111, 276; Thomas 73
Crugion (*see* Criggion)
Crystal Palace 114
Cundy, Thomas 24
Cunedda Wledig *352-3*, 353
Cyrn y Brain 88
Cwm *33*
Cwm Amarch 258
Cwm Bychan *248*
Cwm-Cefn-y-Gaer 315
Cwmciprwth *169*
Cwmcloch 165
Cwm Croesor 165
Cwm Cynllwyd *226*
Cwm Cywarch 226
Cwmdauddwr, Rhayader 312
Cwm Eigiau 164
Cwm Elan *311*, 312
Cwm-glas *162*
Cwmhir 242
Cwm Hirnant 223
Cwm Idwal *163*
Cwm Llafar 164
Cwm Maen Gwynedd 269
Cwmorthin 233
Cwm Penamnen *121*
Cwm Penmachno 119
Cwm Pennant 165, *168*, 169
Cwm Prysor 230
Cwm-y-glo 150
Cwm-y-llan 162
Cwmystradllyn 169, 170
Cwmystwyth 311
Cyff Eilian 206
Cymer Abbey *242*
Cymmrodorion Society 205
Cymyran Bay 215, *219*
Cynan 141
Cynfal Fawr 231
Cynlas 224
Cynllaith 265, 267
Cynwyd 45, *221*

Dadford, Thomas and John 275
Dafydd ab Ifan ab Einion 245, 250
Dafydd ap Gruffydd 163, 359
Dafydd ap Gruffydd Fychan 289
Dafydd Ddu Hiraddug 45
Dafydd Gam 300

Dafydd Nanmor 153
Dafydd y Garreg Wen (*see* Owen, David)
Danvers, Sir Charles 287
Darowen *298*
Darwin, Charles 163
Dashwood, Thomas 320
David's Well 317-18
Davies, David, Llandinam 292, 296, 298, *301*, 303; family, Croes Foel 52, 65, 71, 72, 92; family, Llandinam 303; Gwendoline *292-3*, 302; John (*see* Robber's Grave); Lord 289, 292, 300, 302; Margaret *292-3*, 302; Rev. Randolph 277; Robert 41; Rev. Thomas 112; Thomas, Governor of the Gold Coast 280; W. 124
Davis, W. 100
Davison, George 246
Dawpool 236
Dduallt, 194, 233
Dduallt (mountain) 226
Deacon, George Frederick 272, 273
De Barri, William 355
De Boulers, Baldwin 286
De Braose, William 135
De Breos, Philip 322; William 334
Dee, 21, 23, 32, 38, 45, 60, 72, 73, 74, 77, 79, 81, 82, 84, 85, 86, 87, 88, 89, 91, 94, 117, 221, 222, 223, 226
Defferd, James 155, 213, 218
De Freney, Gilbert 36; William 35
Degannwy *109*
De Grey, Reginald 53
De Lacy, Henry, Earl of Lincoln 97
De Montgomery, Earl Roger 286
De la Pole family 281
Denbigh 21, 43, 58, *97-100*, 101, 115; Castle *97*, 117; 8th Earl of (*see* Feilding, Viscount); Moors 110
Denbighshire 21, 47, 55, 56, 74, 77, 79, 104, 110, 111, 117, 223, 265
Derfel 223
Derwen 54. *55*
Derwen-las *300*
Deva 73, 363
Devannor *315*
Devil's Bridge 311
Devonport, Lord 115
De Walden, Lord Howard 92
Dibdin, Charles 264
Dickens, Charles 204
Diffwys 249
Digby, Sir Kenelm 44
Dinas 155
Dinas Bran 261
Dinas Dinlle *174*
Dinas Emrys *154*
Dinas Gynfor *207*
Dinas Mawddwy *255*, 256, 298
Dinas Oleu 252
Dinbaud (*see* Castelldinboeth)
Dinbych (*see* Denbigh)
Dingey and Son 169
Din Llugwy *205*
Dinmael (*see* Maerdy)
Dinorben *104*
Dinorwic 121, 233; quarries 139, 140, *150*, 151
Dinsylwy Hill Fort *208*
Discoed 318, 321
Diserth 30, 33
Disserth Church 325, *328*
Dodd, A. H. 302
Dolanog 273
Dolau Gwyn 262
Dolbadarn Castle *152*
Dolben 116
Dolbenmaen *167-8*
Doldowlod House 329
Dolfor *295*, 319
Dolforwyn Castle *290*
Dolgarrog 110, *125*
Dolgellau 226, *228-9*, 241, 256, 259, 264, 299
Dolgoch 262
Dol-llys *304*
Dolmelynllyn *241*
Dolobran *277-8*
Dolwar Fach 273
Dolwyddelan *121*, 157, 233; Castle 121
Dominican Order 36
Donne, John 287
'Dorothea' Quarry 157
Double-naved Churches 32, 33, 36, 42, 44, 45, 50, 51, 52, 54, 57, 86, 96, 97, 103, 104, 110, 112, 116, 124, 183, 186, 189, 191, 219, 353
Douglas, John 23, 24, 25, 26, 27, 33, 38, 39, 44, 50, 52, 53, 56, 60, 73, 74, 75, 77, 106, 107, 109, 113, 116, 130, 139, 191, 192, 233, 234, 253, 274, 290, *353*
Dovey 264; Estuary 263; Valley 255, 259, 298
Downing 29, *31*
Doyle, J. F. 108
Drapers' Company 99
Drayton, Michael 153

Drelincourt, Mary 68
Drew, Mary 38
Droitwich 262
Δροσης, Δ. 102
Druids 215
'Druids' Circle', Moelfre 133
Drws Bach 255
Drws-y-coed 156, 166
Drybridge Lodge 30
Dugdale, Thomas 93
Dugoed Valley 255, 289
Dulas Harbour 205; Valley, Denbs. 113; Valley, Merioneth 259; Valley, Montgoms. 305
Dulyn *125*
Dumas, A. 252
Dunawd, Abbot, of Bangor 74
Dwyfor 168, 169, 190
Dwygyfylchi *133*
Dwyryd 234, 235, 242-3
Dyer, John 295
Dyfed 13
Dyffryn Ardudwy *250*, 251
Dyffryn Edeirnion 89
Dyffryn Meifod *226-7*
Dyffryn Mymbyr 153
Dylife 304; mines 300, 305
Dysynni 259, 261, 262

Earp, Thomas 99, 102, 103, 105, 276, 287, 289
Eaton Hall 71, 214
Edern *179*
Edge, John 75
Edisbury, Joshua 71
Edw 330, 331
Edward I, King 13, 23, 29, 35, 36, 53, 93, 97, 110, 128, 129, 143, 144, 178, 191, 197, 199, 217, 245, 261, 281, 335, 357, 359, 363
Edward II 36, 144
Edward IV 245, 352
Edward VII 58
Edward the Confessor 321
Edwards, J. C. & Company 91, 267
Edwards, Mrs. of Nanhoron 187; Lewis 224; Llewelyn 45; Thomas (*see* Twm o'r Nant,); William 119
Efenechtyd *55*
Égalité, Duke of Orléans 174
Eginton, Francis 50, 73, 102
Eglwysbach *110*, 112
Eglwyseg 82, 87, 88
Eglwys Fair 277
Eglwys Gwyddfarch 277
Eglwys Seion, Cricieth 191
Eglwys Tysilio 277
Eglwys Wen (*see* Whitchurch)
Egryn Abbey *251*
Eifion Wyn 168
Eigg, Hebrides 181
Eisteddfa Gurig *306*
Eisteddfodau 45, 78, 85, 225, 240, 247, 267, 350, *354*, 356
Elan Reservoirs 310, *310-11*; River 313; Valley *311*, 312, 324; Village *313*
Elen 141
Elidir Fach 150
Elidir Fawr 163
Eliseg, King 87, 278; Pillar of *87*
Elizabeth I, Queen 28, 45, 88, 217, 245, 253, 354
Elkingtons 281
Ellesmere 76
Ellice, Peter 69
Ellis, Thomas Edward *224*
Elwy 101, 114, 116
Emes, William 72, 93, 201
Emral Hall 75, 236
Epynt 329
Erbistock *77*
Erddig 65, 66, *71*, 72, 73, 93
Erwood 334
Eryri (*see* Snowdonia)
Eryrys 60
Esclusham Mountain 70, 78, 88
Estreldis 290
Evans, brothers 296; David 94, 138, 275, 277, 285, *354*; Ellis Humphrey 240; Evan (*see* Glan Geirionydd, Ieuan); Grace 280; John 80; Rev. J. 150; Mari, y Fantell Wen 243-4; Ruth 273
Evelyn, John 76
Everton Water Tower 272
Evins, J. H. 334
Ewloe *25*, 261

Faenol Bach *104*
Fairbourne 260; Railway 260
Fairy Glen, Conwy Falls *119*
Fan Pool 304
Fathew Valley 262, 263
Fawnog Valley 258
Fechan, Ednyfed 107
Feilding, Viscount 29, 30
Felton, George 108
Fenton, Richard *355*
Ferodo Works, Caernarfon 145
Ferrey, Benjamin 66, 80, 81, 116, 224, 270, 273, 277; E. B. 121, 220, 224, 227, 261
Festiniog Railway 153, 193, *194*, 233, 234, 236;

Ffarm, 114
Fferm *41*
Ffestiniog 119, 224, 230, *231*, 238, 243, 244; Vale of *233*
Ffon Dderfel 233
Ffon-y-cawr 126
Ffordd Môn 190
Ffrith 42
Ffrwd Fawr *304*
Ffynnon Beuno *46*
Ffynnon Eidda 119
Ffynnon Fair 28, 35, *116*
Ffynnon Gelynnin 127
Ffynnongroyw *31-2*
Ffynnon Lloer 164
Ffynnon Llugwy 164
Fiennes, Celia 27
Firbank, Thomas 153
Fishguard 355
Fitzhugh family 70
Fitzmaurice, Hon. Thomas 58-9
Flannel-making 29, 85, 279, 293, 302
Flint *23*, 25, 26, 35, 36, 45
Flintshire 21, 30, 36, 40, 48, 63, 73, 101
Foel *255*, 289
Foel Cynwch 227
Foel Fenlli 48
Foel Goch 163
Forden 284, *285*
Forden Gaer *285*, 286
Fordham 253
Forest, Friar 223
Forrest and Bromley 284
Forts (*see* Hill-forts *and* Roman Forts)
Fort Belan 166, 174
Fort Williamsburg 174
Foryd Bay 166
Foulkes, Sidney Colwyn 47, 104, *106*, 130
Four Mile Bridge 215
Four Stones, Walton *321*
Fowkes, Francis 336
Fowler, Hodgson 76, 241; family 314; Richard 307
Fowler's Armchair *317*
Fox, George 323
Foxes' Path 259, 260
Franciscan Order 30
Fron *84*
Fron Goch *229*
Frontinus 141
Frost family, of Colwyn 107
Fulljames 100
Furness 29
Furse, Mr. and Mrs. A. W. 43
Gadeon 141
Gadlys 26
Gain Valley, Merioneth 240; Montgoms. 274
Gallen Valley 113
Galloway 138
Gam, Dafydd (*see* Dafydd Gam)
Gamlan 241
Gandon, James 80
Ganllwyd 241
Gapper, R. L. 229
Garibaldi 114
Garn Dolbenmaen 166
Garnedd Goch 166
Garner, M. J. 321
Garreg, Flints 31; Merioneth 237-8
Garreg Ddu 312
Garregelldrem 238
Garrick, David 79
Garrison Chapel, Caernarfon 144-5
Garthbeibio (*see* Foel)
Garthewin *114*
Gaskell, Mrs. 231
Gee, Thomas 100; W. H. 283
Gelert 154
Gelli, The 25
George I, King 282
George III 49, 227
George IV 213
George V 188
George, David Lloyd 145, *190-1*, 302; Museum 191
Gibberd, Sir Frederick 229
Gibbons, Grinling 44
Gibbs, A. 44, 58, 74; John 323
Gibson, John, architect *67*, 70, 103
Gibson, John, sculptor, *49-50*, 113, 129
Gilbert, Alfred 301
Giler *118*
Gilfach Copper mine 169
Gill, Eric 92
Gillot's Tower 35
Giraldus Cambrensis 156, 249, 288, 316, 322, 350, *355*, 360
Girouard, Mark 110
Gladestry *332*
Gladstone family 355; Memorial Chapel 25;'s Rock 162; Sir Stephen 24; W. E. 24, 25, 38, 39, 134, 162
Glamorgan 13, 350
Glanadda 139
Glanaled, Iorwerth (*see* Iorwerth Glanaled)
Glan Alyn School 47
Glan Geirionydd, Ieuan 124

Glanllyn 224
Glanmule 287
Glansevern 289, *290*
Glanydon 30
Glan-yr-Afon *220*
Glanywern 58
Glasbury *336*
Glascoed 267
Glascwm 331
Glasgow 101, 246
Glaslyn 161
Glaslyn, River 154, 155, 194
Glendower, Owen (*see* Owen Glendower)
Gloddaeth *109*, 136
Glyder Fach *163*
Glyder Fawr *163*
Glyders 142, 148, 153, *162-3*, 163, 249
Glyn, Anglesey *204*
Glyn, Merioneth 244
Glyn Ceiriog 91, *94*, 221
Glyndyfrdwy *89*
Glynllifon Park 173, *174-5*
Glynne, Sir Stephen 24, 331
Goch Eryri, Rhys 154
Goch, Iolo *267-8*
Goddard's Plate Palace 178
Godwin 322
Golden Grove 32
Gold-mining 240-1, 254
Goodhart-Rendel, Henry Stuart 25, 32, 33, 47, 103, 279, 323, *355*
Goodman, Dr. Gabriel 52-3, 53
Gop Hill *32*
Gordon, Alex 187; Dr. Mary 86
Gorsedd 29, 33; Ceremony of 354; Circle 188
Gorseddau Quarries 170
Gors Graianog 166
Gotha Canal 197
Goytmor, Hywel (*see* Hywel Goytmor)
Graig Lwyd 133
Gratian, Emperor 141
Graves, Dr. Percival 244; Robert 244
Gray, Thomas 328
Great Orme's Head 107, 203, 208
Greaves, John Whitehead 231, 232; R. M. 192
Gredington *76*
Green, W. J. 110
Gregory, P. S. 187
Gregynog *292-3*, 302
Gresford 60, *61*, 65; Colliery 63; Lodge 65
Gresham, Sir Thomas 46
Grey, Reginald, third Lord of Ruthin 52
Griffith family of Devannor 315; family of Penrhyn 136; Moses 31; Nehemiah 40; Sir William 136
Griffiths, Ann 273, 274
Griffiths, Grace 33; Robert 119
Grimthorpe, Lord 38
Gronw 239
Grosvenor, Lord 26; Lodge 67
Groves, Thomas 311
Gruffydd ap Cynan 235, 239, 243; ap Dafydd Goch 120, 122; ap Gwenwynwyn 281; ap Madoc 86; ap Rhys ap Tewdwr 183
Guildhall, London 26
Guild of St. George 252
Guilsfield *278*-9
Gummow, Benjamin 43, 55; J. R. 67
Gun Cliff, Llanddwyn Island 218
Gunpowder Plot 189
Gurn Ddu 176
Guyard, Auguste 252
Gwaenynog *100*
Gwaenysgor *32*
Gwendolen, Queen 290
Gwen o'r Ddol 153
Gwent 13
Gwerful Goch 56
Gwernafield *40*
Gwernol Valley 262
Gwernymynydd 47
Gwersyllt Church 69; Park 65
Gwespyr 32
Gwibernant (*see* Wybrnant)
Gwrych Castle 105, 114
Gwyddelwern *55*
Gwydion 234, 239
Gwydir Castle 78, 111, *123*, 136; Forest 120
Gwydir Uchaf Chapel *123*
Gwylfa Hiraethog 115
Gwylltion Cochion Mawddwy 255
Gwyn, King of the Fairies 324
Gwynedd 13, 107, 135, 138, 191, 351, 358, 361, 363; Owain (*see* Owain Gwynedd)
Gwyneddigion Society 56
Gwynfynydd *240*
Gwynne, Eliza 193; family 187
Gwysaney *40*
Gwyther, W. W. 40
Gwytherin *112*
Gyffin 127, 128, *130-1*, 131
Gyffylliog *96*
Gyrn Castle 32

Haddon 318
hafod 17
Hafod-dwyryd 120
Hafod Garegog 153, 238
Hafod Llwyfog *153*
Hafodunos *113*
Hafoty 203
Haig, Caton 235
Hakewill, Henry 113
Halghton Hall *75*
Halkyn 27; Castle *26*; Mountain 26, 27
Hall, E. S. 301; John 201; Joseph 24
Hampton Court 104
Hanbury-Tracy, Hon. H. 292, 293
Hanmer *76*; family 76; Margaret 245; Richard 361; Sir Thomas 76
Hanmer Hall 76
Hansom, Joseph Aloysius 46, 103, 201
Happy Valley, Llandudno *108-9*
Hardman 30, 105, 289, 322
Hare, H. T. 139
Harlech 23, 230, 243, *244-6*, 250, 264, 318; Castle 244, *245-6*; Dome 249; Lord 244
Harley Dingle 323
Harp Inn, Old Radnor *322*
Harris, Howell 356
Harpton Court 323
Harries, Rev. Gilbert C. F. 350-1
Harrison, James 25, 38; Thomas 49, 63, 76, 93, 211, 213, *356*, 362
Hausburg 284
Hawarden 25, 355; Castle *24*
Hawkins, Rhode 221
Hawthorne Hill 320
Haycock, Edward Sen. 229, 252-3, 300, 319, *356*; Edward Jun. 286, 289, 295, *356*
Hay-on-Wye 309, 337
Hazeldine, William 77, 84, 122
Heaton, Butler and Bayne 26, 255, 315
Heber, Bishop 270
Hebog range 156
Hedd Wyn (*see* Evans, Ellis Humphrey)
Helen, Queen 238
Hell's Mouth 134, 185
Helperthorpe Church, Yorks. 293
Henblas 32
Hen Ddinbych 115
Hen Domen 286
Hendre Cenin 190
Hendwr 221
Hengwm 255, 256
Hengwrt *242*, 261
Henllan *115*, 116
Henrietta Maria, Queen 76
Henry I, King 183, 286, 360
Henry II 350, 361, 364
Henry III 286, 333, 358, 359
Henry VI 245
Henry VII 18, 28, 30, 118, 137, 210, 252, 278, 285, *298-9*, 349, 364, *367*
Henry VIII 13, 28, 223, 263, 349
'Hên Waliau' 142
Herbert, Sir Edward 281; Edward 287; George 287; family of Montgomery Castle 286, 287; Henrietta 282; Lord, of Chirbury 283, 286; Magdalen 287; Sir Richard 245; Richard 287
Hereford 102, 318, 321, 329, 334, 336
Heseltine, Philip 291
Hesketh, Lloyd 105; Robert Bamford 105
Hetherington, Henry 302
Hewitt, Capt. Vivian 208
Heyop Church *319*
Hilbre Island 208
Hill-forts 26, 48, 49, 58, 86, 89, 104, 125, 133, 154, 174, 176, 181, 203, 207, 214, 218, 251, 285, 286, 315, 316, 321
Hindwell Pool 321
Hiraethog, Gwilym (*see* Rees, William)
Hirgwm Valley 254
Hirnant *272*
Hitler 191
Hoare, Sir Richard Colt 227
Hodge, Vernon 68
Holiday, Henry 38
Holland, Samuel 231
Hollins, Peter 103
Holme, F. V. 273
Holt 66, 69, *72*, 73
Holyhead 85, 129, 198, *213*, 214, 215, 219, 353, 356; Hut Circles *214*
Holyhead-Liverpool Telegraph System 205, 208; Mountain 212, *214*
Holy Island 181, 212, 214, 215, 219, 353
Holywell 21, 24, 26, *27*, 29, 30; Junction Station *29*, 30; Well 27, 116
Honeywood File 23
Hooton Hall 236
Hope *42*, 60; Mountain 42

Hopkins, Gerard Manley 27, 47, 49, 97, 101, 116
Hopper, Thomas 71, 104, 136-7
Horon 187
Horseshoe Falls *88*; Pass 88, *161*
Hound of Heaven, The 30
Houses of Parliament 211, 284
How, Walter 43
Howard of Effingham, Lord 42
Howell, Thomas 99-100
Howell Saer 120, 122
Howell the Good *356*
Howell's School *99*
Howse, W. H. 308
Hugh of Avranches, Earl of Chester 202
Hughes, Rev. Edward 104; H. R. 58, 104; Henry Harold 150, *350*; I. 119; Rev. John 273; John Ceiriog 296
Hugo, Victor 252
Hunt, Leigh 56
Hutchinson 31
Huw Llwyd *231*; 's Pulpit *231*
Huw Morus, Eos Ceiriog 94, 267
Hyde, Elizabeth 43
Hywel ap Gruffydd ap Cynan 251
Hywel Goytmor 111
Hywel Sele 226

Iaen 298
Iâl 50, 51
Idris 258
Idwal 163
Ignatius, Father 32
Impney, Droitwich 262
Iolo Morganwg 155, 354, *356*
Iorwerth Glanaled 114
Iron-working 63f., 69-71, 84, 94, 278
Isycoed *73*
Ithon 315, 326, 327, 328; Valley 295
Ivy Bridge 239, 242
Iwan, Dafydd 128

Jackson, Sir T. G. 39, 65
'Jack the Ripper's Church' 108
James I, King 45, 52, 153
James II 28, 123, 267
James of St George, Master (*see* St George, James of)
Jelf, Rev. W. E. 253
Jesse, John 49
Jesus College, Oxford *357*
Joan of Arc 13
Joan, Princess 135, 201, 358
John, Sir W. Goscombe 68, 145, 224
John, King 135, 201, 278, 358
Johnson, Dr. S. 31, 45, 46, 100, 101, 133; 's Cottage 100
Joicey, Lord 292-3
Joldwynds 291
Jones, Barbara 99; David 124; Griffith 350, *357*; Hugh 151; Inigo 35, 42, *111*, 250; Jenny 259; John 114; Col. John 88, 249; Rev. John *157*; Mary 262; Maurice of Ddol 96-7; Michael C. 225; Morris Charles 280; Owen (elder) 56; Owen (younger) 56; Robert 57; Robert (architect) 145; Robert Rhoslan 191; Thomas 32, 37, 40, 48, 61, 95, 102, 103, 104, 127, 232, 246, 253, *357*; Thomas, Pencerrig 325, 328
Jones-Brydges, Sir Harford 320
Jonson, Ben 250
Julitta 147, 305

Kanovium 126
Katheryn of Berain 115
Keating, the Misses 184
Kelham 113
Kemp, Edward 284
Kempson, F. R. 289
Kendall 103
Kennedy, Henry 52, 112, 126, 131, 136, 149, 150, 152, 173, 177-8, 180, 183, 187, 212, 216, 231, 246, 250, 294, 357
Kenyon family 77; George, Second Lord 77; Lord 75, 76
Kerry, Montgomeryshire 49, *287-8*; Hills 287
Kilvert, Rev. Francis 313-14, 314 329, 332, 334, 336, 337, *357*
King's Sutton Church 103
Kinmel 58, *104*
Knighton 309, 317, 318, *318-19*, 322
Knucklas 319; Viaduct *319*
Kossuth 114

Labouchere, Violet 86
'Ladies Mount' 281
Lake Vyrnwy 223, 226, 229, 255, *272-3*, 312
Lamartine 252
Lancing College 46
Landor, W. S. 50
Lanscroon 282, 283
Lansdowne, Marquess of 58
Laud 136
Lawrence, T. E. 154
Lay, Benjamin 273, 281

Lead-mining and working 24, 26, 29, 44, 47, 63f., 69, 146, 185, 271, 304, 305, 306
Leeswood *41*, 50, 71
Leete, The 44, 48
Leicester, Earl of 97; 's Church *97-8*
Leighton *283-4*, 285; Hall 279, 283, *284*
Leinster 171
Leopold Gate 25
Lewis, Mary 174; Memorial Cross, New Radnor *323*; S. 94, 182, 238
Liddell family 109
Lincoln 136
Lighthouses 32, 182, 185, 205, 208, 214, 217
Lindisfarne College (*see* Wynnstay)
Linnaeus 31
Little Orme's Head 107
Liverpool 15, 205, 206, 208, 225, 229, 272
Llanaber *251-2*, 253
Llanaelhaearn *176*
Llananno *316*
Llanarmon Church *189*
Llanarmon Dyffryn Ceiriog *95*, 296
Llanarmon-yn-Iâl 50
Llanasa *32*
Llanbabo 203, *209*
Llanbadarn Fynydd *316*
Llanbadarn-y-garreg Church *330*
Llanbadrig Church *207*
Llanbeblig Church *143*
Llanbedr *247*, 249, 250, 251
Llanbedr Hill *334*
Llanbedr Dyffryn Clwyd *49*, 56
Llanbedr Painscastle *333-4*
Llanbedrog *186*, 261
Llanbedr-y-Cennin *125*
Llanberis 140, *150-1*, 152, 232; Pass 153, 162; Path *161*, 162
Llanbister *315*
Llanbrynmair *298*, 304
Llandaff 99, 120
Llandanwg 244, *246*
Llanddaniel-fab 216
Llandderfel *222-3*
Llanddeusant 209
Llanddewi *112*, 113; Brefi 353; Fach *333*; Ystradenny 315
Llanddoged *112*
Llanddona 203
Llanddulas 105
Llanddwyn Bay *217*; Island *217-18*
Llanddwywe Church *251*
Llandecwyn *243*
Llandegfan 199
Llandegla *50*, 102
Llandegley *323*
Llandegwning *185*
Llandeilo Graban *334-5*
Llandinam 292, *300-1*, 305
Llandrillo *221-2*
Llandrillo-yn-Rhos 95, 107, 143
Llandrindod Wells 295, 310, 317, 320, 324, *325-6*, 327
Llandrinio *276*
Llandudno 37, *107-9*; Bay 107; Borough Council 125; Junction *109-10*, 113, 233
Llandudwen *179-80*
Llandwrog 173
Llandygai 45, *135*, 137, 149
Llandyrnog *57*
Llandysilio, Denbs. 88; Montgoms. 276
Llandyssil *290*
Llanedwen Church *216*
Llanegryn 259, *261*
Llaneilian Church *206*
Llaneilian-yn-Rhos *106-7*
Llanelidan *54*
Llanelli 319
Llanelltud *241-2*, 255, 259
Llanelwedd quarries 329
Llanelwy (*see* St Asaph)
Llanenddwyn *250*
Llanengan 181, *185*, 261
Llanerchydol 279, *281*, 288
Llanerchymedd *209-10*, 210
Llanerfyl *289*
Llaneugrad Church *204*
Llaneurgain *25*
Llanfachreth *227*
Llanfaelog 219
Llanfaelrhys Church *184*
Llanfaes Friary 201, 210
Llanfaglan 166, *167*
Llanfair 243, 244, *246-7*, 249; Caereinion 288-9, 292; Dyffryn Clwyd *51*
Llanfairfechan 126, *134*, 135
Llanfairisgaer *140*
Llanfair Mathafarn Eithaf *204*
Llanfair Pwllgwyngyll (gogerychwyrndrobwllllandysiliogogogoch) *211-12*, 215
Llanfair Talhaearn *114*
Llanfarchell (*see* Whitchurch)
Llanfaredd Church *335*
Llanfechain *274*
Llanferres *48*
Llanfigael *209*

Llanfihangel Glyn Myfyr *56*; Helygen 324, *327*
Llanfihangel-yng-Ngwynfa *273*
Llanfihangel-y-Pennant *168*, *262*
Llanfihangel-y-Traethau *243-4*, 244
Llanfor *220-1*, 223
Llanfrothen 234, *237*
Llanfwrog *55*
Llanfyllin *273-4*, 303
Llanfynydd *42*
Llangadfan *289*
Llangadwaladr Church *218*, 351
Llangaffo 212
Llangammarch Wells 326
Llangar *221*
Llangedwyn 79, *270-1*, 271
Llangefni 209, *210*
Llangeinwen *216-17*
Llangelynnin, Caerns 127; Merioneth 260
Llangernyw *113*
Llangian 185
Llangollen 66, 81, 82, 84, *85*, 87, 89, 90, 94, 354; Canal *84*, 88; 'Ladies of' 85-6; Vale of *82*f., 91
Llangristiolus Church *212*
Llangurig *305*, 310
Llangwnnadl *180-1*, 183
Llangwyfan, Anglesey 219; Denbs. 58
Llangwyllog Church *210*
Llangybi 189
Llangynhafal *57*
Llangynog 223, *271*
Llangywer *226*
Llanhychan *56*
Llanidan (old) Church *216*
Llanidloes 293, 296, 297, *302-5*, 305, 313, 314, 315
Llaniestyn, Anglesey 203; Caerns. 180, *186*
Llanilltyd Fawr 356
Llanllechid *149*, 231
Llanllugan *290*
Llanllwchaearn *295*, 354
Llanllyfni 167
Llanmerewig *291-2*
Llannefydd *116*
Llannerch Panna 77
Llanover, Lady 280
Llanrhaeadr-ym-Mochnant 120, *268-9*, 270
Llanrhaeadr-yng-Nghinmeirch 95, *96*, 97
Llanrhudd *52*, 57
Llanrhwydrys Church *208*
Llanrhychwyn *124-5*
Llanrug *150*
Llanrwst 66, 109, 110, *111*, 112, 123, 124, 150
Llansanffraid Glan Conwy *110*; Glynceiriog (*see* Glyn Ceiriog); Glyndyfrdwy *89*
Llansanffraid-ym-Mechain *274-5*, 277
Llansannan *114*
Llansilin *265-7*, 267, 268
Llanstephan *336*
Llantrisant Church *209*
Llanuwchllyn *225*, 226, 240, 256
Llanwddyn 273
Llanwenllwyfo 205
Llanwnda 167
Llanwnog *296*, 315
Llanwrthwl *324*
Llanwrtyd 326
Llanyblodwel 292
Llanycil *224*
Llanymawddwy 224, 226, 255
Llanymynech *275*, 276
Llanynys *57*
Llanyre 324, 327
Llanystumdwy 190, *190-1*, 191
Llawlech 251
Llawr-y-Betws 220
Llechfraith 254
Llech Idris *240*
Llechog 162
Llechwedd quarries 192, *232*
Lledr 121; Valley 110
Llefelys 154
Lleiniog 202
Lletyau 41
Lleu Llaw Gyffes 239
Lleweni Hall 45, *58*, 116
Lleyn 15, 31, 171-94, 197, 261
Llifon 174
Llithfaen 177, 178
Lliw 225
Lliwedd 162
Llowes Church *336*
Lloyd, T. Alwyn 187, 300; Charles 277; Edward 49; Emmeline Lewis 307; Evan 50; family, Merioneth 248; family, Mont. 277-8; Major General Henry 248; J. Y. W. 305; John 38, 42, 144; Richard 191; Sampson 278; Thomas 41; Thomas 278
Lloyd's Bank 278
Lloyd-Williams and Underwood 99, 112, 114, 119
Lludd, King 154
Llugwy, 123, 146, 147, 164; Burial Chamber *205*
Lhuyd, Edward 256

Llwyd, David 299; Evan 243; family (*see* Lloyd family, Merioneth)
Llwydiarth *273*
Llwyngwril 260
Llwyn-y-Cil 93
Llyn Aled Reservoir 114, 115
Llyn Bodlyn 251
Llyn Bwch-llyn *334*
Llyn Cau 258
Llyn Celyn *229*, 230
Llyn Cerrig Bach hoard 212
Llyn Conwy 119
Llyn Cowlyd 125, 164
Llyn Crafnant 125
Llyn Cwellyn *157*, 166
Llyn Cwm-Silyn 166
Llyn Dinas *154*
Llyn Dulyn 251
Llyn Ebyr *297*
Llyn Eigiau 125
Llyn Geirionydd 125
Llyn Gwernan 259
Llyn Gwyn 324
Llyn Gwynant 153
Llyn Gynwch 228
Llyn Hywel 250
Llyn Lliwbran 256
Llyn Llydaw 161
Llyn Maelog 219
Llyn Mair 234
Llyn Nantlle Uchaf 156
Llynnau Cregennen 259, 260
Llynnau Mymbyr 147
Llyn Ogwen *147*, 164
Llyn Padarn *150*, 151
Llyn Peris 151, 152
Llyn Stwlan 165, 233
Llyn Tecwyn-uchaf 243
Llyn Tegid *223*, 255, 256, 258
Llyn Tryweryn 230
Llyn-y-Cwn 163
Llyn-y-Dywarchen *156*
Llyn y Foel 164
Llyn y Gadair 156, 258, 259
Llyn-y-Gafr 259
Llyn-y-Morynion *230-1*, 239
Llyn y Pandy 44, 48, 69
Llyn Ystradau 238
Llŷr 244
Llysdinam 324
Llysdulas 205
Llys Euryn 107
Llysfaen *105*
Llys Gwenllian 100
Llyswen 336
Llywelyn Fardd 263
Llywelyn the Great 107, 111, 121, 124, 135, 152, 201, 251, 261, 333, *358*; the Last 25, 121, 122, 152, 163, 197, 281, 290, 314, 320, 335, *358*; 's Old Church 124
Lockwood, T. M. 126, 130, *359*
Locrine, King 290
Loggerheads 44, 47; Inn *48*
Londonderry family 299; Marquess of 299
London Lead Company 26
Long Mountain *283*
Louis Philippe of France 174
Lover's Leap, Llandrindod 326
Lowther College (*see* Bodelwyddan Castle)
Ludlow 129, 352
Lugar, Robert 336
Lugg 313, 320; Valley 317, 318, 321
Lutyens, Edwin 117, 134
Luxmore, Bishop of St Asaph 102; family 102, 103
Lymore 287

Mabinogion 140, 218, 234, 239, 244, 351, *359-60*
Machno 119, 120
Machynlleth 255, 256, 259, 264, 298, *299-300*, 302, 305; Garden Village 300
Mackintosh, C. R. 246
Macsen Wledig 140-1, 143
'Madam's Chapel' 68
Madocks family 61; John 58; John 61; William 61, 179, *192*, 193, 194, 235, 236, 237, 241
Madog ap Llywelyn 245
Madryn Castle *180*
Maelor Saesneg 21, 60, 73, *73-4*
Maen Achwyfan 31
Maenan *110*, 111, 128
Maen Beuno *289*; Huail 52
Maentwrog *233-4*, 238, 239, 242
Maen-y-Bardd *126*
Maerdy 56, 117
Maesgwm Valley 237
Maeshafn *47*
Maesllwch Castle *336*
Maesmawr Hall *295-6*
Maes-y-garnedd *249*
Maes-y-Neuadd *244*
Maesyronnen Chapel 336
Maesyrychen Mountain 87
Magnus Maximus (*see* Macsen Wledig)
Malltraeth Marsh 212, *218*
Mallwyd 255, 298
Malory 349
Malpas 74

'Mam Cymru' (*see* Katheryn of Berain)
Manafon *290*
Manning 29
Manod Mawr 231
Manorbier Castle 355
'Marble Church' 67, 103
Marchell 280
Marches, Council of the 28
Marchlyn Mawr 151
Marchwiel *78*
Maredudd ab Ieuan 121
Marford *61*
Margaret, Queen 245
Maria Stella, Lady Newborough (*see* Wynn, Thomas)
Market Hall, Llanidloes 303
Martial 243
Martin, Theodore 88
Mary of Modena 28
Math, son of Mathonwy 239
Mathafarn 298
Mathews, Charles 50
Matholwch, King 244
Mathrafal *278*
Maughan, John 190
Mawddach 226, 227, 240, 241, 242, 253; bridge 260; Estuary *253*, 258, 260; Ferry 260; Valley 240
Mawson, T. H. 192
Mazzini 114
Mead, Clement 46
Meifod *277*, 278
Meifod Valley 274
Meirchion 116
Meliden *33*
Melin-y-Wig *56*
Meller, John 71
Memorial Arch, Holyhead 213
Menai Bridge (town) *198*, 199, 210, 211; Bridge 84, 129, *197-9*, 209; Straits 128, 137, 138, 140, 143, 166, 174, 179, 195, 197, 199, 201, 202, 211, 215, 216, 217
Mendham, J. B. 260
Merddin Emrys Engine 236
Merioneth 36, 55, 56, 79, 89, 119, 121, 164, 220-64, 224, 227, 229, 255, 289
Merlin 154
Merrifield, L. S. 240
Mersey 207
Merseyside 21, 201
Meurig Fychan 228
Michaelchurch-on-Arrow *337*
Middleton 102
Mid-Wales Railway 319, 335
Migneint 249
Mileham, C. H. R. 104
Mill Farm 70
Millichope Park, Shrop. 356
Mills, W. and T. 99
Milton, John 290
Minera 69, *70*, 88
Miners' Bridge *146*; Track, Snowdon *161*, 162
Minffordd 235, 236
Mochdre 295
Mochras 247
Moel Bentyrch 289; Ddu 156; Fama 44, *48*, 49, 356; Fferna 89
Moelfre 133, 204, 205, 251
Moel Hebog 154, *165*, 169, 170; Hiraddug 180; Lefn 165; Siabod 153, *164*
Moel Sych 269
Moelwyn Range 156, *164-5*, 238; Bach *165*; Mawr *165*, 233
Moel-y-don 216
Moel y Dyniewyd 153, 154
Moel-y-Gaer 26, 49
Moel y Gest 194
Moel y Golfa 276
Moel y Mab 284
Mold 21, 38, *39*, 40, 41, 43, 47, 50, 53, 58, 100, 218
Molinduna 'Abbey' 31
Monacella (*see* St Melangell)
Monastic Houses (*see also clasau*) 29, 32, 36, 74, 87, 100, 110, 128-9, 155, 182, 185, 202, 242, 279, 290, 314
Monaughty *318*
Monmouth, Geoffrey of 102
Monmouthshire 203, 353
Montgomery, *286-7*, 333; Castle 286, 290
Montgomeryshire 79, 223, 265-306, 271, 272, 275, 276, 288, 293, 294, 309, 316; Canal *275*, 279, 289, 290, 303; Waterway Restoration Group 275
Moore, Leslie 100
Morfa Bychan *192*; Dinlle 166; Dyffryn 247; Gwyllt 237; Harlech 243, 246; Nefyn 179; Rhuddlan, Battle of 35
Morgan, William, Bishop of St Asaph 18, 53, 102, *120*, 269
Morgan Llwyd 231
Moriah Chapel 140
Morris Brothers Memorial *205*
Morris, James 235; Lewis 205; William 134, 214; William, and Co. 285
Mortimer, Sir Edmund 245, 287,

Mortimer [*Contd.*]
318; family 286; Roger 93, 294
Morus, Huw (*see* Huw Morus)
Mostyn, Bishop of Menevia 32; Charlotte Theophila 44; 'Christ' 138; Dock 30; Hon. E. M. L. 108; Estate 30, 108; family 23, 30, 44, 109; Hall *30*; Lord 138; Dame Mary 111; Sir Pyers 32; Station 30
Mountain Lodge 78
Mount Sion *69*
Mumford, Lewis 235
'Mur Castell' (*see* Tomen-y-Mur)
Muriau'r Gwyddelod *246*
Museums 137, 138, 141, 151, 191, 198, 280, 293, 303, 326
Myddelton Family 92, 93, 100; Sir Hugh 193; Mary 65-6, 69
Myfanwy Fechan 86
My Life and Times 72
Mylne, R. W. 324
Mynydd Anelog 181; Bodafan *205*; Carnguwch 127; Cefnamlwch *180*; Cilan 185; Drws-y-coed 156, 166; Eilian *205*, 208; Enlli 182; Hiraethog 96, 114; Mawr 156, 157, *166*, 167, 181; Nefyn 178; Perfedd 151-2, 163; Rhiw 185; Tal-y-mignedd 166; y Dref (*see* Conwy Mountain)

Nanhoron 187
Nanmor 153, 164, 238; Valley *153*
Nannau *226-7*, 227, 228
Nannerch *44*
Nanney 227
Nant 187
Nantclwyd Hall *54*
Nantcol *249*
Nant Conwy, Lord of 121; Ffrancon 147, 148, 157
Nantglyn *115*
Nant Gwrtheyrn 177; Gwyllt 311, 312, 313; Gwynant *153*, 154, 162; Iago *306*
Nantlle 156, 167; Quarries *156-7*; Ridge *165-6*, 169
Nantmel 324
Nant Peris *152*
Nant-y-Belan Tower 81
Nant-y-Garth Pass *51*
Nant-y-Pandy 89
Napoleon 248
Nash, John 24, 323; Paul 293
Naylor family 284; Georgina 284; John 283, 284
Neath 29
Nefyn 176, *178*, 187
Neill, A. 138
Nelson, B. 108; Joseph 182; Lord 211
Nercwys *42*; Hall *43*, 236
Nerquis (*see* Nercwys)
Nesfield, Willam Eden 35, 57-8, 104, 109, 292, 301, *360*
Nest, 353, *360*
Newborough *217*, 218; family 174, 182-3; Forest 217, 218; Mausoleum 174-5; Thomas, First Lord 174; Warren *217*
Newbridge, Ruabon 80
Newbridge, Radn. *324*
New Brighton 70
New Delhi 150
Newenham, T. G. 291, 295
New Grange, Ireland 219
New Lanark 294
Newman 37
Newmarket (*see* Trelawnyd)
Newnham Paddox 29
Newport 293
New Radnor 320, *322-3*, 329; Castle 322
Newtown 273, 287, 288, *293-5*, 296, 300, 302, 303, 315, 317; Hall 295
Newtown and Machynlleth Line 298
Nicholson, T. 285, 337
'Nimrod' 72
Nithsdale, Lady 280
Noble, Matthew 211
Nollekens, Joseph 81
Non 353
Normal College, Bangor *139*
North, Herbert Luck 105, 110, 126, 127, 131, *134*, 135, 139, 229, 270, 350
North Wales Mental Hospital *100*
North Wales Quarrying Museum *151*
Norton Water Tower, Cheshire 272
Norton, Radn. *320*

Oakeley Arms *234*; family of Tan-y-Bwlch 232, 234; Quarries *232*
Oates, John 38
Ocean Coal Company 301
O'Connor 103, 115
Odelau 243
Offa's Dyke 33, 42, 70, 87, 93, 275, 285, 306, 319-20, 321, *360*
Ogilvie, R. M. 217
Ogof Owain Glyn Dŵr 165
Ogwen 162, 163, 164; Bank 149; River 149

Old Radnor *321-2*
Oliver, Isaac 283; R. C. B. 325
Olliphant, F. W. 45, 118
Ordovices 141, 351, *360*
Ormes Bay (*see* Llandudno Bay)
O'Shea *37*, 205
Oswell, A. E. Lloyd 289
Oswestry 95, 265, 281
Overton 74, *77*; Bridge *77*
Owain Goch 152
Owain Gwynedd 25, 51, 56, 163, 243, 251, *360-1*
Owen, Athelstaine 264; family 189; Glendower 13, 52, 76, 90, 165, 191, 226-7, 245, 264, 267, 280, 287, 289, 300, 314, 318, 320, 322, 329, *361*
Owen Glendower Institute 300
Owen Glendower's Mount 89
Owen, David 192; Goronwy (architect) 146-7, 149; (poet) 204; Hugh 189; Col. Hugh 218; John 153, *189*; Sir John 136, 169, 192; Robert 294, 302; William Scott 293
Oxford 154; Museum 37, 101, 205; Town Hall 139

Pace, George 323
Padarn 351
Padeswood Cement Works 39
Paget, Lord Clarence 211
Painscastle 323, *332-3*
Pale *222*, 223
Pales Meeting House 323
Paley and Austin 111, 122
Paley, E. G. 353
Palmer and Holden 108
Pandy *94*
Panorama Walk *253*
Pantasaph *29*
Pant-y-dwr 317
Paradws 218
Parciau Estate 204
Parker, Rev. John 15, 86, *291*, 292, 302
Parker, Thomas Netherton 86, 291
Parkgate 45
Parliament House *300*
Parry, Harry 119, 150, 159; Richard 97
Parsons, S. 285
Parys Mountain Mines 104, *206*
Patagonia 225-6
Paulinus 353
Paxton 284
Peacock, Thomas Love 231, 248
Pearson, J. L. 44, 319, 320, 351
Peblig 143
Pelagius 74, 353
Pembroke, Earl of 281
Pembrokeshire 15, 171, 197, 243
Penamnen 152
Pencerrig 325, *328*
Penegoes 298, *299*
Peniarth 242, *261*
Penisa'rnant 149
Penlan Street, Pwllheli 187, 188; Chapel *188*
Penley *76*
Penllech Church *180*
Penmachno *119*, 120, 150
Penmaen Bach 133
Penmaenmawr 105, *133-4*
Penmaenpool 254, *259*
Penmaenrhos 105
Penmon 198, 202, 203; Point *203*; Priory *202-3*
Penmorfa Church *192*
Penmount Methodist Chapel *188-9*
Penmynydd 201, *210*
Penn, William 228, 324
Pennal 263, *264*
Pennant 269; Caroline, Lady 31; Louise 29; Richard, First Lord Penrhyn (*see* Penrhyn); Thomas 31, 81, 111, 112, 133, 136, 156, 175, 178, 182, 247, 248, *362*; Melangell 271, *271-2*; Valley 169
Pennarth Fawr *189*, 190
Penrallt 145
Penrhos (Anglesey) *213*
Penrhos (Mont.) *276*
Penrhyd 110
Penrhyn Castle 135, 136, *136-7*, 137; Estate 119, 146, 148
Penrhyn, First Lord 136, 137, 147, 148-9, 149; Lady 149; Second Lord 137; Quarries 139, 148
Penrhyndeudraeth 155, 165, *234-5*, 235, 237
Pensarn 247
Penson, R. K. 52, 67, 271, 273, 274, 296, *362*; Thomas 67, 69, 77, 78, 97, 99, 114, 274, 275, 281, 286, 290, 294, 301, *362*; Thomas (the Elder) 49, 56, 77, *362*; T. M. 229, 235, 251, 287, 359, *362*
Pentir 152
Pentraeth 139, 204, 212
Pentre Bach 95; Berw 212; Eiriannell Farm 205; Foelas 115, *118*
Pentrehobin *41*

Pentre Saeson *69*
Pentrobin *38*, 297
Penybont *317*, 324; Common 323
Penybontfawr *271*, 272
Pen-y-Bryn, Aber *135*
Pen-y-bryn, Mont. *271*
Pen-y-Cloddiau *58*
Pen-y-Dinas 251
Pen-y-Fan, Brecon Beacons 256
Penyfron mine 44
Penygadair 258
Pen-y-Gaer *125-6*
Penygarreg *312*
Penygroes 156, 157, 166, *167*
Pen-y-Gwryd *153*, 161
Penylan 277
Pen-y-Mwd 135
Penymynydd (*see* Pentrobin)
Pen y Pass 153, 161
Pen-yr-helgi-du 147, 164
Perrins, Mrs. Dyson 253
Petit, John Louis 253, 254
Petre, Fr 123
Philip, J. Birnie 280
Phillips family 336
Phillott 102
Phylips family 247; Gruffyd 247; Phylip Siôn 247; Rhisiart 247; Siôn 247
Picell Arthur 126
Pickhill *73*
Pierce, Dr. Evan 99
Piercy, Benjamin 253, 298
Piers 108, 139, 169
Pilleth *318*
Pilleth, Battle of 318, 320
Pin Mill 110
Pinnacles, The 161, 162
Piozzi, Gabriele 45, 46; Mrs. (*see* Mrs. Thrale)
Pistyll *178*; Cain *240*, 241; Rhaeadr *269-70*
Pite, Beresford 134
Pitt's Rock 156
Pius IX 305
Plas 215; Berw *212*; Brondanw *237*; Clough *100*; Coch *216*; Cwmllan 162; Dinam *301*; Du *189*; Grono 66, 72; Gwyn, Bangor 139; Iolyn 118; Machynlleth *299-300*; Madoc 112; Mawr, Conwy 111, 121, *130*, 349; Mynach 253; Newydd, Anglesey 193, 211, 215, 216; Newydd, Llangollen 85; Penmynedd 210; Power 65, 70; Têg *41*, 111; Uchaf 88, *221*
Plas-y-Brenin *147*
Plas-yn-Cefn 116
Plas yn Llan 67
Plas-yn-Rhiw *184-5*
Plas-yn-Yale 41
Plas-yn-y-pentre *85*
Pochin, Henry 110
Point Lynas *206*
Point of Air 32
Pollen, John Hungerford *37*, 118
Ponsonby, Hon. Sarah 85-6
Pont Aberglaslyn 153
Pont-ar-Eden 241, 311
Pont ar Ledr 120
Pont Cyfyng 146, 164
Pontcysylltau Aqueduct *83-4*, 275
Pontffriddlwyd 190
Pontllogail (*see* Llwydiarth)
Pont Rhyd-gôch 169; Rhyd-Llanfair *119*; Rhythallt 150
Pontrobert *273*, 277
Pont-y-Blew *94*
Pont y Bodkin *50*
Pont-y-Meibion 94, 267
Pont-y-Pair *123*
Pontypridd 119
Pont yr Afanc *120-1*
Pool Park *55*
Pool Quay *279*
Port Dinorwic *139*, 151, 216
Porthaml 217
Porth Dafarch *214-15*; Dinllaen *179*, 190, 192
Porth Dinllaen Turnpike Trust 179; Llanlleiana *207*
Porth Madryn, Patagonia (*see* Puerto Madryn); Nefyn *178-9*; Oer 181; Trecastell *219*; Trefadog 208; Trwyn 208; Swtan 208; Wen 207; y Nant 177
Portmadoc 155, 157, 167, 173, 192, *193-4*, 238; Embankment 236
Portmadoc Harbour Act 194
Portmeirion 43, 54, 75, *235-6*
Portofino 235
Port Penrhyn *137*
Portreuddyn Castle 156
Potter, Joseph 215
Poundley, John Wilkes 37, *49*, 53, 277, 287, 288, 297, 298, 300, 314
Powell's 53, 266, 274
Powell, Vavasor 280
Powis Castle 271, 279, 281, *281-3*, 288; 2nd Earl of 280; 6th Earl of 282; 3rd Lord 281-2; William Baron 281; Woods 283
Powys 13, 15, 267, 276, 288, 358, 359, 361, *362-3*; John Cowper 19, 232

Powys, Princes of 87, 271, 278, 281, *362-3*
Powysland Museum *280-1*
Poynter Ambrose 23, 30, 31, 44; E. J. 266
Precipice Walk *227-8*, 241
Preedy, F. 322
Prestatyn 30, *33*
Presteigne 318, 319, *320-1*
Price, Rev. John of Efenechtyd 55; Rev. John of Llanbedr 334; Sir Richard Green 320; Richard John Lloyd 220-1, 229; William 189
Prichard, John 299, *363*
Prichard and Seddon 333
Priestholm, Prior of 202
Priestley, Joseph 70
Prince's Oak *276*
Princetown Prison, Dartmoor 214
Prior's House, Penmon 202
Pritchard, M. T. 187; T. F. 66, 79; Mr, of David's Well 317
Prothero 66, 102
Provis 198
Pryce, Sir John 295
Pryce-Jones 294
Pryderi 234
Prys, Edmund 234; Thomas 118
Pryse 326
Puerto Madryn 226
Puffin Island 202, *203*, 208
Pugh, Owen 300
Pugin, A. W. N. 29, 92, 93, 284; E. W. 80
Puleston family 75
Pullan, R. P. 39
Pumlumon 306, 310
Purdie 30
Pusey 350
Pwlldefaid 188
Pwllheli 167, 171, 173, 179, 186, 187, *187-9*, 189, 247
Pwllycrochan 105
Pwyll 234
Pyg Track, Snowdon *161*

Quaker Company 26
Quakers 323-4
Queensferry *23*
Queen's House, Greenwich 214
Quest for Corvo, The 28

Radnor 309; Forest 317, 318, 321, *323*; Lords of 322
Radnorshire 21, 220, 295, 304, 307-37, 317, 319, 323, 325, 328, 331. 334, 336.
Raggi, M. 99
Raikes, Henry 39
Railways (Narrow-Gauge) 151, 155, 157, 161, 194, 238, 260, 262-3, 288
Raleigh, Sir Walter 93
Randles, Mr, of Marford 61
Rea of Monaughty 318
Rebecca Riots 305, 310, *363*
'Red Altar, The, 125
Red Wharf Bay 203, 204
Reed, Charles 199
Rees, Abraham 298; Alwyn D. 273; Henry 114; William *114*
Rehoboth *187*
Reilly, Sir Charles 106
Rendel, Lord 355
Rennie, John 197, 213
Repton, Humphrey 117, 319; J. A. 319; 's 281
Reynolds, Sir Joshua 81
Rhaeadr Bach *135*; Cynfal 231; Ddu (Ganllwyd) *241*; Ddu (Ivy Bridge) *242*; Fawr *135*; Mawddach *240*, 241
Rhaeadr-y-Bedd 114
Rhaeadr-y-Cwm *230*
Rhayader 305, 309, *310*, 311, 312, 313 317, 324
Rhewl 96
Rhianfa 138, 199
Rhiannon 245
Rhinog Range 239, 240, 249; Fach 249, 250; Fawr 249
Rhiw 184, *185*
Rhiw, River 290; Saeson 298
Rhiwabon (*see* Ruabon)
Rhiwlas 189, 190, *221*; Brush Works 220
Rhobell range 226; Fawr 226
Rhodri Mawr 356, *363*
Rhondda Valley, Upper 301
Rhonwydd Valley 264
Rhos 107
Rhoscolyn 215
Rhos Fynach weir 107
Rhosgadfan *167*
Rhosgoch *332*; Common 332, 335
Rhosllannerchrugog *78*
Rhosneigr *219*
Rhos-y-glascoed 277
Rhosymedre 90
Rhual *40*, 43
Rhuddlan 23, *35*, 36, 46, 101, 144; Priory 138; Statute of 13
Rhulen *330-1*
Rhuthun (*see* Ruthin)
Rhyd 234
Rhyd-ddu 155, *156*, 157, *162*, 165, 166, 167, 169

Rhydonnen 56-7, 57
Rhydspence 337
Rhydwhiman 286
Rhyd-y-Carw 297
Rhydycroesau *265*
Rhydymwyn *43*, 44, 48
Rhygyfarch 353
Rhyl 21, 33, *37*, 105, 107
Rhys ap Gruffydd (The Lord Rhys) 322, 361, *364*
Rhys ap Meredydd 118, 153
Robert ap Meredydd 118
Sir Rhys ap Thomas 364
Richard I, King 350; II 23; III 30, 43
Richards family 256
Richardson, Edward 280
Richmond, Sir William 25
Rickman 31, 37
Ridge, Thomas 303
Ridolfi Plot 189
'Rivals', The 176, 177, 217
Robber's Grave 287
Roberts, David 139; Kate 167; Robert, 43; Samuel 298; W. 53
Robertson, Henry, M.P. 83, 91, 222
Rochford, Earl of 282
Rock Park, Llandrindod *326*
Rodney, Admiral 276
Rodgers, Charles 317
Rogers of Tyluggan 318
Rolfe, Frederick (*see* Corvo, Baron)
Roman Bridge Station *122*
Roman Forts and Camps 126, 141, 146, 153, 167, 213-14, 224, 238-9, 264, 285, 296, 297, 306, 326, 363
Roman Steps *248-9*, 249
Roscoe family 113
'Rosebriars', Llanfairfechan 134
Rossett *60*
Rothschild, Nathan Meyer 194
Roubiliac, L. F. 66, 69
Roundabout, The 333
Ro-wen *126*
Rowland, Daniel *364*; John (*see* Stanley, H. M.)
Rowlandson 234
Rowley-Conwy, Conwy Grenville Hercules 35
'Royal Charter' 204
Royal Commission on Ancient Monuments 55, 107, 209
Royal Exchange 46
Royal St David's Golf Club 246
Royal Welsh Show 328-9
Royal Welsh Warehouse, Newtown 294
RSF 95
Ruabon 77, *78*, 79, 81, 84, 90, 91; Mountain 78
Rug 51, 55, 57, *117*
Runcorn Suspension Bridge 197
Ruskin, John 38, 100, 155; -ian 205, 252
Russell, Bertrand 168, 207
Ruthin 21, 40, 47, 48, 50, 51, *52*, 53, 54, 55, 96, 97, 117, 303
Rysbrack 40, 81

Sabrina 290
Saeson 95
Saint, River 141, 143, 166
St Aelhaearn 278
St Aelhaearn's Well 176
St Aelrhiw's Church 185
St Asaph 101; (town) 21, 36, 49, 100, *101*, 113; Bishop's Palace *103*, 218; Cathedral 50, 97, *101-2*, 137, 280, 288
St Augustine 74
St Beuno 27, 46, 166-7, 175, 178, 234, 289, *350*; 's Stone, Clynnog Fawr *175*; 's Stone, Holywell 28; 's Well, Tremeirchion 46; 's Well, Clynnog Fawr *175*
St Cadfan 263, *351*
St Cadwaladr 218
St Clears 224
St Collen's Chuch, Llangollen 86
St Curig 147, 305, 306
St Cybi 214, *353*; 's Well *189*
St Cynlas 202
St Cyricus 147, 305
St David 179, 331, 353
St Davids 138, 288, 353, 355; Head 181
St Deiniol 138; 's Library *25*
St Doged 112; 's Well 112
St Dogfan 269
St Dominic 36
St Dwynen 217; 's Well 217
St Dyfnog's Well 97
St Eilian 206
St Eilian's Chapel 206
St Enclydwyn 119
St Fagan's 221, 289
St Garmon (*see* St Germanus)
St George (village) *104*
St George, James of 23, 35, 128, 199, 200-1, 245, *357*
St Germanus 40, 74, 95, 314
St Gwenfaen's Well *215*
St Gwynhoydl 180-1

St Harmon *313-4*
St Hilary's Chapel, Denbigh *99*
St Hywyn 183
St Iestyn 209
St Illtyd 241, *356*
St John of Jerusalem, order of 118
St Kentigern 101
St Llonio Lawhir 300
St Llwchaearn 292
St Martin's 94
St Mary, Tal-y-llyn *219*
St Melangell 271-2
St Mungo (*see* St Kentigern)
St Pabo 203, 209
St Padarn *362*
St Peris Church, Nant Peris 152
St Seiriol 202; 's Well *202-3*
St Teilo's Barn 334
St Tudclud 119
St Tudno 108
St Tudwal's Islands *185*
St Tudwen 179
St Twrog 234
St Tysilio 277, *367*; 's Church *210-11*
St Wddyn 273
St Winefride 27-8, 113, 350
St Winifred's School, Llanfairfechan 134
Salesbury, William 114
Salisbury Cathedral 87, 136
Salt Island 213
Saltney 21
Salusbury family (of Bachegraig and Lleweni) 45, 58, 97
Salusbury family (of Bachymbyd) 96; Hester Lynch (*see* Mrs. Thrale); John 116; William 117
Salvin, Antony 145, 360
Sandbach, H. R. 113
Sandby, Thomas 59
Sankey 322
Sant 353
Sarn (Lleyn) *186*
Sarn (Mont.) *287*
Sarn Badrig *247-8*; Bridge 75; Helen 141
Savigny, Order of 29
Scoles, J. J. 28
Scott, Sir Gilbert 25, 33, 36, 37, 39, 56, 87, 100, 101, 102, 103, 113, 115, 118, 129, 138, 140, 179, 214, 220, 274, 280, 305, 349, 350, *364-5*; Sir Giles 25, 229, 320, *365*; John Oldrid 42, 108, 112, 138, 275, *365*; Sir Walter 85; Walter 273
Sealand 23
Sedding, J. D. 51, 55, 256
Seddon, John Pollard 363, *365*
Sédille, Paul 156
Sedgwick 163
Segontium 126, *141*, 238, 363
Seiont, River (*see* Saint)
Seithenyn 108, 248
'Seven Wonders of Wales' 61, 65, 77, *365*
Severn, River 276, 279, 285, 286, 289, 293, 294, 302, 304; Valley Mills 293-4
Shakespeare 23, 287, 300
Shaky Bridge *326-7*
Shaw, C. and J. 134; R. Norman 35, 236, 360
Shayler, F. H. 294, 303
Shelley 85, 193, 311, 313
Shepherd's Well, 323
Sheridan, R. B. 79
Shipley, Bishop of St Asaph 102; Dean of St Asaph 102
Shirley, James 66
Shotton *23*
Shrewsbury 81, 113, 276, 279, 286, 296, 336
Shropshire 63, 74, 75, 91, 94, 265, 285, 287, 292, 318, 319; Union Canal 84, 88, 91, 275, 279; Union Canal Society 275
Skeffington, Bishop 138
Skerries *208*
Slate-quarrying 148, 150-1, 156-7, 164, 165, 168, 169, 177, 194, 231-3, 238, 246, 259
Smirke, Sir Robert 282, 320; Sidney 276
Snetzler 80
Smith, Francis 79; S. Pountney 221, 222, 279, 319
Snowdon 140, 146, 147, 150, 153, 156, 159, 237, 246; Horseshoe 159, 162, 165; 'Ranger' 157, 162; 'Ranger' Path *162*; Mountain Railway 161; Station 150, 159
Snowdonia 15, 45, 48, 88, 89, 110, 115, 119, 122, 125, 146, *146-70*, 150, 155, 159, *160-2*, 164, 165, 176, 197, 199, 201, 211, 215, 246, 249, 270, 291
Sodom *47*
Soughton Hall *26*
Southey 270
South Stack Lighthouse *214*
Spaull, W. H. 269, 292
Speed, John 307
Spence, Sir Basil 239
Stanage Park *319*

Stanley, H. M. 100; Embankment *212-13*; Lord, of Alderley 207, 213; Tomb 214
Stanlow 207
Stanner Rocks 321
Stansty Park 65, 69, 72
Stanton, William 66
Staylittle 304
Stein 116
Stephenson, George 91, 128, 203, 211, 213
Strata Florida Abbey 305, 311, 313, 324
Strata Marcella *279*, 280
Street, G. E. 32, 61, 63, 76, 89, 104-5, 105, 276, 278, 280, 286, 288, 301, 304
Sudeley, Charles, first Lord 292
Suetonius Paulinus 217
Summer Hill *69*
Swallow Falls 122
Swansea 60, 326
Swch-cae-Rhiw 95
Sweeney Hall, Oswestry 291
Swettenham, W. N. 279
Switzer 41
Sycharth *267-8*
Sychnant Pass *131-2*, 132
Sychtyn Hall *26*
Sylfaen Valley 288
Symons, A. J. A. 28
Szlumper and Aldwinkle 301

Tacitus 215
Tait, T. S. 114
Talacre 32; Abbey *32*
Talbot, Gilbert and John 245; Mrs. G. T. 252
Talerddig *297-8*
Talgarth (Merioneth) 264
Talgarth (Mont.) 297
Talhaiarn (*see* Jones, John)
Talhenbont Estate 190
Taliesin 125
Tallarn Green *75*
Talsarnau *243*
Tal-y-bont 137, 251
Talycafn *110*, 127
Tal-y-llyn 223, 258; Church *258*-9; Lake 262; Railway *262*, 263
Talysarn *157*
Tanat, River 270, 275; Valley 271
Tan-y-bwlch *234*, 238; Station 234
Tan-y-graig 179
Tanygrisiau 151, *233*
Tanyrallt *193*
Tattersall, George 80
Taylor, A. J. 36, 143
Tea in the Heather 167
Tegfryn Gallery, Menai Bridge 198
Teifi, River 153; Valley 293
Telford, Thomas 83, 86, 88, 89, 91, 92, 117, 122, 128, 139, 147, 157, 197, 198, 203, 209, 210, 212, 213, 215, 366
Teme Valley 318, *319*; Valley Foxhounds 318, 319
'Temple of Peace', the 24
Ternouth 102
Teulon and Cronk 77
Tewdric Mawr 280
Theed, W. 41, 63, 129
Thelwall, Ambrose 52; Edward 116; John 52
'Thetis' submarine 204
Thirlwall, Connop *366-7*
Thomas, Archdeacon 107; John 211; John Evan 281; Sir Percy 139; R. G. 143, 281; R. S. 290
Thompson, Francis (architect) 29, 30, 138; Francis (poet) 30
Thornycroft, Hamo 214
Thorwaldsen 116
Thrale, Mrs. 45, 137
'Three Sisters', The 96
Toddington, Glos. 292
Tomen y Bala 224; y Faerdre 50
Tomen-y-mur 238, *238-9*, 240
Tomen y Rhodwydd *51*
Tonfanau 261
Tooth, Arthur 257; Charles 256-7; Mrs. 256
Torrent Walk 256
Tour de Constance, Aigues Mortes 23
Tower *41*
Towyn 105
Traeth 237
Traeth Bychan *204*
Traeth Coch (*see* Red Wharf Bay)
Traeth Mawr 179, *193*, 243
Trannon Valley 297
Trawscoed Hall *278*; Hen 278
Trawsfynydd 225, 230, *239-40*, 240; Nuclear Power Station *239*
Treardcur Bay 215
Trefeglwys *297*, 301
Trefnant *100*
Trefor 176; Bishop 85; Bridge 85; Rocks 88; Uchaf 84, *85*, 88
Trefriw *124*; Spa 124
Tregunter, Breconshire 193
Tregynon 292, *293*
Trelawnyd 32, *33*
Trelystan Church *285*

Tremadoc 156, 166, 170, *192*, 235, 286; Races 192
Tremeirchion *45*, 46, 47
Tre'r Ceiri *176*
Treuddyn *42*
Trevalyn Hall *60*
Trevor family 61, 93, 111; Sir John 42, 60
Trevor-Roper, Patrick 42
Trinity House Depot, Holyhead *213*
Trofarth *113*
Tros-y-marian *203*
Troughton, Rev. J. E. 39, 296
Trubshaw, Richard 73, 74
Trum y Ddysgl 166
Tryfan 147, 159, *162-3*
Trystion, River 221; Falls 221
Tryweryn Valley 229
Tudur Aled 114
Tudweiliog *179*
Tu Hwnt i'r Bont 111
Turner, Edwin 108; J. M. W. 152, 299; Joseph 24, 25, 39, 53, 54, 71, 93, 103, 114
Twll Du 163
Twm o'r Nant 97
Twthill 35, 145
Twymyn 298, 304
tyddyn 17
Tyddyn Tudur 56
Ty Hyll *146*
Tyluggan 318
Ty Mawr *120*
Ty'n-y-Celyn 124
Tyn-y-Groes 93, 126
Tyrau Mawr 260
tŷ-unnos 26, 38
Tywyn 153, 223, 258, 261, *262-3*, 351

Underwood, Martin 99
Unit System 30, 123, 367
University Church, Dublin 37
University College of North Wales *138-9*
Usk 349

Viaducts 42, 91, 121, 230, 319
Valle Crucis 86, *87*, 265
Valley 147, 208, 212, 215; Airfield *212*, 219
Van lead mines 296, 304
Van Der Hagen 76, 90, 251
Van Dyck 76
Varley, Cornelius 252
Vaughan, E. M. Bruce 133; Catherine 227; Edward 270; family of Cors-y-Gedol 250, 251; family of Derllys Court 350; family of Nannau 226; Griffith 250, 251; Griffith 252; Katherine 270; Robert 242; Rowland 224-5; William 250; William 112; Sir Robert Williames *227*
Vaynol *139-40*, 150
Vaynor Park *290*
Venables, Archdeacon 324
Verelst 199
Veronese 282
Verrio 282
Viceroy's House, Delhi 117
Victoria, Queen 137, 294
Voelas 37, 118, 119
Vortigern 154, 177, 314
Vosper, Sidney Curnow 249
Voysey 134
Vyrnwy, Lake (*see* Lake Vyrnwy)
Vyrnwy, River 273, 275, 276, 277

Waen (*see* Gwernafield)
Wailes 25, 39, 53, 69, 101, 274
Wales, Prince of 52, 144, 359; Statute of 36
Walker, David 37, 40, 49, 53, 280, 295, 297, 298, 300, 314; Leonard 293
Waller, Messrs. 61
Walton 319, *321*; George 246
Warden (Hill) 320
Ward and Hughes 102, 270
Warenne, John de, Earl of Surrey 72
Warlock, Peter (*see* Heseltine, Philip)
Warwick School 189
Water-break-its-neck 323
Waterfalls 33, 88, 95, 114, 135, 221, 230, 231, 240, 241, 242, 262, 269, 304, 323
Waterhouse, Alfred 134
Waterloo, Battle of 211, 259; Bridge, Betws-y-Coed 122; Tower 80
Watkin, Sir Edward 162; Path, *162*; Zigzags 161
Wat's Dyke 367
Watstay (*see* Wynnstay)
Watt, James, Jun. 324
Waunfawr 159, 167
Webb, Sir Aston 292, 295
Webb, Philip 290-1; Thomas 71
Webster, George 38
Wehnert and Ashdown 108
Weightman, Hadfield and Goldie 138
Weightman and Hadfield 202

Welch, John 24, 44, 108, 110, 114, 183, 185, 201, 216
Wellington, Duke of 85; Memorial, Manchester 211
Wells, 27, 35, 46, 76, 97, 107, 112, 116, 119, 124, 127, 175, 176, 181, 189, 202, 215, 217, 316
Welsh Highland Railway *155*, 238
Welshpool 275, 276, 278, *279-81*, 283, 284, 286, 288, 289, 302, 303; and Llanfair Caereinion Railway *288*
Welsh Whiskey Distillery 200, 329
Wern *192*; Fawr 246; Gof Uchaf farm 147
Wesley, John 303
West, Frederick 53, 54
Westmacott, Sir Richard 31, 61, 73, 102, 136
Westminster Abbey 136; College, Cambridge 139; first Duke of 26, 353; second Duke of 88
Weyman, Stanley 52
Whall, Christopher 51
Wharf Station, Tywyn 263
Whitchurch 73, *97*, 99
White, Gilbert 31; William 295
Whitford 30, *31*
Whitland, Carm. 356
Wheatley 32
Whistler, Rex 215
whitefish 223
Whitewell 75
Whithorn 138
Whitland 279
Wigfair 116
Wilkinson, Isaac 64, 70; John 44, *64*, 66, 69, 70; William 69, *70*
William III, King 282
William ap Gruffydd 137
William Rufus 239; the Conqueror 286
Williams and Jones 108
Williams, David 235; 'David', Pwllheli 188
Williams, Edward (*see* Iolo Morganwg); family of Bodelwyddan Castle 102, 103; family of Cochwillan 136; Herbert 100; Hugh 305; John, Archbishop 45, *136*; John, Hafod Llwyfog 153, 155; John, Tremadoc 193; Kyffin 198-9; Rice 51; S. W. 324, 329; Sir Watkin (*see* Williams-Wynn, 3rd Baronet); William, Brondanw 237; William, Pant-y-celyn 368; Sir William *267*
Williams-Ellis, Sir Clough 54, 75, 113, 118, 119, 168, 183, 189, 191, 221, 232, 235, 236, 237
Williams-Wynn, Charles, M.P. 270; family 68, 78, 79, 80, 116, 224, 261, 269, 270, 273; Lady Henrietta 81; Marie Nesta 270-1; Sir Watkin, 3rd Barrnet, 78-9, 267, 270; Sir Watkin, 4th Baronet 79, 80, 81; Sir Watkin, 5th Baronet 79; Sir Watkin, 6th Baronet 271
Willoughby de Broke, Lady 103
Wilson, F. R. 247; Henry 134, 228, 256-7; John 197; Richard 47, 48, 72, 156, 258, 299, 328
Winchester 102; College Chapel 75
Winde, William 282, 283
Wirral 21
Withers, R. J. 295, *368-9*
Wleder 243
Wnion 226, 228, 242
Wolsey, Cardinal 118
Wolves 118, 333
Womaston 321
Wood, Abram 260; John 79; and Kendrick 294; and Turner 38
Woodall, S. 277
Woodchester, Glos. 110
Woodward, Benjamin 205
Wool 29, 85, 293, 302
Woolner, Thomas 66
Wordsworth, W. 57, 85, 129
World's End 78, *88*
Worthenbury *74*, 353
Worthington, Percy 106
Wrexham 40, 51, 60, 61, *63-8*, 66, 69, 71, 72, 73, 74, 77, 78, 99, 281, 303
Wrexham-Ellesmere Railway 65
Wroxeter 285
Wyatt, Arthur *369*; Benjamin *136*, 137, 145, 147, 149, 369; Benjamin, Weeford *369*; James 63, 65, 71, 73, 80, 136, 215, *369*; Jeffry (*see* Wyatville, Jeffry); Lewis William 136, *369*; Mathew 28; Samuel 104, 137, 218, 236, *369*; T. H. 29, 31, 33, 42, 44, 47, 90, 149, 207, 290, *369*; William *369*
Wyatville, Sir Jeffry 81, 356, *369*
Wybrnant 120
Wyddel, Osbwrn 250
Wye 305, *310*, 324, 328, *329*, 330, 335; Valley 305, 307, 309, 311, 329, 332, 334, 335, 336
Wylfa Nuclear Power Station 207, 213

Wynn family of Boduan Hall 187; family of Glynllifon 173; family of Gwydir 81, 123, 136; Sir John, 5th Baronet of Gwydir 78, 112, 121, *123*, 193; John 43; Maurice 116; Sir Richard 111, 112; Sir Richard 123; Thomas, first Lord Newborough (*see* Newborough); Rev. William 40
Wynne, Bishop 26; Ellis 244, 246; family, Garthewin 114; family, Peniarth 261; Father, of Voelas 37; Sir George 299; Katherine, Branes 222; Robert 81, 92, 121, 130, 192; Dame Sarah 112; T. 44; W. W. E., Peniarth 242, 251, 252, *261*, 351
Wynne-Finch family 118
Wynne-Thomas, Dan 139
Wynnstay *78*, 79, 90, 91

Yale, Elihu 51, 65, 66, 71, 72; University 51, 66; Chapel 51
Yale (*see* Iâl)
Yardro *322*
Y Cronicl 298
Yenn, John 274
Y Faner 100
Y Garn 163, 166
Y Garth 237
Y Gegin Fawr *183-4*
Y Gribin 163
Y Lasynys *244*
Y Llethr 250
Y Lôn Goed 191
Ynys Cyngar *192*, 243
Ynyscynhaearn *192*
Ynys Dulas 205; Enlli (*see* Bardsey Island); Gifftan 244; Gybi (*see* Holy Island); Maengwyn 262, 263
Ynyspandy Slate Mill 169
Ynys Towyn 194
York 136
Yorke, Philip 71; Philip 73; Simon 71, 73
Yr Amserau 114
Yr Aran 154, 162
Yr Eifl (*see* 'the Rivals')
Yr Elen 164
Yr Wyddfa (*see* Snowdon)
Yr Wyddgrug (*see* Mold)
Ysbyty Ifan *118*, 119, 230
Ysgeifiog *44*
Ysgethin 251
Ystrad 100
Ystwyth 371
'Y Tŷ Gwyn yn Bermo' 252

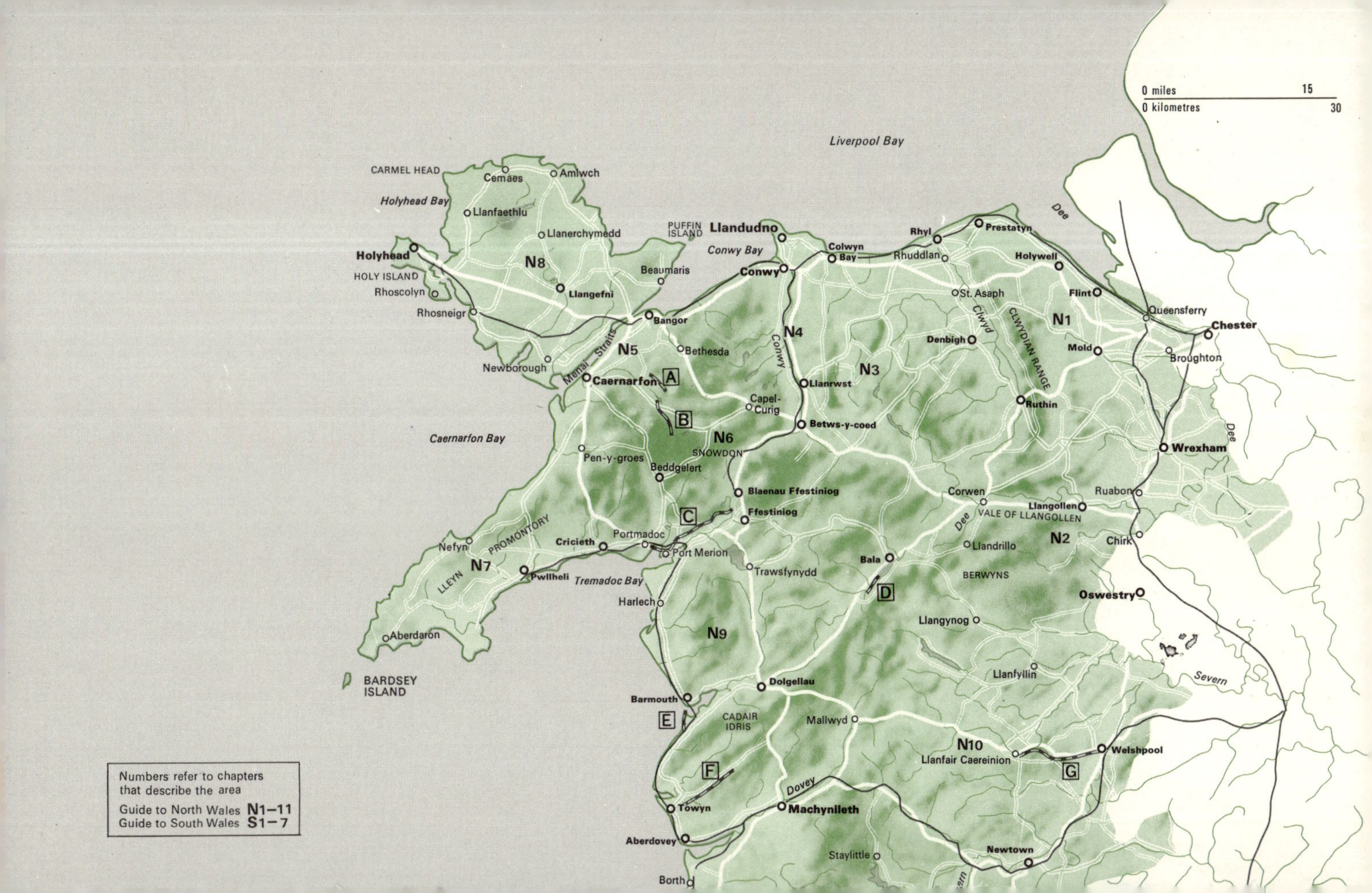

Numbers refer to chapters that describe the area
Guide to North Wales N1–11
Guide to South Wales S1–7